The
Supreme Court
Yearbook

1999–2000

The justices of the Supreme Court. From left are Justices Sandra Day O'Connor, Anthony M. Kennedy, and Antonin Scalia; Chief Justice William H. Rehnquist; and Justices David H. Souter, Ruth Bader Ginsburg, Clarence Thomas, Stephen G. Breyer, and John Paul Stevens.

The
Supreme Court
Yearbook

1999–2000

CQ PRESS

A Division of Congressional Quarterly Inc.
Washington, D.C.

CQ Press
A Division of Congressional Quarterly Inc.
1414 22nd Street, N.W.
Washington, D.C. 20037

(202) 822-1475; (800) 638-1710

www.cqpress.com

Book design: Debra Naylor, Naylor Design Inc.

Cover: Chiquita Babb, Septima Design

Printed and bound in the United States of America

03 02 01 00   5 4 3 2 1

Photo credits: frontispiece, 307, 311, Congressional Quarterly; 10, 43, 53, 59, 67, 81, AP/Wide World Photos; 38, KRT; 47, courtesy J. Daniel Kimel; 63, Alex Brandon; 71, courtesy Zev David Fredman; 78 (left), Reuters; 78 (right), Newsmakers; 309, Supreme Court; 305, 313, 316, 320, Collection, the Supreme Court Historical Society; 315, White House; 318, R. Michael Jenkins.

ISBN: 1-56802-596-3
ISSN: 1054-2701

Contents

Preface

The Supreme Court marked the new millennium by establishing its own Web site: www.supremecourtus.gov. The site, which went on-line April 17, 2000, provided lawyers, litigants, and the general public with instant access to the Court's opinions, orders, argument calendar, and other information. In September the site was expanded to include the Court's automated docket, informing users of status, names, and contact information for every pending case.

The Court also marked the new millennium with a burst of dramatic opinions on emotionally contentious issues ranging from abortion and gay rights to police interrogation and states' rights. Court watchers struggled to find words to convey the impact of the 1999–2000 term; "blockbuster" was used early and often.

Again this year, all of the Court's decisions—in cases big and small—are reported and analyzed in this, the eleventh edition of the *Supreme Court Yearbook*. The book opens with an overview of the term (Chapter 1) and proceeds with accounts of ten of the most important cases (Chapter 2), capsule summaries of each of the Court's decisions (Chapter 3), a preview of the upcoming term (Chapter 4), and excerpts of the major decisions (Appendix).

My thanks again go to the many lawyers, reporters, and experts whose comments and writings inform my own coverage. The Court's public information office, under Kathy Arberg, continues to provide diligent, professional assistance in helping inform the press and public about the Court's work. And at CQ Press, thanks to Christopher Anzalone and Talia Greenberg for their work in bringing the book into print.

Kenneth Jost
Washington, D.C.

Chapter 1

A "Most Extraordinary" Term

Abortion. Gay rights. Aid to parochial schools. School prayer. Violence against women. Police interrogation. Campaign finance. Tobacco. Grandparents' rights. Hate crimes.

This list of hot-button issues could readily consume an entire legislative session and challenge the policymaking ability and political skills of even the wisest lawmakers. In the United States, however, the responsibility for making public policies on those and many other issues does not lie entirely with elected legislators or executive officials. Courts—in particular, the Supreme Court of the United States—often have the final word.

In its 1999–2000 term, the Supreme Court exercised its final-word power on all those issues. And even though a majority of justices professed a commitment to judicial restraint, the Court did not hesitate to override the actions of Congress and state legislatures, federal agencies and local school boards, and state supreme courts across the country.

From the traditional opening on the first Monday in October to a less hectic than usual conclusion in the final week of June, the Court flexed its constitutional muscles on many of the most divisive issues of the day. The Court:

- Struck down a Nebraska law banning a procedure that opponents called "partial-birth abortions"—casting doubt on similar laws enacted in thirty other states by overwhelming legislative majorities.

- Blocked the state of New Jersey from enforcing a state civil rights law to require the Boy Scouts of America to admit homosexuals as members.

- Overturned a new federal law giving victims of "gender-motivated violence" the right to sue their attackers for damages in federal courts.

- Invalidated a thirty-two-year-old federal law aimed at overriding the Court's famous *Miranda* decision requiring police to warn suspects of their constitutional rights before interrogation.

- Barred a local school board in southeastern Texas from adopting a policy of allowing student-led prayers at high school football games.

- Stopped the federal Food and Drug Administration (FDA) from trying to regulate cigarettes in order to reduce youth smoking.

- Limited the scope of a Washington State law giving grandparents and others the right to seek court-ordered visitation with young children.

- Made it harder for states or the federal government to increase sentences for people convicted of committing "hate crimes."

The Court's decisions had teeth even when they upheld the actions made by the other, so-called "political branches" of government. The Court opened the door to wider use of public funds at parochial schools by rejecting a challenge to a federal program that Louisiana taxpayers said amounted to unconstitutional government establishment of religion. And in a Missouri case, the Court gave state and local governments a green light to set low caps on campaign contributions by dismissing a political interest group's claim that the limits unconstitutionally infringed its freedom of speech. *(See Table 1-1.)*

The successive demonstrations of judicial power left commentators of all ideological stripes agape. "I can't remember any time when the Court has been more assertive, more aware of its own prerogatives," commented A. E. (Dick) Howard, a professor at the University of Virginia Law School and longtime Court watcher.

All nine justices were united in asserting the Court's primacy, according to John Yoo, a conservative professor at the University of California in Berkeley's Boalt Hall School of Law. "If there is anything the Court as a whole agrees on and to which they all adhere," Yoo told the *Christian Science Monitor*, "it is the idea of judicial supremacy—that the Supreme Court is the final arbiter of the Constitution to the exclusion of the other branches."

"I don't accept the premise that this is a Court that is committed to judicial restraint," remarked Erwin Chemerinsky, a liberal professor at the University of Southern California Law School. "This is a Court that is much more about judicial power than about judicial deference."

Table 1-1 CQ's Major Cases: U.S. Supreme Court, 1999–2000 Term

CQ each term selects the major cases for the Supreme Court's term. The selection is based on such factors as the rulings' practical impact; their significance as legal precedent; the degree of division on the Court; and the level of interest among interest groups, experts, and news media. Accounts of the major cases appear in Chapter 2; excerpts from the decisions can be found in the Appendix.

Name of Case	Vote	Holding
Stenberg v. Carhart [pp. 34–41]	5-4	Invalidates Nebraska's ban on "partial-birth abortions"
United States v. Morrison [pp. 41–46]	5-4	Bars federal court suits for "gender-motivated" crimes
Kimel v. Florida Board of Regents [pp. 46–51]	5-4	Blocks federal age bias suits against state governments
Dickerson v. United States [pp. 51–57]	6-3	Reaffirms *Miranda* rule on police interrogation
Food and Drug Administration v. Brown & Williamson Tobacco Corp. [pp. 57–61]	5-4	Blocks FDA from regulating tobacco products
Mitchell v. Helms [pp. 61–66]	6-3	Allows use of public funds for computers at parochial schools
Santa Fe Independent School District v. Doe [pp. 66–70]	6-3	Bars prayers at public high school football games
Nixon v. Shrink Missouri Government PAC [pp. 70–75]	6-3	Upholds state limits on campaign contributions
Boy Scouts of America v. Dale [pp. 75–79]	5-4	Backs Boy Scouts' right to exclude homosexuals
Troxel v. Granville [pp. 80–84]	6-3	Limits courts' power to order third-party visitation

Here are some other especially noteworthy cases: *Hill v. Colorado:* permits curbs on protests at abortion clinics; *Apprendi v. New Jersey:* strengthens jury trial rights on sentencing; *Illinois v. Wardlow:* allows "stop and frisk" of fleeing suspect; *City of Erie v. Pap's A.M.:* upholds nude dancing ban; *California Democratic Party v. Jones:* bars state's "blanket primary."

The Court's assertiveness was borne out in headline-making decisions that began early in the term with a ruling in January that state governments cannot be sued for damages by their workers for violating the federal law against age discrimination. By the end of the month, the Court had filled out its argument calendar for the term by agreeing to hear the partial-birth abortion, gay Boy Scout, and *Miranda* cases. All three were set to be heard in April and due for decision before the summer.

Court watchers—such as the *New York Times'* Pulitzer Prize–winning reporter Linda Greenhouse—began talking or writing about a "blockbuster" term. In early spring, Pepperdine University Law School announced plans for its retrospective on the Court's year, to be held in September. The program's title: "The Supreme Court's Most Extraordinary Term."

As the justices left Washington for their summer travels, conservative and liberal advocates and interest groups were left to count up their wins and losses. The Court's generally conservative cast was well established and well known. A conservative majority consisted of Chief Justice William H. Rehnquist and four associate justices: the centrist-leaning Sandra Day O'Connor and Anthony M. Kennedy and the more doctrinaire Antonin Scalia and Clarence Thomas. Aligned on the opposite side in two-thirds of the Court's 5–4 rulings were four more or less liberal justices: John Paul Stevens, David H. Souter, Ruth Bader Ginsburg, and Stephen G. Breyer.

Among the seventy-four signed decisions for the term, conservatives counted as victories rulings that cut back the federal government's powers, decisions that took a narrow view of civil liberties and civil rights remedies, and criminal law cases that for the most part backed law enforcement. But liberals won a major victory in the partial-birth abortion case and counted an unexpected number of wins in rulings that backed rights for criminal defendants and suspects, including the reaffirmation of the *Miranda* rule.

"There were lots of big issues, but the outcomes did not predominate one way or another," said Thomas Baker, a professor at Drake University Law School. "Everyone got something out of this term in the sense of winners and losers."

"There were both liberal and conservative victories, but they were not so much in either direction that they were profoundly out of the mainstream," said Douglas Kmiec, a conservative professor at Pepperdine Law School. With a few exceptions, Kmiec said, the Court's decisions were "within the range of reasonableness."

Some Court watchers also said the major decisions were in some sense less important than headlines suggested. "This is a term that could have been a blockbuster," said Barry Friedman, a professor at New York University Law School. "It didn't end up being a blockbuster. That's because the Court is deciding cases on very narrow grounds and leaving options open."

Laurence Tribe, the prominent Harvard Law School professor and frequent Supreme Court advocate, agreed. "If you really step back and ask historically: Is this term going to be remembered because any new direction was established, because any major surprises occurred, because the Court established some landmark in a novel area—then I think the true answer is no," Tribe remarked on the PBS *NewsHour*. "It was not a term that made new law."

Whether making new law or reaffirming old doctrines, the Court in the 1999–2000 term was playing a role that Chief Justice John Marshall created nearly two centuries earlier. "It is, emphatically, the province and duty of the judicial department to say what the law is," Marshall wrote in the landmark 1803 decision, *Marbury v. Madison*.

"This is a conservative Court, but conservative can mean a lot of different things," explained Mark Levy, a Washington lawyer who follows the Court closely. "One of the things that conservative traditionally means is deference to other branches of government. The Court was not conservative in that sense in this term."

The Rehnquist-O'Connor Court

The Court's work during the 1999–2000 term bore the unmistakable stamps of two of its members. Rehnquist's influence was evident in the Court's selection of cases—especially federalism issues—and its generally conservative orientation. But O'Connor played an equally important role as the pivotal justice during the year. She provided critical votes for the conservative majority in federalism and criminal cases, but also helped give the liberal minority its most important victories during the term in the abortion, school prayer, and *Miranda* cases.

Rehnquist, in his fourteenth term as chief justice, had long since moved from his position as a conservative dissenter in the 1970s to the leader of a conservative majority in the 1990s. And the Court continued during the term to build Rehnquist's likely legacy: reshaping the relationship between the federal government and the states by using two of the Constitution's states' rights provisions—the Tenth and Eleventh Amendments.

In his most important opinion for the term, Rehnquist led the 5-4 majority in striking down the provision of the Violence Against Women Act that allowed federal court suits by victims of gender-motivated crimes. Upholding the law, Rehnquist wrote, would invite Congress to use its power over interstate commerce to "completely obliterate the Constitution's distinction between national and local authority. . . ."

In a second federalism ruling, however, Rehnquist upheld a federal law that barred state governments from selling personal driver's license information. State governments were subject to congressional regulation, Rehnquist said in the unanimous decision, because they engaged in interstate commerce by selling the information to a variety of individuals and businesses.

Rehnquist surprised—and displeased—some of his conservative admirers by writing the Court's 7–2 decision reaffirming the *Miranda* rule despite his long record of criticizing and trying to restrict the decision. Disinterested experts, however, said Rehnquist's decision to take the assignment for himself reflected loyalty to the Court as an institution. "He does put on his chief justice hat in some circumstances," commented Richard Lazarus, director of Georgetown University Law Center's Supreme Court Institute.

In the third of his major opinions for the term, Rehnquist wrote the Court's 5–4 decision upholding the right of the Boy Scouts of America to exclude homosexuals. Rehnquist said that enforcing a state civil rights law to require the admission of homosexuals would "significantly burden the organization's right to oppose or disfavor homosexual conduct."

Among the rest of his nine majority decisions for the term were several in criminal law cases—generally upholding convictions against constitutional law claims. In an Illinois case, Rehnquist led a 5–4 majority in upholding the right of police to stop and frisk a fleeing suspect. But he also authored the 7–2 decision that ruled a federal drug agent violated a bus passenger's Fourth Amendment rights by feeling his soft-sided luggage to see if it contained any drugs.

As chief justice, Rehnquist dissented rarely—only eight times—and sparingly. In his most notable dissenting opinion, he complained that the decision barring prayer at high school football games reflected "hostility" to religion. But Rehnquist refrained from writing his own dissent in the partial-birth abortion case. And he deserted his conservative colleagues in some major cases—for example, the 6–3 rulings that reaffirmed the constitutionality of campaign contribution limits and upheld a Colorado law limiting anti-abortion protests.

Rehnquist and O'Connor were closely aligned throughout the term: they voted together in 95 percent of the cases, the closest alignment of any two justices. *(See Table 1-2.)* O'Connor's pivotal role could be seen in another statistic. She dissented in only four cases—the fewest number of any justice for the term and equal to the record low of four dissenting votes that Kennedy cast in the 1993–1994 term. *(See Table 1-3.)* "She's the center of the Court," Professor Baker observed.

Table 1-2 Justices' Alignment, 1999–2000 Term

This table shows the percentage of decisions in which each justice agreed with each of the other members of the Court. Of the seventy-four signed decisions for the 1999–2000 term, twenty-nine (or 39 percent) were unanimous.

The voting pattern continued to indicate a general division between a conservative bloc consisting of Chief Justice Rehnquist and Justices O'Connor, Scalia, Kennedy, and Thomas, and a moderately liberal bloc of Justices Stevens, Souter, Ginsburg, and Breyer.

In comparison to previous years, however, the figures suggested a slight shift toward the center by Rehnquist from the right and Breyer from the left. Rehnquist voted most often with the centrist-leaning O'Connor (nearly 95 percent agreement) and less frequently with Scalia and Thomas than in past years. Breyer agreed with Rehnquist in 73 percent of the cases—compared to 63 percent in the previous term. And he voted with his liberal colleagues somewhat less frequently than in the previous term.

Rehnquist and O'Connor were the most closely aligned pair of justices. Scalia and Thomas also continued to be closely aligned, voting together in 90 percent of the cases. Among the liberal justices, Stevens and Ginsburg voted together in 92 percent of the cases; Stevens and Souter agreed nearly 90 percent of the time.

The widest gap was between Ginsburg on the left and Scalia on the right. They voted together in fewer than half of all the cases and in only seven out of forty-five divided decisions. Stevens and Scalia were also far apart. They agreed in eight of the nonunanimous decisions.

	Rehnquist	Stevens	O'Connor	Scalia	Kennedy	Souter	Thomas	Ginsburg	Breyer
Rehnquist		20.0	91.1	68.9	82.2	35.6	73.3	33.3	55.5
		51.3	94.6	81.1	89.2	60.8	83.8	59.5	73.0
Stevens	20.0		28.9	17.8	31.1	82.2	26.7	86.7	62.2
	51.3		56.8	50.0	58.1	89.2	55.4	91.9	77.0
O'Connor	91.1	28.9		64.4	80.0	44.4	71.1	42.2	60.0
	94.6	56.8		78.4	87.8	66.2	82.4	64.9	75.7
Scalia	68.9	17.8	64.4		75.6	22.2	84.4	15.6	42.2
	81.1	50.0	78.4		85.1	52.8	90.5	48.6	64.9
Kennedy	82.2	31.1	80.0	75.6		33.3	73.3	31.1	48.9
	89.2	58.1	87.8	85.1		59.5	83.8	58.1	68.9
Souter	35.6	82.2	44.4	22.2	33.3		33.3	84.4	44.4
	60.8	89.2	66.2	52.8	59.5		59.5	85.7	66.2
Thomas	73.3	26.7	71.1	84.4	73.3	33.3		24.4	35.6
	83.8	55.4	82.4	90.5	83.8	59.5		54.1	60.8
Ginsburg	33.3	86.7	42.2	15.6	31.1	84.4	24.4		68.9
	59.5	91.9	64.9	48.6	58.1	85.7	54.1		81.1
Breyer	55.5	62.2	60.0	42.2	48.9	44.4	35.6	68.9	
	73.0	77.0	75.7	64.9	68.9	66.2	60.8	81.1	

Note: The first number in each cell represents the percentage of agreement in divided decisions. The second number represents the percentage of agreement in all signed opinions.

Table 1-3 Justices in Dissent, 1999–2000 Term

Justice	Division on Court				Total	Percentage
	8–1	7–2	6–3	5–4		
Rehnquist	1	—	2	5	8	10.8%
Stevens	1	6	5	16	28	37.8
O'Connor	—	—	1	3	4	5.4
Scalia	1	5	4	4	14	18.9
Kennedy	—	1	3	4	8	10.8
Souter	—	3	4	14	21	28.4
Thomas	—	4	4	3	11	14.9
Ginsburg	—	4	5	15	24	32.4
Breyer	—	1	2	16	19	25.7

Note: Totals reflect cases where the justice dissented in whole or in part from the result or the major legal holding. There were seventy-four signed opinions during the 1999–2000 term.

In her nineteenth year on the Court, O'Connor continued as a reliable conservative vote on issues ranging from states' rights and federal regulation to criminal law and civil rights litigation. Her opinions on those issues this term also reflected her position in the middle of a closely divided Court.

O'Connor led the 5–4 majority in protecting state governments from age discrimination suits by their workers. Congress could not use its power under the Fourteenth Amendment to override the states' sovereign immunity from suits, O'Connor explained, because age discrimination did not amount to a constitutional violation. In another 5–4 decision, O'Connor wrote the opinion blocking the FDA from regulating the sale and marketing of cigarettes and smokeless tobacco. Despite the seriousness of the problem, O'Connor said, Congress had "clearly precluded" the agency from exercising jurisdiction over tobacco.

Among her other majority opinions, O'Connor upheld a new law Congress passed to help states get out from under federal court supervision of prison conditions. The 5–4 decision rejected arguments that the law unconstitutionally infringed on the power of the judiciary. She also wrote for a five-justice majority in a complex habeas corpus case that upheld another congressional restriction on federal judges' power—in this instance, a higher standard for reviewing state inmates' constitutional challenges to their convictions or sentences.

O'Connor played a distinctive role in several other cases that found the justices even more divided. In the grandparents' rights case, she wrote for a plurality of four justices in concluding that a Washington State court judge had gone too far in ordering visitation over the mother's objections. But she stopped short of holding the state law allowing third parties to petition for court-ordered visitation flatly unconstitutional. In another important case, she wrote a critical concurring opinion that upheld the use of federal funds to lend computers and other equipment to parochial schools. But she refused to join a broader plurality opinion, written by Thomas, that called for even lower barriers to government funding of church-affiliated schools.

In another case, O'Connor fashioned a majority opinion for upholding laws to ban nude dancing—a decade after the Court had issued a badly fractured ruling on the question.

O'Connor also cast the decisive fifth vote to strike down Nebraska's so-called "partial-birth abortion ban." In her concurring opinion, she agreed the law amounted to an "undue burden" on a woman's right to abortion—a standard that O'Connor had helped write into law in the joint opinion written with Kennedy and Souter in the 1992 *Planned Parenthood of Southeastern Pennsylvania v. Casey.* But O'Connor also said that a more narrowly drafted law could be constitutional.

In her only dissenting opinion for the term, O'Connor disagreed with the 5–4 decision to strengthen jury trial rights in hate crime cases. Of her three other dissenting votes, only one came in a major case. She dissented from the 5–4 decision to strike down a federal law regulating sexually explicit programming on cable television.

Along with O'Connor, Kennedy had held a pivotal position between the conservative and liberal blocs in his thirteen years on the Court. In the past term, though, he shifted slightly but perceptibly to the right—most significantly, with his dissent in the partial-birth abortion case. He also strengthened his role as a supporter of First Amendment claims in a range of settings, including anti-abortion protests, campaign finance regulation, and sexual programming on cable television.

The generally mild-mannered Kennedy ended the term with sharply written dissents in two abortion-related cases. In the partial-birth abortion case, Kennedy accused the majority of ignoring the "profound concerns" about a procedure found "abhorrent" by "many decent and civilized people." And he evidently felt betrayed after having joined O'Connor and Souter in the pivotal opinion in the *Casey* abortion case. "Kennedy is wondering whether the compromise that he understood is not the same compromise that O'Connor understood," Professor Baker remarked.

In a second ruling on the final decision day of the term, Kennedy also dissented from the decision upholding Colorado's law curbing protests—

Anti-abortion demonstrators protest in front of the Supreme Court building as the justices hear arguments on a Nebraska law banning so-called "partial-birth abortions." The Court's decision invalidating the law seemed likely to doom similar statutes in thirty other states.

including so-called "sidewalk counseling"—at abortion clinics. Emphasizing his disagreement by reading portions of the opinion from the bench, Kennedy complained that the law "bars a private citizen from passing a message, in a peaceful manner and on a profound moral issue, to a fellow citizen on a public sidewalk."

Kennedy sided with First Amendment interests in another notable dissent. He voted to invalidate Missouri's restrictive law on campaign contributions and to overturn the Court's controversial 1976 decision *Buckley v. Valeo*, which barred limits on campaign spending but allowed limits on contributions. The ruling should be scrapped, Kennedy argued, because it had resulted in a "serious distortion of the First Amendment."

Kennedy wrote for the majority in two other First Amendment cases. He led a 5–4 majority in striking down a federal law that effectively forced many cable television systems to limit sexually explicit channels to late-night hours. The law was more restrictive than necessary, Kennedy said. In another case, he allowed state universities to use funds from mandatory student fees to support lobbying and political advocacy organizations. Kennedy said the system served First Amendment purposes by ensuring support for a diversity of viewpoints in an academic setting.

In other areas, Kennedy was reliably conservative. He wrote the 7–2 decision striking down a Hawaii law that allowed only "native Hawaiians" to vote for members of an office that administered programs to benefit descendants of the state's native people. He wrote five criminal law decisions, all but one of them upholding convictions and sentences. And—with the exception of the school prayer case—he sided with the Court's conservatives in all of the Court's other most newsworthy decisions.

Scalia and Thomas had long been paired as the Court's most consistent conservatives. They also had a long record of close voting alignment since Thomas joined the Court in 1991, five years after Scalia. In this term, though, they split in seven cases, for a 91 percent voting alignment—somewhat lower than in some recent years. "People still think of them as joined at the hip," Mark Levy remarked. "That's not right. They're not clones."

Between the two, Thomas made the greater mark during the term with his bold plurality opinion on aid to parochial schools and his strong dissenting opinions in the campaign finance and partial-birth abortion cases. "His written work product is very interesting, very worth reading, and very forcefully, cogently, and logically argued," said Eugene Volokh, a conservative professor at UCLA Law School. "He is in some sense the most radical justice in the sense that he's willing to go to the roots of a problem and pull out the source of an incorrect doctrine."

In the parochial school aid case, Thomas advocated changing the standard used in Establishment Clause cases to allow government assistance as long as it was generally available on a nondiscriminatory basis to all types of schools: public, private, or parochial. "If the religious, irreligious, and areligious are all alike eligible for governmental aid," Thomas wrote in the thirty-eight-page opinion, "no one would conclude that any indoctrination that any particular recipient conducts has been done at the behest of the government."

Thomas's dissent in the partial-birth abortion case the same day was even longer—forty-four pages—and stronger. Thomas unflinchingly described the medical procedure, likening it to "infanticide." He said the state law banning the procedure "expresses a profound legitimate respect for fetal life" and should pass muster under the "undue burden" test adopted in the *Casey* decision. "If this statute is unconstitutional under *Casey*," he added acidly, "then *Casey* meant nothing, and the Court should candidly admit it."

Earlier in the term, Thomas wrote another lengthy dissent in the campaign finance case: a twenty-two-page opinion that forcefully called for scrapping all limits on campaign contributions or on spending "[C]ontribution caps, which place a direct and substantial limit on core speech, should be met with the utmost skepticism and should receive the strictest scrutiny," Thomas wrote.

Thomas's majority opinions came in mostly minor cases and reflected a general conservative orientation. In his only 5–4 decision, he took a literalist approach to a federal bank robbery statute in order to reject a defendant's attack on the jury instructions in the case. In some other cases, though, Thomas found himself aligned with the more liberal justices. In line with his strengthening support for First Amendment claims, he voted with the liberals to strike down the cable indecency law. And, in dissent, he voted with three of the Court's liberals to block on federal preemption grounds state court suits against automakers for failing to install air bags before federal regulations required them.

Scalia remained the Court's most vocal conservative, both in oral arguments and in written opinions, but he authored none of the term's most newsworthy decisions. Of his eight majority opinions, only one made major headlines: a ruling to strike down California's so-called "blanket primary election." But he wrote dissents in several of the major decisions, including the *Miranda* ruling and the two abortion-related cases—each one filled with Scalia's distinctively trenchant criticism of opposing views.

In the *Miranda* case, for example, Scalia strenuously insisted that the Court had no constitutional basis for the original ruling and therefore no basis for invalidating Congress's effort to overturn the decision. "By disregarding congressional action that concededly does not violate the Constitution," Scalia wrote, "the Court flagrantly offends fundamental principles of separation of powers. . . ."

Writing in the partial-birth abortion case, Scalia called it "simply absurd" to contend that the Constitution prevents states from banning "this visibly brutal means of eliminating our half-born posterity." And on the same day, he bitterly attacked the Colorado law curbing protests at abortion clinics as another in a line of "aggressively proabortion novelties" from the Court in recent years. "Does the deck seem stacked?" Scalia asked, reading his dissent from the bench. "You bet it does."

Scalia also dissented from the grandparents' rights case. In that opinion, he argued against extending two decisions from the 1920s that first established parents' constitutional rights to control their children's education and upbringing. Parental rights, he said, should left to state legislatures to define rather than to the courts.

The ruling in the California case struck down a primary election scheme that allowed voters to cast ballots for nominees for various offices from different parties rather than from a single party. The system, Scalia said, violated political parties' First Amendment freedom of association by forcing them to allow "unaffiliated voters to participate in their selection of candidates."

Among his other majority opinions, Scalia wrote the 7–2 decision protecting states from private suits for fraud or waste in use of federal funds. He also wrote an important 5–4 decision that made it harder to use the federal Voting Rights Act to attack election law changes that discriminated against racial minorities but did not leave minority voters worse off than before. And in a significant business case, Scalia wrote a unanimous opinion making it harder for manufacturers to use trademark law to protect the design of a product.

Scalia also had the satisfaction of seeing one of his strongly held views adopted by a majority, though another justice—Stevens—wrote the main opinion. In a decision ordering a new sentence for a New Jersey man convicted of a racially motivated hate crime, the Court held, 5–4, that a defendant was entitled to a jury trial on any fact that could increase a sentence beyond the statutory maximum for the offense. Scalia had advocated that position in a dissenting opinion several years earlier. In summarizing the opinion from the bench, Stevens—typically on opposite sides of Scalia in closely divided cases—acknowledged his conservative colleague's contribution by closing with a quote not from his own opinion but from Scalia's concurrence.

The (Somewhat) Liberal Minority

The Court's liberal minority included two justices appointed by Republican presidents—Stevens and Souter—and the only two Democratic appointees—Ginsburg and Breyer, both named by President Bill Clinton. None of the four, however, was as consistent in doctrine as the liberal justices who had retired in the 1990s: William J. Brennan Jr., Thurgood Marshall, and Harry A. Blackmun. "There is no Brennan, there is no Marshall, there is no Blackmun," Professor Chemerinsky noted. "The liberals are much more moderate liberals."

Outvoted in most of the Court's 5–4 decisions, the liberals were left to complain that the conservative majority was distorting precedent in their federalism rulings and unduly restricting protections for defendants and suspects in criminal cases. The few major victories for the liberal bloc—notably, the abortion, *Miranda*, school prayer, and campaign finance rulings—largely reaffirmed earlier rulings rather than creating new legal doctrines.

Stevens, at eighty the oldest and the longest serving of the liberal justices, marked his twenty-fifth year on the bench with several important majority opinions and, as usual, a large number of dissenting opinions: eighteen, the most of any of the justices. He also cast the largest number of dissenting votes: twenty-eight. One day, he genially took note of his frequent dissents as he began announcing a decision following two others where he had been in dissent. "I'm happy to say I'm in the majority in this case," Stevens said with a smile.

Among his majority opinions, Stevens wrote the 6–3 decisions in the high school prayer case and the abortion-protest ruling. In the prayer case, Stevens rejected the local school board's effort to distance itself from the student-led "invocations" at football games. "[T]he religious liberty protected by the Constitution is abridged when the State affirmatively sponsors the particular religious practice of prayer," Stevens explained. In the abortion case, Stevens upheld the Colorado law that limited the ability of protesters to approach patients or staff entering any "health care facility." Stevens called the law a "modest," content-neutral restriction to protect patients from "unwanted encounters, confrontations, and even assaults. . . ."

In two other important decisions, Stevens expanded rights for criminal defendants. The 5–4 decision on the New Jersey hate crimes law had the potential for affecting sentencing under many laws—both federal and state—that gave judges discretion to consider as sentencing factors allegations not specifically tried to the jury. Stevens said that due process required a jury trial and proof beyond a reasonable doubt of any fact that could expose a defendant to a punishment greater than the statutory maximum for the offense. In the other case, Stevens backed an argument by the former Clinton administration official Webster Hubbell that Independent Counsel Kenneth Starr violated his privilege against self-incrimination by using business records obtained under a grant of immunity to prosecute him on tax and fraud charges.

Stevens's dissenting opinions reflected generally liberal views on a wide range of issues. He led the liberal bloc in dissenting from 5–4 decisions to bar age discrimination suits by state government employees, to uphold the Boy Scouts' exclusion of homosexuals, and to affirm death sentences in two separate Virginia capital murder cases. He also wrote the main dissents in a pair of First Amendment cases—supporting the free speech claim in the ruling to allow bans on nude dancing while opposing the political parties' freedom of association argument in the decision to strike down California's blanket primary election.

All told, Stevens wrote thirty opinions—the most of any justice. His prolific output combined with his hale appearance on the bench to cast some doubt on speculation about his possible retirement. "He shows no signs of slowing up," Professor Baker commented.

In his tenth term, Souter continued his role as a fairly consistent liberal vote—espousing views surprisingly close to those of the justice he succeeded in 1990, Brennan. "I don't think there's a single case where his vote would have been different from what Brennan's would have been," Professor Lazarus remarked.

Souter's most important opinions for the term came in his dissents from the rulings to strike down the Violence Against Women Act and to uphold federal aid to parochial schools. Each one was long and dense with history and legal argument. In the first case, he strenuously argued that the conservative majority was resurrecting the idea of limiting Congress's power to regulate interstate commerce in hopes of returning to a "federalism of some earlier time." In the school aid case, he argued that Thomas's plurality opinion contradicted the established rule from prior cases: "no aid supporting a sectarian school's religious exercise or the discharge of its religious mission."

In his most important majority opinion, Souter wrote the 6–3 decision upholding Missouri's limits on campaign contributions. Souter reaffirmed the reasoning in *Buckley v. Valeo* that contribution limits were justified by the government's interest in preventing corruption or the appearance of corruption among political candidates. "Leave the perception of impropriety unanswered," Souter explained, "and the cynical assumption that large donors call the tune could jeopardize the willingness of voters to take part in democratic governance."

Among his other majority opinions, Souter wrote a significant unanimous decision that barred the use of the federal employee benefits law to sue health maintenance organizations (HMOs) for making treatment decisions to try to hold down costs. And he also wrote the unanimous decision striking down on federal preemption grounds a Massachusetts law imposing sanctions on companies that did business with the authoritarian government of Myanmar (formerly Burma).

In another case, Souter helped forge a majority for an approach he had advocated a decade earlier on the issue of nude dancing—even though he disagreed with the Court's disposition of the case. In the earlier case, Souter had said that a ban on nude dancing could be justified on grounds of preventing so-called "secondary effects," such as prostitution. In the new decision, the Court adopted Souter's rationale to uphold an Erie, Pennsylvania, ordinance. Souter joined part of the Court's opinion but said the city needed to present stronger evidence on the issue for the ordinance to be upheld.

Souter continued to emerge as a pointed questioner during oral argument, frequently sparring with the conservative Scalia on his immediate left. But the heft of his opinions discomfited some Court watchers. "I wish he could get to a point quicker," Professor Baker commented. "It takes him four pages to tell the time of day."

Breyer and Ginsburg had been closely aligned since Breyer joined the Court in 1994, one year after Ginsburg. In the past term, though, Breyer moved a bit to the right, joining with the conservatives in several criminal cases and some First Amendment disputes. He remained, however, a stalwart member of the liberal bloc in defending congressional prerogatives and federal powers and in taking a broad view of civil rights remedies and individual rights.

In his most important opinion, Breyer wrote the 5–4 decision striking down the Nebraska partial-birth abortion statute. Breyer opened his twenty-seven-page opinion with a seemingly balanced précis of what he called the "virtually irreconcilable points of view" on the issue. But in his first abortion-related opinion, Breyer made clear his agreement with the rulings from *Roe v. Wade* through *Casey* that, as he put it, "the Constitution offers basic protection to the woman's right to choose." From there, Breyer proceeded methodically to describe the medical procedures for abortions and then to conclude that the Nebraska law imposed an "undue burden" on abortion rights because it lacked an exception for the mother's health and because it could be applied to prohibit a common and safe procedure for abortions in the late second trimester of pregnancy.

In another 5–4 decision, Breyer wrote for the majority in holding that federal regulations that limited automakers' obligation to equip cars with air bags had the effect of preempting state court suits for failing to install the safety devices. In another important federal regulatory case, Breyer wrote the unanimous opinion upholding Interior Department regulations for livestock grazing on public lands that western ranchers said infringed on statutorily protected rights.

Breyer's support for expansive federal powers emerged in other, higher-profile cases. He wrote for the four dissenters in the ruling that blocked the FDA from regulating cigarettes. He also wrote a secondary dissenting opinion in the decision to strike down the Violence Against Women Act's provision for federal court damage suits. In both opinions, Breyer, a former congressional aide, indicated confidence that the issues were best dealt with in the political branches of government rather than in the courts.

The same trust in the political process led Breyer to reject First Amendment claims in most free speech–related cases during the term. In voting to uphold campaign contribution limits, Breyer explicitly said that legislatures had "greater institutional expertise" on the issue than courts. He led four dissenters in arguing that the decision to strike down the cable indecency law had unduly restricted Congress's power to deal with the issue. "He takes a looser view of First Amendment restrictions," Professor Volokh observed. "He's a balancer."

Ginsburg began her seventh term on the Court three weeks after undergoing surgery for colon cancer in September. She completed the term without missing a single Court session, even while undergoing what was termed "precautionary" chemotherapy from January through June. "A remarkable display of will power," Professor Baker commented.

Nonetheless, Ginsburg, who turned sixty-seven in March, appeared weak or tired on the bench during some arguments. And her written work was somewhat diminished. Of her eight majority opinions, six were unanimous decisions, and none was a major ruling. Altogether, she wrote eighteen opinions—the third lowest number of any of the justices (after O'Connor with fifteen and Rehnquist with sixteen).

In the most important of her majority opinions, Ginsburg gave environmental organizations a rare victory by upholding the right of citizen groups to sue alleged polluters under the Clean Water Act even if any financial penalties are to be paid to the federal government. Civil penalties "afford redress to citizen plaintiffs," Ginsburg wrote, because they "encourage defendants to discontinue current violations and deter them from committing future ones."

In a second significant opinion, Ginsburg led a unanimous Court in limiting the ability of police to use anonymous tips to justify stopping and frisking a suspect on the street. Allowing police to do so with nothing more than an anonymous tip, Ginsburg said, could subject innocent citizens to "an intrusive, embarrassing police search" without cause. Ginsburg also wrote another unanimous criminal law decision, narrowly construing the federal arson statute so as not to cover the torching of a private residence.

While typically siding with defendants in closely divided criminal law cases, Ginsburg did write for herself and three conservatives in dissenting from a decision to limit prosecutors' ability to use changes in evidentiary laws enacted after an offense has been committed. The majority said that use of relaxed evidentiary standards to convict a defendant in a Texas child abuse case violated the Constitution's Ex Post Facto Clause. Ginsburg said the law was not the kind of retroactive change that the Constitution prohibits.

Among her few concurring opinions, Ginsburg, a longtime women's rights advocate before her appointment to the bench, did write briefly in the partial-birth abortion case. But she criticized the Nebraska law banning the procedure mainly by quoting from another judge's opinion—a dissenting opinion by federal appeals court Judge Richard Posner from a decision to uphold similar laws in Illinois and Wisconsin.

Presidential Politics

Vice President Al Gore was campaigning for president in Ohio on June 28 as the Supreme Court was issuing its final decisions for the term in Washington. As Gore learned of the Court's 5–4 decision to strike down Nebraska's partial-birth abortion ban, the presumptive Democratic nominee scrapped a planned speech on energy and the environment and decided instead to talk about the role the next president would play in shaping the Court's future direction.

"The next president will nominate at least three and probably four, perhaps four, justices to the Supreme Court," Gore told his audience in the Columbus suburb of Blacklick. "One extra vote on the wrong side," he said, "would change the outcome, and a woman's right to choose would be taken away."

The warning was something of an exaggeration, as veteran legal affairs reporter Stuart Taylor Jr. noted in his account of the speech in *Newsweek*. Six justices supported the Court's basic abortion-rights decisions—the five in the majority in the Nebraska case plus dissenter Kennedy. Still, Gore was correct in his basic appeal. The Court was closely divided on a range of issues, and even one new justice could make a difference. And Gore's listing of his favorite justices—liberals Thurgood Marshall and William J. Brennan Jr.—was aimed at energizing moderate and liberal constituencies who might fear more conservative appointments if Gore's Republican opponent, Texas governor George W. Bush, made it to the White House.

For his part, Bush was not pushing the composition of the Court as an issue. When asked, Bush listed the conservatives Scalia and Thomas as his favorite justices and promised to name justices who would "strictly interpret" the Constitution. He declined to give his opinion of Souter, who had evolved into a liberal after his appointment in 1990 by Bush's father, President George Bush.

The presidential contenders' pronouncements came amidst the widely shared assumption that one or more of the justices would retire during the term of the next chief executive. The speculation naturally focused on the Court's three oldest and longest serving members: Chief Justice Rehnquist, who was to turn seventy-six in October at the start of his thirtieth term; Stevens, who marked his eightieth birthday in April; and O'Connor, who turned seventy in March. Ginsburg was counted by some as a fourth possible departure because of her bout with colon cancer.

History as well as actuarial tables suggested the likelihood of a retirement sometime soon. By the end of the summer, the nine justices had served together for six full years—the Court's longest period of unchanged membership since an eleven-year stretch of no vacancies from 1812 to 1823.

Still, some Court watchers cautioned against expecting any imminent departures. "I don't see any of the members as candidates for retirement," Professor Kmiec said. Joan Biskupic, the respected Supreme Court reporter who moved from the *Washington Post* to *USA Today* toward the end of the term, agreed. "They look great. They seem quite healthy. They're quite vigorous," she said. "No one seems like they're in a hurry to step down."

The justices themselves were saying nothing publicly. But the *Los Angeles Times'* Supreme Court correspondent, David Savage, reported one tidbit to suggest that the justices were watching the political developments. He quoted one justice as remarking early in the year: "There's a sense of everyone around the building holding his breath, awaiting the outcome of the November election."

Whatever the results of the presidential race, the possibility of an ideological shift on the Court turned on a host of imponderables. Gore's options could be limited by the likelihood of a Republican-controlled Senate. "I'm not sure he can get a Marshall or a Brennan through," Professor Baker commented. More likely, he said, "you're looking at someone who's confirmable, more middle of the road."

As for Bush, his record of judicial appointments in Texas during his two terms as governor confounded easy predictions, according to a number of observers quoted by the *New York Times* in July. "The people he picked were sort of moderate conservatives," Anthony Champagne, a political scientist at the University of Texas in Dallas, told the *Times*. "Like he is."

The justices' decisions themselves could be shaped by the outcome in November. The common speculation was that Rehnquist was all but certain to retire if the Republican Bush was elected but somewhat less likely if the Democrat Gore won. But to outlast a hypothetical four-year Gore administration, Rehnquist would have to stay in office past the age of eighty. Rehnquist's outside interests—he has written two books of Supreme Court history—suggested he might be loath to keep a full-time job that long.

Finally, the president's ability to accurately discern the future votes of a Supreme Court nominee was subject to some doubt. For the most part, justices generally conformed to expectations at the time of their confirmations. Republicans Richard Nixon, Ronald Reagan, and Bush had named the five justices that formed the Court's conservative majority, while Ginsburg and Breyer were voting in line with the moderate-to-liberal views of the "New Democrat" president who appointed them, Clinton. But there were exceptions—notably Souter and Stevens on the current Court, both more liberal than the presidents who appointed them, Bush and Gerald Ford.

The past term's decisions underscored the uncertainties, according to one expert. "The justices defied any simple political typecasting," Kathleen Sullivan, dean of Stanford Law School and a liberal constitutional law expert, wrote in the *New York Times* following the final rulings. "This term's decisions should make politicians wary of simple ideological labels."

"This is a world in which the issues are changing a great deal," Professor Friedman added. "It makes for a volatile situation for judicial appointments."

Chapter 2

The 1999–2000 Term

"Justice Breyer has the opinion of the Court in number 99-830, *Stenberg against Carhart*."

The time was shortly after 10 o'clock in the morning on June 28. Moments earlier, the nine justices of the Supreme Court of the United States had emerged from behind thick maroon velvet curtains, taken their places behind the Court's carved mahogany bench, and stood solemnly as the Court's marshal, Dale Bosley, intoned the brief invocation with its famous closing: "God save the United States and this Honorable Court."

Without further preliminaries, Chief Justice Rehnquist introduced the first of four decisions the Court had to announce before concluding the 1999–2000 term. The rulings promised to add weight to an already momentous year. Of the four cases, none was more anxiously awaited by interest groups on opposing sides than *Carhart*. LeRoy Carhart, a Nebraska surgeon, was challenging a state law that banned so-called "partial-birth abortions"—the name that anti-abortion forces had coined for a rare but controversial procedure and that abortion rights supporters insisted was misleading and deceptive. The state's attorney general, Donald Stenberg, had personally argued the case before the Court barely two months earlier.

"This case concerns the right to abortion," Breyer began, reading the summary of his opinion with an extra measure of formality. "We understand the intensely controversial nature of the problem," he continued, his remarks evidently aimed at a wider audience than the few hundred visitors in the courtroom that day.

Millions of Americans, Breyer said, believe that abortion is "like causing the death of an innocent child." Other millions, he said, fear that a law forbidding abortion "would condemn many American women to lives that lack dignity, depriving them of equal liberty and leading those with least resources to undergo illegal abortions with attendant risk of death and suffering." Despite those "virtually irreconcilable points of view," Breyer continued, the Court—"in the course of a generation"—had recognized a constitutional right to abortion. "We shall not revisit those basic legal principles," he declared. "Here, we shall simply apply these principles to the circumstances here."

Over the next seven minutes, Breyer declared that the Nebraska law— comparable to those in thirty other states—was unconstitutional for two reasons. First, it was "too broad." The statutory definition could be read to encompass a common and safe abortion procedure used for women after their thirteenth week of pregnancy. Second, the law did not contain an exception to permit the challenged procedure when necessary for the preservation of the mother's health.

As he closed, Breyer noted that four justices had filed dissenting opinions: Rehnquist, Scalia, Kennedy, and Thomas. Seated to his immediate right, Thomas spoke next. "It behooves me to say a few words in dissent," Thomas said. For the next eight minutes, Thomas attacked the majority's decision calmly but bitterly. The American people—"unlike the members of this Court"—were not deeply divided on the issue of partial-birth abortions, Thomas said. Nebraska had passed its law with only one dissenting vote, thirty states had passed similar laws, and most doctors who perform abortions decline to use the procedure.

Unflinchingly, Thomas described the procedure. The fetus is pulled almost completely from the mother's womb, its skull is pierced with scissors or some other instrument, and the doctor "literally sucks the brain from the fetus's skull." The Constitution, Thomas said, "does not prohibit a state from banning this horrifying and rarely used procedure that many find hard to distinguish from infanticide."

"The Court's decision is indefensible," Thomas concluded. "I respectfully dissent."

Three more decisions followed, with more drama. Thomas announced a bold opinion in a closely watched case involving aid to parochial schools. His opinion envisioned greater leeway for the government to provide assistance to church-affiliated schools, but it gained only three other votes— one short of a majority. Two other justices—O'Connor and Breyer—had a narrower opinion that upheld the federal program at issue in the case, but maintained existing rules for drawing the line between permissible and impermissible aid.

In a third case, Stevens announced the Court's decision upholding a Colorado law curbing demonstrations at abortion clinics. Scalia and Kennedy each read strongly written dissents complaining that the ruling

Table 2-1 Laws Held Unconstitutional

The Supreme Court issued nine decisions during the 1999–2000 term that held unconstitutional federal laws or state laws or constitutional provisions. The rulings brought the number of decisions by the Rehnquist Court striking down federal laws on constitutional grounds to thirty-one. The total number of such decisions by the Court throughout history was 153.

Decisions (in chronological order)	Law Held Invalid
Federal Laws	
Kimel v. Florida Board of Regents [p. 148]	Age Discrimination in Employment Act (Private suits against state governments)
United States v. Morrison [p. 144]	Violence Against Women Act (Private suits in federal court)
United States v. Playboy Entertainment Group, Inc. [p. 139]	Telecommunications Act (Cable indecency provision)
Dickerson v. United States [p. 113]	*Miranda* override (18 U.S.C. §3501)
State Laws	
Hunt-Wesson, Inc. v. Franchise Tax Board of California [p. 150]	Limit on interest deductions for out-of-state corporations
Rice v. Cayetano [p. 120]	"Native Hawaiian" requirement to vote for Office of Hawaiian Affairs
California Democratic Party v. Jones [p. 119]	Blanket primary
Apprendi v. New Jersey [p. 115]	Hate crime law (sentencing provisions)
Stenberg v. Carhart [p. 141]	Nebraska "partial-birth abortion" ban

amounted to an unprecedented restriction on freedom of speech on an issue of profound political and moral importance. Then Rehnquist read the Court's final decision: a 5–4 ruling upholding, under the First Amendment's freedom of association, the Boy Scouts' policy of excluding homosexuals. A gay ex–Eagle Scout had challenged the policy under a New Jersey law prohibiting discrimination on the basis of sexual orientation.

The four decisions were of a piece with the rest of the term. Liberals and conservatives each counted victories in two of the four cases. All four were closely divided, and all four brought forth strongly opposed views from the Court's opposing ideological groupings. Similarly mixed patterns appeared in the Court's cases on federalism, individual rights, and criminal law.

The Court did not hesitate to strike down either federal or state laws on federal constitutional grounds. *(See Table 2-1.)* It sided with law enforce-

Table 2-2 Reversals of Earlier Rulings

The Supreme Court issued one decision during the 1999–2000 term that explicitly reversed a previous ruling by the Court. The ruling brought the number of such reversals during the Court's history to at least 217.

New Decision	Old Decision	New Holding
Mitchell v. Helms	Meek v. Pittenger, Wolman v. Walter	Public money may be used to provide equipment for parochial schools

ment in most criminal law decisions, but gave civil liberties and criminal defense advocates some significant victories. It backed First Amendment claims in two cases, but rejected them in several others. In cases involving religion, church-state separationists cheered the Court's decision to bar prayers at public high school football games, but regretted the last-day decision on aid to parochial schools. That ruling overturned two of the Court's precedents from the 1970s that limited government assistance to parochial schools. *(See Table 2-2.)*

"This term forced us to make a much more nuanced appraisal of the Rehnquist Court," University of Southern California law professor Erwin Chemerinsky said. "In some areas, it remains a very activist, conservative Court. In other areas, it was bitterly disappointing to conservatives."

Moreover, despite the ideological divisions, the Court continued to draw generally favorable reviews from lawyers and observers for judicial craftsmanship. "It's a very smart Court, a very well prepared Court," said attorney Mark Levy. "The oral arguments are very engaging. You can see the justices dealing with the problems."

"It's a Court of judges," said John Roberts, a Washington attorney and former Rehnquist law clerk, noting that all of the justices except Rehnquist had previously served on a federal or—in O'Connor's case—a state appeals court. "I think they do look at each case and let the chips fall where they may," Roberts said.

Individual Rights

The Court's decision to strike down Nebraska's partial-birth abortion ban cheered civil liberties advocates. But two other last-day rulings illustrated the difficulty of defining the stakes in individual rights cases. The justices had to choose between conflicting rights in a pair of unrelated cases. In one, they favored the Boy Scouts' freedom of association over an antidiscrimination claim by a gay former Scout leader. In the other, the Court favored access rights to abortion clinics over free speech claims by anti-abortion protesters.

In his opinion in the partial-birth abortion case, Breyer said he was simply applying the Court's prior abortion rights ruling by finding that the law imposed an "undue burden" on a woman's choice in violation of the 1992 *Casey* decision and failed to include a health exception as required by *Casey* and the landmark 1973 decision *Roe v. Wade*. Dissenting justices insisted the ruling went beyond the Court's precedents.

Anti-abortion leaders vowed to draft new laws with features from O'Connor's pivotal concurring opinion: a narrower definition of the procedure covered and a health exception. "It seems to me that such a law could be upheld," said James Bopp, general counsel of the National Right to Life Committee. But Simon Heller, legal director of the Center for Reproductive Law and Policy, who argued the case before the Court, predicted that anti-abortion organizations would not be satisfied with more tightly written laws. "They do not want to prohibit a narrow technique," he said.

The health exception could also prove to be a stumbling block. Anti-abortion groups "don't want to have a full-fledged health exception," Heller said. "Over and over, they have announced that they view women's health as a loophole." Bopp acknowledged the concern. A law "probably" would not be worth passing "if you had to write the exception too broadly," he said.

For their part, lower federal courts continued to reject partial-birth abortion measures following the Court's decision. Within a month, federal courts blocked partial-birth abortion measures in New Jersey, Virginia, and West Virginia. The Court itself ordered the federal appeals court in Chicago to reconsider its decision upholding laws in Illinois and Wisconsin. Heller said that courts had blocked all but eight of the thirty-one partial-birth abortion laws and that the laws not yet challenged were not being enforced.

First Amendment cases also saw the justices closely divided, sometimes across normal ideological lines. The results were mixed. The Court rejected free speech claims in five of six cases, but upheld freedom of association arguments in two decisions.

The Court struck down a federal law regulating sexual programming on cable television, but upheld a local ordinance banning nude dancing. It upheld the Colorado law curbing anti-abortion protests and a Missouri law limiting campaign contributions—rulings that found liberal justices in the majority and conservatives backing free speech arguments in dissent.

In another closely watched case, the Court rejected a challenge to the use of mandatory student fees to fund political and ideological advocacy groups at public colleges and universities. And the Court also rejected a First Amendment attack on a Los Angeles ordinance that denied commercial businesses access to police department arrest records.

Besides the Boy Scouts case, the Court also backed a freedom of association argument in ruling that a so-called "blanket primary"—an election that allowed voters to vote to nominate a candidate of one party for one position and a candidate of another party in another race—infringed on political parties' First Amendment rights.

The Boy Scouts ruling cheered conservative interest groups. The American Center for Law and Justice said the ruling allowed "all private organizations, including religious groups, to define their own mission and set their own criteria for membership." But the American Civil Liberties Union (ACLU) criticized the decision. "The Court has essentially said that freedom of speech gives an organization the right to discriminate on the basis of an individual's identity," it said.

The term's two religion cases also featured conflicting results. In a Texas case, the Court barred a local school board's policy of permitting student-led prayers at high school football games. The majority rejected the school board's argument that barring the prayers would violate the students' free speech rights. In a second case, the Court turned aside a taxpayers' challenge to the use of federal funds to provide computers and other instructional equipment to parochial schools. The justices in the majority found no improper establishment of religion. The 6–3 ruling not only opened the door to more public support for parochial schools but also gave school voucher supporters encouragement that at least four of the justices—and perhaps six—could be counted on to approve such plans.

The Court issued only one signed decision in a traditional civil rights dispute: a 5–4 ruling that made it harder for minority groups to use the federal Voting Rights Act to challenge election law changes that do not leave minority voters worse off than before. Civil rights groups counted one significant victory: a ruling in an age discrimination case that eased the burden on plaintiffs to rebut an employer's defense in job bias suits. Experts said the ruling would also likely be applied to suits brought under the broader Title VII of the Civil Rights Act of 1964, which prohibits discrimination in employment based on race or sex, among other factors.

Finally, civil liberties groups on both the left and right were pleased with the Court's parental rights decision in a Washington State case overturning a judge's order to grant visitation rights to the grandparents of two young girls over the mother's objections. Justices in the majority criticized the state's third-party visitation law as too broad, but the fractured ruling left unsettled whether grandparents or other relatives could use narrower laws to win visitation rights under some circumstances.

States and Federal Government

The Court continued building on its framework of federalism rulings limiting the powers of Congress and strengthening the role of state governments. "The Rehnquist Court is serious about dual sovereignty," Pepperdine Law School professor Douglas Kmiec remarked. At the same time, though, the Court backed federal over state powers in federal preemption cases and struck down five state laws or constitutional provisions on federal constitutional grounds.

The two major federalism rulings expanded Rehnquist Court precedents limiting Congress's powers under the Commerce Clause and the Fourteenth Amendment and protecting states from private damage suits under the Eleventh Amendment. The Court said that the Violence Against Women Act's provision for federal court damage suits went beyond Congress's authority to regulate interstate commerce to invade the states' traditional police powers. It also rejected the argument that the law could be justified under the Fourteenth Amendment.

The dissenting justices noted that some thirty-six states had joined the federal government in urging the Court to uphold the law. "States will be forced to enjoy the new federalism whether they want it or not," Souter wrote. Former U.S. solicitor general Walter Dellinger said the Court appeared more interested in curbing Congress than in aiding the states. "The states are sometimes a stick that the Court uses to beat Congress when Congress stumbles into an area that the Court regards as its domain," he said.

The decision to protect state governments from federal age discrimination suits by their workers extended Eleventh Amendment protections to limit Congress's power to enforce traditional equal rights legislation against the states. Congress could not use the Fourteenth Amendment to override states' sovereign immunity, O'Connor wrote for the 5–4 majority, because age discrimination did not amount a constitutional violation. "Congress cannot redefine the constitutional right in the name of protecting it," Kmiec explained.

Attorney Mark Levy, a former assistant U.S. solicitor general, said the rulings represented "the fruits of seeds that were planted years earlier" and predicted more such rulings in the future. "There are now a lot of doctrines that the Court has developed that all lead to the result of a federal action being declared unconstitutional," Levy said. "The more established these doctrines become, the more likely that we're going to see other federal statutes declared unconstitutional."

The Court issued two other rulings favoring states in closely watched federalism disputes, but relied on statutory rather than constitutional grounds. In one, the Court held that private individuals could not use the federal False Claims Act to sue states to recover money in cases of fraud or waste involving federal funds. The 7–2 decision said that states were not included as "persons" subject to suit under the terms of the law. The Court also narrowly construed the federal arson statute to bar a federal prosecution for torching a private residence. That ruling was unanimous.

In another clash of state and federal powers, however, the Court unanimously upheld a provision of the Driver's Privacy Protection Act that barred state governments from selling driver's license lists. "This is not a traditional state function," Kmiec explained. "This is not an invasion of sovereign immunity."

The Court had scheduled arguments in another federalism dispute testing whether states could be subject to damage suits by workers under the Americans with Disabilities Act (ADA), but the case was settled and pulled from the docket. The justices quickly found another case raising the issue, however, and put it on the Court's calendar for the coming term. Disability rights advocates hoped to amass stronger evidence of discrimination against workers with disabilities to save the law. For his part, Kmiec noted that the Court in prior rulings had given somewhat closer scrutiny to laws affecting people with disabilities—possibly suggesting a greater willingness to view the ADA as a valid exercise of Congress's Fourteenth Amendment power to enforce constitutional rights.

The federal preemption rulings came in four cases brought by business groups challenging state regulations or state court suits. The Court rejected pleas from state governments in striking down a Massachusetts economic sanctions law and parts of Washington State's oil tanker regulations and barring state court product liability suits involving automobile airbags and railway crossings. "If they were really concerned about protecting states' rights, you would see more rulings backing states on preemption," Professor Chemerinsky remarked.

The Court's decisions striking state laws on constitutional grounds arose in a variety of settings and differing ideological contexts. A liberal majority struck down the partial-birth abortion ban by a 5–4 vote. Breyer's opinion applied prior abortion rulings, which he said were based on "the Constitution's guarantees of fundamental individual liberty." In his dissent, Kennedy complained that the Court "substitutes its own judgment for the judgment of Nebraska and some 30 other States and sweeps the law away."

Other rulings were less sweeping and had cross-ideological coalitions. A majority formed of three liberals and conservatives Scalia and Thomas struck down parts of New Jersey's hate crimes sentencing scheme for giving too much power to judges rather than juries. Criminal law experts disagreed—as did the justices—on the likely impact of the ruling on other state and federal sentencing laws.

The Court's conservative bloc, along with liberals Souter and Breyer, voted to strike down California's so-called "blanket primary" as an invasion of political parties' First Amendment freedom of association. Two other states—Alaska and Washington—had similar primaries that allowed voters to choose candidates of different parties for different positions. Dissenting justices Stevens and Ginsburg warned the ruling could also jeopardize the more common "open primary"—which allows voters to vote in a party primary without registration prior to the day of the election.

The Court struck down a Hawaii constitutional provision that allowed only "native Hawaiians" and their descendants to vote for members of the Office of Hawaiian Affairs. The vote was 7–2, with Stevens and Ginsburg again in dissent. The ruling, based on the Fifteenth Amendment's prohibition against racial discrimination in voting, seemed unlikely to have much impact on other affirmative action–type issues.

In a final decision, the Court struck down a California tax provision that limited interest deductions for out-of-state corporations. The unanimous ruling relied on well-established Commerce Clause principles prohibiting states from discriminating against interstate commerce.

Criminal Law

The Court's decision to reaffirm the *Miranda* rule on police interrogation came as no surprise to most experts or to many of the critics of the ruling. "It was a long-shot effort," remarked Kent Scheidegger, legal director of the California-based Criminal Justice Legal Foundation, which filed a brief urging the justices to uphold Congress's anti-*Miranda* law. Overall, however, the Court's criminal law rulings during the term did produce a measure of surprise: "Criminal defendants fared unusually well," the ACLU said in its end-of-term wrap-up.

Statistically, the justices agreed to hear a greater proportion of appeals from defendants or inmates than in recent years—seventeen cases compared to eleven appeals by the government—and ruled for defendants or inmates in twelve of the cases—a somewhat higher victory rate for defendants (42 percent) than in the recent past. The defense victories were also more important than the pro-prosecution decisions, although some rulings for inmates in habeas corpus cases had mixed legal outcomes that could restrict federal court challenges to state convictions in the future.

The *Miranda* ruling left intact the thirty-four-year-old decision requiring police to warn suspects of their rights before conducting interrogation. "[T]he warnings have become part of our national culture," Rehnquist said in his opinion for the seven-justice majority. Defense lawyers said, however, that *Miranda*'s impact had been blunted over the years. "Law enforcement knows how to deal with *Miranda*, and the Court has cut back on it anyway," said University of New Mexico law professor Barbara Bergman, who follows the Court for the National Association of Criminal Defense Lawyers.

Defendants won a second important—and unexpected—victory with the Court's 5–4 ruling somewhat limiting judges' role in favor of juries in statutory sentencing schemes. The ruling invalidated portions of a New Jersey hate crime law because it allowed a sentence-enhancing factor— racial motivation—to be determined by a judge based on a preponderance of the evidence rather than by the jury using the beyond-the-reasonable-doubt standard. Defense lawyers immediately began looking for other statutes subject to similar challenges. "It's going to be a major effort to determine which things the legislature can shift to the sentencing phase," said Ron Wright, a professor at Wake Forest University Law School. But Wright discounted the warning by the dissenting justices that the ruling jeopardized the federal Sentencing Guidelines.

The Court backed Fourth Amendment claims by defendants in three out of four search and seizure decisions during the term. In one case, the Court rejected an effort by the state of Florida—backed by the Clinton administration—to allow police to stop and frisk a suspect based on an anonymous tip that he or she was carrying a firearm. In a second case, the Court said that a federal drug agent stepped over the line when he looked for drugs by feeling a bus passenger's soft-sided, carry-on luggage. And in an unsigned decision, the Court refused to create a "crime scene exception" to the general rule requiring a warrant to search private property. The government's only victory in search and seizure issues came in a ruling in an Illinois case giving police broad leeway to stop and frisk a fleeing suspect. "We've turned a little bit of a corner on the Fourth Amendment," Professor Friedman said.

In habeas corpus cases, the Court continued to interpret provisions of the 1996 law—the Anti-Terrorism and Effective Death Penalty Act—that Congress intended to restrict inmates' ability to challenge state court convictions in federal court. The Rehnquist Court had also been tightening habeas corpus rules, but this term inmates prevailed in three cases dealing with complex procedural issues.

In the most important, the Court ruled that a Virginia death row inmate, Terry Williams, deserved a new trial because of inadequate legal representation at trial. In reaching that result, the Court applied a provision of the 1996 law aimed at limiting federal courts' power to override state court rulings on constitutional claims: it adopted a restrictive standard, but rejected a more stringent test used by the lower federal appeals court in the case. "The Court is saying that federal courts will still remain involved in reviewing state court convictions," Wright said. In the two other rulings— including one filed by another Virginia death row inmate, Michael Williams (no relation)—the Court eased curbs on repeat habeas corpus petitions by inmates.

The Court rejected habeas corpus petitions by two other Virginia death row inmates who challenged procedures used in the capital sentencing phases of their trials. In both cases, the Court backed trial judges' handling of jury instruction issues: an ambiguous instruction on how to consider mitigating circumstances in one case, a failure to tell a jury that a defendant might be ineligible for parole in the other. Both rulings came on 5–4 votes, with the conservative bloc aligned against the four liberal justices. By the same division, the Court refused late in the term to block the execution of a Texas death row inmate, Gary Graham, who had gained national support for his attack on the evidence used in his 1981 murder conviction.

Defendants won victories in some other cases. In a Texas case, the Court limited prosecutors' ability to retroactively apply laws relaxing evidentiary burdens in trials involving offenses committed before enactment of the laws. In another, the Court ruled that Independent Counsel Kenneth Starr violated the Fifth Amendment rights of former Clinton administration official Webster Hubbell by using business records that Hubbell turned over under a grant of immunity. Prosecution victories were more limited and less noteworthy. One ruling, in a California case, softened the requirement on defense lawyers to file appeals for indigent defendants if they believe there are no grounds to contest a conviction. Another decision limited defendants' ability to appeal a pretrial ruling on the admissibility of prior criminal convictions if the defendant later acknowledges the conviction while testifying.

Business, Labor, and Consumers

The tobacco industry won a major victory against federal regulators with the Court's 5–4 decision barring the restrictions proposed by the Food and Drug Administration (FDA) on the sale and marketing of cigarettes and smokeless tobacco. But politically sensitive business groups left it to the tobacco industry itself to handle the litigation. "We weren't involved," noted Stephen Bokat, vice president and general counsel for the U.S. Chamber of Commerce. And experts doubted that the ruling had broad implications for other regulatory disputes.

The ruling "was not a sea change in the Court's approach to reviewing agency action," said Glenn Lammi, president of the pro-business Washington Legal Foundation. David Vladeck, director of the Public Citizen Litigation Group, agreed. "I can't imagine this case having long legs," Vladeck said. "It's a reasonably narrowly written opinion that's quite careful in most respects not to make broad pronouncements on administrative law."

Overall, business groups counted the year's rulings as generally favorable. "It was a good term for business," Bokat said. "There were a lot of decisions that we considered as positive." At the top of the Chamber's list were rulings in four unrelated cases that challenged state laws or state court suits as "preempted" by federal law. Business advocates have favored federal preemption in recent years in order to reduce the burdens of dealing with separate regulations enacted by various states. "Trying to deal with regulation of your business on a fifty-state basis is almost an impossibility to comply with," Bokat explained.

In the most closely watched of the cases, the Court ruled, 5–4, that auto accident victims could not bring product liability suits against automakers in state court for failing to install air bags before they were required by federal regulation. Breyer said that a Department of Transportation regulation that permitted a gradual phasing in of air bags protected automakers from product defect suits even though Congress had provided that compliance with federal regulations did not affect liability in personal injury actions. In a second case, the Court held, 7–2, that railroads cannot be sued for inadequate warning signs at rail crossings when the signs are paid for with federal funds.

The Court also unanimously backed federal preemption arguments in two cases with foreign policy implications. It struck down a Massachusetts law imposing economic penalties on companies that did business with the authoritarian government in Myanmar (formerly Burma). Souter said the state sanctions measure was preempted by a narrower law passed by Congress. The Court also barred oil tanker regulations adopted by the state of Washington after the *Exxon Valdez* oil spill in 1989. Kennedy said that federal laws as well as international treaties indicated Congress's intention for "national uniformity regarding maritime commerce."

In another business victory, the Court barred the use of the federal employee benefits law known as ERISA—Employee Retirement Income Security Act—to sue health maintenance organizations (HMOs) for cost-saving treatment decisions. In a unanimous opinion, Souter said that allowing such suits would mean the end of for-profit HMOs and would federalize medical malpractice litigation. "This is a Court quite skeptical of civil litigation as a method of social ordering," attorney Dellinger said of the ruling.

Businesses also won two victories in rulings involving civil suits brought under the federal antiracketeering law commonly known as RICO (Racketeer Influenced and Corrupt Organizations Act). In one, the Court held that a fired employee ordinarily cannot leverage a wrongful termination claim into a more potent, treble-damage RICO suit. In the other, the Court rejected an expansive time period for plaintiffs to file RICO suits when they belatedly learn of evidence needed to allege a "pattern" of racketeering as required under the law.

The Court handed business groups two defeats in cases involving job discrimination litigation and environmental suits. In the first case, the Court made it harder for employers to keep a case from the jury by presenting a business-reason defense for the allegedly discriminatory action. The ruling, in an age discrimination case, was likely to be extended to other federal job bias suits, experts agreed.

In the environmental case, the Court made it easier for individuals or advocacy groups to file so-called "citizen suits" against companies under antipollution laws such as the Clean Water Act. The ruling was "a huge win for the environmental community," according to Georgetown law professor Richard Lazarus, an environmental law expert. Lammi agreed. "The ruling enhances the power of activist groups that sue businesses," he said.

The Court also issued a significant pro-consumer ruling in a trademark-related, business-on-business dispute. The unanimous ruling made it harder for manufacturers to claim so-called "trade dress" protection for product designs. The decision set aside a $1.6 million jury award won by an apparel manufacturer, against Wal-Mart Stores for selling low-cost "knockoffs" of one of its signature designs.

Abortion

"Partial-Birth Abortion" Ban Is Struck Down

Stenberg, Attorney General of Nebraska v. Carhart, decided by a 5–4 vote, June 28, 2000; Breyer wrote the opinion; Thomas, Rehnquist, Scalia, and Kennedy dissented.

LeRoy Carhart began his career as an abortion doctor at the request of a nurse who worked at a Nebraska clinic where Carhart had been performing vasectomies following his retirement as an Air Force physician in 1985. Over time—and especially after founding his own clinic in the Omaha suburb of Bellevue in 1991—Carhart became a crusader of sorts, a fervent believer in the right to an abortion as an integral part of women's health care.

By 1999 Carhart was one of only three physicians performing abortions in Nebraska—and the only one who performed the operation on women more than sixteen weeks pregnant. In some twenty or so cases per year, Carhart used a procedure described in medical terminology as "dilation and extraction," or D&X. In this procedure, the woman's cervix is dilated and the fetus brought feet first from the uterus into the vagina. Then, because the head is too large to pass through the cervix, the doctor pierces the fetal skull, suctions out the contents, and crushes or collapses the skull to complete removal of the fetus.

The procedure had been developed years earlier as an alternative to the somewhat risky process of induced labor for late second-trimester abortions. The American College of Obstetrics and Gynecology viewed the procedure as a variant of the more common "dilation and evacuation" or D&E procedure, in which the fetus is dismembered as it is brought through the cervical opening into the vagina. But anti-abortion organizations disagreed. The National Right to Life Committee in 1995 coined a new name for the D&X procedure: "partial-birth abortion." Using graphic pictures of nearly intact fetuses with their brains spilling out of collapsed skulls, the anti-abortion forces likened the procedure to infanticide and mounted lobbying campaigns in state capitals and in Washington to enact laws prohibiting the operation.

The movement succeeded in the legislative arena. Some thirty-one states, including Nebraska, enacted laws aimed at prohibiting so-called "partial-birth abortions." But abortion rights advocates challenged the laws in courts—successfully, for the most part. Carhart, the challenger in one of those cases, filed suit to invalidate Nebraska's partial-birth abortion ban not long after its enactment in 1997. Two lower federal courts agreed with Carhart that the law was unconstitutional. This term, so did the Supreme Court, in a 5–4 ruling that gratified abortion rights advocates but provoked outrage from anti-abortion groups—as well as from the dissenting justices.

Background. The Court first recognized a woman's right to an abortion in 1973 in the controversial decision *Roe v. Wade*. The ruling guaranteed women an unfettered right to an abortion during the first three months of pregnancy. But it allowed states to impose regulations to protect a woman's health or safety during the second trimester. States could also ban abortion altogether during the final trimester—when the fetus was thought capable of living on its own—as long as the law permitted exceptions to protect the woman's life or health.

The *Roe* ruling pleased abortion rights advocates, but also mobilized opponents of abortion to mount protests and sustained political efforts to undo or limit the ruling. Most states prohibited post-viability abortions altogether. In addition, anti-abortion forces won enactment of a host of state laws regulating the procedures for women to obtain a pre-viability abortion or for doctors to perform the procedure. The Court sustained some of the provisions and struck others down. In one case, the Court in 1976 struck down a Missouri law that prohibited what was then the most common—and safest—procedure for second-trimester abortions: saline amniocentesis. But in 1989 the Rehnquist Court upheld a provision in a later Missouri law that required doctors to determine the viability of a fetus before permitting an abortion on a woman believed to be as much as twenty weeks pregnant.

Four justices in the 1989 case signaled their willingness to reconsider or overrule *Roe v. Wade*. Abortion rights advocates feared that Thomas's appointment in 1991 would create a majority to overrule the decision.

But in 1992, the Court in *Planned Parenthood v. Casey* reaffirmed *Roe*—by a 5–4 margin—while permitting states to regulate procedures as long as they did not impose an "undue burden" on a woman's right to abortion by posing a "substantial obstacle in her path" to the procedure.

Abortion rights advocates worried that the new standard weakened the protections against restrictive legislation. The Court over the next several years passed up opportunities to flesh out the meaning of the phrase. The Court issued two decisions somewhat limiting the rights of anti-abortion protesters, but it declined to take up for full consideration any cases involving regulation of abortion procedures. One of those cases involved the Ohio law—the first in the nation—seeking to ban "partial-birth" abortions; a federal appeals court struck the law down, and the justices rejected the state's petition to review the decision. *(See* Supreme Court Yearbook, 1997–1998, *pp. 68–69.)*

The Case. Nebraska adopted its partial-birth abortion ban in 1997 with only one dissenting vote in the state's unicameral legislature. The law defined "partial-birth abortion" as "deliberately and intentionally delivering into the vagina a living unborn child, or a substantial portion thereof, for the purpose of performing a procedure that the person performing such procedure knows will kill the unborn child and does kill the unborn child." The procedure was prohibited except when "necessary to save the life of the mother." A doctor violating the law faced up to twenty years in prison, a fine of up to $25,000, and the loss of his or her medical license.

In his suit challenging the law, Carhart claimed that by its terms the provision covered not only the D&X but also the D&E procedure. In both procedures, Carhart testified, the doctor brought a "substantial portion" of the fetus into the vaginal canal while it was still alive. Carhart's lawyers emphasized that the Nebraska legislature had rejected an amendment to the bill to refer specifically to "dilation and extraction" instead of "partial-birth abortion."

The state's attorneys countered that the language of the statute as well as the legislature's intent clearly established that the statute applied only to the D&X procedure. In a D&E procedure, the state argued, the doctor does not intend to deliver an "unborn child." As for the "substantial portion" phrase, the state argued it was used only to prevent abortion doctors from creating a loophole in the law.

Carhart and the state argued on one other major issue: the lack of an exception to permit the procedure to protect the health of the mother.

Carhart's attorneys argued that *Roe* clearly mandated a health exception. But the state's lawyers argued no health exception was needed: a partial-birth abortion was never medically necessary, they argued, because safe alternative methods were available. Carhart disagreed, insisting that the D&X procedure was the only safe alternative in some cases.

A federal district court judge in Omaha agreed with Carhart that the law was unconstitutional because it applied to all D&E procedures and because it failed to include a health exception. On appeal, the Eighth U.S. Circuit Court of Appeals in September 1999 also ruled the law unconstitutional, but solely on the first ground: that the statute imposed an "undue burden" on abortion by prohibiting D&E as well as D&X procedures.

The ruling coincided with most other court decisions on partial-birth abortions, including the earlier federal appeals court decision striking down the Ohio law. But in October the Seventh U.S. Circuit Court of Appeals upheld partial-birth abortion bans enacted in two states: Illinois and Wisconsin. Meanwhile, Congress had twice passed bills including partial-birth abortion bans only to have the measures vetoed by President Bill Clinton. The conflict between the two federal circuits, along with the continuing controversy over the issue, made it harder for the justices to ignore the dispute.

The Court agreed on January 14 to take up the Nebraska case—in time to hear arguments in April and rule before the end of the term. Predictably, the case drew a flood of amicus briefs—more than two dozen altogether—from advocacy groups on both sides of the issue. The Clinton administration filed a brief supporting Carhart's challenge to the law and asking to join the argument before the justices. The Court almost always grants the government's request to participate in arguments, but this time it declined—without explanation—to let the administration participate.

Arguments. A majority of the justices—the four liberals plus O'Connor—voiced strong doubts about Nebraska's law during the April 25 argument. On the other side, only Scalia was openly supportive of the statute.

Nebraska attorney general Donald Stenberg opened by saying that the state was seeking to prohibit "a little used method of abortion that borders on infanticide." Ginsburg quickly interjected that the case only concerned fetuses before viability, since the state separately prohibited post-viability abortions except to save the life of the mother. Stenberg quietly agreed.

O'Connor dealt Stenberg's argument a more telling blow when she questioned the distinction between the D&X and the D&E procedures,

Dr. LeRoy Carhart, the Nebraska physician who challenged the state's ban on so-called "partial-birth abortions," leaves the Supreme Court following the decision in his favor striking down the law.

which Stenberg said was untouched by the law. "They're both rather gruesome procedures," O'Connor said. "For purposes of the statute, the one is very similar to the other."

Later, O'Connor and Breyer both emphasized the lack of a health exception in the state law. Stenberg said the procedure was "not used by most abortionists" and there were "always alternatives available." Stevens followed up, noting that the lower court had found that D&X was the most appropriate procedure for ten to twenty cases per year in the state. Stenberg disagreed. "The overwhelming weight of medical opinion," he said, "is that the procedure is never necessary to save the life of the mother."

As he concluded, Stenberg was sharply questioned by Ginsburg and Souter on the state's justification for the law. Ginsburg said the law did not protect the health of the mother or the potential viability of the fetus—the two purposes that she said the Court had recognized for regulating abortions. Stenberg had no good answer as his time expired.

Representing Carhart, Simon Heller, litigation director of the Center for Reproductive Law and Policy in New York, said the Nebraska law was "so broadly written that it could prohibit most second-term abortions." Scalia challenged him, asking whether "breaking off a leg and dismembering an arm"—as in a D&E operation—was the same as "delivering an unborn child," the definition of partial-birth abortion in the statute. Eventually, Heller in effect said yes. Carhart testified, the lawyer said, that he tries to deliver as much of the fetus as possible into the vagina to avoid the risk of tearing or perforation of the uterus.

Scalia continued as the only justice closely questioning Heller. Toward the end, Scalia challenged Heller's assertion that the state law served no valid purpose. "Why isn't it a legitimate interest that the state is concerned about rendering society callous to infanticide?" Scalia asked. "Every abortion procedure, previability, involves fetal demise," Heller responded. The state's argument, he concluded, "could authorize a statute to prohibit all abortions."

Decision. Breyer's opinion for the Court striking down the Nebraska law—on June 28, the Court's final decision day for the term—began by acknowledging "the controversial nature of the problem" and the "virtually irreconcilable points of view" on the issue. In the remainder of his twenty-seven-page opinion, however, Breyer proceeded unemotionally through medical and legal details in concluding that the law was unconstitutional both because it was too broad and because it did not include a health exception.

By contrast, the dissenting justices railed against the decision with indignation. The ruling, Thomas said as he read portions of his dissenting opinion from the bench, was "indefensible."

Breyer said the ruling was based on an application of the principles of *Roe* and *Casey*. He carefully detailed the state's eight arguments for omitting a health exception and rejected them one by one. "[A] statute that altogether forbids D&X creates a significant health risk," Breyer concluded. "The statute consequently must contain a health exception."

On the scope of the statute, Breyer again detailed and then rejected the state's interpretation. "[U]sing this law, some present prosecutors and future Attorneys General may choose to pursue physicians who use D&E procedures," he explained. "All those who perform abortion procedures using that method must fear prosecution, conviction, and punishment. The result is an undue burden on a woman's right to make an abortion decision."

Four justices joined Breyer's opinion: Stevens, O'Connor, Souter, and Ginsburg. In a concurring opinion, O'Connor briefly recapped the reasons for holding Nebraska's law unconstitutional and then signaled her willingness to accept a more carefully drafted statute. "[A] ban on partial-birth abortion that only proscribed the D&X method of abortion and that included an exception to preserve the life and health of the mother would be constitutional in my view," O'Connor wrote.

In briefer concurrences, Stevens and Ginsburg both said they saw no legal distinction between the D&E and D&X procedures. "[T]he notion that either of these equally gruesome procedures performed at this late stage of gestation is more akin to infanticide than the other, or that the State furthers any legitimate interest by banning one but not the other, is simply irrational," Stevens wrote.

Thomas wrote the longest of the four dissenting opinions—forty-four pages—and emphasized his disagreement by reading much of it from the bench. "Today, the Court inexplicably holds that the States cannot constitutionally prohibit a method of abortion that millions find hard to distinguish from infanticide and that the Court hesitates even to describe," Thomas declared. The ruling "cannot be reconciled with *Casey's* undue-burden standard," he said. Instead, it represented "a reinstitution of the . . . abortion-on-demand era in which the mere invocation of 'abortion rights' trumps any contrary societal interest."

After describing abortion procedures in graphic detail, Thomas insisted that the majority was misreading the "plain language of the statute" to apply to D&E abortions and, in any event, was wrong to substitute its interpretation for the attorney general's. As for the health exception, Thomas said the majority was wrong to require an exception merely because a woman or a doctor preferred one procedure to another. "The exception entirely swallows the rule," Thomas wrote. "[T]here will always be *some* support for a procedure and there will always be some doctors who conclude that the procedure is preferable."

Scalia, who joined Thomas's opinion, and Kennedy, who did not, both wrote separate dissents. Kennedy, who had joined the *Casey* majority in reaffirming abortion rights, said the new ruling "repudiates" the "understanding" that states could enact laws "to promote the life of the unborn and to ensure respect for all human life and its potential." In a shorter but sharper opinion, Scalia likened the ruling to the Court's prior decisions in upholding slavery *(Dred Scott)* and permitting the wartime internment of Japanese Americans *(Korematsu)*. Rehnquist wrote a brief dissenting opinion, explaining that he still considered *Casey* "wrongly decided" but believed that Thomas and Kennedy had both "correctly applied *Casey's* principles" and joined their opinions.

Reaction. Abortion rights advocates applauded the Court's ruling but emphasized the narrowness of the margin. "It's a very significant victory, but a very fragile victory," Janet Benshoof, president of the Center for Reproductive Law and Policy, said on PBS's *NewsHour*. Abortion opponents were dismayed. James Bopp, general counsel of the National Right to Life Committee, called the decision "a radical expansion of the right to abortion."

In Lincoln, Attorney General Stenberg said the ruling showed that the Court's majority would support any form of abortion "no matter how barbarous, no matter how unjustified." Gov. Mike Johanns and other state officials promised to pass another law to try to meet the requirements O'Connor laid out in her opinion.

For his part, Carhart, who came to Washington to be in the courtroom for the decision, said he was pleased but also chastened by the one-vote margin. "It's a true wake-up call to the American people," he told reporters outside the building afterward. "If they want to keep abortion for their children and themselves, they need to go out and vote for choice."

Congressional Powers

Court Bars Federal Suits for "Gender-Motivated" Attacks

United States v. Morrison, decided by a 5–4 vote, May 15, 2000; Rehnquist wrote the opinion; Souter, Stevens, Ginsburg, and Breyer dissented.

Christy Brzonkala had just enrolled at Virginia Polytechnic Institute—Virginia Tech—in September 1994 when she met two members of the varsity football team, Antonio Morrison and James Crawford. She claimed that on the evening of September 21, the two men raped her in a room in her dormitory.

The accusation touched off a series of difficult and ultimately disappointing legal battles for Brzonkala. Morrison, who claimed he had had consensual sex with Brzonkala, was initially suspended from school, but the suspension later was lifted. Brzonkala's complaint against Crawford was dismissed for lack of evidence. Brzonkala, who had waited months to report the incident, did not press for criminal charges.

Thanks to a recently enacted federal law, however, Brzonkala was able to file a suit in federal court seeking money damages from the two men. The law—part of the Violence Against Women Act of 1994—authorized victims of "gender-motivated" violence to bring suit in federal court seeking compensatory or punitive damages from their attackers.

Lawyers for the two men responded by claiming that Congress had exceeded its powers in enacting the federal court suit provision. And this term the Court agreed in a sharply divided, 5–4 decision that continued the Rehnquist Court's trend of curbing Congress's authority to expand the powers of the federal government.

Background. The Violence Against Women Act included a host of provisions to deal with what Congress called an "escalating problem" of gender-motivated attacks against women. The law authorized money for the states to maintain shelters for battered women and improve law enforcement and educational programs. The act also criminalized interstate acts of domestic violence or interstate violations of protective orders against harassment.

The practice of federally criminalizing offenses committed across state lines had become well established, though it was still controversial. Rehnquist himself had chided Congress for converting too many offenses into federal crimes. Lower federal courts, however, uniformly upheld the act's criminal provisions, and the Court declined to take up the issue.

The act's damage suit provision opened by declaring that all persons "have the right to be free from crimes of violence motivated by gender." Lawmakers justified the federal court remedy by detailing the effects of violence against women on interstate commerce and the purportedly inadequate protections for women in state courts. The provision attracted only modest controversy in Congress, but drew legal challenges quickly after the first suits were filed.

The legal challenges came against the backdrop of several decisions by the Rehnquist Court over the previous decade limiting expansion of federal powers by Congress. In one of those cases, *United States v. Lopez*, the Court in 1995 struck down a law making it a federal crime to possess a gun near a school. The law had nothing to do with interstate commerce, Rehnquist wrote for the majority. Dissenters said the decision represented a reversal from a half-century of precedents upholding Congress's discretion to define the scope of its power under the Constitution's Commerce Clause.

The Case. Brzonkala viewed Virginia Tech's handling of her complaint against Morrison and Crawford as a perfect example of the inadequate legal protections at the state level for women against gender-motivated violence. Morrison was initially found guilty of sexual assault and suspended for two semesters. He won a new hearing and was convicted and suspended again, but this time for "using abusive language." Then the university lifted the punishment and allowed Morrison back for the 1995–1996 school year.

Brzonkala, meanwhile, had be- come depressed, stopped attending classes, and attempted suicide. She withdrew from school, but was plan- ning to return in September 1995 un- til she learned that Morrison would be returning. Fearing for her safety, she dropped out. By fall 1999 she was living in Washington and working as a waitress; she had not returned to college.

Frustrated with Virginia Tech's handling of the case, Brzonkala filed suit in December 1995 against Mor- rison and Crawford for the alleged attack under the Violence Against Women Act provision and against the university for permitting a sexu- ally hostile environment. A federal district court judge barred the suit against Morrison and Crawford. He said the law exceeded Congress's powers under the Commerce Clause because it did not regulate interstate commerce and was not directed at

Christy Brzonkala, with one of her at- torneys, Kathryn Rodgers of the NOW Legal Defense Fund.

economic activity. The judge also said the damage suit provision could not be justified under Congress's power to enforce the Fourteenth Amend- ment's Equal Protection Clause because that amendment was directed at actions by government, not private individuals.

Initially, a three-judge panel of the Fourth U.S. Circuit Court of Ap- peals reversed the decision and reinstated the suit. But the full appeals court in March 1999 voted 7–4 to strike down the damage suit remedy. The majority agreed with the trial judge that the law exceeded Congress's power to regulate interstate commerce or enforce the Fourteenth Amend- ment. Both Brzonkala and the Justice Department asked the Court to re- view the decision.

Arguments. The justices' questions during the January 11 argument con- firmed the continuing division between the conservative majority's deter- mination to contain Congress's broad assertions of federal power and the liberal minority's opposition to those moves. Supporters of the law had hoped to capture O'Connor's vote because of her concern with women's rights issues, but her questions placed her in the opposite camp.

Representing Brzonkala, Julie Goldscheid of the National Organization for Women (NOW) Legal Defense and Education Fund opened her defense of the law by quoting Congress's description of gender-based violence as "one of the most persistent barriers to women's full participation in the national economy." Scalia interrupted. "If they can do this, they could enact a general federal robbery statute," he said. No, Goldscheid answered, "discrimination is uniquely a matter of federal concern." The law leaves "traditional" law enforcement areas "exclusively and entirely" in states' control.

Solicitor General Seth Waxman also tried to minimize the law's impact on the states. "Congress was not on a tear to deal with the states as bad actors," he said. But O'Connor was dissatisfied. "Your approach, it seems to me, would justify a federal remedy for alimony or child support or even contract disputes," she said.

Arguing for Morrison, Michael Rosman, a lawyer with the conservative Center for Individual Rights, played to the conservatives' fear of unchecked federal power. Congress cannot regulate all violent crime, and it cannot regulate purely private behavior under the Fourteenth Amendment, he said. Under the theory advanced by the law's defenders, he said, Congress can "relegate the states to a trivial role."

Liberal justices tried to punch holes in the argument. Breyer questioned Rosman's argument that Congress could not regulate "noneconomic" activity. "There are many, many instances of noncommercial activity," the justice said, "that could have substantial effect on interstate commerce." Ginsburg said the law did not "displace" any state policies. Congress was "just complementing what the states do," she said. "Why can't Congress do that?"

Rosman closed, however, by insisting that the law stretched the federal commerce power into the states' domain. "This is not commerce," he said. "This is interpersonal violence, the kind of thing that the states have had the exclusive responsibility to legislate since the [writing of] the Constitution."

Lawyers and justices alike were so occupied with the commerce power debate that they virtually ignored the alternate basis for upholding the law: the Fourteenth Amendment. Waxman literally ran out of time as he was about to turn to the issue. Rosman dealt with it at the very end of his half-hour, stressing that—unlike traditional civil rights laws—the suits for gender-motivated violence had no requirement to prove state action as the basis for a federal remedy.

Decision. Court watchers in the audience on May 15 knew the result as soon as Rehnquist announced, after three lesser cases, that he had the Court's decision in *Morrison*. Firmly but without evident emotion, Rehnquist summarized his twenty-eight-page opinion rejecting the government's effort to uphold the Violence Against Women Act either under Congress's power over interstate commerce or under its power to enforce the Fourteenth Amendment.

On the Commerce Clause issue, Rehnquist said that gender-motivated crimes "are not, in any sense of the phrase, economic activity" and also could not be regulated by Congress on the basis of their "aggregate effect" on the national economy. "If Congress may regulate gender-motivated violence, it would be able to regulate murder or any other type of violence," Rehnquist wrote.

On the Fourteenth Amendment issue, Rehnquist cited what he called "the time-honored principle" that the amendment "prohibits only state action." On that basis, Rehnquist said the civil suit provision was invalid: "[I]t is directed not at any State or state actor, but at individuals who have committed criminal acts motivated by gender bias."

Rehnquist acknowledged that Brzonkala claimed in her complaint that she was the victim of "a brutal assault." If the allegations were true, the chief justice continued, "no civilized system of justice could fail to provide her a remedy for the conduct of respondent Morrison. But under our federal system that remedy must be provided by the Commonwealth of Virginia, and not by the United States."

The Court's four other conservatives—O'Connor, Scalia, Kennedy, and Thomas—joined Rehnquist's opinion. In a brief concurrence, Thomas said he would go further and reconsider the doctrine that Congress can regulate activities that have "substantial effects" on interstate commerce.

For the dissenters, Souter accused the majority of intruding on Congress's powers and silently revising its own precedents. Congress has the power to regulate activity that has a substantial effect on interstate commerce, Souter said, and to determine "the fact of such a substantial effect." The courts, he said, should review Congress's assessment "not for soundness but simply for . . . rationality. . . ." And in this case, Souter concluded, Congress's judgment was amply supported by "the mountain of data" assembled to show the effects of violence against women on interstate commerce.

As for the Court's prior rulings, Souter said that the majority was committing "error" by trying to establish "categorical exclusions" from what had often been held to be Congress's "plenary power" over interstate commerce. The majority was using "formalistic" distinctions in order to serve "a conception of federalism" as limiting national power "in favor of preserving a supposedly discernible, proper sphere of state autonomy. . . ." But Souter said those issues should be left to the political arena. And he noted what he called "not the least irony" that the states themselves—thirty-six of them—had urged the Court to uphold the law, with only one state asking that the law be struck down.

Stevens, Ginsburg, and Breyer joined Souter's opinion. In a separate dissent, Breyer argued that because of the difficulty of drawing lines in Commerce Clause cases, "Congress, not the courts, must remain primarily responsible for striking the appropriate state/federal balance." He also voiced doubts about the Court's ruling on the Fourteenth Amendment issue, noting that the law was aimed at remedying the states' failure to adequately protect women's rights. Stevens and Ginsburg joined the first part of his opinion, but not the second.

Reaction. Opposing lawyers predictably viewed the opinion differently. Rosman said the decision was a welcome reminder that "democratic majorities are limited by the text of the Constitution." But Kathryn Rodgers, executive director of the NOW Legal Defense and Education Fund, said the ruling "took the federal government out of the business of defining civil rights and creating remedies."

On Capitol Hill, Sen. Joseph Biden (D-Del.), a prime sponsor of the 1994 act, also criticized the ruling. "The Supreme Court has become bolder and bolder in stripping the federal government of the ability to make decisions on behalf of the American people," he said. Asked by the Associated Press whether there were any changes that could be made to make federal rape lawsuits legal, Biden replied succinctly: "Yes, two new justices."

States

Age Discrimination Suits Against States Barred

Kimel v. Florida Board of Regents, decided by a 5–4 vote, January 11, 2000; O'Connor wrote the opinion; Stevens, Souter, Ginsburg, and Breyer dissented.

Physics professor J. Daniel Kimel was one of thirty-six faculty members and librarians at two Florida state universities who claimed they had been discriminated against on the basis of age when they lost out on promised salary increases in the early 1990s.

J. Daniel Kimel

The Kimel case was one of many suits state governments around the country were facing under the federal Age Discrimination in Employment Act (ADEA). It was progressing through lower federal courts when the Supreme Court handed down an important states' rights decision in 1996 that limited individuals' right to file damage suits against states for violating federal law.

Applying the new ruling, the federal appeals court in Atlanta dismissed the Kimel case. The plaintiffs, backed by the Clinton administration, asked the Court to reverse the decision. The Court agreed to hear the case, but ruled—by the same 5–4 majority as in a string of other recent federalism rulings—that Congress had exceeded its power in authorizing public employees to sue state governments for violating the age discrimination law.

Background. Congress passed the age discrimination law in 1967 to combat what it called "the common practice" among employers of setting "arbitrary age limits" for jobs based on "stereotypes" and "generalizations." The act originally applied only to private employers but was extended to state and local governments in 1974. Congress gave the Equal Employment Opportunity Commission (EEOC) power to enforce the law but also authorized private suits by employees. The law allowed employers to take age into account in making job decisions if it was a "bona fide occupational qualification" for a position.

The Court upheld Congress's decision to apply the age discrimination law to state governments in a 1983 decision, *EEOC v. Wyoming*. In a concession to state governments, Congress had included in the law an exemption for mandatory retirement policies for law enforcement and firefighting personnel. In a series of cases, the Court rejected arguments by public employees that those policies amounted to unconstitutional governmental discrimination. "Age is not a suspect classification under the Equal Protection Clause," O'Connor wrote in *Gregory v. Ashcroft* (1991).

Age discrimination litigation—against private businesses as well as government employers—sharply increased during the 1990s. Some of the suits against private employers produced lucrative awards for plaintiffs. State governments saw an avenue of legal protection, however, when the Rehnquist Court began limiting suits by private individuals against state governments for alleged violations of federal law.

In the first of those decisions, the Court held in *Seminole Tribe of Florida v. Florida* (1996) that Congress could not use its power over interstate commerce under Article I of the Constitution to authorize private suits against state governments. Three years later, the Court also protected states from suits for violating constitutional rights under the Fourteenth Amendment. The ruling in *Florida Prepaid Postsecondary Educational Expense Board v. College Savings Bank* (1999) held that Congress could not authorize private suits against state governments for due process or equal protection claims unless it identified a "pattern" of constitutional violations and made any remedy "proportionate" to the violations.

The Case. State governments around the country began invoking the *Seminole Tribe* decision as a defense in age discrimination cases not long after the ruling came down. Most federal appeals courts to rule on the issue rejected the states' arguments, generally holding that Congress had expressly "abrogated" the states' sovereign immunity and had properly invoked its Fourteenth Amendment enforcement power to allow private suits under the age discrimination law.

The Kimel case had its origins in the changing economics of the marketplace for college and university professors. Private and public universities alike in the late '80s and early '90s found that they had to raise starting salary offers to attract new faculty members. Older faculty members were left at a disadvantage because their salaries had not risen accordingly. In a complex sequence of events, long-term faculty in Florida's state university system were granted compensatory salary adjustments through collective bargaining, but administrators at two campuses refused to make the adjustments.

The plaintiffs in the Kimel suit claimed that the two universities' refusal to raise their salaries amounted to discrimination on the basis of age. The state sought to dismiss the case by citing the Eleventh Amendment's restriction on federal court suits against state governments, as interpreted in the Court's *Seminole Tribe* decision. The lower federal court rejected the state's argument and kept the case alive. The Eleventh U.S. Circuit Court of Appeals took up the case and combined it with two other age discrimination suits: one filed by a Florida prison guard, Wellington Dickson, and the other by two Alabama state university professors.

The three-judge appeals panel voted to bar the suits, but the two judges in the majority used different grounds. One judge said that the age discrimination law did not reflect an unambiguous decision by Congress to "abrogate" or override the states' sovereign immunity against suits—as required under a series of Eleventh Amendment rulings by the Court. The other judge said that Congress had no power to authorize the suits under its Article I power to regulate interstate commerce or under the power granted in section 5 of the Fourteenth Amendment to enact legislation to enforce the amendment's due process and equal protection provisions.

Five other federal appeals courts around the country had ruled that states could be subject to federal age discrimination suits; only one other panel agreed with the Eleventh Circuit decision. The Justice Department asked the Court to review the Eleventh Circuit's decision in order to clarify what the solicitor general's brief called Congress's "comprehensive remedial power" under the Fourteenth Amendment.

Arguments. The arguments in the case—on October 13, in the second week of the Court's new term—went badly for the plaintiffs and the government. Conservative justices made it clear that they thought Congress had stepped on the Court's own prerogatives by trying to declare age discrimination to be a constitutional violation. Liberals, seemingly sensing another 5–4 defeat, hardly put up a fight.

Jeremiah Collins, the Washington lawyer representing the university professors, opened his argument by contending that Congress "unequivocally" authorized suits against states in the age discrimination law and had the power to do so under the Fourteenth Amendment. O'Connor and Scalia quickly disagreed.

Both justices said the law went beyond constitutional requirements. "Congress just went ahead on its own and identified this serious constitutional violation, the existence of which is not mentioned in any opinion of this Court," Scalia said. O'Connor saw no pattern of age discrimination by the states. "There's very little that indicates there was a need to reach discrimination by state and local government," she said.

In her argument, Deputy Solicitor General Barbara Underwood contended Congress had what she called "extensive evidence" of "irrational discrimination" against older workers. But Rehnquist said that Underwood's argument would allow Congress to use the Fourteenth Amendment to permit federal suits against any form of irrational discrimination. O'Connor interjected to note that most states had their own age discrimination laws anyway.

In his turn, the state's attorney, Jeffrey Sutton, said that Congress had little justification for allowing private suits against states for age discrimination. "When it comes to Fourteenth Amendment equal protection against discrimination by state employers, the record shows absolutely nothing," said Sutton, a former Ohio state solicitor who continued to represent state interests before the Court as a private lawyer in Cleveland.

The liberal justices challenged Sutton only mildly. Ginsburg and Breyer concentrated on the question whether Congress had unmistakably authorized suits against the states. Souter pointed to several provisions in the age discrimination law—such as the defense for bona fide job qualifications—that suggested the remedy was "proportional" to the problem Congress was trying to solve. But veteran reporters and observers left the courtroom with little doubt that the states were going to win—and Congress was going to lose.

Decision. The Court's decision came only three months later, on January 11, and it largely followed the established pattern in other federalism cases. After agreeing (on a 7–2 vote) that Congress intended to authorize age discrimination suits against the states, the Court held 5–4 that the law was "not a valid exercise of Congress's power under §5 of the Fourteenth Amendment."

For the majority, O'Connor reviewed the prior decisions holding that age discrimination did not amount to a per se violation of the Constitution. Then looking at the evidence before Congress when it extended the law to state governments, O'Connor said the lawmakers "never identified any pattern of age discrimination by the States, much less any discrimination that rose to the level of constitutional violation." On that basis, she concluded, the law was "an unwarranted response to a perhaps inconsequential problem."

The Court's four conservatives—Rehnquist, Scalia, Kennedy, and Thomas—joined that part of O'Connor's opinion. In a separate opinion written by Thomas, he and Kennedy disagreed with O'Connor's conclusion that the law included a clear override of the states' sovereign immunity.

Stevens wrote a short, seven-page dissenting opinion devoted to re-arguing the sovereign immunity issue that the liberals had lost in the *Semi-*

nole Tribe decision four years earlier. "There is not a word in the text of the Constitution," Stevens wrote, "supporting the Court's conclusion that the judge-made doctrine of sovereign immunity limits Congress' power to authorize private parties . . . to enforce federal law against the States." Souter, Ginsburg, and Breyer joined his opinion.

Reaction. The Court's ruling left state governments covered by the substantive provisions of the federal age discrimination law, and O'Connor noted at the end of her opinion that state workers might be able to sue under their own state laws. But Laurie McCann, a lawyer with the American Association of Retired Persons (AARP), said the ruling left older workers with "virtually no federal protection against age discrimination." The decision, McCann said, "sends a message that if age discrimination is a civil right at all, it's a second-class right."

In Florida, a spokesman for the Florida Board of Regents seconded O'Connor's suggestion about the availability of state remedies. "The right place for this is with the states," Keith Goldschmidt said. In that vein, the state's Commission on Human Rights did agree after the Court's ruling to investigate Kimel's age discrimination claim. But Kimel's local attorney, Thomas Brooks, voiced concern that the agency might ultimately rule that it had no jurisdiction over the matter.

Criminal Law

"Miranda" Rule on Police Interrogation Reaffirmed

Dickerson v. United States, decided by a 7–2 vote, June 26, 2000; Rehnquist wrote the opinion; Scalia and Thomas dissented.

The Supreme Court came under fierce political attack in 1966 when it handed down its famous *Miranda* decision requiring police to tell suspects of their rights before conducting interrogation. Over the next three decades, however, the warnings became a routine procedure for police and a familiar and accepted practice for most of the American public.

But Paul Cassell, a University of Utah law professor and former federal prosecutor and Justice Department official, remained unreconciled. In a series of academic writings, he sought to prove that the ruling resulted in thousands of lost convictions and reduced sentences for criminals. Defying conventional wisdom, he also defended the constitutionality of a law that

Congress passed in 1968 in an effort to override *Miranda*, at least in federal court.

Cassell's campaign hit paydirt in February 1999 when the federal appeals court in Richmond, Virginia, invoked the *Miranda* override statute in an otherwise routine bank robbery case to allow prosecutors to use a suspect's statement that a federal judge ruled had been obtained without proper warnings. The Supreme Court agreed to hear the case and—in a rare procedure—gave Cassell the opportunity to defend the law after the Justice Department refused. But this term the Court rejected Cassell's argument. By a 7–2 vote, the Court reaffirmed *Miranda* and nullified Congress's attempt to override it.

Background. The *Miranda* decision followed three decades of intermittent efforts by the Court to crack down on the use of third-degree techniques by police to obtain confessions from suspects. In some thirty cases decided between 1936 and 1964, the Court ruled that the Due Process Clause prohibited the use of "involuntary" confessions and determined the voluntariness of a suspect's statement by looking case by case at the "totality of the circumstances."

Frustrated with this approach, the Court agreed in 1965 to hear a group of four unrelated cases involving challenged confessions—including Ernesto Miranda's appeal of his 1963 kidnap-rape conviction in Arizona. In a 5–4 ruling issued on June 13, 1966, the Court said that uniform safeguards were required to protect what Chief Justice Earl Warren called the Fifth Amendment's "cherished" principle against self-incrimination. Before conducting custodial interrogation, the Court said, police must advise a suspect that he had the right to remain silent, the right to an attorney, and the right to an appointed attorney if he could not afford one, and that any statement given after waiving those rights could be used against him in court. Warren said the Constitution required those warnings unless "equally effective safeguards" were created.

Police criticized the decision but were obliged to comply. In Congress, lawmakers immediately began efforts to undo the ruling. The result in 1968 was a law—§3501 of the U.S. criminal code—that declared that a confession "shall be admissible" in federal court "if it is voluntarily given." Judges were to determine voluntariness by considering all the circumstances. Five factors were specifically mentioned, including how much time elapsed between the defendant's arrest and arraignment; whether the defendant had been informed of the nature of the charge, his right to remain silent, and his right to a lawyer; and whether the suspect had no lawyer when questioned.

Paul Cassell, right, a professor at the University of Utah Law School, meets with reporters after arguments in his effort to uphold a 1968 law limiting the Miranda decision on police interrogation. Attorney Paul Kamenar of the Washington Legal Foundation is with him.

The law went all but completely ignored. Cassell, while working in the Justice Department's Office of Legal Counsel during the Reagan administration, argued unsuccessfully for seeking a case to test its constitutionality. He maintained his interest in the law as a federal prosecutor in Virginia and then after 1992 as a law professor. Critics sharply disputed Cassell's assumptions and techniques in claiming that the ruling had hurt law enforcement. Cassell also insisted that §3501 was constitutional since the Court itself had opened the door to a legislative alternative. Most legal experts disagreed, however, and the Justice Department itself continued to ignore the law.

The Case. The opportunity to test the constitutionality of §3501 arose when a federal prosecutor in Alexandria, Virginia, cited the law in an effort to use a statement given by a suspect, Charles Dickerson, in a 1997 bank robbery. Dickerson contended that the FBI agent who interrogated him did not give him the *Miranda* warnings before he gave a statement linking him to the truck identified as the get-away vehicle in the robbery. The FBI agent said he had, but the judge believed Dickerson and ruled the statement inadmissible.

In seeking reconsideration, the prosecutor cited §3501 as a separate reason for admitting the statement; the judge reaffirmed his decision without addressing the issue. The government appealed the decision to the Fourth U.S. Circuit Court of Appeals, but—in line with Justice Department policy—did not rely on §3501. Cassell, however, filed a brief on behalf of the conservative Washington Legal Foundation as a "friend of the court" urging the appeals court to use the law to admit Dickerson's statement.

In a 2–1 decision, the appeals court agreed with Cassell. It described *Miranda* as a "judicially created rule" that was not required by the Constitution and that Congress had the power to overrule. It went on to find Dickerson's statement voluntary and therefore admissible. Dickerson's lawyer promptly asked the Supreme Court to review the decision. The Justice Department joined Dickerson in urging the Court to hear the case and to rule §3501 unconstitutional. For his part, Cassell again filed a brief defending the law. The Court in December agreed to hear the case and— given the Justice Department's position—appointed Cassell as an *amicus curiae* to defend the appeals court's decision.

Arguments. Liberal justices relentlessly grilled Cassell during his defense of the anti-*Miranda* law in the April 19 argument. By contrast, Dickerson's lawyer, James Hundley, and Solicitor General Seth Waxman got off with mostly mild questions except from one justice: Scalia.

Hundley opened his allotted ten minutes with what he later called "a subtle distinction" as to *Miranda*'s constitutional basis. Even though the warnings were "not constitutionally mandated," Hundley said, "the constitutional threshold represented by those warnings is constitutionally required."

Scalia quickly pounced: Could a police officer be sued for violating a suspect's constitutional rights by failing to give *Miranda* warnings? "I'd be very surprised," he said, answering his own question. On that basis, Scalia concluded, the rights appeared to be "procedural" and not "substantive"— and, by implication, within Congress's power to amend.

Hundley stood his ground, however. *Miranda* provided "a more objective, concrete, clear-cut procedure" for protecting suspects' rights than §3501, which he said "reverts" to the "unworkable" totality-of-the-circumstances test.

In his turn, Waxman also defended *Miranda*'s constitutional status. The ruling, he said in reply to an O'Connor question, was based on the Court's "power to interpret and apply the Constitution." The 1968 law, he continued, could be upheld only if the Court was willing to overturn *Miranda*, a precedent of thirty-four years' standing that he said had proven to be "workable" and produced "benefits to the administration of justice."

Cassell began with his strongest point: the Court's statements in numerous decisions that *Miranda* was not a constitutional requirement. Under questioning by Rehnquist, Cassell offered his own subtle distinction as to the ruling's basis, calling it "the Court's provisional judgment about how to go about enforcing Fifth Amendment rights."

The four liberal justices, however, sharply questioned Cassell when he tried to defend §3501 as an "equally effective" alternative to *Miranda*. With Breyer and Souter asking overlapping questions, Cassell emphasized that some of *Miranda*'s requirements were themselves incorporated into the law, providing "clear incentives to law enforcement agents to deliver warnings." Souter interjected: "Incentive is not required." "There is a difference," Cassell acknowledged. "You bet," Souter concluded.

Hundley had two minutes remaining after Cassell had finished. "It is this Court that sets the limits of the Bill of Rights, not Congress," the defense lawyer told the justices. Congress, he said, "attempted to roll the clock back. That's the reason this statute fails."

Decision. Rehnquist opened his announcement of the Court's decision on June 26 by reciting the famous *Miranda* warnings themselves—dramatic evidence of the place that the decision had come to have in American law and society. Proceeding through his tersely written, fifteen-page opinion, Rehnquist explained that *Miranda* had established "a constitutional rule" that Congress "may not legislatively supersede."

Citing one of his own opinions from the early 1970s, Rehnquist acknowledged that some of the Court's decisions had suggested that the *Miranda* protections were not constitutionally required. But the Court could not have applied the *Miranda* rule to state cases except to enforce constitutional rights, Rehnquist explained. Subsequent decisions creating "exceptions" to *Miranda* simply proved that "no constitutional rule is immutable," he continued.

As for §3501, Rehnquist said that it did not satisfy the Court's criterion of being "equally effective" as *Miranda* in safeguarding suspects' rights. Even combined with other new remedies for "abusive police conduct," the law was not "an adequate substitute for the warnings required by *Miranda*," the chief justice concluded.

Rehnquist also rejected the Court's overruling *Miranda* itself—citing the doctrine of *stare decisis*, or respect for precedent. "Whether or not we would agree with *Miranda*'s reasoning and its resulting rule, were we addressing the issue in the first instance, the principles of *stare decisis* weigh heavily against overruling it now," Rehnquist wrote. The warnings have become "embedded in police practice," he explained. In addition, the Court's subsequent cases "have reduced the impact of the *Miranda* rule on legitimate law enforcement while reaffirming the decision's core ruling. . . ."

Six justices joined Rehnquist's opinion: Stevens, O'Connor, Kennedy, Souter, Ginsburg, and Breyer. None wrote separately—as though to avoid diluting the force of Rehnquist's opinion.

Scalia dissented in an acerbic opinion, joined by Thomas, that was half again longer than the Court's. The majority's description of *Miranda* as a "constitutional rule" implied that the Court had the power "not merely to apply the Constitution but to expand it," Scalia wrote. "That is an immense and frightening antidemocratic power," he continued, "and it simply does not exist."

Miranda itself was "objectionable for innumerable reasons," Scalia said, in part because of its "palpable hostility toward the act of confession *per se*." Subsequent decisions limiting the ruling's impact simply proved that a *Miranda* violation was not itself a violation of the Constitution. And the Court's enforcement of the rule in state court cases, Scalia concluded, was merely "evidence of its ultimate illegitimacy."

"Far from believing that *stare decisis* compels this result," Scalia concluded, "I believe we cannot allow to remain on the books even a celebrated decision—*especially* a celebrated decision—that has come to stand for the proposition that the Supreme Court has power to impose extraconstitutional constraints on Congress and the states." For good measure, Scalia added that he would defy the ruling by continuing to apply §3501 "in all cases where there has been a sustainable finding that the defendant's confession was voluntary."

Reaction. The Court's ruling drew praise from the nation's highest law enforcement officer, Attorney General Janet Reno. "Today's decision recognizes *Miranda* has been good for law enforcement," Reno said. "Most importantly," she added, "it will continue to provide a public sense of fairness in our criminal justice system."

In Utah, Cassell voiced bitter disappointment that his long legal campaign had come to naught. "It's a sad day for victims of crime and law-abiding Americans," Cassell said. The National Association of Police Organizations was similarly critical, saying that the ruling allows suspects to go free because of "one misstep—not giving a suspect a *Miranda* warning."

Dickerson himself remained free on pretrial supervised release. But the U.S. attorney's office in Alexandria went forward with his prosecution despite the suppression of his statement. The four-day trial ended on October 6 with Dickerson's conviction on three counts (bank robbery, conspiracy, and a gun charge).

Federal Regulation

FDA Blocked from Regulating Tobacco

Food and Drug Administration v. Brown & Williamson Tobacco Corp., decided by a 5–4 vote, March 21, 2000; O'Connor wrote the opinion; Breyer, Stevens, Souter, and Ginsburg dissented.

For decades, the tobacco industry fought off or softened federal efforts to regulate the sale and advertising of cigarettes. In the 1990s, however, public attitudes toward smoking—and toward the tobacco industry—hardened.

Tobacco companies came under particular scrutiny when internal documents surfaced suggesting that executives had long known of the health risks from smoking and the addictive effects of nicotine and that manufacturers may have manipulated nicotine levels to try to keep smokers hooked. Relying on this new evidence, the FDA in 1996 adopted stiff regulations to control how cigarettes and smokeless tobacco were sold and marketed.

The tobacco industry challenged the regulations in court, contending in part that the rules went beyond the FDA's statutory power to regulate "drugs." The Supreme Court this term agreed. By a 5–4 vote, the justices told the agency that it had to go to Congress for explicit authority if it wanted to take on the tobacco issue.

Background. Congress created the FDA in 1906 in the midst of public concern about unsafe food and somewhat expanded the agency's authority in 1938 in a retitled Food, Drug and Cosmetic Act. Neither of the authorizing charters mentioned tobacco; Congress in fact turned aside a proposal in 1930 to include tobacco within the FDA's jurisdiction.

The FDA itself repeatedly disclaimed any power over tobacco during the decades of controversy that began with the surgeon general's famous 1964 report linking smoking to lung cancer and other diseases. Agency officials under Democratic and Republican presidents alike said that cigarettes did not fall within the law's definition of "drugs" because manufacturers made no claims for health benefits from smoking. In any event, FDA officials said, the issue was for Congress, not the agency, to decide.

The FDA changed its stance under Dr. David Kessler, an aggressive commissioner originally appointed by President George Bush and retained in the post by President Clinton. Emboldened by the evidence from tobacco company files, Kessler hinted to Congress in 1994 that the agency might regulate nicotine as a drug and might be forced to ban nicotine altogether since it could not be found to be "safe" as food and drug laws require.

When Congress took no action, Kessler proceeded to act on his own. He unveiled proposed FDA regulations at a White House ceremony in August 1995—with Clinton at his side. The proposed regulations made it a federal offense to sell cigarettes to anyone under eighteen, prohibited billboards advertising cigarettes near schools and playgrounds, and barred brand-name sponsorship by tobacco companies of entertainment and sporting events. The proposals drew a record number of 95,000 individual comments on both sides, but the FDA adopted them virtually unchanged in August 1996.

The Case. The tobacco industry—major manufacturers and a trade association of retailers—challenged the regulations in federal court in North Carolina, the heart of tobacco country. In a mixed ruling, Judge William L. Osteen in April 1997 held that the FDA had the power to regulate access to tobacco but not to control marketing or promotion practices.

Both sides appealed, and the case went before a three-judge panel of the predominantly conservative Fourth U.S. Circuit Court of Appeals in June 1998. Outgoing solicitor general Dellinger personally argued for the government—an unusual appearance by the government's top appellate advocate in an intermediate-level appellate court.

The appeals court handed the tobacco industry a clear-cut victory only two months later. "Congress did not intend to delegate jurisdiction over tobacco products," Judge H. Emory Widener wrote for the 2–1 majority. He listed a half-dozen "internal inconsistencies" in the FDA's interpretation of the statute—notably, the agency's failure to ban tobacco even though the statute calls for barring any product found to cause "serious adverse health consequences or death."

The Justice Department promptly asked the Court to review the decision. If the appeals court decision was allowed to stand, the government argued, "an unparalleled opportunity to curb tobacco use by children and to reduce the disease and death associated with such use will be lost." Tobacco

Two teenagers smoke and talk in front of a video-game parlor at a strip shopping center in Robbinsville, North Carolina. The Supreme Court struck down Food and Drug Administration regulations aimed at curbing teenage smoking.

companies responded by insisting that Congress had given the agency "no role" on tobacco issues. The FDA was "short-circuiting an ongoing political process," the industry argued. As expected, the justices agreed to hear the case, setting the stage for a showdown early in the 1999–2000 term.

Arguments. The justices appeared decidedly skeptical of the FDA's arguments when they heard the case on December 1. "It just doesn't fit," O'Connor said early in Solicitor General Waxman's defense of the regulations—and several times thereafter. Rehnquist, Scalia, and Kennedy signaled their doubts as well, while only Stevens and Breyer seemed strongly inclined to support the agency.

Waxman opened by carefully fitting tobacco within the terms of FDA's governing statute. Nicotine was a "highly addictive substance," he said, that functioned as "a sedative, stimulant, and appetite suppressant"— "quintessentially" drug-like characteristics, he added.

Drugs have to be "safe and effective," O'Connor interrupted. "Is it the position of the government that tobacco is safe and effective?" Without taking a breath, O'Connor answered her own question: "It's not."

For their part, Rehnquist and Scalia zeroed in on the FDA's long-held position that it had no power to regulate tobacco. "Thirty years ago, no one suggested" the FDA could regulate cigarettes, Rehnquist said. When Waxman insisted the agency acted because of the new evidence about the industry's conduct, Scalia demurred. Weren't the dangers of smoking clear enough in the 1960s to sustain regulation? Scalia asked.

Waxman got a more sympathetic but equally troubling question from Souter, who said he could accept the government's "technical arguments" but still had "a problem with the totality of it." Given the long history of nonregulation and the enactment of other tobacco-related statutes, the FDA's decision to regulate "does not seem to me to be reasonable," Souter concluded.

When he began his allotted half-hour, the industry's lawyer, Richard Cooper, seemed to many observers to have the case already won. Echoing O'Connor's questions, Cooper, a lawyer with a big Washington firm and a former FDA general counsel, contended that tobacco products "simply do not fit" within the agency's statute.

Cooper stuck to his guns under extended questioning from Breyer, who approvingly outlined the agency's rationale for regulation. Nicotine's effects on the body were well known, Breyer said—both to the industry and to smokers. That fit the definition of a drug, the justice continued. Cooper countered that tobacco companies were not claiming that nicotine produced any health benefits. That did not matter to smokers, Breyer retorted. "Once you say it's a cigarette, they've got the point."

Cooper stood his ground, though. He closed his argument by insisting the FDA's regulation was "lawless"—"however admirable its intentions and motivation."

Decision. O'Connor spoke for the Court in announcing the decision March 21 to bar the FDA regulations. She began by acknowledging tobacco to be "one of the most troubling public health problems facing our Nation today." But, she continued, "we believe that Congress has clearly precluded the FDA from asserting jurisdiction to regulate tobacco products."

At length, O'Connor tracked her reasoning from the oral arguments. She cited food-and-drug law provisions governing labeling and classification of drugs and then declared, "were the FDA to regulate cigarettes and smokeless tobacco, the Act would require the agency to ban them." But Congress had "foreclosed" that option. Well aware of tobacco's health effects, Congress had approved some half-dozen tobacco-specific statutes but "stopped well short of ordering a ban," O'Connor concluded.

O'Connor conceded that the Court ordinarily defers to an agency's interpretation of a statute that it is charged with administering. But this, she said, was "no ordinary case." Given the "unique political history" of tobacco, she said, "we are obliged to defer not to the agency's expansive con-struction of the statute, but to Congress' consistent judgment to deny the FDA this power." Rehnquist, Scalia, Kennedy, and Thomas joined her opinion.

For the dissenters, Breyer maintained that tobacco fit well within the definitions in the FDA's governing statute, which should be given a broad interpretation because of the public health risks at stake. "The upshot is that the Court today holds that a regulatory statute aimed at unsafe drugs and devices does not authorize regulation of a drug (nicotine) and a device (a cigarette) that the Court itself finds unsafe," Breyer concluded. "Far more than most, this particular drug and device risks the life-threatening harms that administrative regulation seeks to rectify." Stevens, Souter, and Ginsburg joined his opinion.

Reaction. The Court's ruling did nothing to quiet the push for stronger regulation of tobacco. Vice President Al Gore, the presumptive Demo-cratic presidential nominee, and his Republican counterpart, Texas gover-nor George W. Bush, both called on the Republican-controlled Congress to enact stricter regulations. For his part, Kessler, who had gone to become dean of Yale Medical School, said that Congress had "a moral responsibil-ity to act." But Republican leaders in both the House and the Senate sig-naled that tobacco legislation was a nonstarter.

Tobacco industry officials, however, appeared somewhat conciliatory. Steven Parrish, senior vice president of Philip Morris Cos., the biggest to-bacco manufacturer, said the ruling was "an opportunity . . . to come up with a tough, sensible, common-sense approach to the regulation of ciga-rettes." Analysts noted that the industry was paying into a twenty-five-year, $250 billion settlement to reimburse the states for tobacco-related health care costs and facing a comparable suit by the Justice Department. "The industry wants peace," Mary Aronson, a longtime tobacco analyst, re-marked. But no regulatory proposal advanced in Congress.

Church and State

Fractured Ruling Allows Expanded Aid to Parochial Schools

Mitchell v. Helms, decided by a 6–3 vote, June 28, 2000; Thomas wrote the main opinion; O'Connor and Breyer concurred in the judgment; Souter, Stevens, and Ginsburg dissented.

Mary Helms and Marie Schneider were public school parents in suburban Jefferson Parish, Louisiana, in 1985 when they began wondering why public school buses were transporting kids to parochial schools. Their inquiry led to a broad legal challenge claiming that government aid to the parish's thirty Catholic schools violated the First Amendment's prohibition against government establishment of religion.

Their case followed a tortuous path through federal courts in Louisiana over the next thirteen years. It came to focus on a program known as Chapter 2 that used public funds to lend instructional equipment ranging from film projectors to computers to public and private schools. A group of parents of parochial school students, including Guy Mitchell, joined the case to defend the program. One federal judge agreed that the program violated church-state principles, but after his retirement a second judge disagreed.

The federal appeals court in New Orleans eventually ruled for the plaintiffs. The Supreme Court, which had been easing the restrictions on aid to parochial schools, agreed to hear the case. This term, the justices voted 6–3 to allow the program to resume.

Background. The Supreme Court's Establishment Clause cases had gone back and forth since its first ruling in 1930—also in a Louisiana case—upholding public aid for parochial schools. Gov. Huey Long persuaded the state's legislature to approve lending textbooks to pupils in public and parochial schools. The Court upheld the program on the ground that it benefited the children, not the schools themselves.

Four decades later, in *Lemon v. Kurtzman* (1971), the Court set out a three-part test for permitting assistance to parochial schools: aid had to be secular in purpose and effect and must not entangle the government in its administration. Textbook loans passed muster under that test, but the Court barred state governments from providing instructional materials in two cases: *Meek v. Pittenger* (1975) and *Wolman v. Walter* (1977). In 1985 the Court struck down two other programs that provided remedial services to students in parochial schools. One case—*Grand Rapids School District v. Ball*—involved a local aid scheme. The other—*Aguilar v. Felton*—involved a federal program known as Title II established in 1965 to provide aid to schools in disadvantaged areas.

The Court gradually weakened the strictures against public aid to church-affiliated schools over the next decade or so while also criticizing the *Lemon* test as being too rigid. In two cases—one in 1986, the other in 1993—the Court allowed government assistance to students with disabilities attending church-affiliated schools. Each time, the Court stressed that the aid went to the individual, not the school. Then in 1997, the Court opened the door wider by upholding, 5–4, aid to parochial schools under the federal Title II program that the Court had restricted twelve years earlier in *Agostini v. Felton*.

The Case. The aid program challenged in Jefferson Parish originated as Title VI of the 1965 education aid act and was renamed Chapter 2 in a 1981 reauthorization. Under the law, the federal government provided funds via state education departments to local school systems to buy instructional materials to be lent to public or private schools. Separationist groups such as the ACLU and the National Education Association did not oppose the program at its creation, but—like Helms and Schneider—came to view it as a drain on

The Supreme Court decision in a Louisiana case allows parochial schools like this one to use computers provided with public funds.

public school funds and a form of direct aid to religious schools.

Five years after the case was filed, the chief federal district court judge in New Orleans ruled in 1990 that the program was unconstitutional because it violated the second part of the *Lemon* test: it had the primary effect of advancing religion. Four years later, he issued a permanent injunction barring aid to church-affiliated schools under the program. After his retirement, however, a new judge got the case. He looked at the Supreme Court's more recent rulings and concluded that the aid to parochial schools was permissible because the benefits were "neutrally available without reference to religion" and the aid did not have the primary effect of advancing religion.

The plaintiffs appealed that decision to the Fifth U.S. Circuit Court of Appeals, which ruled in their favor. In its decision in 1998, the appeals court acknowledged the Supreme Court's apparent change of doctrine in the *Agostini* decision one year earlier. But it concluded that it had to follow the two cases from the 1970s that barred providing instructional materials to parochial schools unless the Supreme Court itself reversed them.

Arguments. Justices and lawyers alike struggled during the December 1 arguments to draw the line between permissible and impermissible aid to parochial schools. "We're groping for a distinction," Souter declared at one point. The overall tenor of the justices' questioning, however, seemed to favor greater discretion for the government in providing aid to parochial schools.

Michael McConnell, a University of Utah law professor, opened his argument by defending the Chapter 2 loan program as secular and neutral and criticizing the distinction between textbooks and instructional materials as "counterproductive." But Stevens and Souter quickly turned to another distinction in the cases between permissible "supplementing" of parochial school programs and impermissible "supplanting" of core parochial school spending.

McConnell said that aid should not be "automatically unconstitutional" if it supplanted some parochial school spending. Would that allow the government to build a new parochial school as part of a general school construction program, Rehnquist asked. McConnell hesitated before replying no. Doesn't that mean, Rehnquist said, that "supplanting" plays some role in evaluating parochial school aid?

Representing Helms, Lee Boothby, a Washington lawyer associated with Americans United for Separation of Church and State, opened by invoking what he called "our historical commitment that taxpayers must not be forced to subsidize the sectarian mission of religious schools." But he had difficulty justifying the rule against providing computers to parochial schools. "Computers today are what textbooks were thirty years ago," Breyer said. Scalia agreed. "A lot of the precedents don't stick together," he said.

McConnell made good use of two minutes of rebuttal time. The arguments against aid to parochial schools, he said, were "mired in the technology of the 1970s and the jurisprudence of the 1970s." Allowing secular aid to parochial schools on a neutral basis, he told the justices, would be "in the finest tradition of the First Amendment."

Decision. The Court's ruling June 28 gave a green light to the computer loan program—formally overruling the two 1970s decisions that disallowed such aid—but without a majority opinion. Four justices went so far as to say that any neutral, secular aid program would be constitutional. But two others—O'Connor and Breyer—concurred more narrowly; they said courts must examine whether the publicly provided equipment had been used for religious purposes.

The three dissenters said there was adequate evidence of "diversion" in Jefferson Parish to block the aid. More broadly, the dissenters said the plurality opinion threatened to allow wholesale, direct government aid to parochial schools in violation of previous Establishment Clause decisions.

Writing for the plurality, Thomas said that government aid was permissible if it was available without regard to religious affiliation. "Nothing in the Establishment Clause requires the exclusion of pervasively sectarian schools from otherwise permissible aid programs," he wrote. Thomas, a Roman Catholic, added that the opposition to aid to church-affiliated schools stemmed from "pervasive hostility" to the Catholic Church; the doctrine, he said, was "born of bigotry." Rehnquist and the Court's two other Catholics—Scalia and Kennedy—joined Thomas's opinion.

In her opinion concurring in the judgment, O'Connor agreed that the aid program in Jefferson Parish did not run afoul of the requirements that she set out in her opinion for the Court three years earlier in *Agostini*. She listed six factors: the aid must be allocated on the basis of "neutral, secular criteria," and must supplement rather than supplant non-federal funds; no funds could "reach the coffers of religious schools"; and the aid must be secular, with only minimal evidence of diversion to religious purposes and with adequate safeguards against such diversion. Thomas's opinion, O'Connor said, went too far. "The plurality opinion foreshadows the approval of direct monetary subsidies to religious organizations, even when they use the money to advance their religious objectives," she wrote. Breyer joined her opinion.

For the dissenters, Souter also sharply criticized Thomas's opinion. The neutrality principle, he said, amounted to "a formula for generous religious support." As for the aid to Jefferson Parish's parochial schools, Souter said there was sufficient evidence that the schools had used publicly provided materials for religious purposes to curtail the program. And he closed by criticizing what he called Thomas's "imputations of bigotry and irreligion." Stevens and Ginsburg joined his opinion.

Reaction. Parochial school supporters praised the decision. "Children who go to private, religiously affiliated schools will continue to share in the benefits of the changes in educational technology," Mark Chopko, general counsel of the U.S. Catholic Conference, told the *Washington Post*. But church-state separation groups criticized the ruling. "Taxpayers will now be forced to pay for an endless parade of computers and other expensive equipment for religious schools," said Barry Lynn, executive director of Americans United.

The ruling stirred speculation about the Court's likely attitude on school vouchers. "We see six potential votes for vouchers," said Clint Bolick, director of the pro-voucher Institute for Justice, referring to the four justices in the plurality plus O'Connor and Breyer. But Steven Green, legal director for the anti-voucher Americans United group, said O'Connor's position was less certain. He noted that O'Connor repeatedly referred in her opinion to "true" private choice plans. "Every single school voucher program in existence doesn't meet her criterion of providing a true universe of options for parents," Green said.

Freedom of Religion

No Organized Prayer at High School Football Games

Santa Fe Independent School District v. Doe, decided by a 6–3 vote, June 19, 2000; Stevens wrote the opinion; Rehnquist, Scalia, and Thomas dissented.

Marian Ward received a standing ovation at the Santa Fe, Texas, high school football team's season opener in September 1999 after she delivered a pregame prayer asking for good sportsmanship from the players and the fans. But families of two students at the small Gulf Coast town's school— one Catholic, the other Mormon—saw football game prayers as part of a pervasive policy of improperly injecting religion into school life.

The two families had won a federal appeals court ruling that barred the Santa Fe school board's policy of allowing prayers at football games. Ward, daughter of a Baptist minister, had won a reprieve of sorts by filing her own free speech lawsuit while the school board was asking the Supreme Court to reverse the appeals court decision.

School prayer advocates saw the case as an opportunity to affirm that student-led prayers in public schools were constitutional despite the Court's controversial decisions four decades earlier banning school-sponsored religious observances. But the Court dashed their hopes this term with a 6–3 ruling that found the Santa Fe school system's policy violated the Constitution's prohibition against government establishment of religion.

Background. School prayer had been a contentious issue for the Court ever since its rulings in the early 1960s—*Engel v. Vitale* (1962) and *Abington*

A handful of fans pray before the start of the Santa Fe, Texas, high school's first home football game following the Supreme Court's decision barring student-led prayers over the loudspeakers.

School District v. Schempp (1963)—that barred organized prayer or Bible reading in public school classrooms. Critics tried but failed repeatedly to pass a constitutional amendment to overturn the decisions. Public opinion polls registered continuing opposition to the decisions decades later.

Despite the controversy, the Court did not retreat from the decisions. In a 1985 case, *Wallace v. Jaffree*, the Court invalidated an Alabama "moment-of-silence" law that called for "meditation or voluntary prayer" at the start of the school day. The decision left unsettled whether a more neutral moment of silence law could be upheld.

A new issue reached the Court in the 1991–1992 term: prayer at high school graduation ceremonies. With a conservative majority on the Court, school prayer advocates hoped for a different result from the earlier cases. But in a 5–4 decision, the Court in *Lee v. Weisman* (1992) held that schools could not invite clergy members to deliver invocations at commencement ceremonies. Kennedy wrote the opinion.

School prayer advocates said the Court's decision left open the possibility that students themselves could deliver prayers at graduation ceremonies or invite speakers to do so. Within the year, the Fifth U.S. Circuit Court of Appeals, ruling in a Texas case, allowed the practice; the justices declined to review the ruling. Later, two other federal appeals court disagreed, but the Court left the conflict unresolved.

The Case. The football prayer issue reached the Court as part of a broad legal challenge to religious practices at the high school in Santa Fe, an overwhelmingly white, predominantly Baptist town of about 8,500 people midway between Houston and Galveston. The two Mormon and Catholic families claimed in their suit, filed in April 1995, that school officials had encouraged students to attend revival meetings or join religious clubs and that some students had been chastised for minority religious beliefs.

The next month, a lower federal court judge in Galveston issued an interim order that prohibited a variety of practices—such as the use of "blatantly religious denominational" lesson material in classes—but allowed students to select a speaker to deliver a "non-denominational" prayer at graduation. Over the summer, the school board adopted a comparable policy for students to vote on whether to have invocations at football games and—if approved—then to elect one student for that role for the season. As adopted, the policy made no specification about the content of the invocation. But it included a fallback provision in the event of a court challenge to require any invocation to be "nonsectarian and nonproselytizing."

The students voted to have invocations at games and then elected a student to deliver them. But the judge blocked the policy, saying that it "coerces student participation in religious events." On appeal, the Fifth Circuit—by a 2–1 vote—held that the school board could allow graduation prayers only if they were "nonsectarian and nonproselytizing" and barred prayers from football games altogether. "Football games are hardly the sober type of annual event that can be appropriately solemnized with prayer," the court said.

The school district asked the Supreme Court to review the decision. Texas governor George W. Bush, then campaigning for the Republican nomination for president, signed a brief for the state urging the justices to review the decision. The justices agreed to hear the case, but limited the issue to whether "student-led, student-initiated" prayers were permissible at football games.

Arguments. Lawyers representing the school district and the state sought to convince the justices in the March 29 argument that the school's football game policy was constitutional because it was neutral toward religion. But they encountered deep skepticism from several of the justices.

Jay Alan Sekulow, chief counsel for the conservative American Center for Law and Justice, opened by saying that the school's policy was "neutral as to secular or religious speech." Echoing the school board's policy statement, he said that the pre-game invocation "serves important and legitimate goals of solemnizing the event, promoting good sportsmanship and safety, and establishing the appropriate environment for competition."

Souter and Stevens were skeptical. "I'm not sure what solemnizing a football game is," Souter said. Stevens questioned what was meant by "a secular invocation." Souter referenced the history of the policy. "We're not required to close our eyes to the context in which the policy arose," he said.

Kennedy jumped in with his own doubts about the election of a student to deliver the invocation. The campaign would be based on whether to have prayer at the games, the justice said. "That's the kind of thing the Establishment Clause was designed to keep out of our schools," he concluded.

In his turn, Texas attorney general John Cornyn argued that the policy should be allowed to go into effect to see whether it could be applied constitutionally. Breyer was skeptical. "As soon as it's in place, with the first prayer, the lawsuit is back," he said.

The parents' lawyer, Anthony Griffin, faced sharp questions from Rehnquist and Scalia about the reason why the plaintiffs had requested anonymity. Griffin explained that the families had feared intimidation. The two justices appeared unconvinced, but let Griffin move on to the main issue. The school's policy was unconstitutional, the attorney said, because it "endorses religion. Its whole purpose is religious."

Scalia countered that what he called the "rigid rule" of the graduation prayer case might not apply to football games. Rehnquist followed later by asking whether students were required to attend football games. Griffin said that, in fact, attendance was mandatory for band members, cheerleaders, and team members.

In any event, Griffin concluded, football games play an important part in high school. "There's not a school district in the country who wouldn't cringe if I got up and said, 'This is just football. Let's let [students] do what they want.'"

Decision. The Court's June 19 ruling decisively rejected the school district's effort to defend the policy as neutral toward religion. "[T]he delivery of a pregame prayer has the improper effect of coercing those present to participate in an act of religious worship," Stevens said. Five justices joined his opinion: liberals Souter, Ginsburg, and Breyer, along with O'Connor and Kennedy.

Stevens minimized the importance of the students' role in the policy. The invocations, he said, "are authorized by a government policy and take place on government property at government-sponsored school-related events." The policy, he continued, "invites and encourages religious messages." And the policy would not be saved even if attendance at football games were completely voluntary. The school district cannot require "religious conformity" from a student as the price of joining classmates at a game, Stevens wrote.

Stevens stressed—both in his written opinion and in his summary from the bench—that the Constitution does not bar all religious activity in public schools. Nothing stops "any public school student from voluntarily praying at any time before, during, or after the school day," Stevens wrote. The dissenters were not mollified. The majority's opinion, Rehnquist wrote, "bristles with hostility to all things religious in public life."

The rest of Rehnquist's dissent, however, was short—only eight pages—and narrow. The school's policy had "plausible secular purposes," he said, and could have been implemented in a neutral manner. On that basis, Rehnquist said, the policy should have been allowed to go into effect and blocked only if it was applied in an unconstitutional manner. Scalia and Thomas joined his opinion.

Reaction. Griffin, the plaintiffs' lawyer, called the Court's ruling a victory for religious freedom. "Religious belief and expression is flourishing in our country," he said, "precisely because America has . . . resisted the temptation for the government to endorse religion." But Sekulow said the decision showed "hostility toward student speech." "It is the free speech of students that has been censored," he said. Nationally, Vice President Gore said through a spokesman that he supported the decision, while Bush called the ruling "disappointing."

In Santa Fe itself, school board member and one-time chairman John Couch also called the ruling disappointing. "We tried to be as neutral as possible," Couch said. But the board was also facing criticism from the parents of the high school's only Jewish student, who said he had been harassed because of his religion throughout the school year. Two fellow students were facing misdemeanor charges for allegedly threatening the boy, but the boy's parents said one school board member had dismissed the incident in a television interview as a prank.

Campaign Finance

Court Upholds Low Contribution Limits for State Races

Nixon, Attorney General of Missouri v. Shrink Missouri Government PAC, decided by a 6–3 vote, January 24, 2000; Souter wrote the opinion; Thomas, Scalia, and Kennedy dissented.

Zev David Fredman was a thirty-four-year-old political neophyte when he declared his candidacy for the Republican nomination for state auditor in 1997. A conservative attorney friend with a political action committee descriptively titled Shrink Missouri Government PAC saw Fredman as a good standard-bearer for its cause and decided to back him.

Under Missouri's recently enacted campaign finance law, however, the committee was limited to making a contribution of no more than $1,075 to Fredman. With no war chest of his own and no broad base of support, Fredman decided that the contribution limit was preventing him from taking his message to the voters. So he filed suit—along with the political action committee—claiming that Missouri's law infringed his freedom of speech under the First Amendment.

Zev David Fredman

The case reached the Supreme Court after a federal appeals court agreed with Fredman and invalidated the Missouri law. But the Court voted 6–3 to reinstate the law. The majority justices said that contribution limits help prevent political corruption. But three dissenters said the limits unduly restrict political expression and called for overruling the Court's controversial decision that upheld such laws.

Background. Campaign spending limits for federal elections had been on the books since the early 1900s, but the levels were unrealistically low and the law went largely unenforced. Congress in 1971 enacted a new law, the Federal Election Campaign Act, and then strengthened it three years later in the wake of the Watergate scandal. The revamped law tightened disclosure requirements and set new limits on individual, committee, and party donations to federal campaigns. It also provided a system of public campaign financing for presidential campaigns and established the Federal Election Commission (FEC) to enforce the law.

Two years later, the Court cut a major hole in the law by striking down the limits on campaign spending as an unconstitutional infringement of free speech. The ruling in *Buckley v. Valeo* (1976) upheld contribution limits, however, by citing the government's interest in preventing corruption.

Candidates themselves could make unlimited expenditures from their own funds.

The Court's ruling left supporters and opponents of campaign finance regulation dissatisfied. Congress considered various bills over the years to revise the system, but the proposals—including efforts to raise the contribution limits—died in partisan stalemates. Meanwhile, several states were passing new laws with contribution limits lower than the $1,000 for individual donations set in federal law.

The Court returned to the subject in 1996 in a case challenging political party contributions to congressional candidates. In *Colorado Republican Federal Campaign Committee v. Federal Election Commission* (1996), the Court voted 7–2 to allow parties to make unlimited "independent" expenditures on behalf of a candidate. Breyer, in a plurality opinion, skirted the constitutional issues in the case. But Thomas wrote a separate opinion calling for overruling *Buckley* and striking down all campaign contribution limits.

The Case. Missouri's campaign contribution limits stemmed from widespread revulsion with the state's record $20 million gubernatorial race in 1992. The legislature in early 1994 passed a law that set contribution limits ranging from $1,000 for statewide offices down to $250 for legislative seats. Some campaign finance reform proponents were satisfied, but others pushed a more stringent measure as an initiative on the November 1994 ballot. The measure—setting a maximum contribution of $300 for statewide races—won approval from 74 percent of Missouri voters.

The Eighth U.S. Circuit Court of Appeals invalidated the initiative, however. The effect was to restore the legislature's version. Under a cost-of-living adjustment, the limits stood at $1,075 for statewide races when Fredman was campaigning for auditor. His legal challenge brought him a measure of relief in the form of a temporary injunction against enforcement of the law. That allowed him to collect one donation in excess of $2,000. But he raised less than $5,000 in total and was crushed in the voting.

Fredman's legal challenge continued, however. And in 1998 the Eighth U.S. Circuit Court of Appeals sided with him in a 2–1 decision striking the law down. The appeals court majority said the state had too little evidence of real corruption; one of the judges said the limits were too low anyway.

The state argued the appeals court had misapplied *Buckley* and asked the Court to review the decision. The justices agreed to hear the case. Significantly, though, they turned aside a second petition, filed by an individual legislator, that urged the Court to reconsider *Buckley* itself.

Arguments. The justices appeared both divided and uncertain during the hour-long argument October 5. Liberal justices seemed supportive of the law: Breyer and Souter, in particular. Scalia and Kennedy voiced strong doubts. And at the very end of the session, Thomas—who rarely speaks during oral arguments—signaled his continuing opposition to contribution limits by asking the state's lawyer, with evident incredulity, whether the government could combat political corruption by limiting the amount of money that news organizations receive for political ads.

In his opening remark, Missouri attorney general Jay Nixon depicted the case as "a direct challenge to the validity of the *Buckley* rule." Rehnquist quickly turned to the specifics, asking whether the $1,000 limit approved in *Buckley* was out of date because of inflation. Nixon said that some limits might be too low, but insisted that the opponents of the law had not shown that Missouri's limits had impaired political speech.

That answer did not satisfy Scalia and Kennedy. "I thought the burden was on you to show that there's a subsisting, existing interest that's served by the statute," Kennedy remarked. Scalia asked what evidence the state had of "this spectre of corruption."

Representing Fredman and Shrink Missouri Government, Bruce La Pierre, a law professor at Washington University in St. Louis, sought to re-inforce those doubts. He noted that the only evidence in the record about political corruption was a single affidavit from one Missouri legislator—a stark contrast to the ample evidence of corruption Congress had before it in enacting the 1974 law.

But Souter countered that no evidence was necessary to show the corrupting effects of political contributions. "Most people assume, and I do, certainly, that someone making an extraordinarily large contribu-tion gets something extraordinary in return," Souter said. Contribution limits helped promote "confidence in the integrity of the system," he concluded.

Breyer saw another purpose in the law: equalizing access to the political system. "A big megaphone can drown out a smaller one," he said. But La Pierre disagreed. "The government should not limit the voice of some to protect the rights of others," he said.

Decision. Souter announced the Court's decision January 24 in an eighteen-page opinion that reaffirmed *Buckley*'s approval of contribution limits—with or without adjustment for inflation. "We hold *Buckley* to be authority for comparable state regulation, which need not be pegged to *Buckley*'s dol-lars," Souter wrote.

After summarizing *Buckley*, Souter tracked the course of his questioning. The law was not void for lack of evidence, Souter said. "There is little reason to doubt that sometimes large contributions will work actual corruption of our political system," he wrote, "and no reason to question the existence of a corresponding suspicion among voters." As for the dollar amounts in the Missouri law, Souter said that *Buckley* "specifically rejected" the idea of some "constitutional minimum below which legislatures could not regulate." Rehnquist and O'Connor—who had given mixed signals in the argument—joined his opinion, as did Souter's fellow liberals: Stevens, Ginsburg, and Breyer.

In a brief concurrence, Stevens—who joined the Court later in the year *Buckley* was decided—registered his agreement with the ruling. Money, he said, "is property . . . not speech"—and therefore not entitled to the same First Amendment protections as speech. In a longer concurrence, Breyer argued that the issue was better left to legislatures than to courts. "[T]he legislature understands the problem—the threat to electoral integrity, the need for democratization—better than do we," he wrote. Ginsburg joined his opinion.

Forcefully dissenting, Thomas again called for overruling *Buckley* and accused the majority of weakening what he called "the already enfeebled constitutional protection" for campaign contributions. The majority, he said, "blindly adopts *Buckley*'s flawed reasoning" and retreated from the ruling's announced standard of review: "closest scrutiny." Missouri had no evidence of true "quid pro quo" corruption to justify its law, only "vague and unenumerated harms," he said. And the limits in the Missouri law were "much more restrictive" than those approved in *Buckley*, Thomas said, especially when inflation is taken into account. Scalia joined Thomas's opinion.

In a separate dissent, Kennedy said he agreed with Thomas on overruling *Buckley*, which he said had driven "a substantial amount of political speech underground" as contributors sought out ways—such as unregulated "soft money"—to circumvent the donation limits. But Kennedy left open the possibility that Congress or state legislatures could "attempt some new reform if, based upon their own considered judgment of the First Amendment, it is possible to do so."

Reaction. Supporters of stricter campaign finance regulations hailed the Court's ruling. The opinion "keeps open the door for states to pass reasonable contribution limits," said Scott Harshbarger, president of the citizens' group Common Cause. The cosponsors of a broad reform bill—Sens.

John McCain (R-Ariz.), and Russ Feingold (D-Wis.)—both said the ruling would help the measure's prospects. Opponents of the bill minimized the decision. "The Court issued a narrow decision that explicitly refused to address issues beyond the Missouri state candidate limits," said Sen. Mitch McConnell (R-Ky.).

In Missouri, Attorney General Nixon called the ruling "a big win." "Elections are not auctions," Nixon said, "and candidates are not to be sold to the highest bidder." But Fredman said that the ruling hurt democracy. "It's in the politician's interest to reduce competition," Fredman said, "and I can't think of anything that reduces competition in a more effective way than campaign finance limits."

Freedom of Association

Boy Scouts Can Exclude Homosexuals as Leaders

Boy Scouts of America v. Dale, decided by a 5–4 vote, June 28, 2000; Rehnquist wrote the opinion; Stevens, Souter, Ginsburg, and Breyer dissented.

James Dale loved Scouting. He joined the Cub Scouts in Matawan, New Jersey, in 1978 at the age of eight and eventually attained the Boy Scouts' highest rank: Eagle Scout. When he turned eighteen in August 1988, he was asked to become an assistant scoutmaster; the Boy Scouts' national office approved his application for adult membership.

In July 1990, however, the local Monmouth Boy Scouts Council summarily expelled Dale after learning from a newspaper article that Dale is gay. Boy Scouts of America (BSA) had successfully defended its policy on homosexuality in several state courts. But the New Jersey Supreme Court ruled in August 1999 that the Scouts were subject to the state's public accommodation law and ordered Dale reinstated.

The Scouts' appeal to the U.S. Supreme Court set up an emotional confrontation between civil rights groups seeking to broaden the reach of anti-discrimination laws and an array of conservative groups defending First Amendment protections for private organizations. The Court this term sided with the Scouts, ruling by a 5–4 vote that application of New Jersey's public accommodation law would violate the Boy Scouts' "freedom of expressive association."

Background. The First Amendment does not mention "freedom of association," but the Court recognizes it as implicit in the guarantees of freedom of speech and of assembly. In the 1980s, however, the Court ruled that state and local antidiscrimination laws could override the associational rights of private clubs in some circumstances.

In two cases—*Roberts v. United States Jaycees* (1984) and *Board of Directors of Rotary International v. Rotary Club of Duarte* (1987)—the Court unanimously ruled against private civic clubs with membership policies excluding women. The Court found that excluding women was not essential to the Jaycees' or Rotary's stated purposes and concluded that any incidental effects were outweighed by the states' interests in promoting equal treatment of women.

Critics of the Boy Scouts' policy of barring homosexuals as Scout leaders mounted legal attacks in several states with civil rights laws that prohibited discrimination on the basis of sexual orientation. But through 1998 all state supreme courts that ruled on the issue had held that BSA was not a "public accommodation" subject to antidiscrimination provisions.

The Supreme Court also had given gay rights advocates no encouragement on the question. In 1986, the Court ruled in *Bowers v. Hardwick* that homosexuals could not claim a "right of intimate association": to prevent states from enforcing antisodomy laws. A decade later, the Court ruled unanimously in *Hurley v. Irish-American Gay, Lesbian and Bisexual Group of Boston* (1995) that Massachusetts could not use an antidiscrimination law to require the organizers of Boston's St. Patrick's Day parade to allow a gay group to join the procession.

The Case. Dale did not seek out a confrontation with the Scouts' policy. After "coming out" at Rutgers University in Newark, he became copresident of the campus's gay and lesbian alliance. The local newspaper ran a photograph of Dale on July 18, 1990, with a story on a seminar on gay health issues. When officials of the Monmouth Scout Council saw the article, they promptly revoked Dale's membership. "Boy Scouts of America does not admit avowed homosexuals to membership in the organization," a BSA lawyer wrote after Dale requested an explanation.

The Boy Scouts' policy on homosexuals had solidified over time. A BSA internal advisory written in 1978 stated simply, "We do not believe that homosexuality and leadership in Scouting are appropriate." After defending the policy in court in the 1980s, the Scouts issued more official pronouncements. In one policy statement issued in 1991, homosexual conduct was declared to be "inconsistent" with the requirements in the Scout oath and Scout law to be "morally straight" and "clean."

The New Jersey legislature amended its public accommodations law in 1991 to include sexual orientation in the list of protected categories.

Eleven days later, Dale filed a complaint against the Boy Scouts, alleging that his exclusion violated the state law and asking for reinstatement as well as compensatory and punitive damages. In an interview with the *New York Times*, he tied his legal action to lessons he learned as a Scout. "Being proud about who I am is something the Boy Scouts taught me," he said.

The trial judge ruled against Dale. He said that Boy Scouts was not subject to the public accommodation law and, in any event, that requiring Scouts to admit homosexuals would violate the organization's First Amendment rights. But an intermediate appellate court disagreed, voting 2–1 that the Scouts had no First Amendment right to bar Dale because of his homosexuality. The New Jersey Supreme Court upheld that ruling in a carefully constructed decision in August 1999. After surveying Scouting materials and policy statements, the justices acknowledged that Boy Scouts "expresses a belief in moral values," but concluded that Scouting's members had no "shared goal" of promoting the view that homosexuality is immoral.

Arguments. In their briefs and opposing arguments, lawyers for the Scouts and for Dale continued to argue about whether the Scouts' policy on homosexuals was central to its mission. For their part, the justices seemed uncertain during the hour-long session April 26 both about the Scouts' policy and the implications of a ruling either way.

"This case is about the freedom of a voluntary association to choose its own leaders," the Scouts' lawyer, George Davidson, began. "Being openly homosexual conveys the concept that homosexuality is OK," said Davidson, a Wall Street attorney who had also represented the Scouts in the California case on the issue.

Liberal justices, however, seemed unconvinced. Ginsburg asked skeptically whether a heterosexual who lived with someone outside marriage would be barred from serving as adult leader. "I don't understand the policy," she said. Souter, who had authored the *Hurley* decision, asked why the policy was not spelled out in the Scouts' Handbook or troop leaders' manual. "This is not a stealth policy," Davidson answered.

Later, Souter contrasted Dale with the gay group seeking to join the St. Patrick's Day parade. "Mr. Dale is not proposing to carry a banner," the justice said. "He put a banner around his neck when he appeared in the newspaper," Davidson replied. "He can't take it off."

Representing Dale, Evan Wolfson, a senior attorney with the Lambda Legal Defense and Education Fund, opened by saying the Scouts were asking the Court to "specially excuse" it from New Jersey's civil rights law. Rehnquist voiced doubts. If a state prohibited discrimination against ex-

James Dale

convicts, could the Scouts be required to appoint one as scoutmaster? the chief justice asked. Breyer was also troubled. The Scouts' position, Breyer said, could mean that "a Catholic organization has to admit Jews, the B'nai B'rith has to admit Catholics."

"What they have failed to show is that their expressive message is burdened," Wolfson replied. But Scalia sharply disagreed. "To require the Boy Scouts to have as a scoutmaster someone who embodies a contradiction of their message—how can that be?" Scalia said.

Kennedy was also skeptical. "Who is better qualified to determine the expressive purpose of the Boy Scouts: the Boy Scouts or the New Jersey courts?" he asked. "It's their burden," Wolfson responded, "to show that their central message is significantly burdened."

Outside the Court, one demonstrator held a placard that read, "A homosexual Boy Scout leader is like asking a fox to guard the chickens." Inside, however, Davidson acknowledged under questioning that the Scouts did not contend that a homosexual leader posed any special risk to boys in the program.

Dale told reporters after the argument that he felt his actions had been faithful to the Scout Law. "That's what morally straight is about: standing up for yourself and being honest," he said.

A demonstrator holds an antigay placard as the Supreme Court hears arguments on the Boy Scouts' policy of excluding homosexuals. The Court ruled the Scouts have a First Amendment right to bar homosexuals.

Decision. The justices divided along conservative-liberal lines in their 5–4 decision June 28 in favor of the Scouts. For the majority, Rehnquist seemed to soften the test for finding a burden on a group's freedom of association. "The forced inclusion of an unwanted person in a group infringes the group's freedom of expressive association," Rehnquist wrote, "if the presence of that person affects in a significant way the group's ability to advocate public or private viewpoints."

The chief justice acknowledged that government could override a group's associational rights in order to serve a "compelling interest." But he also said that courts must "give deference to an association's assertions regarding the nature of its expression" and to its "view of what would impair its expression." And after surveying the Scouts' policy, Rehnquist concluded, "Dale's presence in the Boy Scouts would, at the very least, force the organization to send a message . . . that the Boy Scouts accept homosexual conduct as a legitimate form of behavior." O'Connor, Scalia, Kennedy, and Thomas joined Rehnquist's opinion.

Dissenting justices disagreed primarily with the majority's view of the facts, not the law. Quoting from the Scouts' Handbook, Stevens declared, "It is plain as the light of day that neither one of these principles, 'morally straight' and 'clean,' says the slightest thing about homosexuality." The Boy Scouts, he said, "has, at most, simply adopted an exclusionary membership policy. . . ." Souter, Ginsburg, and Breyer joined Stevens's opinion.

Justices on both sides stressed that their votes signaled no view on the wisdom of the Scouts' policy. "The First Amendment protects expression, be it of the popular variety or not," Rehnquist wrote. In a dissent joined by Ginsburg and Breyer, Souter wrote similarly: "Whether the group appears to this Court to be in the vanguard or rearguard of social thinking is irrelevant to the group's rights."

Reaction. The Scouts took the decision as vindication for their position. "We can now continue in our mission of providing character building experiences for young people," BSA spokesman Greg Shields said. But Ruth Harlow, deputy legal director of the Lambda legal defense group, called the ruling a "hollow, Pyrrhic" victory for the Scouts. "The Boy Scouts have fought long and hard for something that has marginalized the institution," Harlow said.

Dale himself, who had moved to New York and was working as advertising director for a magazine for people who are HIV-positive, was disappointed both with the ruling and with his beloved Scouts. "The Boy Scouts are making themselves extinct," Dale told reporters, "and it's a very sad thing."

Family Law

Grandparents Lose Bid for Court-Ordered Visitation

Troxel v. Granville, decided by a 6–3 vote, June 5, 2000; O'Connor wrote the main opinion; Stevens, Scalia, and Kennedy dissented.

Gary and Jenifer Troxel thought of themselves as devoted, loving grandparents to their young granddaughters, Isabelle and Natalie. But the girls' mother, Tommie Granville Wynn, viewed them as overbearing and resisted the grandparents' pleas to spend more time with the girls.

Unlike most interfamily disputes, this one found its way into the court system. Invoking a broadly written Washington State child visitation law, the Troxels asked a state court judge to order Wynn to allow them to have the girls at their home for overnight stays twice a month. The trial judge agreed after cutting the number of overnight visits to one a month.

On appeal, however, the Washington Supreme Court ruled that the visitation law was unconstitutional because it infringed on parents' fundamental rights to bring up their children. The Supreme Court's decision to hear the Troxels' appeal took the justices into the largely uncharted waters of grandparents' rights. Their ruling, however, settled little more than the Troxels' case. By a 6–3 vote, the Court rejected the Troxels' plea for court-ordered visitation, but the narrow and fractured decision left most questions to be decided in future cases.

Background. All fifty states had laws on the books giving grandparents some visitation rights. The laws dated from the mid-1960s and varied widely. Many permitted court-ordered visits only under limited conditions—for example, if the parents were deceased, divorced, or unmarried. But others allowed for court-ordered visitation even if the nuclear family was intact. Some but not all of the laws required proof of some close relationship between the grandparents and the child.

Washington's child visitation law—adopted in 1973—was the broadest of any. It allowed "any person"—not just grandparents or other relatives—to petition a court for visitation "at any time" and allowed the court to grant visitation rights whenever "visitation may serve the best interest of the child."

The Court rarely deals with custody disputes, but it had recognized parental rights to control their children's upbringing in a pair of education-related cases from the 1920s. In *Meyer v. Nebraska* (1923), the Court invalidated a law that barred the teaching of foreign language to young children. Two years later, in *Pierce v. Society of Sisters* (1925), the Court struck down

Jenifer and Gary Troxel leave the Supreme Court following arguments in their effort to gain visitation rights to their two young granddaughters. The Court upheld the right of the children's mother to limit their time with their grandparents.

an Oregon law requiring parents to send their children to public schools. Both laws were held to violate the Due Process Clause by interfering with what the Court in *Meyer* called "the liberty of parents and guardians to direct the upbringing and education of children under their control."

The Court also relied on the Due Process Clause in its only prior ruling on grandparents' rights. In that case, *Moore v. City of East Cleveland* (1977), the Court overturned a local zoning ordinance that would have prevented a woman from having two grandsons—cousins, not brothers— live with her in her home. Under the Rehnquist Court, however, the use of so-called "substantive due process" to expand individual rights lost favor. In one custody-related case, the Court in 1989 rejected a California man's due process challenge to a law that blocked him from trying to establish paternity of a child born to his wife while she was married to another man.

The Case. The Troxels' case arose against the backdrop of a complex, and tragic, web of relationships in the rural northwestern town of Anacortes.

Their son Brad fathered two children with Tommie Granville, although the two never married. They separated in 1991—before the younger daughter, Isabelle, was born. Tommie became the primary caregiver for the two girls, but Brad kept them from time to time—sometimes at his parents' house.

Brad committed suicide in 1993. The Troxels wanted to stay in their grandchildren's lives. Tommie never tried to cut off their access to the children. But as she was about to marry Kelly Wynn, she came to view the Troxels' requests as interfering with her efforts to build a new family and limited the visits to one weekend day a month with no overnight stays. Dissatisfied, the Troxels went to court in 1995. The trial judge granted them one overnight visitation a month, one week during the summer, and four hours on each of the children's birthdays.

The intermediate-level Washington Court of Appeals reversed the visitation order in 1997 by ruling that nonparents had no standing under the law to petition for visitation unless a custody proceeding was pending. The Troxels appealed to the Washington Supreme Court, which issued a broader ruling in 1998. By a 5–4 vote, the state justices ruled the visitation law unconstitutional. The government could not overrule a parent's "fundamental rights," the state high court ruled, except to prevent harm to the child.

The Court granted the Troxels' petition to review the decision on September 28, just before the opening of the new term. The case drew broad attention. The AARP, which filed a legal brief supporting the Troxels, released a survey on the eve of arguments showing that more than 80 percent of grandparents questioned had seen their grandchildren within the previous month. On the other side, the liberal ACLU and the conservative American Center for Law and Justice both supported Wynn's argument that the visitation order violated her parental rights.

Arguments. The justices' questions during the January 12 argument left little doubt that most believed the Washington statute went too far. "This is a breathtakingly broad provision," O'Connor declared. But some justices worried about giving parents what Stevens called "an absolute veto" over the rights of grandparents or other relatives.

Representing the Troxels, Seattle attorney Mark Olson insisted the Washington Supreme Court went too far in requiring a showing of harm before a court could order visitation. He said the visitation order for the Troxels amounted to a "very slight" infringement of Wynn's rights and emphasized that the grandparents had no religious or educational agenda for the two girls.

O'Connor, Scalia, and Souter all criticized the Washington law as too broad. Souter asked why "any person walking off the streets" should be able to petition for visitation. Scalia criticized the standard the law set for ordering visitation. "It might be in the best interest of the child to take children away from a lot of parents," Scalia said, "but the parents have rights."

In her turn, Catherine Smith, the Seattle attorney representing Wynn, argued that courts should have no power to intervene "absent a showing to harm" to the child. Stevens pressed her: "Even if the order was only for 20 minutes every six months?" Smith said yes. Breyer followed: "Do you want to say that we're giving a constitutional veto to the mother?" Again, Smith answered yes.

Smith turned to the facts of the case to illustrate the problems of judicial intervention. The visitation order had gone into minute details, she said, amounting to "micromanagement." And Wynn had been forced to spend a lot of money to defend the case and was unlikely to recover any of the expense through an award of attorney fees.

She closed by returning to her opening theme: parental rights over their children's upbringing. "We let parents make these decisions—how much candy the children eat, how much television to watch," Smith said. "We don't take that decision away from them."

Decision. O'Connor began her announcement of the decision on June 5 by confessing the justices' divisions. "Unfortunately, the members of this Court were no more able to reach a resolution than the parties to this case," O'Connor said. The decision stopped short of declaring the Washington law unconstitutional. Instead, O'Connor said in the main opinion only that the statute—"as applied to Granville [Wynn] and her family in this case"— unconstitutionally infringed on her "fundamental parental right" concerning the care, custody, and control of her children.

O'Connor stressed that the Troxels had not claimed that Wynn was an unfit parent, that Wynn had never refused the Troxels all visitation, and that the Washington court had given no special weight to her views. The judge's order, O'Connor said, "directly contravened the traditional presumption that a fit parent will act in the best interest of his or her child." Three justices joined her opinion: Rehnquist, Ginsburg, and Breyer.

Given the breadth of the statute, O'Connor said that the Court did not have to decide whether a nonparental visitation statute must require a showing of harm before courts could intervene. Souter, concurring in the judgment, said he would have upheld the Washington Supreme Court's decision that the state law was unconstitutional on its face, without regard to the specific facts in the case. But he too said the Court did not have to decide whether a showing of harm was constitutionally required for non-parental visitation.

In a separate opinion concurring in the judgment, Thomas called for applying the most stringent constitutional standard—"strict scrutiny"—before allowing courts to infringe on "fundamental parental rights." Under that test, a court would need a "compelling interest" to intervene. In this case, Thomas said, the court had no "legitimate governmental interest . . . in second-guessing a fit parent's decision. . . ."

The three dissenters took somewhat different approaches. Stevens and Kennedy both faulted the Washington court for rejecting what Kennedy called the "well recognized" best-interest-of-the-child standard. Children's interests, Stevens wrote, "must be balanced in this equation." Kennedy said the Court should "proceed with caution" in fashioning constitutional rules in the area. Both said they would remand the case for further proceedings.

For his part, Scalia directly challenged the whole idea of judicially enforced parental rights. He said the issues should be left to state legislatures and warned against "ushering in a new regime of judicially prescribed, and federally prescribed, family law."

Reaction. Family law experts disagreed on the likely impact of the ruling. David Hudson, a lawyer with the First Amendment Center at Vanderbilt University in Nashville, said the case was unlikely to have much impact beyond the Washington statute. Other experts, however, predicted that the ruling would lead to more challenges to grandparent visitation statutes and that some state laws might need to be rewritten.

In Washington State, Wynn told reporters that she was "relieved" with the victory, but called the case "a huge waste of time, money, and emotion." For their part, the Troxels voiced plaintive disappointment at having to bow to the limited time with the girls. "If one afternoon a month is what we get, we'll be happy with that," Jenifer Troxel said. "We miss them. They're still part of our family."

Chapter 3

Case Summaries

A strange legal drama heavy with political and diplomatic implications held Americans' attention for seven months beginning in November 1999 after a six-year-old Cuban boy fleeing his native country with his mother and a raftful of other refugees was rescued from waters off the Florida coast.

Elian Gonzalez's mother and ten other passengers on the raft drowned in their effort to reach the United States. Once ashore, Elian became the focus of an intrafamily immigration case pitting his Miami relatives, who sought asylum for him to stay in the United States, against Elian's father, who wanted the boy returned to him in Cuba.

For months, television news crews staked out the Miami relatives' home to bring Americans continuous updates on Elian's every move. Immigration authorities and lawyers representing Elian's great-uncle, Lazaro Gonzalez, in Miami and his father, Juan Miguel Gonzalez, in Cuba sharply contested what course—asylum or repatriation—was in Elian's best interest and who had authority to speak for the boy. After tortuously complicated legal proceedings, the Eleventh U.S. Circuit Court of Appeals in Atlanta in early June backed the Clinton administration's position that Elian's father had sole authority to speak for his son—and therefore the power to withdraw the asylum application that Lazaro Gonzalez had filed on the boy's behalf.

Still, the drama was not over. The Miami relatives made one last appeal—to the Supreme Court. They filed a petition on June 26 seeking an asylum hearing and asking for an order to keep Elian in the United States. Justice Anthony M. Kennedy, who oversaw cases from the Eleventh Circuit, referred the petition to the full Court, which issued a one-sentence order on June 28 denying the relatives' plea.

The Court's action removed the last legal barrier to Elian's return to Cuba. And so it was that on the same day that the Supreme Court ended

its 1999–2000 term with important rulings on abortion rights, aid to parochial schools, abortion protests, and gay rights, the justices shared TV
newscasts and headlines with images of a six-year-old boy and his father
boarding a chartered plane to return to Cuba.

Legal observers doubted that the Court would take up Elian's case. It
was the type of fact-intensive dispute with inchoate legal issues that the
Court, in its discretion, leaves to lower federal courts to sort out. But the
juxtaposition of the day's news stories underscored the truism that the Supreme Court has impact on Americans' lives not only when it decides to
hear a case and issue a ruling but also when it decides not to.

The Court's case selection process is shrouded in secrecy. The justices'
reasons for passing up a case can sometimes be inferred, but often times
not. What is known, however, is that the justices in the last decade or so
have been taking up fewer and fewer cases than in years past even while the
number of cases brought to the Court has continued to increase.

The Court received a record number of 8,445 petitions for review and
appeals during the 1999–2000 term: a 4½ percent increase over the previous year. Despite the increase, the Court issued signed decisions in only
seventy-four cases—substantially lower than the 100 or more cases typically
decided as late as the early 1990s and the lowest number since the 1953–
1954 term, when the Court decided only sixty-five cases. *(See Figure 3-1.)*

Among the various explanations for the Court's shrinking calendar, one
new suggestion came this term from attorney Thomas Goldstein, who for
several years has compiled unofficial statistics on the Court's caseload and
justices' voting patterns. "I expect that in coming years the Court will generally hear arguments in around 80 cases per term," Goldstein wrote in the
end-of-term wrap-up he distributed to the Supreme Court press corps.
The argument calendar, he noted, "provides slots for approximately 80
cases if two cases are heard each argument day." Put more bluntly, the justices seem to have settled into a pattern of finishing arguments by noon and
leaving their afternoons free for other work, such as drafting opinions.

In refusing to take up cases, the Court sometimes seemed to be sending
mixed signals to courts below. At the start of the term, the Court left standing a Knoxville, Tennessee, school board policy requiring drug testing for
school teachers. But at the end of the term, it refused to consider reinstating a Louisiana law requiring drug testing for elected officials. The Court
cheered advocates of aid to parochial schools by leaving in place an Arizona
tax credit for people who contributed to church-affiliated schools. But it
also refused an effort by parents of parochial school students in Maine to
take advantage of a tuition reimbursement program offered to students at
nonreligious schools.

Figure 3-1 Supreme Court Caseload, 1960 Term–1999 Term

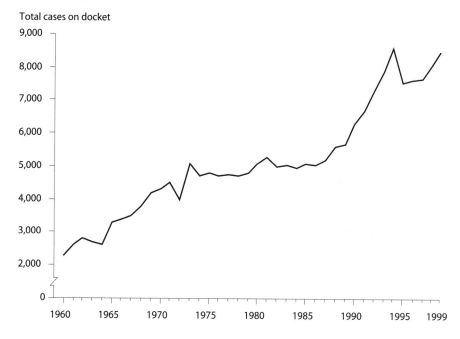

Total cases on docket

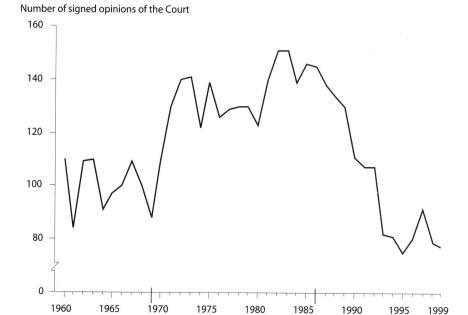

Number of signed opinions of the Court

In the vast majority of cases, the Court's orders declining to grant "certiorari"—the legal term for the review of a lower court opinion—consist of a single sentence, with no explanation for the action. Occasionally, however, a justice may issue a statement "dissenting from the denial of certiorari." Justice Thomas, for example, dissented when the Court refused to take up a California man's appeal of a state court injunction barring him from using derogatory terms for Latinos at the car rental agency where he worked. In another case, Justice Scalia, joined by Thomas, complained about the Court's refusal to hear an appeal by a group of anti-abortion clergy members challenging an injunction against their efforts to boycott a women's health clinic where abortions were performed.

One closely watched appeal produced opposing statements from justices on whether the Court should have taken up the issue. The case involved parallel appeals by death row inmates in two states raising the question whether lengthy delays in waiting for a death sentence to be carried out were unconstitutional under the Eighth Amendment's prohibition against "cruel and unusual punishments." In a nine-page opinion, Justice Breyer said the Court should hear the cases. "Both of these cases involve astonishingly long delays flowing in significant part from constitutionally defective death penalty procedures," Breyer wrote. "Where a delay, measured in decades, reflects the State's own failure to comply with the Constitution's demands, the claim that time has rendered the execution inhumane is a particularly strong one."

Thomas answered with a five-page opinion: "I am unaware of any support in the American constitutional tradition or in this Court's precedent for the proposition that a defendant can avail himself of the panoply of appellate and collateral procedures and then complain when his execution is delayed." Thomas went on to blame the delays on what he called "this Court's Byzantine death penalty jurisprudence." Recognizing an Eighth Amendment claim, he said, "would further prolong collateral review by giving virtually every capital prisoner yet another ground on which to challenge and delay his execution."

The Court did agree to decide one unsettled death penalty question: whether execution by electrocution is unconstitutional under the Eighth Amendment. The justices in October agreed to hear a Florida death row inmate's appeal raising the issue. Florida had had some famously botched electrocutions, and the Florida Supreme Court had upheld the practice only by a one-vote margin: 4–3. After the Court agreed to hear the case, however, the Florida legislature changed its law to provide for execution by lethal injection unless an inmate specifically requested electrocution. With that action, the Court dismissed the appeal.

Figure 3-2 Vote Divisions on Cases Decided in 1999–2000 Supreme Court Term

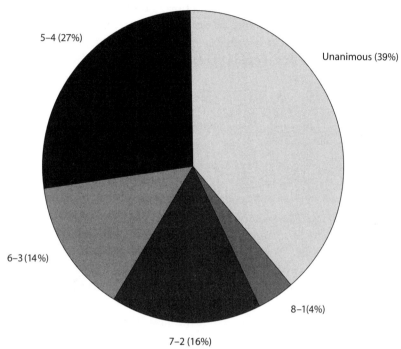

Among the Court's seventy-four signed decisions was one that only barely counted. In considering a Pennsylvania man's federal habeas corpus petition, the Court decided to "certify" to the Pennsylvania Supreme Court a state law question that the justices said would help them decide the case. The Court also decided four cases with unsigned—or *per curiam*—opinions, all of them unanimously and three without hearing arguments. The Court also issued an unsigned opinion announcing a deadlock in one case: an important but technical dispute involving federal court jurisdiction over class action suits. O'Connor recused herself, and the other justices divided 4–4. The tie vote left in place a lower court decision that favored business groups by making it easier to move class actions into federal court; but the Court's action set no precedent on the issue for future cases.

Overall, the Court divided 5–4 in twenty out of the seventy-four signed decisions for the term: a somewhat higher proportion, 27 percent, than in recent years. The number of unanimous decisions—twenty-nine—represented a somewhat lower proportion, 39 percent, than in recent years. There were three decisions with a single dissenter, twelve with two dissenting votes, and ten with three dissenters. *(See Figure 3-2.)*

Following are summaries of the seventy-four signed opinions and five *per curiam* opinions issued by the Court during the 1999–2000 term. They are organized by subject matter: business law, courts and procedure, criminal law and procedure, election law, environmental law, family law, federal government, First Amendment, individual rights, labor law, states, and torts.

Business Law

Bankruptcy

Hartford Underwriters Insurance Co. v. Union Planters Bank, N.A., decided by a 9–0 vote, May 30, 2000; Scalia wrote the opinion.

Unsecured creditors cannot seek payment of a claim against a bankrupt estate by using a Bankruptcy Code provision that allows the trustee to recover administrative costs before secured creditors are paid.

The ruling blocked an effort by Hartford Underwriters Insurance Co. to collect more than $5,000 in unpaid workers' compensation insurance premiums owed by a bankrupt Missouri company from the company's primary lender, Union Planters Bank. As a secured creditor, the bank had first priority on any of the company's assets. But Hartford sought payment for the claim from the bank by invoking a provision of the Bankruptcy Code — §506(c) — that allows the trustee in bankruptcy to recover so-called "administrative expenses." A bankruptcy judge allowed the claim, but the Eighth U.S. Circuit Court of Appeals reversed the decision. It ruled that an administrative claimant could not use the provision to collect on a claim.

Unanimously, the Court held that only the bankruptcy trustee could invoke §506(c) to recover administrative expenses. The "most natural reading" of the law, Scalia wrote, "supports the conclusion that entities other than the trustee are not entitled to use" the section.

Raleigh v. Illinois Department of Revenue, decided by a 9–0 vote, May 30, 2000; Souter wrote the opinion.

The Court eased the burden on local or state taxing authorities to collect unpaid taxes in bankruptcy proceedings.

The ruling backed the Illinois Department of Revenue in a dispute stemming from an unpaid use tax for the purchase of an airplane by a defunct Illinois company. The president of the company, William Stoecker, later filed for bankruptcy. Illinois law makes a corporate officer responsible for willful failure to pay a tax and places the burden of proof on the taxpayer to disprove a claim. Stoecker claimed he had no knowledge of the failure to pay the tax. The bankruptcy trustee then argued that the state should be required to prove its claim just as most creditors do in bankruptcy proceedings. The Seventh U.S. Circuit Court of Appeals disagreed.

Unanimously, the Court held that state law governs the burden of proof on tax claims in federal bankruptcy proceedings. The basic rule in bankruptcy, Souter wrote, is that state law governs claims, and the bankruptcy code "makes no provision for altering the burden on a tax claim."

Taxation

Baral v. United States, decided by a 9–0 vote, February 22, 2000; Thomas wrote the opinion.

The three-year period established by the federal tax code for seeking a refund begins on the normal due date for the taxpayer's return, not when the return is actually filed.

The ruling blocked taxpayer David Baral from getting a $1,175 credit for overpaid taxes for 1989. Baral filed his return, including the request for the refund, in 1993, four years late. The issue in the case was whether Baral's tax was "paid" on the due date of his return in 1989—as the Internal Revenue Service contended—or upon the filing of his return, as Baral argued.

Unanimously, the Court held that federal income taxes are considered to have been paid on the due date regardless when the return was actually filed. Thomas cited the "plain language" of a "nearby provision" that said withheld taxes or estimated taxes are "deemed to have been paid" on the normal due date for the return.

Drye v. United States, decided by a 9–0 vote, December 7, 1999; Ginsburg wrote the opinion.

Someone eligible to inherit money or property cannot circumvent a federal tax lien on the value of the estate by disclaiming his right to the inheritance.

The ruling rejected an effort by an Arkansas man, Rohn F. Drye Jr., to block enforcement of a $325,000 federal tax lien on the $233,000 estate that he stood to inherit after his mother's death in 1994. Drye exercised his right under state law to "disclaim" the inheritance, which meant that the estate then passed to his daughter. But a lower federal court and the Eighth U.S. Circuit Court of Appeals ruled that the move did not prevent the government from levying on the estate for Drye's unpaid back taxes.

In a unanimous decision, the Court agreed that federal rather than state law determined the outcome. "The control rein [Drye] held under state law,"

Ginsburg wrote, "rendered the inheritance 'property' or 'rights to property' belonging to him [under federal law], and hence subject to the federal tax liens."

Trademarks

Wal-Mart Stores, Inc. v. Samara Brothers, Inc., decided by a 9–0 vote, March 22, 2000; Scalia wrote the opinion.

The design of a product is not ordinarily protected by trademark law.

The ruling set aside a $1.6 million jury award won in a trademark infringement suit by a clothing manufacturer, Samara Brothers, against the giant retailer Wal-Mart Stores. Wal-Mart sold close copies—so-called "knockoffs"—of Samara's signature line of distinctively designed one-piece seersucker suits. Samara brought suit under a provision of the federal trademark law, the Lanham Act, that protects "trade dress." That term was originally applied to product packaging, but some courts expanded it also to cover product design. A jury ruled in Samara's favor, and the Second U.S. Circuit Court of Appeals upheld the verdict.

Reversing the appeals court ruling, the Court unanimously held that the design of a product is not ordinarily distinctive enough to qualify for trademark protection. "A product's design is distinctive, and therefore protectible," Scalia wrote, "only upon a showing of secondary meaning"—that is, that consumers identify the design with the maker of the specific product rather than merely with the product itself.

Courts and Procedure

Appeals

Weisgram v. Marley Co., decided by a 9–0 vote, February 22, 2000; Ginsburg wrote the opinion.

A federal appeals court may set aside a jury verdict and enter a judgment in favor of the losing party if it rules expert testimony was improperly admitted at trial.

The ruling upheld the action of the Eighth U.S. Circuit Court of Appeals in barring a new trial in a product liability suit brought by the family of a North Dakota man who blamed his death from carbon monoxide poisoning on an allegedly defective room heater. A jury ruled in the family's favor and ordered the manufacturer of the heater to pay $500,000 in damages. The appeals court ruled, however, that the expert testimony used to prove the heater defective was too speculative and should not have been admitted. The court went on to rule that the remaining evidence was insufficient to sustain a verdict and ordered the trial judge to enter a judgment in favor of the defendant. The family contended the action went beyond an appeals court's power under the Federal Rules of Civil Procedure.

Unanimously, the Court rejected the family's argument. "The authority of courts of appeals to direct the entry of judgment as a matter of law," Ginsburg wrote, "extends to cases in which, on excision of testimony erroneously admitted, there remains insufficient evidence to support the jury's verdict."

Arbitration

Cortez Byrd Chips, Inc. v. Bill Harbert Construction Co., decided by a 9–0 vote, March 21, 2000; Souter wrote the opinion.

The Court gave parties to an arbitration wide discretion as to where to file a court action to enforce, modify, or set aside the arbitrator's award.

The ruling allowed a Mississippi company, Cortez Byrd Chips, to file a court action contesting a $275,000 arbitration in federal court in Mississippi rather than have the case heard in Alabama, the home state of the other company in the dispute. The federal court in Alabama and the Eleventh U.S. Circuit Court of Appeals had both interpreted the venue provisions of the Federal Arbitration Act to require that an action to contest an arbitration award be filed in the federal district where the arbitration was heard.

Unanimously, the Court held that the law allowed an action to confirm, modify, or vacate an arbitration to be filed in any court where venue would be proper under general federal law. Souter said the arbitration act, enacted in 1925, had been intended to liberalize arbitration procedures, and that the law should be treated "as permitting, not limiting, venue choice today."

Class Actions

Free v. Abbott Laboratories, Inc., affirmed on a 4–4 vote, April 3, 2000; *per curiam* opinion; O'Connor did not participate.

The Court upheld on a tie vote a federal appeals court decision making it easier for defendants in certain class action suits to have the cases tried in federal courts.

The ruling stemmed from a class action price fixing suit filed by a Louisiana couple, Robin and Renee Free, in state court against a number of infant formula manufacturers. The companies removed the case to federal court under the federal "diversity of citizenship" jurisdiction, which allows federal courts to try cases involving parties in different states. The Frees sought to have the case sent back to state court. They claimed that federal jurisdiction was improper because the unnamed plaintiffs did not meet the minimum $75,000 amount required for diversity jurisdiction. The Fifth U.S. Circuit Court of Appeals held federal jurisdiction was proper because of a 1990 statute giving federal courts "supplemental jurisdiction" over claims related to one that was properly within federal jurisdiction.

The 4–4 vote left the appeals court decision standing but established no precedent on the issue. The Court does not announce how the justices vote in deadlocked cases. O'Connor recused herself because she owned a small amount of stock in one of the companies named as defendants.

Judgments

Nelson v. Adams USA, Inc., decided by a 9–0 vote, April 25, 2000; Ginsburg wrote the opinion.

A court cannot add a party to a lawsuit after judgment and simultaneously make him subject to the judgment without giving him an opportunity to contest liability.

The ruling stemmed from a dispute over attorneys' fees in an unsuccessful patent infringement suit brought by Ohio Cellular Products Corp. (OCP) against Adams USA, Inc. A federal district court dismissed the suit and ordered OCP to pay Adams $178,888.51 in attorneys' fees and costs. Adams then moved to add OCP's president and sole shareholder, Donald Nelson, as a defendant. The court granted the motion and at the same time made Nelson personally liable for the award. Nelson argued the ruling violated his rights to due process, but the U.S. Court of Appeals for the Federal Circuit held that he had not been prejudiced by the procedure.

Unanimously, the Court held that the procedure violated due process rights set out in the Federal Rules of Civil Procedure. "Due process . . . required that Nelson be given an opportunity to respond and contest his personal liability for the award after he was made a party and before the entry of judgment against him," Ginsburg wrote.

Criminal Law

Appeals

Martinez v. Court of Appeal of California, decided by a 9–0 vote, January 12, 2000; Stevens wrote the opinion.

Criminal defendants have no federal constitutional right to represent themselves in appealing their convictions.

The ruling barred an effort by a self-taught paralegal, Salvador Martinez, to represent himself in appealing his embezzlement conviction in California for pocketing $6,000 from a client of a law firm where he worked. Martinez argued that the Supreme Court's 1975 decision, *Faretta v. California*, guaranteeing a defendant the right to represent himself at trial should be extended to appeals. But a state appeals court and the California Supreme Court both refused to let Martinez handle his own appeal.

Unanimously, the Court upheld the decision. Stevens said the state's "overriding interest in the fair and efficient administration of justice" outweighed the defendant's "interest in acting as his own lawyer."

Seven justices joined Stevens's opinion. Scalia, concurring in the judgment, said he based his vote solely on the fact that there is no federal constitutional right to an appeal at all. Scalia also criticized Stevens for appearing to question the validity of the earlier decision regarding self-representation at trial. In a separate concurring opinion, Kennedy also defended *Faretta*. Breyer, however, noted in another concurring opinion that trial judges had criticized *Faretta* but stopped short of calling for a reconsideration of the decision.

Ohler v. United States, decided by a 5–4 vote, May 22, 2000; Rehnquist wrote the opinion; Souter, Stevens, Ginsburg, and Breyer dissented.

A defendant cannot appeal a judge's pretrial ruling to allow evidence of a prior criminal conviction if the defendant takes the stand and acknowledges the conviction herself in her direct testimony.

The ruling upheld the drug conviction and thirty-month prison sentence of a California woman, Maria Ohler, for bringing eighty-one pounds of marijuana into the state from Mexico inside a van. Before trial, the judge granted the government's motion to allow the introduction of Ohler's prior drug conviction if she testified. At trial, Ohler took the stand: she denied any knowledge of the marijuana and acknowledged the prior conviction. The jury found her guilty. On appeal, Ohler challenged the judge's decision to allow use of the prior conviction, but the Ninth U.S. Circuit Court of Appeals said she waived her objection by introducing the evidence herself.

By a 5–4 vote, the Court agreed. "[A] defendant who preemptively introduces evidence of a prior conviction on direct examination may not on appeal claim that the admission of such evidence was error," Rehnquist wrote.

Writing for the dissenters, Souter said the ruling would unfairly discourage a defendant from introducing evidence of a prior conviction herself. "Allowing the defendant to introduce the convictions on direct examination . . . tends to promote fairness of trial," Souter wrote, "without depriving the Government of anything to which it is entitled."

Smith, Warden v. Robbins, decided by a 5–4 vote, January 19, 2000; Thomas wrote the opinion; Souter, Stevens, Ginsburg, and Breyer dissented.

A lawyer for an indigent criminal defendant does not have to file a full appellate brief or try to identify potentially valid grounds for attacking a conviction if he believes the appeal is frivolous.

The ruling rejected a federal habeas corpus petition by a convicted murderer, Lee Robbins, who claimed that a California procedure for indigent appeals conflicted with the requirements set out by the Supreme Court. In a 1967 case, *Anders v. California*, the Court held that a lawyer for an indigent defendant could withdraw from a purportedly frivolous appeal only after first filing a brief noting anything that might arguably support an appeal. In 1979, however, California adopted a procedure that allowed an attorney in such a situation simply to file a summary of the case with an appeals court with a request that the court conduct a full review. A lower federal court and the Ninth U.S. Circuit Court of Appeals agreed with Robbins that the procedure did not adequately protect his right to counsel on appeal.

By a 5–4 vote, the Court held California's procedure was constitutionally sufficient. Thomas said the previous ruling, *Anders*, set out "merely one method" for handling the issue and that states were free to adopt other methods if they ensured "that an indigent's appeal will be resolved in a way that is related to the merit of that appeal." After examining the California procedure, Thomas concluded that it "affords adequate and effective appellate review for criminal indigents."

Writing for the four dissenters, Souter said the California procedure "fails to assure representation by counsel with the adversarial character demanded by the Constitution." In a separate dissent, Stevens, joined by Ginsburg, said the ruling "effectively overruled" *Anders* and amounted to "a sharp departure from settled law."

Capital Punishment

Ramdass v. Angelone, Director, Virginia Department of Corrections, decided by a 5–4 vote, June 12, 2000; Kennedy wrote the plurality opinion; O'Connor concurred in the judgment; Stevens, Souter, Ginsburg, and Breyer dissented.

The Court somewhat limited the due process requirement that jurors in capital cases be told of a defendant's ineligibility for parole if the prosecution cites future dangerousness to justify a death sentence.

The ruling upheld a death sentence imposed on a Virginia man, Bobby Lee Ramdass, for the September 1992 robbery-murder of a convenience store clerk. At the time of sentencing, Ramdass had been convicted by juries of two armed robberies committed around the same time; in one of the cases, but not the other, a judge had entered a final judgment of conviction. In appealing the murder conviction, Ramdass argued that the judge should have told the jury that he was ineligible for parole under Virginia's three-strikes law, which bars parole for a defendant upon a third conviction for certain violent crimes. He cited as precedent a Supreme Court decision, *Simmons v. South Carolina* (1994), requiring such an instruction if the prosecution argues the defendant might be a danger to society if released. The Virginia Supreme Court rejected Ramdass's argument. Ramdass then sought to set the death sentence aside with a federal habeas corpus petition, but the Fourth U.S. Circuit Court of Appeals similarly rejected his position.

By a 5–4 vote, the Court ruled that Ramdass was not entitled to a parole ineligibility instruction. In the main opinion, Kennedy said that the instruction was not required under *Simmons* because the second of the two robbery convictions had not yet become final. Ramdass "was not ineligible for parole as a matter of state law at the time of his sentencing trial," Kennedy wrote. Three justices joined his opinion: Rehnquist, Scalia, and Thomas. O'Connor concurred in the judgment in a narrower opinion. Applying a recently enacted federal habeas corpus statute, she said that Ramdass was not entitled to habeas corpus relief because the Virginia Supreme Court's decision was not "contrary to, nor an unreasonable application of" the *Simmons* decision.

Writing for the dissenters, Stevens said Kennedy's opinion was based on "an arbitrary line." The ruling, he added, undercut the rationale of the *Simmons* decision, which he described as "the need for capital sentencing juries to have accurate information about the defendant in the particular area of parole eligibility."

Weeks v. Angelone, Director, Virginia Department of Corrections, decided by a 5–4 vote, January 19, 2000; Rehnquist wrote the opinion; Stevens, Souter, Ginsburg, and Breyer dissented.

The Court rejected a Virginia death row inmate's argument that the trial judge had failed to give the jury clear instructions on how to choose between imposing the death penalty and life imprisonment.

The ruling upheld the death sentence imposed on Lonnie Weeks Jr. for the 1993 murder of a state trooper after a traffic stop for speeding. Prosecutors sought the death penalty by citing two aggravating circumstances, while the defense presented a variety of mitigating circumstances. During deliberations, the jury asked for a clarification of its discretion to impose a life sentence even if one of the aggravating circumstances had been proven. The judge responded by pointing to the paragraph in his original instruction on the issue. After another two hours of deliberation, the panel returned with the death sentence. After Weeks's conviction and sentence were upheld in state courts, he filed a federal habeas corpus petition claiming constitutional error in the judge's failure to clarify his instructions. A lower federal court and the Fourth U.S. Circuit Court of Appeal refused to set aside the sentence.

By a 5–4 vote, the Court held that the judge had committed no constitutional error. Rehnquist rejected Weeks's argument that the sequence of events indicated the jury was confused about its role. "At best, [Weeks] has demonstrated only that there exists a slight *possibility* that the jury considered itself precluded from considering mitigating evidence," he wrote.

Writing for the dissenters, Stevens said the evidence showed "a virtual certainty" that the jury did not understand its discretion to reject a death sentence. "[T]he judge refused to tell them that *even if* they found one of those [aggravating] circumstances, they did not have a 'duty to issue the death penalty,'" Stevens wrote. Ginsburg and Breyer joined all of Stevens's opinion; Souter joined most of it.

Criminal Offenses

Carter v. United States, decided by a 5–4 vote, June 12, 2000; Thomas wrote the opinion; Ginsburg, Stevens, Souter, and Breyer dissented.

A person charged under the major federal bank robbery statute is not entitled to ask the jury to consider a bank larceny charge as a lesser offense.

The ruling upheld the conviction of a New Jersey man, Floyd Carter, for stealing $16,000 from a bank in Hamilton Township in September 1997. Carter, unarmed, entered the bank wearing a ski mask, ran to the tellers' cages, swept about $16,000 in cash into a bag, and fled. The government charged him under a federal law that makes it illegal to "take" anything of value from a bank "by force and violence, or by intimidation." Carter did not dispute the description of the events, but asked that the jury be instructed under a lesser statute that makes it illegal to "take and carry away" anything of value from a bank "with intent to steal." The trial court refused the instruction on the lesser offense, the jury convicted Carter under the robbery statute, and the Third U.S. Circuit Court of Appeals affirmed the conviction.

By a 5–4 vote, the Court held that Carter was not entitled to the jury instruction on the lesser of the two offenses. Thomas acknowledged that the two statutory offenses corresponded to the common law crimes of robbery and the lesser offense of larceny. But he said that the larceny-type offense under the federal law included elements not included in the robbery provision—specifically, carrying away and the intent to steal. For that reason, he said, the lesser offense could not be regarded as "included" within the robbery-type provision.

Writing for the dissenters, Ginsburg called the majority's interpretation of the law "woodenly literal." In enacting the bank robbery law, she said, Congress "did not intend to depart from [the] traditional understanding" that larceny is a lesser and included offense of robbery.

Castillo v. United States, decided by a 9–0 vote, June 5, 2000; Breyer wrote the opinion.

The Court made it harder for federal prosecutors to use a provision in a firearms statute that imposes a mandatory, thirty-year prison sentence for using a machine gun while committing a violent crime.

The ruling set aside long prison sentences imposed under the firearms provision on several members of the Branch Davidian religious sect after their convictions for voluntary manslaughter in the deaths of four federal agents in the 1993 raid on the group's compound near Waco, Texas. (Four received thirty-year terms for use of a machine gun; a fifth received a ten-year sentence for use of a grenade.) On appeal, the defendants argued the machine gun provision amounted to a separate offense that had to be charged and tried to a jury separately from the underlying crime. The government disagreed, saying use of a machine gun was a factor for a judge to consider at sentencing. The Fifth U.S. Circuit Court of Appeals agreed with the government.

Unanimously, the Court held that the machine gun provision amounted to a separate offense. "[T]he difference between the act of using or carrying a 'firearm' and the act of using or carrying a 'machinegun' is both substantive and substantial," Breyer wrote. That conclusion, he said, "supports a 'separate crime' interpretation."

Fischer v. United States, decided by a 7–2 vote, May 15, 2000; Kennedy wrote the opinion; Thomas and Scalia dissented.

The federal bribery statute can be used to prosecute someone for defrauding a hospital that receives reimbursements from the federal Medicare program.

The ruling upheld the convictions of a Florida man, Jeffrey Fischer, for fraud and kickback charges stemming from a $1.2 million loan from the West Volusia Hospital Authority, the municipal agency responsible for operating two hospitals in the city. Fischer, who was president and part owner of a company that performed billing audits for health care organizations, used the loan for business and investment purposes and paid a $10,000 kickback to the agency's chief financial officer. He eventually defaulted on the loan. The government prosecuted him under the federal bribery statute, which prohibits defrauding organizations that receive more than $10,000 in "benefits" under a federal program in any one year. After a federal jury convicted him of thirteen counts, Fischer argued on appeal that the hospital's receipt of Medicare reimbursements did not amount to "benefits" for purposes of the federal bribery statute. The Eleventh U.S. Circuit Court of Appeals disagreed and upheld his convictions.

By a 7–2 vote, the Court ruled that Medicare payments do constitute "benefits" for purposes of invoking the federal bribery statute. After detailing "the role and regulated status" of hospitals under Medicare, Kennedy concluded that "the providers themselves derive significant advantage by satisfying the participation standards imposed by the government. These advantages constitute benefits within the meaning of the federal bribery statute. . . ."

In a dissenting opinion, Thomas argued that Medicare payments are only reimbursements for services, not benefits to hospitals. He also warned that the ruling "could be applied to any federal assistance program that provides funds to any organization." In his opinion, Kennedy discounted the warning.

Jones v. United States, decided by a 9–0 vote, May 22, 2000; Ginsburg wrote the opinion.

A federal law prohibiting arson or bombing of property used in interstate commerce does not cover arson of an owner-occupied private residence.

The ruling set aside one count of a three-count conviction of an Indiana man, Dewey Jones, for using a Molotov cocktail to set fire to a home owned and occupied by his cousin. Jones was charged under a federal law passed in 1970 and amended in 1982 that prohibited damaging or destroying "by fire or an explosive, any . . . property used in interstate or foreign commerce or in any activity affecting interstate or foreign commerce." After his conviction on that and two other counts, Jones argued that the law did not apply to arson of a private residence occupied by the owner. The Seventh U.S. Circuit Court of Appeals disagreed and affirmed his convictions on all three counts.

Unanimously, the Court ruled the law applied only to arson of property actively used for commercial purposes. Under the government's broader interpretation, Ginsburg explained, "hardly a building in the land would fall outside the federal statute's domain." The narrow interpretation of the statute, she added, made it unnecessary to decide the constitutional question whether Congress has the power to convert arson—"a paradigmatic common-law state crime"—into a federal offense.

Detainers

New York v. Hill, decided by a 9–0 vote, January 11, 2000; Scalia wrote the opinion.

A defense lawyer can waive or give up a defendant's right to a speedy trial under a provision of an interstate agreement governing the transfer of a prisoner from one state to another.

The ruling reinstated the second-degree murder and robbery convictions of Michael Hill, who had been arrested in Ohio and brought to New York under the Interstate Agreement on Detainers. The agreement—tantamount to a federal law—provides for a state to request transfer of a prisoner being held in another state, but allows the prisoner to demand that he be brought to trial within 180 days. Hill made such a request, but his lawyer agreed to a trial date past the expiration of the 180-day period. The New York Court of Appeals, the state's highest court, reversed Hill's convictions, saying that he had not waived his right to a speedy trial under the interstate agreement.

Unanimously, the Court held that the defense lawyer's agreement to the delayed trial date was a valid waiver of Hill's rights. "Requiring express assent from the defendant himself for such routine and often repetitive scheduling determinations would consume time to no apparent purpose," Scalia wrote.

Ex Post Facto Laws

Carmell v. Texas, decided by a 5–4 vote, May 1, 2000; Stevens wrote the opinion; Ginsburg, Rehnquist, O'Connor, and Kennedy dissented.

The Court reversed some of a Texas man's child abuse convictions because prosecutors used a state law aimed at easing prosecution of sex crimes that was passed after some of his offenses.

The ruling had the effect of invalidating convictions on four out of fifteen counts against Scott Carmell for various sexual offenses against his teenaged stepdaughter from February 1991 to March 1995. A Texas law that went into effect on September 1, 1993, made it easier to obtain convictions for sexual offenses against teenagers. Previously, Texas law required corroboration of a victim's testimony unless the victim was younger than fourteen. The new law raised the age to eighteen. After Carmell was convicted, he argued that application of the law violated the Constitution's Ex Post Facto Clause, which prohibits retroactive use of some types of laws in criminal or other cases. Four of the offenses—though not the most serious—were allegedly committed when Carmell's stepdaughter was over fourteen and after the law went into effect. Texas courts rejected Carmell's argument.

In a closely divided decision, the Court said use of the law violated the Ex Post Facto Clause. "A law reducing the quantum of evidence required to convict an offender," Stevens wrote, "is as grossly unfair as, say, retrospectively eliminating an element of the offense, increasing the punishment for an existing offense, or lowering the burden of proof."

Writing for the dissenters, Ginsburg argued that the Texas law was a permissible change in evidentiary rules regarding the competency of witnesses to testify in sexual offense trials. The law, she said, "does nothing more than accord to certain victims of sexual offenses full testimonial stature. . . ."

Habeas Corpus

Edwards, Warden v. Carpenter, decided by a 9–0 vote, April 25, 2000; Scalia wrote the opinion.

A state prisoner in a federal habeas corpus case ordinarily cannot use a claim of inadequate legal representation that was filed too late in state courts to excuse a failure to raise other claims.

The ruling blocked an effort by an Ohio man, Robert Carpenter, to attack his convictions for aggravated murder and robbery on grounds of insufficient evidence. Carpenter failed to raise the issue on appeal. Ohio courts then ruled he was too late in filing a postconviction petition seeking to litigate the issue on grounds of ineffective assistance by his first appellate lawyer. In his federal habeas corpus case, however, a lower court and the Sixth U.S. Circuit Court of Appeals both agreed that Carpenter's lawyer was inadequate and that the ineffective-assistance claim excused his failure to raise the evidentiary issue on time in state court.

Unanimously, the Court ruled the case had to be returned to lower courts. In an opinion for seven justices, Scalia said that ineffective-assistance claims are not "uniquely immune" from ordinary procedural-default rules. An inmate cannot satisfy the normal requirement to exhaust state remedies, Scalia explained, if he fails to present an ineffective-assistance claim "in the manner that state law requires."

In an opinion concurring in the judgment, Breyer, joined by Stevens, agreed that Carpenter's petition should be returned for further proceedings, but disagreed with the Court's holding. "Why should a prisoner . . . lose his basic claim because he runs afoul of state procedural rules governing the presentation to state courts of the 'cause' for his not having followed state procedural rules?" Breyer wrote.

Fiore v. White, Warden, decided by a 9–0 vote, November 30, 1999; Breyer wrote the opinion.

The Court asked Pennsylvania's highest court to resolve a state law question needed to decide a Pennsylvania man's federal habeas corpus claim that he had been improperly convicted of operating a hazardous waste facility without a permit.

The rarely used, interim procedure sent back to Pennsylvania courts a habeas corpus petition filed by William Fiore. Fiore had a permit for a hazardous waste facility, but was found guilty because he had "deviated significantly" from its terms. Later, a trial court ruled in a codefendant's case that failure to follow the terms of the permit did not amount to a violation of the state law. Fiore then claimed in a habeas corpus petition that he had been unconstitutionally convicted, but the federal appeals court in Philadelphia said state courts were not required to apply the later interpretation of the law retroactively.

In a unanimous action, the Court "certified" to the Pennsylvania high court the question whether the interpretation of the law in the codefendant's case was "a correct interpretation of the law of Pennsylvania at the date Fiore's conviction became final." The answer, Breyer wrote, would help "our Court's determination of the federal constitutional question raised" in the case.

Slack v. McDaniel, Warden, decided by a 7–2 vote, April 26, 2000; Kennedy wrote the opinion; Scalia and Thomas dissented.

A state prisoner is ordinarily not barred from filing a second federal habeas corpus petition if his first petition is dismissed on procedural grounds so that he can return to state courts to raise his claims.

The complex ruling reinstated an effort by a Nevada man, Antonio Slack, to challenge his second-degree murder conviction in federal court. Slack filed an initial federal habeas corpus petition in 1992, but the judge dismissed it "without prejudice" so that Slack could litigate claims not yet presented to state courts. When he returned to federal court in 1995, however, the judge dismissed Slack's case, saying it amounted to a prohibited "second or successive" petition. The Ninth U.S. Circuit Court of Appeals refused to consider Slack's appeal, saying it raised "no substantial issue."

By a 7–2 vote, the Court held that the lower court was wrong to dismiss Slack's petition. "A habeas petition filed in the district court after an initial habeas petition was unadjudicated on the merits and dismissed for failure to exhaust state remedies is not a second or successive petition," Kennedy wrote.

Before reaching that issue, the Court had to resolve two preliminary questions. First, it ruled—by a 6–3 vote—that Slack's appeal was governed by the habeas corpus provisions of a 1996 law, the Anti-Terrorism and Effective Death Penalty Act. That law made it somewhat more difficult for a state prisoner to appeal a dismissal of a habeas corpus petition. The Court said the law applied to appeals filed after its enactment even if the petition was filed before the law took effect; Stevens, joined by Souter and Breyer, disagreed. On the second issue, the Court held that a state prisoner was entitled to appeal a ruling on a procedural issue if he made out an adequate case on both the procedural and the substantive questions raised.

Dissenting on the main issue, Scalia, joined by Thomas, said the ruling would encourage "vexatious litigation" by state prisoners. The decision, Scalia wrote, "would allow federal petitions to be repeatedly filed and dismissed for lack of exhaustion . . . with no help in sight from supposed limitations on 'second or successive' petitions."

Williams v. Taylor, Warden (Michael Williams), decided by a 9–0 vote, April 18, 2000; Kennedy wrote the opinion.

A Virginia death row inmate was given a chance to show juror misconduct in his murder trial as the Court gave a relaxed interpretation to a recent law aimed at restricting federal habeas corpus hearings.

Michael Wayne Williams filed a federal habeas corpus petition challenging his conviction for the 1993 robbery-abduction-murder of a rural Virginia couple on several grounds. He said the prosecution failed to turn over a psychiatric report on his codefendant or to disclose a plea bargain with the codefendant in exchange for testimony against Williams. In addition, Williams alleged juror misconduct because the jury's foreperson failed to disclose that she had been married several years earlier to a deputy sheriff who testified in the trial and that one of the prosecutors had represented her in the divorce. The state argued that Williams was not entitled to a federal court hearing on his allegations because of a provision in the 1996 habeas corpus law—the Anti-Terrorism and Effective Death Penalty Act—that generally barred hearings if an inmate "failed to develop the factual basis of a claim in State court proceedings. . . ." The Fourth U.S. Circuit Court of Appeals rejected Williams's claim on the plea bargain issue and denied him hearings on the other two issues, saying his attorneys had "failed to develop" the claims because of a lack of diligence.

Unanimously, the Court ruled that Williams was entitled to a hearing on the juror misconduct issue. In reaching the conclusion, Kennedy rejected the state's argument that the habeas corpus law denied a hearing on any claim that an inmate did not raise in state court. Instead, Kennedy said, the law barred a hearing "unless there is a lack of diligence, or some greater fault, attributable to the prisoner or the prisoner's counsel." Applying that standard, Kennedy said there was "no evidence that would have put a reasonable attorney on notice" of the juror's failure to disclose her relationship with the deputy sheriff and prosecutor.

Williams v. Taylor, Warden (Terry Williams), decided by 6–3 and 5–4 votes, April 18, 2000; Stevens wrote the main opinion; O'Connor wrote an opinion for the Court on one legal issue; Stevens, Souter, Ginsburg, and Breyer disagreed with the Court's ruling on that issue; Rehnquist, Scalia, and Thomas dissented in part.

Federal courts cannot grant a state inmate's habeas corpus petition unless a state court decision was contrary to clearly established Supreme Court precedent or was an objectively unreasonable application of Supreme Court precedent to the facts of the case.

The ruling, interpreting a newly enacted provision of federal habeas corpus law, made it somewhat more difficult for state inmates to challenge their convictions in federal courts. But the Court nonetheless reinstated a claim by a Virginia death row inmate, Terry Williams, that his constitutional rights had been violated because of ineffective assistance of counsel during the sentencing phase of his trial. And it also rejected a more restrictive interpretation of the law adopted by a federal appeals court in denying Williams's petition.

Williams was convicted and sentenced to death for the 1985 robbery-murder of an elderly man in Danville, Virginia. In a state habeas corpus proceeding, Williams claimed that his trial counsel failed to introduce mitigating evidence in the death penalty phase of the trial, including a history of childhood abuse and neglect and a diagnosis as "borderline mentally retarded." The trial judge agreed, but the Virginia Supreme Court ruled that Williams was not entitled to a new sentencing hearing under the U.S. Supreme Court's precedents defining ineffective assistance of counsel.

Williams then filed a federal habeas corpus petition. The federal trial judge again ruled Williams was entitled to a new sentencing hearing, but the Fourth U.S. Circuit Court of Appeals rejected his petition. It relied on a provision of a 1996 habeas corpus reform law—the Anti-Terrorism and Effective Death Penalty Act. The law barred federal habeas corpus relief on any claim raised in state court unless the state court decision was "contrary to, or involved an unreasonable application of, clearly established Federal law, as determined by the Supreme Court of the United States." The appeals court defined "unreasonable" to mean "in a manner that reasonable jurists would all agree is unreasonable." Applying that definition, the appeals court said the Virginia Supreme Court's decision could stand.

In a complex decision, the Court unanimously rejected the appeals court's reading of the law and adopted instead, by a 5–4 vote, a somewhat narrower interpretation. By a different 6–3 vote, however, the Court ruled that the Virginia Supreme Court's decision nonetheless was an unreasonable application of prior rulings on ineffective assistance of counsel.

Stevens wrote the main opinion for the Court, but O'Connor wrote for a different majority in interpreting the law. In her opinion, O'Connor said a federal court "should ask whether the state court's application of clearly established law was objectively unreasonable." Rehnquist, Scalia, Kennedy, and Thomas concurred. Stevens, on the other hand, said a federal court could grant habeas corpus relief even if a state-court judgment seemed "entirely reasonable" if "thorough analysis . . . produces a firm conviction that that judgment is infected by constitutional error." Souter, Ginsburg, and Breyer joined that portion of Stevens's opinion.

Applying the law, Stevens said the Virginia Supreme Court decision was unreasonable because the court misread Supreme Court precedent and "failed to evaluate the totality of the available mitigation evidence." O'Connor and Kennedy joined that portion of Stevens's opinion along with the other three justices. In her opinion, O'Connor described the Virginia Supreme Court's failure as "obvious."

Three justices—Rehnquist, Scalia, and Thomas—dissented from the outcome of the case while joining O'Connor's interpretation of the law.

Writing for the three, Rehnquist said it was "not unreasonable" for the Virginia Supreme Court to conclude "that a jury would not have been swayed" by the mitigating evidence that Williams's lawyer failed to introduce.

Jury Selection

United States v. Martinez-Salazar, decided by a 9–0 vote, January 19, 2000; Ginsburg wrote the opinion.

A defendant's constitutional rights are not violated when he chooses to use a peremptory challenge to remove a juror who should have been removed for cause.

The ruling reinstated narcotics and weapons convictions of an Arizona man, Abel Martinez-Salazar, that a federal appeals court had overturned because of an error in the jury selection process. Martinez-Salazar's attorney had challenged one potential juror for cause because of answers suggesting a bias in favor of the prosecution. The judge disallowed the challenge, however, and the defense lawyer instead used peremptory challenge to remove the juror. The Ninth U.S. Circuit Court of Appeals said that the judge was wrong not to remove the juror and that the error deprived Martinez-Salazar of his full complement of peremptory challenges, requiring automatic reversal.

In a unanimous decision, the Court disagreed. "[A] defendant's exercise of peremptory challenges . . . is not denied or impaired when the defendant chooses to use a peremptory challenge to remove a juror who should have been excused for cause," Ginsburg wrote. Six justices joined her opinion. In an opinion concurring in the judgment, Scalia, joined by Kennedy, objected to a passage in Ginsburg's opinion suggesting that the conviction could have been overturned if the defendant had failed to remove the questionable juror.

Parole and Probation

Garner, Former Chairman of the State Board of Pardons and Paroles of Georgia v. Jones, decided by a 6–3 vote, March 28, 2000; Kennedy wrote the opinion; Souter, Stevens, and Ginsburg dissented.

The Court turned aside a Georgia inmate's constitutional challenge to a parole board's retroactive application of a new policy that barred prisoners denied parole from applying again for another eight years.

The ruling came in the case of a twice-convicted murderer, Robert Jones, who challenged the state parole board's action to apply a restrictive policy adopted following his second conviction. The new policy changed to eight years from three years the time period for making a new parole application after an inmate was denied parole. The Eleventh U.S. Circuit Court of Appeals held that applying the policy to Jones violated the Constitution's Ex Post Facto Clause, which generally prohibits retroactive increases in punishments. In its ruling, the appeals court found that the Georgia policy was significantly different from a California parole policy that the Supreme Court had sustained in a 1995 decision, *California Dept. of Corrections v. Morales.*

By a 6–3 vote, the Court ruled that Jones had failed to show that the change in parole policy had "created a significant risk of increasing his punishment." Kennedy stressed that Georgia law gave the parole board "broad discretion" to grant parole at any time between scheduled reconsiderations. The ruling sent the case back to give Jones another opportunity to prove that the policy was likely to affect his time in prison. Four justices joined Kennedy's opinion. In an opinion concurring in the judgment, Scalia said that the Ex Post Facto Clause did not apply at all to the parole board policy.

Writing for the three dissenters, Souter said he would have upheld the appeals court decision blocking retroactive application of the new eight-year policy. "[T]he State provided no evidence," Souter wrote, "that the board's occasional willingness to re-examine cases sufficiently mitigates the substantial probability of increased punishment."

United States v. Johnson, decided by a 9–0 vote, March 1, 2000; Kennedy wrote the opinion.

A federal inmate is not entitled to a reduction of a period of supervised release for time served in prison under a sentence later ruled invalid.

The ruling rejected an effort by a Michigan man, Roy Johnson, to shorten the three-year period of supervised release—essentially the same as parole—that was imposed as part of a fifty-one-month prison sentence on drug and firearms convictions in 1990. The sentences on the firearms counts were thrown out in 1995, but by that time Johnson had already served about two-and-a-half years beyond the term for the drug offenses. He was immediately released and then sought to have his period of supervised release shortened. A lower federal court rejected his plea, but the Sixth U.S. Circuit Court of Appeals ruled in his favor.

Unanimously, the Court held that the federal statute governing supervised release allowed the period to begin only after an inmate was actually released from prison. Kennedy noted, however, that judges have authority to modify the conditions of supervised release or to terminate it altogether after one year.

Prisons and Jails

Miller, Superintendent, Pendleton Correctional Facility v. French, decided by a 5–4 vote, June 19, 2000; O'Connor wrote the opinion; Souter and Ginsburg dissented in part; Breyer and Stevens dissented.

The Court upheld a provision in a newly enacted law limiting federal judges' power to continue enforcement of court-ordered remedies in suits over prison conditions.

The ruling rejected decisions by a lower federal court and the Seventh U.S. Circuit Court of Appeals that the "automatic stay" provision of the Prison Litigation Reform Act of 1995 violated separation of powers principles by intruding on judicial powers. The law established stricter standards to be met before federal judges could order relief in inmates' suits over prison conditions. It also allowed state or local prison officials to move to modify or terminate any existing injunction. Such a motion, the law provided, "shall operate as a stay"—in effect, lift the injunction—after a period of thirty days until a ruling by the judge on the motion. The superintendent of a prison in Indiana invoked the provision to try to get out from under a court-ordered plan to improve conditions dating from 1980. In appealing the Seventh Circuit's decision, the solicitor general's office sought to skirt the constitutional issue by arguing that the law still allowed federal judges to use their so-called "equitable powers" to refuse to issue a stay in some circumstances. Indiana officials said that the law required federal judges to grant a stay and that—under that interpretation—it was constitutional.

By a 5–4 vote, the Court agreed with the state's strict interpretation of the law and upheld it as constitutional. Interpreting the "mandatory stay" provision to be discretionary, O'Connor wrote, "would be plainly contrary to Congress' intent. . . ." Turning to the separation of powers argument, she rejected the inmates' claim that the law interfered with judicial decisionmaking. "The PRLA does not deprive courts of their adjudicatory role," O'Connor wrote, "but merely provides a new legal standard for relief and encourages courts to apply that standard promptly."

In a partial dissenting opinion, Souter, joined by Ginsburg, agreed that the automatic stay provision was mandatory, but said that a strict application of the law might violate due process principles in some cases. He said the case should be sent back to lower courts for further proceedings. In a separate dissent, Breyer agreed with the solicitor general's "reasonable construction" of the statute, which he said would avoid "serious constitutional problems." Stevens joined his opinion.

Right to Counsel

Roe, Warden v. Flores-Ortega, decided by a 6–3 vote, February 23, 2000; O'Connor wrote the opinion; Souter, Stevens, and Ginsburg dissented.

The Court adopted a case-by-case approach to evaluate whether a court-appointed lawyer's failure to file an appeal for an indigent defendant violated the defendant's right to effective assistance of counsel.

The ruling set aside a stricter approach to ineffective assistance of counsel claims adopted by the Ninth U.S. Circuit Court of Appeals in a federal habeas corpus case brought by a California inmate, Lucio Flores-Ortega. Ortega pleaded guilty to second-degree murder, but the guilty plea allowed him to appeal to challenge his sentence. His court-appointed lawyer, however, failed to file the required notice of appeal within the time limit of sixty days. The appeals court ruled that unless the defendant had agreed, a court-appointed lawyer's failure to file an appeal was a per se violation of an indigent defendant's Sixth Amendment right to counsel.

By a 6–3 vote, the Court said the per se rule was "inconsistent" with its previous ruling, *Strickland v. Washington* (1984), requiring case-by-case evaluation of ineffective assistance of counsel claims. "We cannot say, as a *constitutional* matter, that in every case counsel's failure to consult with the defendant about an appeal is necessarily unreasonable, and therefore deficient," O'Connor wrote. Nonetheless, O'Connor said that lawyers would have such a duty "in the vast majority of cases." And she said a defendant would be entitled to a new chance to file an appeal if he showed that "but for counsel's deficient conduct, he would have appealed."

The ruling sent the case back to lower federal courts to apply the Court's test. In a dissenting opinion, Souter, joined by Stevens and Ginsburg, said he would have held that a lawyer's failure to file an appeal for an indigent defendant "almost always" amounted to ineffective assistance to counsel "in those cases in which a plea of guilty has not obviously waived any claims of error."

Search and Seizure

Bond v. United States, decided by a 7–2 vote, April 17, 2000; Rehnquist wrote the opinion; Breyer and Scalia dissented.

Police may not physically manipulate a bus passenger's carry-on luggage to try to determine its contents without a warrant or other legal justification.

The ruling overturned the drug convictions of a bus passenger, Steven Bond, stemming from a search of a canvas carry-on bag by a U.S. Border Patrol agent at a Texas checkpoint. Agent Cesar Cantu squeezed the bag and felt a "brick-like" object; after asking Bond for permission to open the bag, the agent found a "brick" of methamphetamine wrapped in duct tape and rolled in a pair of pants. Bond unsuccessfully sought to suppress the evidence and was then convicted on two drug counts and sentenced to fifty-seven months in prison.

In a brief opinion, the Court held that the agent's action constituted an unreasonable search under the Fourth Amendment because it violated Bond's "reasonable expectation of privacy." Rehnquist acknowledged that a bus passenger might expect other passengers or bus employees to move a bag "for one reason or another." But, Rehnquist continued, "[h]e does not expect that other passengers or bus employees will, as a matter of course, feel the bag in an exploratory manner."

In an equally terse dissent, Breyer, joined by Scalia, disagreed. "An individual cannot reasonably expect privacy in respect to objects or activities that he knowingly exposes to the public," Breyer wrote.

Flippo v. West Virginia, decided by a 9–0 vote, October 18, 1999; *per curiam* opinion.

Police ordinarily need a warrant to search a crime scene unless some other exception to the requirement applies.

The ruling set aside a West Virginia man's murder conviction for the 1996 killing of his wife and gave the defendant, the Rev. James Flippo, a new chance to argue for the suppression of photographs found by police at the scene and introduced as evidence at his trial. The evidence included a photograph that suggested Flippo was having a homosexual relationship with one of the members of his church; the prosecution argued that Flippo's wife's displeasure with the relationship could have been a motive for the slaying. On appeal, the West Virginia Supreme Court upheld the use of the evidence by saying that police have general authority to search a homicide crime scene without a warrant.

In a summary decision issued without hearing argument, the Court unanimously ruled that the West Virginia court's ruling conflicted with a 1978 precedent, *Mincey v. Arizona*, rejecting a "crime-scene" exception to the search warrant requirement. The unsigned ruling left open the possibility that the search could be upheld on other grounds—for example, that Flippo had consented to the search or that use of the evidence, if improper, was nonetheless "harmless error."

Florida v. J. L., decided by a 9–0 vote, March 28, 2000; Ginsburg wrote the opinion.

Police have no automatic right to stop and frisk someone after receiving an anonymous tip that he is carrying a firearm.

The ruling upheld the Florida Supreme Court's decision that Miami–Dade County police officers violated an African American teenager's Fourth Amendment rights on October 13, 1995, when they frisked him after receiving an anonymous telephone tip. The caller said a young black male was standing at a bus stop, was wearing a plaid shirt, and was carrying a gun. Officers dispatched to the location observed the teenager, identified as J. L., and after frisking him found a gun. The teenager was charged with illegal possession of a firearm, but a lower court and the Florida Supreme Court both ruled the gun could not be used as evidence because the pat-down search was illegal. In appealing the decision, the state and the federal government both urged the Court to create a "firearm exception" to the normal rules limiting the use of anonymous tips to justify a police stop or search.

Unanimously, the Court rejected the government's arguments and agreed that the frisk was illegal. "[A]n anonymous tip lacking indicia of reliability . . . does not justify a stop and frisk whenever and however it alleges the illegal possession of a firearm," Ginsburg wrote. Allowing an automatic firearm exception, she said, "would enable any person seeking to harass another to set in motion an intrusive, embarrassing police search of the targeted person simply by placing an anonymous call falsely reporting the target's unlawful carriage of a gun."

Ginsburg limited her opinion by saying that it did not bar public safety officials from using anonymous tips to justify frisks in airports or schools. In a concurring opinion, Kennedy suggested that police could use instant caller identification and recording of telephone tips to trace callers and add reliability to anonymous tips; Rehnquist joined his opinion.

Illinois v. Wardlow, decided by a 5–4 vote, January 12, 2000; Rehnquist wrote the opinion; Stevens, Souter, Ginsburg, and Breyer dissented as to the result.

Police may have sufficient cause to stop and frisk a suspect if he runs away upon seeing the officer.

The ruling reinstated a firearms possession conviction against an Illinois man, Sam Wardlow, who was apprehended by police on a Chicago street after running away at the approach of a drug-patrol team. After stopping Wardlow, police conducted a "pat-down" search and found a gun in a plastic bag he was carrying. The Illinois Supreme Court suppressed the evidence and reversed the conviction. It held that a suspect's "unprovoked flight" was insufficient to justify a police stop.

The Court unanimously disagreed with the Illinois court's legal rule, but divided 5–4 in upholding the stop and reinstating the conviction. Writing for the majority, Rehnquist said that police were entitled to consider "nervous, evasive behavior" as a "pertinent factor" in determining suspicion. "Headlong flight," Rehnquist continued, was "the consummate act of evasion: it is not necessarily indicative of wrongdoing, but it is certainly suggestive of such."

Writing for the four dissenters, Stevens agreed that a suspect's flight could justify a stop and frisk under such circumstances, but not in Wardlow's specific case. "I am not persuaded that the mere fact that someone standing on a sidewalk looked in the direction of a passing car before starting to run," Stevens wrote, "is sufficient to justify a forcible stop and frisk."

Self-Incrimination

Dickerson v. United States, decided by a 7–2 vote, June 26, 2000; Rehnquist wrote the opinion; Scalia and Thomas dissented.

The Court invalidated a law Congress passed aimed at overturning the *Miranda* decision requiring police to warn suspects of their rights to remain silent and to be represented by a lawyer before conducting interrogation.

The ruling—a decisive defeat for conservative critics of the famous 1966 decision—reversed a decision by the Fourth U.S. Circuit Court of Appeals upholding the 1968 law. The statute—§3501 of the U.S. criminal code, Title 18—provided that any confession "voluntarily given" would be admissible in criminal prosecutions in federal court. Judges were to determine voluntariness based on "all the circumstances surrounding the giving of the confession." The law contradicted the Court's decision in *Miranda v. Arizona*, which required police to tell suspects that they had the right to remain silent, the right to an attorney, and the right to have an attorney appointed for them, and that any statement given after waiving those rights could be used against them in court. The Fourth Circuit appeals court applied the statute to reject a *Miranda* challenge by Charles Dickerson, a suspect in an Alexandria, Virginia, bank robbery, to the use of a statement he gave to FBI agents. Dickerson appealed the ruling, and the Justice Department joined in urging the Court to rule the law unconstitutional. The Court appointed a University of Utah law professor, Paul Cassell, to defend the statute.

By a 7–2 vote, the Court held the law unconstitutional. Writing for the majority, Rehnquist declared that *Miranda* "being a constitutional decision, may not be in effect overruled by an Act of Congress, and we decline to overrule *Miranda* ourselves." "We therefore hold," Rehnquist continued, "that *Miranda* and its progeny in this Court govern the admissibility of statements made during custodial interrogation in both state and federal courts."

In a biting dissent, Scalia described *Miranda* as "judicial overreaching," insisting that the ruling went beyond the Fifth Amendment's prohibition against use of compelled confessions. "[W]hat today's decision will stand for," Scalia continued, "is the power of the Supreme Court to write a prophylactic, extraconstitutional Constitution, binding on Congress and the states." Thomas joined the opinion. *(See story, pp. 51–57; excerpts, pp. 242–251.)*

United States v. Hubbell, decided by an 8–1 vote, June 5, 2000; Stevens wrote the opinion; Rehnquist dissented.

The Court threw out the tax conviction of a former high-ranking Clinton administration official by ruling that Independent Counsel Kenneth Starr broke an immunity agreement when he used the defendant's subpoenaed business records to build a prosecution.

The ruling sustained the claim by Webster Hubbell, a former associate attorney general, that Starr's office violated Hubbell's privilege against self-incrimination by using the subpoenaed records as the basis of a ten-count indictment charging him with various tax-related crimes and mail and wire fraud. Hubbell had pleaded guilty in 1994 to mail fraud and tax evasion in connection with his billing practices as a private attorney in Little Rock, Arkansas, and had been sentenced to twenty-one months in prison. As part of the plea bargain, he agreed to cooperate with the independent counsel's investigation of the so-called "Whitewater affair" involving President Bill Clinton and his wife, Hillary.

Two years later, the independent counsel subpoenaed Hubbell's business records and granted him immunity after Hubbell refused to turn over the documents by invoking his Fifth Amendment privilege against self-incrimination. Starr's office nonetheless obtained the multicount indictment against Hubbell. A lower court judge dismissed the indictment on the ground that the prosecution stemmed from use of the immunized documents. The U.S. Court of Appeals for the District of Columbia Circuit ruled somewhat differently, saying the indictment could stand if the independent counsel could show "with reasonable particularity" some "prior awareness" of the documents Hubbell had been forced to turn over. Starr's office conceded that it could not meet that test, agreed to a conditional plea bargain with Hubbell, and then asked the Court to review the decision.

In a nearly unanimous decision, the Court held that the indictment against Hubbell had to be dismissed. Stevens noted that the Court in 1976 had ruled that the government could use the contents of records turned over under subpoena in a criminal prosecution. But he said the government could not force a witness to help "to identify potential sources of information and to produce those sources." "[T]he constitutional privilege against self-incrimination protects the target of a grand jury investigation from being compelled to answer questions designed to elicit information about the existence of sources of potentially incriminating evidence," Stevens wrote.

In a concurring opinion, Thomas, joined by Scalia, said he would go further and consider overruling the 1976 decision to bar the government altogether from forcing someone to turn over business records in a criminal investigation.

Rehnquist dissented alone, without writing an opinion.

Sentencing

Apprendi v. New Jersey, decided by a 5–4 vote, June 26, 2000; Stevens wrote the opinion; O'Connor, Rehnquist, Kennedy, and Breyer dissented.

A defendant is entitled to a jury trial and to proof beyond a reasonable doubt of any fact other than a prior criminal conviction that may be used to increase a sentence beyond the statutory maximum.

The ruling invalidated provisions of New Jersey's "hate crime" law, which provided for enhanced sentences for any offense committed "with a purpose to intimidate an individual or group of individuals because of race, color, gender, handicap, religion, sexual orientation or ethnicity." The law gave the responsibility for imposing the sentence to a judge rather than to a jury, and a finding was to be based on a preponderance of the evidence rather than the beyond-a-reasonable-doubt standard required for a criminal conviction. Charles Apprendi challenged the law as a violation of due process after he was given an enhanced prison sentence of twelve years for firing shots into the home of an African American family who had moved into his neighborhood. Apprendi, who is white, denied any racial motivation for the shooting. The New Jersey Supreme Court, in a 5–4 decision, rejected his challenge and upheld the law.

In a closely divided—and unexpectedly broad—decision, the Court held that the law violated the Due Process Clause by bypassing the jury and lowering the standard of proof. Writing for the majority, Stevens said the law was "an unacceptable departure from the jury tradition." Summarizing the holding, Stevens wrote, "Other than the fact of a prior conviction, any fact that increases the penalty for a crime beyond the prescribed statutory maximum must be submitted to a jury, and proved beyond a reasonable doubt."

In a brief concurrence, Scalia rephrased the holding: "[A]ll the facts which must exist in order to subject the defendant to a legally prescribed punishment *must* be found by the jury." Thomas wrote a lengthy concurrence; he called for a broader rule to require a jury finding on any fact that could be used to determine a defendant's sentence, even one within the statutory range for the offense.

In a lengthy dissent, O'Connor said the ruling appeared to invalidate determinate-sentencing schemes—including the federal Sentencing Guidelines and comparable state laws—that typically give judges rather than juries the responsibility for factual determinations used in calculating a defendant's final sentence. "[T]he apparent effect of the Court's opinion," she wrote, "[is] to invalidate with the stroke of a pen three decades' worth of nationwide reform, all in the name of a principle with a questionable constitutional pedigree." Rehnquist, Kennedy, and Breyer joined her opinion. In a shorter dissent, Breyer, joined by Rehnquist, called the ruling "impractical." "There are . . . far too many potentially relevant sentencing factors to permit submission of all (or even many) of them to a jury," Breyer wrote.

Johnson v. United States, decided by an 8–1 vote, May 15, 2000; Souter wrote the opinion; Scalia dissented.

Federal judges can impose a second term of supervised release on a defendant after revoking the defendant's freedom and ordering him to prison for violating the conditions of the release.

The ruling upheld a twelve-month period of supervised release imposed on a Tennessee man, Cornell Johnson, who had originally been sentenced in March 1994 to twenty-five months' imprisonment and three years' supervised release in a credit card misuse case. The judge revoked Johnson's release after he was arrested in Virginia on forgery charges, ordered him to prison for the balance of the supervised release term, and then imposed a new supervised release term of twelve months. A law that took effect in 1994—after Johnson was sentenced—explicitly gave federal judges power to impose a second supervised release term. But Johnson argued that use of the law in his case would amount to retroactive punishment in violation of the Constitution's Ex Post Facto Clause. The Sixth U.S. Circuit Court of Appeals rejected the argument, saying the new supervised release term was punishment for the offenses committed after the law was enacted.

By an 8–1 vote, the Court upheld the second supervised release term even though it agreed that the 1994 law could not be applied retroactively. Instead, the Court held that judges had power to impose a second supervised release term under the pre-1994 law. Souter said that the provision giving judges the power to "revoke" a defendant's supervised release could be interpreted to "leave open the possibility of supervised release after reincarceration."

In a lone dissent, Scalia called the majority's reading of the statute "linguistically and conceptually absurd." He noted, however, that the 1994 amendment had eliminated the issue for the future.

Trials

Portuondo, Superintendent, Fishkill Correctional Facility v. Agard, decided by a 7–2 vote, March 6, 2000; Scalia wrote the opinion; Ginsburg and Souter dissented.

A prosecutor does not violate a defendant's rights by suggesting that a defendant who testifies might tailor his testimony based on having heard the previous witnesses.

The ruling reinstated the sodomy and assault convictions against a New York man, Ray Agard, who had been charged with raping one woman and threatening her and a friend with a gun. Agard, testifying in his own behalf, claimed he had consensual intercourse with the first woman and denied threatening either of them. In her summation, the prosecutor attacked the defendant's credibility in part by noting that he "gets to sit here and listen to the testimony of all the other witnesses before he testifies." New York courts upheld most of Agard's convictions, but the Second U.S. Circuit Court of Appeals granted his federal habeas corpus petition. It ruled that the prosecutor's comments violated Agard's Fifth Amendment privilege against self-incrimination, his Sixth Amendment right to be present at his trial, and his Fourteenth Amendment right to due process.

By a 7–2 vote, the Court rejected Agard's constitutional claims and ordered the convictions reinstated. "It is natural and irresistible," Scalia concluded, "for a jury, in evaluating the relative credibility of a defendant who testifies last, to have in mind and weigh in the balance the fact that he heard the testimony of all those who preceded him."

Four justices—Rehnquist, O'Connor, Kennedy, and Thomas—joined Scalia's opinion. In an opinion concurring in the judgment, Stevens said he found no constitutional violation but added that the prosecutor's comment "should be discouraged rather than validated." Breyer joined his opinion.

In a dissent, Ginsburg, joined by Souter, said the prosecutor's comments were an unfair burden on the defendant's constitutional rights. "The

Court today transforms a defendant's presence at trial from a Sixth Amendment right into an automatic burden on his credibility," she wrote.

Election Law

Campaign Finance

Nixon, Attorney General of Missouri v. Shrink Missouri Government PAC, decided by a 6–3 vote, January 24, 2000; Souter wrote the opinion; Thomas, Scalia, and Kennedy dissented.

States can limit contributions to political candidates by individuals or political committees, as low as $250 for some races, without violating the First Amendment's protections for freedom of speech or association.

The ruling rejected a constitutional challenge to a 1994 Missouri law limiting the amounts that individuals or political action committees could donate to candidates for governor, members of the state legislature, or other state offices. The limits originally were $1,000 for governor and $250 for legislator, but had been adjusted for inflation to $1,075 and $275 respectively by the time of the Court's decision. The law was challenged by a minor candidate for state auditor, Zev Fredman, and a political action committee, Shrink Missouri Government, which said it wanted to contribute more than the legal limit to Fredman's 1998 campaign. A lower federal court upheld the statute on the strength of the Supreme Court's 1976 decision, *Buckley v. Valeo*, upholding individual campaign contribution limits of $1,000 in congressional races. But the Eighth U.S. Circuit Court of Appeals ruled the state law unconstitutional, saying the state had presented insufficient evidence that the law was necessary to prevent political corruption or the appearance of corruption.

The Court upheld the law by a 6–3 vote, rejecting calls from the three dissenters to overrule *Buckley*. "There is no reason in logic or evidence to doubt the sufficiency of *Buckley* to govern the case in support of the Missouri statute," Souter wrote. Souter said that the evidence was sufficient to substantiate Missouri lawmakers' concern about potential corruption from large campaign contributions. He also rejected arguments that *Buckley* prevented states from imposing contribution limits below $1,000. Concurring opinions were written by Stevens and by Breyer, joined by Ginsburg.

In the main dissenting opinion, Thomas, joined by Scalia, said the ruling "unjustifiably discounts the First Amendment interests of citizens and candidates, and consequently fails to strictly scrutinize the inhibition of political speech and competition. . . ." In a separate dissent, Kennedy said that *Buckley* had created "adverse, unintended consequences," and that Missouri's law in any event "does not even come close to passing any serious scrutiny." *(See story, pp. 70–75; excerpts, pp. 186–197.)*

Primary Elections

California Democratic Party v. Jones, Secretary of State of California, decided by a 7–2 vote, June 26, 2000; Scalia wrote the opinion; Stevens and Ginsburg dissented.

A state "blanket primary" law allowing voters to choose freely among candidates for separate offices regardless of party affiliation violates a political party's First Amendment freedom of association.

The ruling invalidated a primary system adopted by California voters in a 1996 initiative and followed in two other states: Alaska and Washington. The "blanket primary" did not require voters to affiliate with a particular party either at the time of an election—as in an "open primary," or beforehand—as in a "closed primary." Instead, voters in a blanket primary received a ballot listing all candidates regardless of party affiliation and could choose a candidate from one party for one position and a candidate from another for a different position. Four political parties—Democratic, Republican, Libertarian, and Peace and Freedom—challenged the scheme as a violation of their right to require affiliation of voters in their respective primaries. The state defended the law by saying it encouraged voter participation and the selection of nominees with "moderate" positions. A lower federal court and the Ninth U.S. Circuit Court of Appeals both upheld the law.

By a 7–2 vote, the Court invalidated the law, saying it imposed a "severe and unnecessary" burden on the parties' freedom of association. The initiative, Scalia wrote, "forces [the parties] to adulterate their candidate-selection process . . . by opening it up to persons unaffiliated with the party. Such forced association has the likely outcome . . . of changing the parties' message. We can think of no heavier burden on a political party's associational freedom."

In a dissenting opinion, Stevens, joined by Ginsburg, called the ruling "novel" and "wholly wrong." The First Amendment's protections, Stevens wrote, "do not encompass a right to exclude nonmembers from voting in a state-required, state-financed primary election."

Territories

Gutierrez v. Ada, decided by a 9–0 vote, January 19, 2000; Souter wrote the opinion.

Guam's governing law does not require a runoff election for governor or lieutenant governor if the leading candidate fails to receive an absolute majority of all ballots cast in the election.

The ruling upheld the results of a closely contested race for governor of the island territory in 1998. Carl Gutierrez appeared to have defeated Joseph Ada for governor, with 51.2 percent of the votes cast in the race. But Gutierrez had only 49.8 percent of all ballots cast in the election. Ada claimed that a runoff was required under a provision of Guam's Organic Act. The provision called for a runoff for governor and lieutenant governor "if no candidates receive a majority of the votes cast in any election. . . ." A lower federal court and the Ninth U.S. Circuit Court of Appeals agreed—in conflict with another federal appeals court's interpretation of an identical provision in the governing law for the Virgin Islands.

Unanimously, the Court held that the runoff provision applied only to votes cast in the gubernatorial election, not to all ballots cast. Souter said that the "obvious reading" of the provision was confirmed by the way the rest of the section was written. In addition, he said it would have been "strange" for Congress to have wanted to "make it hard to select a Governor."

Voting Rights

Rice v. Cayetano, Governor of Hawaii, decided by a 7–2 vote, February 23, 2000; Kennedy wrote the opinion; Stevens and Ginsburg dissented.

A Hawaii law that allowed only people of native Hawaiian ancestry to vote for members of a state agency in charge of programs aimed at benefiting native Hawaiians was struck down as unconstitutional racial discrimination.

The ruling invalidated a provision of the Hawaii Constitution adopted in 1978 regarding the election of nine members of an agency, the Office of Hawaiian Affairs, created for "the betterment of conditions of native Hawaiians . . . and Hawaiians." The agency's funding came from the proceeds of land set aside at the time of Hawaii's annexation by the United States as well as from state and federal appropriations. Voting was limited to people who could trace their ancestry to native peoples who lived in Hawaii before the European explorer Captain James Cook made landfall in 1778. Harold Rice, a white rancher and fifth-generation Hawaiian, challenged the scheme as a violation of the Fourteenth Amendment's Equal Protection Clause and the Fifteenth Amendment, which prohibits racial discrimination in voting. A lower federal court and the Ninth U.S. Circuit Court of Appeals both rejected the challenge.

By a vote viewed as surprisingly lopsided, the Court ruled the voting scheme violated the Fifteenth Amendment. "A state may not deny or abridge the right to vote on account of race," Kennedy wrote for a five-justice majority, "and this law does so." Kennedy rejected the state's argument that the plan was comparable to federal laws providing for special treatment of Indian tribes. He also said the voting scheme was not equivalent to the limitations on voting for special-purpose government bodies such as water or irrigation districts aimed at benefiting specific groups of property owners or citizens.

In an opinion concurring in the result, Breyer distanced himself from the broader passages of the Court's opinion. He said the law could not be justified because the lands that the agency administered had not been set aside as a trust only for native Hawaiians and because the definition of native Hawaiians was too broad. Souter joined his opinion.

Stevens and Ginsburg dissented. In his twenty-two-page opinion, Stevens said the voting scheme did not amount to the kind of racial discrimination prohibited by the Fifteenth Amendment. "[T]here is simply no invidious discrimination present in this effort to see that indigenous peoples are compensated for past wrongs, and to preserve a distinct and vibrant culture that is as much a part of this Nation's heritage as any." Ginsburg, who joined part of Stevens's opinion, said in her own dissent that the voting scheme was "rationally tied to fulfillment" of "Congress' prerogative to enter into special trust relationships with indigenous peoples."

Voting Rights Act

Reno, Attorney General v. Bossier Parish School Board, decided by a 5–4 vote, January 24, 2000; Scalia wrote the opinion; Souter, Stevens, Ginsburg, and Breyer dissented.

Governments covered by the Voting Rights Act's preclearance requirement can obtain federal approval for election law changes as long as the revisions do not leave minority voters worse off than before.

The ruling—a setback for civil rights organizations—upheld a redistricting plan for the Bossier Parish, Louisiana, school board that created none of the twelve districts with a majority of African American voters. African Americans comprised about one-fourth of the parish's population. The Justice Department, acting under the authority of section 5 of the Voting Rights Act, refused to "preclear" the change. Citing the statutory language, the department said that the plan had both the "purpose" and "effect" of "abridging" the rights of minority voters. In an initial ruling, the Supreme Court in 1997 said the Justice Department could not withhold approval solely because an election law change had the "effect" of "diluting" minority voting strength as long as minority voters were not worse off than before—no "retrogressive" effect, as the Court put it *(Reno v. Bossier Parish School Board)*. But the Court sent the case back to a three-judge federal court in Washington to consider whether the government could block the change because of evidence of discriminatory intent. The three-judge court again ruled that the Justice Department had been wrong to refuse permission for the redistricting plan.

By a 5–4 vote, the Court agreed that the preclearance requirement could not be used to block an election law change that had no retrogressive effect on minority voters even if the change was intended to dilute minority voting strength. Scalia said the government could oppose such a change only through the more difficult route of a suit brought under a different provision of the voting law, section 2. "[T]he voting change is no more dilutive than what it replaces," Scalia wrote, "and therefore cannot be stopped in advance under the extraordinary burden-shifting procedures of §5, but must be attacked through the normal means of a §2 action."

Writing for the dissenters, Souter disagreed. "[N]o redistricting scheme should receive preclearance without a showing that it is nondilutive," he wrote. In separate dissents, Stevens, joined by Ginsburg, and Breyer also criticized the majority's interpretation of the act.

In his dissent, Souter set out the history of the redistricting plan at length to show that the school board had sought to prevent the election of African Americans. But in a concurring opinion Thomas noted that in the most recent election three African Americans had been elected to the board despite the lack of any majority-minority districts.

Environmental Law

Friends of the Earth, Inc. v. Laidlaw Environmental Services, Inc., decided by a 7–2 vote, January 12, 2000; Ginsburg wrote the opinion; Scalia and Thomas dissented.

Courts can fine polluters in citizen suits brought under the federal Clean Water Act and can enforce those fines even if the company eliminates any violations while the case is proceeding.

The ruling reinstated a $405,800 fine issued in 1997 against Laidlaw Environmental Services, Inc., for excessive discharges of toxic mercury from a waste-water treatment plant on the North Tyger River in South Carolina. Two environmental groups—Friends of the Earth and a local organization—had filed suit against the company in 1992. Evidence showed violations of mercury discharge levels through 1995. In issuing the fine, the federal judge said the penalty was needed to deter violations, but he declined to issue an injunction against excessive discharges. On appeal, the Fourth U.S. Circuit Court of Appeals set aside the fine and dismissed the case as moot, saying the company had come into compliance with the law.

By a 7–2 vote, the Court upheld the environmental groups' standing to seek the civil penalty and rejected Laidlaw's mootness contention. On the first issue, Ginsburg said civil penalties "may serve . . . to deter future violations and thereby redress the injuries that prompted a citizen suitor to commence litigation." On the second issue, Ginsburg said that a defendant's "voluntary cessation of allegedly unlawful conduct" does not suffice to establish mootness unless "it is absolutely clear the allegedly wrongful behavior could not reasonably be expected to recur."

In dissent, Scalia, joined by Thomas, argued that the environmental groups had not made sufficient allegations of injury to establish standing to bring the suit and in any event that they should not be allowed to seek civil penalties. "The undesirable and unconstitutional consequence of today's decision," Scalia wrote, "is to place the immense power of suing to enforce the public laws in private hands." As for mootness, however, Scalia said he did not disagree with the Court's conclusion.

Family Law

Visitation

Troxel v. Granville, decided by a 6–3 vote, June 5, 2000; O'Connor wrote the main opinion; Stevens, Scalia, and Kennedy dissented.

A Washington State judge went too far in applying a state law to grant visitation rights to the grandparents of two young girls over the mother's objections.

The narrow ruling in a closely watched case set aside a visitation order that a Washington State court judge issued in 1995 requiring that Jenifer and Gary Troxel be allowed overnight visits of their granddaughters Isabelle and Natalie one weekend a month and one week during the summer as well as four hours on each of their birthdays. The girls' mother, Tommie Granville, objected, though she agreed to less frequent visits. (The girls' father, Brad Troxel—Jenifer and Gary Troxel's son—had committed suicide in May 1993; he and Granville had never married.) In issuing the order, the judge relied on a Washington State statute allowing "any person" to petition a superior court for visitation rights "at any time" and authorizing a court to issue such an order whenever "visitation may serve the best interests of the child." On appeal, the Washington Supreme Court held that the statute unconstitutionally interfered with the fundamental rights of parents to rear their children by allowing court-ordered visitation without evidence of harm to the child.

The Court affirmed the Washington court's judgment on a 6–3 vote in a narrower decision that skirted the major constitutional question. Writing for four justices, O'Connor cited the specific facts of the case—including the mother's willingness to permit some visitation by the grandparents—in concluding that the judge's ruling amounted to "an unconstitutional infringement on Granville's fundamental right to make decisions concerning the care, custody, and control of her two daughters." But she put off to future cases the question whether nonparental visitation statutes always violate parents' due process rights. Rehnquist, Ginsburg, and Breyer joined O'Connor's opinion.

In an opinion concurring in the judgment, Souter said he would have upheld the Washington Supreme Court's decision and ruled the state statute "unconstitutional on its face." Thomas, also concurring in the judgment, said he would apply the most stringent level of constitutional review—the so-called "strict scrutiny standard"—in determining the validity of a nonparental visitation order.

Each of the three dissenters wrote separately. Stevens suggested the Washington statute should be rewritten, but that states should be allowed to protect children from "arbitrary parental decisions that neither serve nor are motivated by the best interests of the child." In his opinion, Kennedy said he would have reversed the Washington Supreme Court's decision that a nonparental visitation order was necessarily unconstitutional without evidence of harm to the child and remanded the case for further proceedings. In a broader dissent, Scalia disagreed with Court precedents from the 1920s recognizing parental rights under the Fourteenth Amendment's Due Process Clause and said he would not extend those decisions by using them to question state visitation statutes. *(See story, pp. 80–84; excerpts, pp. 220–231.)*

Federal Government

Federal Regulation

Crosby, Secretary of Finance and Administration of Massachusetts v. National Foreign Trade Council, decided by a 9–0 vote, June 19, 2000; Souter wrote the opinion.

The Court struck down a Massachusetts law imposing economic sanctions on companies doing business in Myanmar, saying the act was preempted by a less stringent federal measure aimed at penalizing the country's dictatorial government.

The ruling came in a suit brought by an organization of companies engaged in foreign commerce contesting a stringent sanctions measure that Massachusetts enacted in June 1996. The law barred any state agency from buying goods or services from any company "doing business in Burma," as the Asian country was formerly called. Congress passed a less restrictive measure in September 1996 that banned direct aid to the Burmese government and authorized the president to bar any new investment by U.S. firms in the country. The foreign trade group challenged the state law on grounds that it was preempted by the federal act, that it improperly restricted foreign commerce, and that it intruded on the president's prerogatives in foreign policy. The First U.S. Circuit Court of Appeals agreed with all three grounds and ruled the act unconstitutional.

In a unanimous but somewhat narrower decision, the Court ruled that the federal sanctions law preempted the Massachusetts statute. "[T]he state Act's provisions conflict with Congress's specific delegation to the President of flexible discretion," Souter wrote.

Food and Drug Administration v. Brown & Williamson Tobacco Corp., decided by a 5–4 vote, March 21, 2000; O'Connor wrote the opinion; Breyer, Stevens, Souter, and Ginsburg dissented.

The Food and Drug Administration (FDA) has no authority under its statutory charter to regulate cigarettes or other tobacco products.

The ruling represented a major victory for the tobacco industry against a Clinton administration initiative to impose advertising and marketing restrictions on manufacturers and retailers of cigarettes and smokeless tobacco. The FDA adopted the regulations in August 1996 after concluding that nicotine amounted to a "drug" and cigarettes and smokeless tobacco "drug delivery devices" as defined in the federal Food, Drug and Cosmetic Act (FDCA). The regulations—aimed at reducing smoking among teenagers—required age verification to buy cigarettes or smokeless tobacco; barred self-service vending machines except in "adult-only" nightclubs; and limited outdoor advertising and print advertising in publications with significant youth readership. Tobacco companies challenged the regulations as beyond the FDA's authority. A federal court judge barred part of the regulations. On appeal, the Fourth U.S. Circuit Court of Appeals agreed with the industry that all of the rules went beyond the FDA's statutory power.

In a closely divided decision, the Court held that Congress had not given the FDA authority to regulate tobacco products. "Reading the FDCA as a whole, as well as in conjunction with Congress' subsequent tobacco-specific legislation," O'Connor wrote, "it is plain that Congress has not given the FDA the authority that it seeks to exercise here." If the FDA could regulate tobacco, O'Connor explained, the agency would have to ban tobacco products altogether as unsafe. But Congress, she said, had passed a number of tobacco-specific laws that stopped short of banning tobacco and that included no provisions for FDA authority over tobacco.

Writing for the four dissenters, Breyer argued that tobacco fit within the food and drug law's definitions of drugs and drug delivery devices and contended that the agency would have discretion under the FDCA to impose restrictions short of a ban. *(See story, pp. 57–61; excerpts, pp. 197–208.)*

Geier v. American Honda Motor Company, Inc., decided by a 5–4 vote, May 22, 2000; Breyer wrote the opinion; Stevens, Souter, Thomas, and Ginsburg dissented.

A federal regulation aimed at encouraging but not requiring airbags protected automobile manufacturers from damage suits by consumers injured in crashes involving cars that were not equipped with the devices.

The ruling in a closely watched business dispute barred a product liability suit stemming from injuries suffered in an automobile crash in 1992 by a Washington, D.C., woman, Alexis Geier, while she was driving a 1987 Honda that was not equipped with an airbag. Geier and her parents sued Honda, claiming that the car was defective because it had no driver's side airbag. Honda argued that the suit—brought under District of Columbia tort law—was preempted by the federal National Traffic and Motor Vehicle Safety Act of 1966 or by a 1984 regulation requiring auto manufacturers to equip some but not all of their cars with passive restraints. Airbags were not required in all cars until 1998. A federal district court judge and the U.S. Circuit Court of Appeals for the District of Columbia both ruled the suit was preempted. In its ruling, the appeals court said that the state-law claim would pose an obstacle to the accomplishment of the objective of the 1984 regulation.

By a 5–4 vote, the Court agreed that the suit was preempted. The regulation, Breyer wrote, "sought a gradually developing mix of alternative passive restraint devices"—either airbags, automatic seatbelts, or some other equipment. A "no airbag" suit, Breyer concluded, "would stand as an obstacle to the accomplishment of that objective."

Writing for the dissenters, Stevens contended that the federal regulation "would not be frustrated one whit by allowing state courts to determine whether in 1987 the life-saving advantages of airbags had become sufficiently obvious that their omission might constitute a design defect in some new cars."

Norfolk Southern Railway Co. v. Shanklin, decided by a 7–2 vote, April 17, 2000; O'Connor wrote the opinion; Ginsburg and Stevens dissented.

Federal law prevents states from applying their own standards in personal injury suits based on allegedly inadequate warnings at railway crossings if federal funds were used in installing the safety devices.

The ruling nullified a $430,765 jury award to Dedra Shanklin, whose husband Jessie was killed in 1993 when a Norfolk Southern Railway train struck his pickup truck at a crossing in rural West Tennessee. The crossing was equipped with flashing lights and a reflectorized X-shaped sign but not with an automatic gate that closes as a train approaches. Federal regulations issued by the Federal Highway Administration (FHWA) under a 1970 law, the Federal Railroad Safety Act, provided funding for installing warning devices and required automatic gates at certain crossings. Devices at other crossings were subject to FHWA approval. The act also expressly preempted state law governing the adequacy of warning devices built with federal funds. A federal court jury agreed with Shanklin's claim that the warning devices at the crossing were inadequate. The railroad argued the federal law preempted the claim, but the trial judge and the Sixth U.S. Circuit Court of Appeals rejected the argument.

By a 7–2 vote, the Court held the state law claim was preempted. "Once the FHWA approved the project and the signs were installed using federal funds," O'Connor wrote, "the federal standard for adequacy displaced Tennessee statutory and common law addressing the same subject. . . ." In a brief concurrence, Breyer said the agency could revise its regulations to allow state court suits.

Writing for the dissenters, Ginsburg said the ruling "defies common sense and sound policy." "No authority, federal or state, has found that the signs in place at the scene of the . . . accident were adequate to protect safety," she wrote.

Public Lands Council v. Babbitt, Secretary of Interior, decided by a 9–0 vote, May 15, 2000; Breyer wrote the opinion.

The Court upheld three revised Interior Department regulations governing livestock grazing on public lands that Western ranchers argued undermined their livelihood and infringed on rights protected under a 1934 federal law.

The ruling rejected a challenge brought by the Public Lands Council, representing livestock ranchers, to three regulations issued in 1995 under the Taylor Grazing Act. The 1934 law gave the secretary of the Interior authority to divide public rangelands into grazing districts; specify the amount of grazing permitted in each district; and issue permits to "settlers, residents, and other stock owners." The three challenged regulations changed the definition of "grazing preference" to make it conform to land use plans; authorized permits to people not engaged in the livestock business; and granted the United States title to all future "permanent" range improvements, such as fences, wells, and so forth. The ranchers' group contended the revisions violated the Taylor Act's requirement that "grazing privileges recognized and acknowledged shall be adequately safeguarded." A federal court agreed, but the Tenth U.S. Circuit Court of Appeals upheld the regulations.

Unanimously, the Court held that the regulatory changes did not exceed the Interior secretary's authority under the grazing law. Breyer said the revised definition of "grazing preference" was lawful because the act made clear that ranchers had no "absolute" interest in "permit stability." In any event, he said ranchers could challenge any loss of grazing permits in individual cases. On the second issue, Breyer said the law did not limit permits to people engaged in the livestock business. Finally, Breyer said the act gave the secretary "the power to set terms of title ownership to . . . improvements . . . just like any landlord." In a brief concurring opinion, O'Connor, joined by Thomas, also emphasized that the ruling left open the possibility of challenging any loss of grazing permits on a case-by-case basis.

Reno, Attorney General v. Condon, Attorney General of South Carolina, decided by a 9–0 vote, January 12, 2000; Rehnquist wrote the opinion.

The federal government can prohibit state governments from selling personal information obtained in issuing driver's licenses.

The ruling upheld the constitutionality of a 1994 law, the Driver's Privacy Protection Act, challenged by a number of states on federalism grounds. The law restricted states from selling such personal information as names, addresses, telephone numbers, Social Security numbers, and the like to most businesses or direct marketing companies. It included exceptions, however, permitting disclosure of personal information to law enforcement, private investigators, and others. Ruling in a challenge brought by the state of South Carolina, the Fourth U.S. Circuit Court of Appeals said the law was unconstitutional because it violated principles of federalism.

Unanimously, the Court ruled that Congress had authority under the Commerce Clause to regulate the states' sale of personal information and that the act did not improperly intrude on the states' sovereignty. The act, Rehnquist wrote in a terse ten-page opinion, "does not require the states in their sovereign capacity to regulate their own citizens. It does not require the South Carolina Legislature to enact any laws or regulations, and it does not require state officials to assist in the enforcement of federal statutes regulating individuals."

Shalala, Secretary of Health and Human Services v. Illinois Council on Long Term Care, Inc., decided by a 5–4 vote, February 29, 2000; Breyer wrote the opinion; Thomas, Stevens, Scalia, and Kennedy dissented.

Nursing homes seeking to challenge Medicare regulations must do so through administrative enforcement proceedings at the Department of Health and Human Services (HHS), not in federal court.

The ruling turned aside a challenge by the Illinois Council on Long Term Care, a trade association of nursing homes, to regulations issued by HHS in 1994 that were part of a crackdown on substandard conditions at long-term care facilities. The trade association attacked the regulations in a federal court suit on a variety of grounds, including vagueness, due process, and administrative procedures. HHS sought to have the suit dismissed because of a Medicare Act provision that required any "action . . . to recover on any claim" to be brought in administrative proceedings instead of in federal court. A lower federal court agreed with the government, but the Seventh U.S. Circuit Court of Appeals said the prohibition against federal court suits did not apply to broad regulatory challenges.

By a 5–4 vote, the Court ruled that the Medicare Act provision did bar the trade association's suit. "The association or its members must proceed . . . through the special review channel that the Medicare statutes create," Breyer wrote.

Writing for the four dissenters, Thomas said the Medicare Act provision barring court challenges applied only when "a particular fact-bound determination is in dispute," not when the validity of instructions or regulations is being challenged. Stevens and Scalia wrote separate, shorter dissenting opinions.

United States v. Locke, Governor of Washington, decided by a 9–0 vote, March 6, 2000; Kennedy wrote the opinion.

Federal laws and regulations generally preempt state regulation of oil tankers.

The ruling invalidated four oil tanker regulations and cast doubt on other restrictions that were part of a stringent regulatory scheme adopted by the state of Washington following the *Exxon Valdez* oil spill off the coast of Alaska in 1989. The state law created an Office of Marine Safety with a mandate to provide "the best achievable protection from damages caused by the discharge of oil." The office promulgated detailed regulations covering working conditions on tankers, worker qualifications, operating procedures, and accident reports. The International Association of Independent Tanker Owners, which represented about 80 percent of the world's independent tanker fleet, challenged the regulations on the ground they were preempted by federal statutes, including the Ports and Waterways Safety Act of 1972 and the Oil Pollution Act of 1990. After a lower federal court upheld the state regulations, the United States intervened on the tanker association's side, arguing that the lower court ruling failed to give sufficient weight to the federal government's substantial foreign affairs interest. The Ninth U.S. Circuit Court of Appeals nonetheless held that the state could enforce all but one of the challenged regulations.

Unanimously, the Court held that the state regulations were "preempted by federal statute and regulations." Kennedy said that the 1972 federal law generally preempted state law and rejected the state's argument that the 1990 act had opened the door to state regulation. The ruling specifically invalidated four regulations covering training requirements, crew English proficiency, navigation watch requirements, and accident reporting. Kennedy said it was "preferable" for the other regulations to be considered again by lower courts in part because the federal government had not participated in the case at the trial level. While rejecting the state's regulations, Kennedy closed by saying that Congress and the Coast Guard should take the views of the states, environmental groups, and local port authorities into account in determining whether the federal regulations are adequate.

Government Contracts

Mobil Oil Exploration and Producing Southeast, Inc. v. United States, decided by an 8–1 vote, June 26, 2000; Breyer wrote the opinion; Stevens dissented.

The Court ordered the government to repay two oil companies $156 million for reneging on contracts for crude oil and natural gas leases off the North Carolina coast.

The ruling backed claims by a subsidiary of Mobil Oil Corp. and the Marathon Oil Co. that the government had repudiated a 1981 contract giving them a conditional right for oil and gas exploration in the environmentally fragile area about forty-five miles off the coast of Cape Hatteras. The companies paid $156 million up front for the leases. The contract was contingent on the companies' compliance with various federal statutes; one of the laws gave a state an opportunity to block exploration in some circumstances. North Carolina officials generally opposed oil and gas drilling off the state's coast. The oil companies submitted an exploration plan in 1990, but the Interior Department refused to act on it because of a law passed that year imposing a thirteen-month moratorium on approval of any such plan. The trial-level Court of Claims ruled the government had broken the contract and had to repay the up-front money. The Court of Appeals for the Federal Circuit disagreed, saying that the state's objection to the plan would have prevented the companies from exploring regardless.

In a nearly unanimous decision, the Court held that the companies were entitled to restitution of the money they paid because the government had repudiated the contract by failing to approve the exploration plan. "We agree that the Government broke its promise," Breyer wrote. "[I]t repudiated the contracts; and it must give the companies their money back."

In a lone dissent, Stevens agreed the government had breached the contract, but said the failure to approve the plan had merely delayed the oil companies' efforts. He said the states' objections would have blocked exploration anyway and called the Court's decision "a draconian remedy."

Social Security

Sims v. Apfel, Commissioner of Social Security, decided by a 5–4 vote, June 5, 2000; Thomas wrote the main opinion; O'Connor concurred in part; Breyer, Rehnquist, Scalia, and Kennedy dissented.

The Court made it easier for people who have been denied Social Security disability benefits to contest the decision in federal court.

The ruling reinstated a federal court challenge by a Mississippi woman, Juatassa Sims, to a decision by an administrative law judge in the Social Security Administration denying disability benefits for a variety of claimed ailments, including carpal tunnel syndrome. After the Social Security Appeals Council upheld the ruling, Sims filed a federal court suit contesting the decision. The Fifth U.S. Circuit Court of Appeals refused to consider two of her three arguments because she had not raised those issues before the agency's appeals body.

By a 5–4 vote, the Court held that a Social Security applicant can raise issues in a federal court suit even if she did not raise them in an administrative appeal. Writing for a plurality of four justices, Thomas emphasized the informal nature of Social Security proceedings in refusing to apply an "issue exhaustion" requirement. "The Council, not the claimant, has primary responsibility for identifying and developing the issues," Thomas wrote. In a partial concurring opinion, O'Connor said the critical factor was the agency's failure to inform claimants that they would give up any issue not raised before the appeals body.

For the dissenters, Breyer argued that the Social Security Administration should be allowed to bar applicants from raising new issues in court when they have been represented by lawyers before the agency. A lawyer should know, Breyer wrote, that "a claimant must raise his objections in an internal agency appellate proceeding or forgo the opportunity later to raise them in court."

First Amendment

Church and State

Mitchell v. Helms, decided by a 6–3 vote, June 28, 2000; Thomas wrote the main opinion; O'Connor and Breyer concurred in the judgment; Souter, Stevens, and Ginsburg dissented.

Governments can lend computers and other instructional equipment to religious and other private schools without violating the constitutional prohibition against establishment of religion.

The ruling—in a fractured decision with no majority opinion—turned aside an Establishment Clause challenge to the operation of the federal government's so-called "Chapter 2" program. Under the program, the federal government provided funds via state education agencies to local school systems, which in turn bought instructional materials and equipment to be lent to public or private secondary and elementary schools. A group of taxpayers in Jefferson Parish, Louisiana, filed a challenge in 1985 to the use of funds under the program to provide equipment to parochial schools. After a lengthy and complex course of litigation, the Fifth U.S. Circuit Court of Appeals ruled in 1998 that the program was improper under two earlier Supreme Court decisions, *Meek v. Pittenger* (1975) and *Wolman v. Walter* (1977), that barred lending instructional materials to parochial schools or parochial school pupils. The appeals court noted, however, that those decisions appeared to be inconsistent with the Court's more recent school-aid ruling, *Agostini v. Felton* (1997).

The Court upheld the program by a 6–3 vote. Four justices joined in a broadly worded opinion to permit aid to parochial schools under any neutral, secular program generally available to all schools. Two other justices took a narrower approach that also examined the effects of the program in terms of advancing or endorsing religion. All six voted to overturn the earlier precedents.

In the plurality opinion, Thomas said that the Chapter 2 program met the criteria established by the later case, *Agostini*, for permitting public aid to church-affiliated schools. "Considering Chapter 2 in light of our more recent case law, we conclude that it neither results in religious indoctrination by the government nor defines its recipients by reference to religion," Thomas wrote. Rehnquist, Scalia, and Kennedy joined his opinion.

In an opinion concurring in the judgment, O'Connor cited a list of several factors in concluding that the program "does not have the impermissible effect of advancing religion." But she criticized the plurality opinion. "[W]e have never held that a government-aid program passes constitutional muster *solely* because of the neutral criteria it employs as a basis for distributing aid," she wrote. Breyer joined her opinion.

Writing for the three dissenters, Souter said the operation of the program violated church-state principles because of evidence of "diversion" of equipment and materials to religious purposes and lack of safeguards to prevent such use. But he reserved his strongest criticism for the broad rule in Thomas's opinion. "[T]he plurality's notion of evenhandedness neutrality as a practical guarantee of the validity of aid to sectarian schools would be the end of the principle of no aid to the schools' religious mission," Souter wrote. *(See story, pp. 61–66; excerpts, pp. 267–281.)*

Santa Fe Independent School District v. Doe, decided by a 6–3 vote, June 19, 2000; Stevens wrote the opinion; Rehnquist, Scalia, and Thomas dissented.

The Court strengthened its restrictions on school-sponsored religious observances by barring a Texas school district's policy permitting an elected student-speaker to deliver an invocation before high school football games.

The ruling invalidated a policy adopted at the start of the 1995–1996 school year by the 4,000 student Santa Fe, Texas, school district but never implemented because of litigation brought by two families with students in the system: one Catholic, the other Mormon. Under the policy, the high school students voted first to allow a student to deliver a prayer at football games and then elected one student to hold that position for the year. The policy—originally entitled "Prayer at Football Games"—was amended in October to omit the word "prayer" and to refer to "messages" and "statements" as well as "invocations." A lower federal court and the Fifth U.S.

Circuit Court of Appeals both ruled that the policy violated the Establishment Clause, which provides that the government "shall make no law respecting an establishment of religion."

By a 6–3 vote, the Court held that a student-led, student-initiated prayer at public high school football games violates the Establishment Clause. For the majority, Stevens rejected the school district's argument that the policy was constitutional because it had a secular purpose of solemnizing football games and because the policy entailed private rather than government speech. The policy was "invalid on its face," Stevens wrote, "because it establishes an improper majoritarian election on religion, and unquestionably has the purpose and creates the perception of encouraging the delivery of prayer at a series of important school events."

Writing for the dissenters, Rehnquist said the policy had a legitimate secular purpose and should not be invalidated on its face because it could be applied in a constitutional manner. *(See story, pp. 66–70; excerpts, pp. 232–241.)*

Commercial Speech

Los Angeles Police Department v. United Reporting Publishing Corp., decided by a 7–2 vote, December 7, 1999; Rehnquist wrote the opinion; Stevens and Kennedy dissented.

The Court turned aside a First Amendment challenge to a California law that limited access to information about arrestees to anyone requesting the data for commercial purposes.

The narrow ruling sent back to lower federal courts a suit brought by a company, United Reporting Publishing Corp., that wanted to collect names and addresses of arrestees for sale to attorneys, insurance companies, driving schools, and drug and alcohol counselors, who could then use the lists to solicit clients or customers. California enacted a law in 1996 that barred law enforcement agencies from releasing the addresses of arrestees unless the person requesting the information declared under oath that it would not use the addresses to "directly or indirectly . . . sell a product or service." The publishing company challenged the law as unconstitutional "on its face"—that is, invalid under any circumstances. A federal district court and the Ninth U.S. Circuit Court of Appeals both agreed.

By a 7–2 vote, the Court ruled that the publishing company could not bring a facial challenge to the law because the statute did not directly infringe on the company's own free speech rights. "For purposes of assessing the propriety of a facial invalidation, what we have before us is nothing more than a governmental denial of access to information in its possession," Rehnquist wrote.

The majority opinion left unanswered whether a so-called "as applied" challenge to the law could be brought by someone who had a direct interest in using the address information for commercial purposes. Two groups of justices in the majority wrote separate concurring opinions disagreeing on the point. Scalia, joined by Thomas, suggested the law might be ruled invalid as an improper restriction on speech. But Ginsburg—joined by O'Connor, Souter, and Breyer—said that "selective disclosure" would not "impermissibly" burden speech.

In a dissenting opinion, Stevens, joined by Kennedy, maintained that the law was invalid. The law, Stevens said, imposed a "discriminatory ban on access to information . . . in an attempt to prohibit persons from exercising their constitutional rights to publish it in a truthful and accurate manner. . . ."

Freedom of Association

Boy Scouts of America v. Dale, decided by a 5–4 vote, June 28, 2000; Rehnquist wrote the opinion; Stevens, Souter, Ginsburg, and Breyer dissented.

The Boy Scouts may continue to enforce a policy prohibiting avowed homosexuals from serving as adult Scout leaders despite a state law prohibiting discrimination in public accommodations on the basis of sexual orientation.

The ruling barred a complaint brought under a New Jersey antidiscrimination law by a former Boy Scout assistant scoutmaster, James Dale, after his local Scout council revoked his membership because of his homosexuality. Dale, a former Eagle Scout, acknowledged his homosexuality while in college. The Monmouth, New Jersey, council learned of Dale's sexual orientation from a newspaper story describing his position as copresident of a gay student organization, and then barred him from continuing as a Scout leader. He sued under the state's public accommodations law. The Scouts sought to have the complaint dismissed on a variety of grounds, including a claim that enforcement of the law would violate the organization's First Amendment rights. The New Jersey Supreme Court ruled that the Scouts were a public accommodation subject to the law and that enforcement of the law would not violate the Scouts' freedom of association.

By a 5–4 vote, the Court held that application of the state's antidiscrimination law would violate the Boy Scouts' "freedom of expressive association." Writing for the majority, Rehnquist accepted the Scouts' contentions that it had an "official policy" disapproving of homosexual conduct and that admitting "an avowed homosexual" as an adult leader would "significantly affect its expression." The state's interests in enforcing the public accommodation law, Rehnquist concluded, "do not justify such a severe intrusion on the Boy Scouts' rights to freedom of expressive association."

Writing for the four dissenters, Stevens disagreed that the Scouts had an established policy of disapproval of homosexual conduct. "Boy Scouts of America is simply silent on homosexuality," Stevens said. "There is no shared goal or collective effort to foster a belief about homosexuality at all—let alone one that is significantly burdened by admitting homosexuals." In his opinion, Stevens took note of increased public tolerance of homosexuality. Souter wrote a brief dissent—joined by Ginsburg and Breyer—agreeing with Stevens's conclusions but stressing that the Boy Scouts' right of expressive association did not turn on the popularity or unpopularity of its views. *(See story, pp. 75–79; excerpts, pp. 281–292.)*

Freedom of Speech

Board of Regents, University of Wisconsin v. Southworth, decided by a 9–0 vote, March 22, 2000; Kennedy wrote the opinion.

Public universities can impose mandatory student activity fees to support political and ideological groups as long as the funds are distributed in a viewpoint-neutral manner.

The ruling generally upheld a scheme used by the University of Wisconsin—parallel to programs at many other public universities—to support an array of extracurricular organizations, including political and ideological advocacy groups. The Wisconsin fee—set at $331.50 for the 1995–1996 academic year—was challenged by several conservative students, who said use of the funds to support liberal groups violated their First Amendment rights. A lower federal court held that the program violated the students' freedom of speech and freedom of association by compelling them to support activities with which they disagreed. The Seventh U.S. Circuit Court of Appeals generally upheld the ruling and barred the university from requiring students to pay the portion of the fee used to fund political or ideological groups.

Unanimously, the Court rejected the objecting students' claim and upheld the bulk of the university's system. Writing for six justices, Kennedy said universities could impose such fees as long as they abided by "viewpoint neutrality as the operational principle." Kennedy explained, "When a university requires its students to pay fees to support the extracurricular speech of other students, all in the interest of open discussion, it may not prefer some viewpoints to others."

In an opinion concurring in the judgment, Souter agreed the university's system was valid, but said he would not impose viewpoint neutrality as "a cast-iron requirement." Stevens and Breyer joined his opinion.

Student government bodies awarded most of the funds under the Wisconsin scheme, but groups could also gain the right to funding through a student referendum. All nine justices agreed that the referendum mechanism had not been adequately considered in the lower courts; the case was remanded for further proceedings on that issue.

City of Erie v. Pap's A.M., decided by a 6–3 vote, March 29, 2000; O'Connor wrote the main opinion; Scalia and Thomas concurred in the judgment; Souter dissented in part; Stevens and Ginsburg dissented.

Cities and states can ban nude dancing.

The ruling revived an ordinance enacted by Erie, Pennsylvania, in 1994 after the opening of a bar in the city's downtown area featuring nude female dancers. The owner of the bar, known as "Kandyland," challenged the ordinance as an unconstitutional limitation on freedom of speech. The Court had upheld a similar ordinance in a fractured decision in 1991, *Barnes v. Glen Theatre, Inc.* In that 5–4 ruling, three justices—Rehnquist, O'Connor, and Kennedy—said a ban on nude dancing was permissible because of its limited impact on free speech; one justice—Scalia—said the ordinance regulated conduct, not speech; and one justice—Souter—said the ban helped prevent secondary effects associated with nude dancing establishments, such as prostitution and sexually transmitted diseases.

Interpreting that decision in the Kandyland case, the Pennsylvania Supreme Court said the ruling was not binding precedent because there was no majority position. The state court then went on to strike down the Erie ordinance. It ruled that the law had to meet the "strict scrutiny" test because the ordinance was aimed at "the erotic message of the dance" and that it failed that test because there were less restrictive alternatives to preventing the secondary effects associated with nude dancing.

In a decision slightly less fractured than its previous ruling, the Court ruled that the ordinance did not violate the First Amendment because it was subject to a lesser "intermediate scrutiny" test used to judge laws that are not aimed at regulating the content of speech. "Erie's asserted interest in combating the negative secondary effects associated with adult entertainment establishments like Kandyland is unrelated to the suppression of the erotic message conveyed by nude dancing," O'Connor wrote for a five-justice majority. She went on to conclude that the Erie city council should be accorded "sufficient leeway" to judge the importance of combating those secondary effects and that the ordinance did in fact advance the goal of preventing public health and safety problems associated with adult entertainment.

Three justices joined all of O'Connor's opinion: Rehnquist, Kennedy, and Breyer. Souter joined the first part of O'Connor's opinion, but said the city had failed to present "factual justification" for the ordinance in terms of "the seriousness of the threatened harm" or "the efficacy of its current remedy." He said he would return the case to the state courts and require the city to make a more detailed showing of the need for the measure.

Scalia and Thomas provided the critical votes for reversing the Pennsylvania Supreme Court's decision in an opinion—written by Scalia—concurring in the judgment. Scalia said the ordinance regulated conduct, not speech, and did not have to be justified on grounds of combating secondary effects. "The traditional power of government to foster good morals. . . , and the acceptability of the traditional judgment . . . that nude public dancing *itself* is immoral, have not been repealed by the First Amendment," he wrote.

In a dissenting opinion, Stevens, joined by Ginsburg, called the ordinance "patently invalid" and criticized the majority for misapplying previous decisions that upheld zoning restrictions on adult entertainment facilities. "Never before have we approved the use of that doctrine to justify a total ban on protected First Amendment expression," Stevens wrote.

Hill v. Colorado, decided by a 6–3 vote, June 28, 2000; Stevens wrote the opinion; Scalia, Kennedy, and Thomas dissented.

The Court upheld a Colorado law that limited leafleting or so-called "sidewalk counseling" at abortion clinics or other health care facilities except with a person's consent or at a distance of at least eight feet.

The ruling—a setback for anti-abortion protesters—rejected a First Amendment challenge to the Colorado statute, passed in 1993. The act made it a misdemeanor for any person within 100 feet of a health care facility's entrance to "knowingly approach" within eight feet of another person, without that person's consent, in order to pass "a leaflet or handbill to, displa[y] a sign to, or engag[e] in oral protest, education, or counseling" with that person. Anti-abortion protesters who had adopted the tactic of "sidewalk counseling" to try to discourage women from having abortions challenged the law as a violation of their freedom of speech. The Colorado Supreme Court upheld the statute. The state high court said the law was a content-neutral, narrowly tailored "time, place, and manner" regulation; it noted that the eight-foot "bubble" was less restrictive than the fifteen-foot "floating buffer zone" approved by the Supreme Court in an earlier decision, *Schenck v. Pro-Choice Network of Western N.Y.* (1997).

The Court also upheld the law over blistering dissents from three of the justices. Writing for the majority, Stevens said the law was "content neutral" because it applied to all protest or counseling—whether or not concerning abortion and whether in support of or in opposition to abortion. He also said the law met the requirement that speech regulations be "narrowly tailored." "A bright-line prophylactic rule may be the best way to provide protection and, at the same time, by offering clear guidance and avoiding subjectivity, to protect speech itself," Stevens wrote. In a concurring opinion, Souter also stressed that the law was content neutral; O'Connor, Ginsburg, and Breyer joined his opinion.

Scalia and Kennedy both wrote strong dissents and emphasized their disagreement by reading portions from the bench. In his dissent, Scalia said the law was "obviously and undeniably content-based," was not narrowly tailored, and was aimed at protecting "an unheard of 'right to be let alone' on the public streets." Thomas joined Scalia's opinion. In his dissent, Kennedy also argued that the majority misapplied First Amendment doctrine in upholding the statute. He concluded, "The Court tears away from the protesters the guarantees of the First Amendment when they most need it."

Telecommunications

United States v. Playboy Entertainment Group, Inc., decided by a 5–4 vote, May 22, 2000; Kennedy wrote the opinion; Breyer, Rehnquist, O'Connor, and Scalia dissented.

The Court struck down on First Amendment grounds a federal law requiring cable channels primarily devoted to sexually explicit programming either to fully scramble their programs or to limit the material to late night and early morning hours.

The ruling invalidated a provision of the Telecommunications Act of 1996—§505—ostensibly aimed at preventing children from inadvertently being exposed to so-called "signal bleed" from cable sex channels. Cable sex channels scrambled their signals to limit service to paying customers, but some audio or visual portions of the scrambled signals might be heard or seen by cable customers even if they did not subscribe to the sex channels. To eliminate the signal bleed problem, Congress required cable channels devoted to "sexually explicit adult programming" to completely scramble their programs—a costly technical procedure—or to limit programs to times when there were not substantial numbers of children in the audience. The Federal Communications Commission adopted a regulation defining that time period to be from 10 P.M. to 6 A.M. The law included another provision—§504—that required cable operators to fully scramble any channel upon a subscriber's request.

Playboy Entertainment—which operated some of the most popular sex channels, including Playboy Television and Spice—challenged the mandatory §505 as an infringement of freedom of speech. A three-judge federal court in Delaware ruled the provision unconstitutional. It held that the government had less restrictive alternatives to serve its interests of preventing children from exposure to sexually explicit programming. Specifically, the court said that the government's interests could be served by the provision permitting subscribers to request complete scrambling if cable operators gave subscribers additional notice of that right through on-air notice and mailings. The government asked the Court to reinstate the law.

By a 5–4 vote that crossed the usual ideological lines, the Court agreed the law was unconstitutional. For the majority, Kennedy said that §505 amounted to a content-based speech restriction that was subject to "strict scrutiny" and could not be upheld if a less restrictive alternative would accomplish the government's goals. If "a plausible, less restrictive alternative is offered," he continued, "it is the Government's obligation to prove that the alternative will be ineffective to achieve its goals."

After noting that relatively few cable subscribers had invoked §504 to demand signal scrambling, Kennedy said that the lower court had been correct to conclude that there was "little hard evidence of how widespread or how serious the problem of signal bleed is." On that basis, Kennedy concluded, "The Government has failed to show that §505 is the least restrictive means for addressing a real problem." Joining in the opinion were three liberal justices—Stevens, Souter, and Ginsburg—along with the conservative Thomas.

In the main dissenting opinion, Breyer said the ruling imposed too great a burden on the government to justify the restriction, which he said "minimized" its impact on adults while helping parents keep "unwanted transmissions" from children. He questioned whether an enhanced right to demand scrambling under the "opt-out" provision—§504—would accomplish what he called Congress's "child-protecting objective." "By finding 'adequate alternatives' where there are none," Breyer concluded, "the Court reduces Congress' protective power to the vanishing point." Rehnquist, O'Connor, and Scalia joined his opinion.

In a separate, lone dissent, Scalia contended the law could be justified as a regulation of the "business of obscenity." Stevens and Thomas wrote brief concurring opinions disputing that position.

Individual Rights

Abortion

Stenberg, Attorney General of Nebraska v. Carhart, decided by a 5–4 vote, June 28, 2000; Breyer wrote the opinion; Thomas, Rehnquist, Scalia, and Kennedy dissented.

The Court invalidated a Nebraska law that sought to ban so-called "partial-birth abortions." It said the statute imposed an undue burden on a woman's right to abortion and failed to include an exception for the health of the mother.

The ruling was a defeat for anti-abortion groups, which had won enactment of similar laws by overwhelming legislative majorities in a total of thirty-one states. Nebraska's statute provided for criminal penalties and automatic revocation of license for any doctor who performed a partial-birth abortion, which was defined as a procedure in which the physician "partially delivers vaginally a living unborn child before killing the . . . child." The act provided an exception if the procedure was necessary to save the life of the mother, but not to preserve the health of the mother. The law was challenged by Dr. LeRoy Carhart, a Nebraska physician who performed what medical authorities and abortion-rights supporters called a "dilation and extraction" or D&X procedure. A lower federal court and the Eighth U.S. Circuit Court of Appeals both ruled the law unconstitutional.

By a 5–4 vote, the Court also held the law unconstitutional, saying that it contradicted holdings in two previous abortion rights decisions: the "undue burden" standard announced in *Planned Parenthood of Southeastern Pa. v. Casey* (1992) and the "health exception" requirement contained in *Roe v. Wade* (1973) and reaffirmed in *Casey*. For the majority, Breyer said the law imposed an undue burden on abortion rights because the prohibition applied not only to the rarely used D&X procedure but also to the more common "dilation and evacuation" or D&E procedure. He also rejected the state's arguments that no health exception was required because of the availability of alternative abortion procedures.

In a concurring opinion, O'Connor said the ruling left open the possibility of upholding "more narrowly tailored" laws. Stevens and Ginsburg

both wrote brief concurring opinions, contending that there was no basis for distinguishing between the D&E and the D&X procedures; each one joined the other's opinion.

All four dissenters disagreed that the law covered any procedure other than partial-birth abortions or that a health exception was required. In the main dissent, Thomas said the law "should easily pass constitutional muster" under *Casey*. Rehnquist and Scalia joined his opinion. In a second lengthy dissent, Kennedy said that the majority "substitutes its own judgment for the judgment of Nebraska and some 30 other states. . . ." Rehnquist joined his opinion. Scalia wrote a shorter dissent, urging that *Casey* be overruled. Rehnquist wrote a short dissent; he called *Casey* "wrongly decided" but also agreed with Thomas and Kennedy that the Nebraska law could be upheld under that decision. *(See story, pp. 34–41; excerpts, pp. 251–266.)*

Affirmative Action

Adarand Constructors, Inc. v. Slater, Secretary of Transportation, decided by a 9–0 vote, January 12, 2000; *per curiam* opinion.

The Court revived a white contractor's challenge to a minority preference program for federal Department of Transportation (DOT) road contracts.

The ruling sent back to lower federal courts a reverse-discrimination case brought by Randy Pech, owner of the Colorado-based Adarand Constructors, Inc., after he lost out to a minority contractor for a DOT contract despite having submitted a lower bid. In an initial ruling, the Court in 1995 ruled that federal minority preference programs must meet the strictest constitutional standard—strict scrutiny—and sent the case to lower federal courts to apply that standard *(Adarand Constructors, Inc. v. Peña)*. A federal judge invalidated the program. In response, DOT revised the rules to allow a preference to any company that experienced racial discrimination. Applying that rule, Colorado's Department of Transportation determined that Adarand itself qualified for the preference. A federal appeals court then dismissed the government's appeal of the earlier decision, saying the case had become moot. Adarand asked the Court to review that decision and revive its original suit.

Without hearing oral argument, the Court unanimously held that the case was not moot. Specifically, the Court said that the federal government might not uphold the state agency's finding that Adarand qualified for the preference. But the Court also suggested the procedure was unfair to Adarand. "It is no small matter to deprive a litigant of the rewards of its effort, particularly in a case that has been litigated up to this Court and back down again," the Court said.

Texas v. Lesage, decided by a 9–0 vote, November 29, 1999; *per curiam* opinion.

A state college or university applicant who claims reverse discrimination because of a race-conscious admissions process cannot recover damages without showing that he would have been admitted to the school or program but for the racial preference.

The summary ruling—issued without hearing argument—threw out the central part of a federal civil rights suit filed by a white student, François Daniel Lesage, after he was denied admission to the University of Texas's graduate program for psychological counseling. A federal district court judge granted summary judgment in favor of the state university after evidence showed that Lesage would not have been admitted even if the admissions process had been completely colorblind. But the Fifth U.S. Circuit Court of Appeals reinstated the suit. It said Lesage could try to show that the university violated his constitutional rights "in the course of operating a racially discriminatory admissions program."

In a unanimous, unsigned opinion, the Court said the appeals court ruling was "inconsistent with [the] well-established framework" for analyzing unconstitutional-motive suits against the government. "[T]he government's conclusive demonstration that it would have made the same decision absent the alleged discrimination precludes any finding of liability," the Court said. The ruling sent the case back to the lower courts to rule on Lesage's amended complaint to bar race-conscious admissions procedures in the future.

Age Discrimination

Reeves v. Sanderson Plumbing Products, Inc., decided by a 9–0 vote, June 12, 2000; O'Connor wrote the opinion.

Workers in federal age discrimination suits do not have to produce direct evidence that an employer fired or demoted them because of age if they cast doubt on the employer's claimed explanation for the action.

The ruling—an important victory for plaintiffs likely to be applied to all federal job discrimination suits—reinstated a $70,000 jury award won by a Mississippi man, Roger Reeves, against his former employer, Sanderson Plumbing Products. The company claimed it fired Reeves in the summer of 1995 for failing to maintain accurate records of the hours worked by employees under his supervision; Reeves said he was dismissed because of his age, in violation of the federal Age Discrimination in Employment Act. The Fifth U.S. Circuit Court of Appeals threw out the jury verdict, saying Reeves had not produced sufficient evidence of unlawful discrimination.

Unanimously, the Court said that the appeals court "misconceived the evidentiary burden" on plaintiffs under the age discrimination law. If a plaintiff offers enough evidence for a judge or jury to reject an employer's explanation for an adverse job decision, O'Connor explained, there is no need for "additional, independent evidence of discrimination." In a brief concurring opinion, Ginsburg said that the ruling meant that the discrimination issue "ordinarily should not be taken from the jury" once the plaintiff makes out a basic case under the law and discredits an employer's defense.

While the decision was limited to the federal age discrimination law, legal experts said it was likely to be extended to suits brought under the main federal civil rights law, which prohibits job discrimination on the basis of race, religion, sex, and other categories.

Damage Suits

United States v. Morrison, decided by a 5–4 vote, May 15, 2000; Rehnquist wrote the opinion; Souter, Stevens, Ginsburg, and Breyer dissented.

The Court ruled unconstitutional a recently enacted federal law giving victims of gender-motivated violence the right to sue their attackers in federal court for compensatory and punitive damages.

The ruling—another in a series of Rehnquist Court decisions citing principles of federalism to limit Congress's powers—struck down the civil damage remedy provision of the 1994 Violence Against Women Act. The law declared a "right to be free from crimes of violence motivated by gender" and authorized private damage suits by victims of gender-motivated violence against anyone who deprived them of that right. Christy Brzonkala, a former Virginia Tech University student, filed suit under the law against two one-time varsity football players, Antonio Morrison and James Crawford, claiming that they raped her while she was a freshman at the school. A lower federal court and the full Fourth U.S. Circuit Court of Appeals both ruled the law exceeded Congress's power to regulate interstate commerce under the Commerce Clause or to protect equal protection rights under the Fourteenth Amendment. The United States intervened in the case after the lower court ruling to defend the statute.

By a 5–4 vote, the Court held the law could not be sustained under either the Commerce Clause or the Fourteenth Amendment. On the Commerce Clause issue, Rehnquist said Congress had no authority to regulate "noneconomic, violent conduct based solely on its aggregate effect on interstate commerce." As to the Fourteenth Amendment, Rehnquist said it gave Congress authority to prohibit discrimination by state or local governments, but not by private individuals. The chief justice ended by saying that any legal remedy for the alleged rape should be sought in Virginia courts, not in the federal court system.

Writing for the four dissenters, Souter said the ruling sought to revive a narrow view of the Commerce Clause used by the Court prior to 1937. The decision, he said, "can only be seen as a step toward recapturing the prior mistakes." Breyer wrote a separate dissent also criticizing the majority's view of the Commerce Clause; Stevens joined all his opinion, Souter and Ginsburg joined part. *(See story, pp. 41–46; excerpts, pp. 209–220.)*

Village of Willowbrook v. Olech, decided by a 9–0 vote, February 23, 2000; *per curiam* opinion.

Someone can bring an equal protection suit against the government for intentional and arbitrary discrimination even if she is not a member of a racial or ethnic minority or other specially protected class.

The ruling allowed an Illinois woman, Grace Olech, to proceed with a federal court suit against the Village of Willowbrook for delaying her request to connect her property to the municipal water supply. Olech claimed the delay was motivated by ill will resulting from a previous unrelated, unsuccessful lawsuit brought by her and her late husband against the village. The village moved to dismiss the suit. It argued that someone who was not a member of a protected class or group—a so-called "class of one"—could not bring suit under the Fourteenth Amendment's Equal Protection Clause. A lower federal court judge agreed, but the Seventh U.S. Circuit Court of Appeals reinstated the suit.

In a unanimous, unsigned opinion, the Court also said that Olech could proceed with her suit. "Our cases have recognized successful equal protection claims brought by a 'class of one,' where the plaintiff alleges that she has been intentionally treated differently from others similarly situated and that there is no rational basis for the difference in treatment," the brief opinion stated. In an opinion concurring in the result, Breyer sought to minimize the possibility that the ruling would allow "run-of-the-mill zoning cases" to be transformed into constitutional cases.

Labor Law

Pensions and Benefits

Harris Trust and Savings Bank v. Salomon Smith Barney Inc., decided by a 9–0 vote, June 12, 2000; Thomas wrote the opinion.

The Court expanded the types of businesses subject to suit under the federal pension protection law for entering into self-interested transactions with pension or employee benefit funds.

The ruling reinstated a suit by a bank serving as trustee of the Ameritech Pension Fund against the brokerage firm of Salomon Smith Barney brought under the federal Employee Retirement Income Security Act, commonly known as ERISA. The brokerage firm provided services to the fund and also sold the fund $21 million in interests in some motel properties that later proved worthless. The bank sued under an ERISA provision that prohibits a pension fund "fiduciary"—an official or adviser of the fund—from approving any transaction with "a person providing services to [an employee benefit] plan." Salomon Smith Barney sought to dismiss the suit, arguing that the ERISA provision applied only to pension fund fiduciaries, not to outside parties—a so-called "nonfiduciary." A federal district court allowed the suit, but the Seventh U.S. Circuit Court of Appeals agreed with the brokerage firm's argument and dismissed the case.

Unanimously, the Court held that the brokerage firm was subject to suit. Thomas explained that ERISA's legal remedy provision was broad enough to permit suits against a nonfiduciary even if the outside party was not itself covered by the prohibition against "party in interest" transactions.

Pegram v. Herdrich, decided by a 9–0 vote, June 12, 2000; Souter wrote the opinion.

Patients covered by employer-provided health insurance plans cannot use the federal law regulating employee benefit plans to sue health maintenance organizations (HMOs) or their physicians for making treatment decisions in order to hold down costs.

The ruling in the closely watched case barred parts of a suit filed by an Illinois woman, Cynthia Herdrich, for an HMO physician's refusal to order an immediate diagnostic test after Herdrich sought treatment for abdominal pain. Before the test could be conducted, Herdrich's appendix ruptured and she suffered peritonitis. Herdrich sued the physician, Lori Pegram, and the Carle Clinic, an HMO that provided health coverage for Herdrich's husband's employer. Herdrich sued originally for malpractice in Illinois state court, but expanded the complaint after it was removed to federal court to include claimed violations of ERISA. Herdrich contended that because of bonus incentives to its physicians, the HMO was violating responsibilities imposed on so-called "fiduciaries" of employee benefit plans—managers, administrators, or financial advisers—to act solely in the interest of the plan's beneficiaries. A federal district court judge dismissed the ERISA counts, but Pegram was awarded $35,000 for malpractice. On appeal, the Seventh U.S. Circuit Court of Appeals reinstated the ERISA counts, saying that an HMO could be held liable if physicians withhold "proper care . . . for the sole purpose of increasing their bonuses."

Unanimously, the Court reversed the decision, saying the HMO was not acting as a fiduciary in making what it called "mixed eligibility and treatment decisions" regarding patients. Since HMOs were created in order to hold down health care costs, Souter explained, allowing such suits "would be nothing less than elimination of the for-profit HMO." In addition, he said, allowing such suits would bring into federal court any medical malpractice case involving an HMO physician. "[T]he Federal Judiciary would be acting contrary to the congressional policy of allowing HMO organizations," Souter added, "if it were to entertain an ERISA fiduciary claim portending wholesale attacks on existing HMOs solely because of their structure. . . ."

Public Employees

Christensen v. Harris County, decided by a 6–3 vote, May 1, 2000; Thomas wrote the opinion; Stevens, Ginsburg, and Breyer dissented.

State and local governments can require public employees to take compensatory time off for having worked overtime.

The ruling backed state and local governments' interpretation of a 1985 law that created an exception to the general time-and-a-half overtime pay provisions of the federal Fair Labor Standards Act (FLSA). Under the 1985 amendments, state and local governments could grant employees time-and-a-half compensatory time off instead of cash for any overtime worked if there was "an agreement or understanding" with employees to that effect. Under the law, employees could choose when to take the accrued time off as long as their absence did not "unduly disrupt" the employer's operations. State and local governments contended that once there was such an agreement, they could dictate when employees took time off. Government employee unions disagreed. Federal appeals courts split on the question. The issue reached the Court in a suit brought by deputy sheriffs of Harris County, Texas, which includes Houston.

By a 6–3 vote, the Court upheld the ruling by the Fifth U.S. Circuit Court of Appeals backing the county's position. "[N]othing in the FLSA or its implementing regulations prohibits an employer from compelling the use of compensatory time," Thomas wrote. The ruling rejected the position taken by the Labor Department in an opinion letter written to the county earlier in the dispute. In a brief concurring opinion, Souter said the Court's ruling would not prevent the department from adopting formal regulations embodying its position.

Writing for the dissenters, Stevens said the ruling misinterpreted the statute's provision requiring government employers and employees to reach an agreement on the issue. "[R]ules regarding both the availability and the use of comp time must be contained within an *agreement*," Stevens wrote.

States

Immunity

Kimel v. Florida Board of Regents, decided by a 5–4 vote, January 11, 2000; O'Connor wrote the opinion; Stevens, Souter, Ginsburg, and Breyer dissented.

Congress has no power to authorize state government employees to sue states for violating the federal law against age discrimination.

The ruling—in a trio of consolidated suits brought by employees of state universities in Alabama and Florida and a Florida prison guard— invalidated as unconstitutional parts of 1974 amendments to the Age Discrimination in Employment Act. The amendments extended the 1967 law to state and local government employees and appeared to authorize them to sue to enforce the law. State governments challenged the provision, saying it violated the Eleventh Amendment's guarantee of sovereign immunity for the states against private damage suits. In a divided ruling, a panel of the Eleventh U.S. Circuit Court of Appeals ruled that the law did not "abrogate"—or override—the states' Eleventh Amendment protections.

By a 5–4 vote, the Court ruled that Congress had no power under the Fourteenth Amendment's enforcement provision to authorize private age discrimination suits against state governments. On a preliminary issue, the Court ruled—with Kennedy and Thomas dissenting—that Congress had intended to authorize private damage suits against states. But O'Connor said the enforcement provision was "disproportionate" to any problem of age discrimination by state governments. "Congress had virtually no reason to believe that state and local governments were unconstitutionally discriminating against their employees on the basis of age," O'Connor wrote.

The ruling did not nullify the substantive provisions of the law as applied to state governments. But writing for the four dissenters, Stevens said Congress had authority to provide for private enforcement of the act. "Congress' power to authorize federal remedies against state agencies that violate federal statutory obligations is coextensive with its power to impose those obligations on the States in the first place," he wrote. *(See story, pp. 46–51; excerpts, pp. 175–186.)*

Vermont Agency of Natural Resources v. United States ex rel. Stevens, decided by a 7–2 vote, May 22, 2000; Scalia wrote the opinion; Stevens and Souter dissented.

States cannot be sued by private individuals under the federal False Claims Act, a Civil War–era statute that permits suits to recover money for false or fraudulent claims against the federal government.

The ruling barred a suit initiated by a former employee of the Vermont Agency of Natural Resources, Jonathan Stevens, against his former agency for allegedly overstating the amount of staff time devoted to a federally funded program in order to increase federal aid to the state for the program. Stevens brought the suit—a so-called "qui tam" action—in the name of the United States with himself listed as a "relator." The False Claims Act, originally enacted in 1863 and significantly amended in 1986, authorized the procedure and provided that a private citizen could be awarded a portion of any funds recovered for the federal government through such a suit. The state sought to dismiss the suit on two grounds. It argued first that a private citizen had no standing to bring such a suit. Second, the state contended that it could not be sued under the law—either because a state was not a "person" subject to suit under the law or because the suit was barred under the Eleventh Amendment's general prohibition against private suits against state governments in federal court. A lower federal court and the Second U.S. Circuit Court of Appeals both rejected the state's arguments.

By a 7–2 vote, the Court ruled on the narrowest ground presented that the law did not include states within the definition of "persons" subject to suit under the act. Scalia said that the text of the law as enacted in 1863, along with a provision in the 1986 amendments for triple punitive damages in suits under the act and other features of the amended law, indicated that Congress did not intend to provide for private suits against states. On that basis, Scalia said it was unnecessary to decide whether states would be constitutionally immune from such suits, but noted, "[T]here is a serious doubt on that score." Five justices joined his opinion. In a brief opinion concurring in the judgment, Ginsburg agreed that the law did not authorize private suits against state governments, but noted that the decision left open whether the federal government itself could bring a suit under the law. Breyer joined her opinion as well as Scalia's.

Writing for the dissenters, Stevens argued that the law did allow suits against states. "[T]he law was intended to cover the full range of fraudulent acts, including those perpetrated by the States," he wrote. Stevens also rejected the state's argument that the Eleventh Amendment would bar such suits.

Taxation

Hunt-Wesson, Inc. v. Franchise Tax Board of California, decided by a 9–0 vote, February 22, 2000; Breyer wrote the opinion.

The Court ruled unconstitutional a California tax provision that limited the interest deduction that out-of-state corporations could take on the basis of the income generated by operations outside the state.

The ruling came in a suit filed by the Chicago-based food processing firm Beatrice Cos., seeking refunds and interest totaling $1.5 million for franchise taxes paid from 1980 to 1982. Beatrice, which later merged with Hunt-Wesson, challenged a provision that allowed an out-of-state corporation to take an interest deduction only to the extent that the amount exceeded out-of-state income arising from unrelated business activity. The company argued that the limit amounted to a levy on income with no "nexus" or connection to the state—so-called "nonunitary income"—that California was constitutionally barred from taxing. A state court of appeal rejected the argument.

Unanimously, the Court said the tax provision violated the Constitution's Commerce and Due Process Clauses. The provision, Breyer explained, "constitutes impermissible taxation of income outside its jurisdictional reach." The ruling seemed likely to have limited effect: Breyer said California's provision was unique among state and federal jurisdictions.

Water Rights

Arizona v. California, decided by a 6–3 vote, June 19, 2000; Ginsburg wrote the opinion; Rehnquist, O'Connor, and Thomas dissented.

The Court rejected an effort by Arizona and California and two local water districts to bar the Quechan Indian tribe from claiming water rights in the long-running litigation over allocating water from the Colorado River.

The ruling stemmed from a case that Arizona brought against California under the Supreme Court's "original" jurisdiction over disputes between states that sought to determine rights to the waters of the Colorado River. The Court resolved the major issues in a ruling in 1963 that allocated the water between seven Western states. One unsettled question was a claim by the Quechan Indian tribe to about 78,000 acre-feet of water per year—a relatively small amount—by virtue of the location of the tribe's Fort Yuma Reservation straddling the river along the Arizona-California border. The states and two local water districts in California argued that the tribe's claim—supported by the Clinton administration—was barred either by the 1963 ruling or by a 1983 consent decree in which the government paid the tribe $15 million to settle a dispute over ownership of 250,000 acres of the reservation. A "special master" appointed by the Court agreed that the claim was precluded by the 1983 consent decree.

By a 6–3 vote, the Court held that neither the tribe nor the government had forfeited its right to litigate the claim. Ginsburg said that the tribe's water rights had not been decided in the 1963 ruling and that the 1983 decree also failed to resolve the issue because it was "ambiguous" as to the tribe's ownership of the disputed lands.

Writing for the dissenters, Rehnquist said the tribe's claim was barred because it could have been decided in earlier proceedings. In her opinion, Ginsburg said that resolution of the Quechans' claim "will enable the Court to enter a final consolidated decree and bring this case to a close."

Torts

Racketeering

Beck v. Prupis, decided by a 7–2 vote, April 26, 2000; Thomas wrote the opinion; Stevens and Souter dissented.

A whistleblower fired from his job ordinarily cannot use a wrongful termination claim as a basis for a federal antiracketeering suit against his employer.

The ruling rejected a triple-damage suit under the federal Racketeer Influenced and Corrupt Organizations Act (RICO) filed by a Florida man, Robert Beck, against officers and directors of his former company, Southeastern Insurance Group. Beck claimed that he was fired after reporting various allegations of financial fraud and that the firing was part of a conspiracy in furtherance of a "pattern of racketeering activity" as defined by the law. The Eleventh U.S. Circuit Court of Appeals held that the firing could not provide the basis for a civil RICO claim unless it was itself an act of racketeering. Federal appeals courts had split on the issue.

By a 7–2 vote, the Court upheld the Eleventh Circuit's decision. "A person may not bring suit under (RICO) for injuries caused by an overt act that is not an act of racketeering or otherwise unlawful under the statute," Thomas wrote.

Writing for the dissenters, Stevens said RICO "does not require that [the plaintiff] be injured in his business or property by any particular kind of overt act in furtherance of the conspiracy."

Rotella v. Wood, decided by a 9–0 vote, February 23, 2000; Souter wrote the opinion.

The Court rejected an expansive rule for calculating the four-year time period for plaintiffs to bring a civil damage suit under the federal anti-racketeering law.

The ruling barred a suit under the federal Racketeer Influenced and Corrupt Organizations Act—commonly known as RICO—brought in 1997 by a Texas man, Mark Rotella, against doctors at a private psychiatric hospital outside Dallas where he had been treated for depression from 1985 to 1986. Rotella claimed that the doctors violated the racketeering law by conspiring to keep him in the hospital solely for financial reasons. The hospital argued the suit was barred by the four-year statute of limitations for RICO suits. Rotella contended that the time period did not begin to run until 1994, when he learned that the hospital's parent company had pleaded guilty to fraud charges. Rotella cited that conduct as the "pattern of racketeering" required for his RICO claim. A lower federal court and the Fifth U.S. Circuit Court of Appeals both held that the time period ended in 1990, rejecting the broader "injury and pattern discovery rule" Rotella advocated.

In a unanimous decision, the Court also rejected the broader statute of limitations. The pattern discovery rule, Souter said, "would extend the potential limitations period for most civil RICO cases well beyond the time when a plaintiff's cause of action is complete."

Chapter 4

Preview of the 2000–2001 Term

S mog and soot do more than foul the air and cloud visibility even on sunny days. Ground-level ozone—the chemical constituent of smog—impairs breathing for children, asthmatics, and other sensitive populations. Soot—microscopically small particles mainly produced from combustion of fossil fuels—also makes breathing more difficult for people outdoors. In addition, the tiny particles can settle in the lungs and cause serious illness or even premature death for elderly persons or people with heart or lung disease.

For years, environmental and public health advocates had been urging the federal Environmental Protection Agency (EPA) to use its power under the Clean Air Act to reduce the levels of ozone and "particulate matter" in the air. The country's biggest industries vigorously resisted. They warned that the most ambitious proposals would cost billions of dollars while achieving only relatively small public health benefits.

In June 1997, following a voluminous rulemaking proceeding at the EPA and an intense lobbying campaign waged within the White House itself, President Bill Clinton personally announced new rules setting stricter smog and soot standards for state and local governments over a ten-year period. "I approved some very strong new regulations today that will be somewhat controversial, but I think kids ought to be healthy," Clinton said at a June 26 conference on families in Nashville, Tennessee. The conference was hosted by Clinton's environment-minded vice president, Al Gore, who reportedly helped win Clinton's approval for the regulations over the opposition of White House economic advisers.

The business and industry groups that had fought the regulations did not give up. A coalition led by the U.S. Chamber of Commerce promptly challenged the regulations before the federal appeals court in Washington, D.C. Two years later, in a surprising ruling, the court sided with the industry groups in blocking the new rules from going into effect.

The outcome of the court case was not so surprising as the reason the two judges in the majority cited: a rarely used constitutional theory called the "nondelegation doctrine." Under the theory, Congress cannot delegate its legislative power to an administrative agency without providing sufficient guidance—an "intelligible principle"—for the agency to follow in adopting regulations. The Supreme Court had twice used the theory in 1935 to invalidate parts of President Franklin D. Roosevelt's New Deal program. But the doctrine lay dormant over the next sixty-plus years, despite the proliferation of broadly written laws for federal agencies to interpret and enforce.

The appeals court majority—two conservative judges appointed by President Ronald Reagan—stopped short of ruling the Clean Air Act itself unconstitutional. Instead, Judges Stephen Williams and Douglas Ginsburg said that the EPA had "construed [the act's key provisions] so loosely as to render them unconstitutional delegations of legislative power." On that basis, the judges said the EPA had to reconsider the rules and come up with its own "intelligible principle" to explain how it had chosen the specific levels for ozone and soot embodied in them. Even with that qualification, Judge David Tatel sharply dissented. The ruling, he said, "ignores the last half-century of Supreme Court jurisprudence."

The decision was all the more surprising in that the three judges unanimously agreed with the EPA on most of the other issues. In particular, the court rejected business groups' insistence that the Clean Air Act should be interpreted to require the EPA to weigh any health benefits of reducing air pollution against the costs. The appeals court had rejected that argument twenty years earlier, and business groups had been fighting the issue in the courts and in Congress ever since—but without success.

Business advocates and environmentalists alike immediately said that the court's decision on the nondelegation doctrine—if upheld—could portend a new era not only for the Clean Air Act but also for administrative law generally. "'If it is saying that EPA can't do it that way, other agencies can't do it this way either," said Robin Conrad, senior vice president of the National Chamber Litigation Center.

Almost exactly a year later, the Supreme Court decided to look at the issue. The justices agreed on May 22, 2000, to hear the government's appeal, filed in the name of EPA Administrator Carol Browner, who had issued the rules in 1997 and defended them vigorously since *(Browner v. American Trucking Associations, Inc.)*. Then, one week later, the justices raised the stakes by also agreeing to hear the business groups' cross-appeal on the cost-benefit issue. *(American Trucking Associations, Inc. v. Browner)*

EPA Administrator Carol Browner

Together, the two actions meant that the justices would consider early in the 2000–2001 term two of the most controversial legal issues in administrative law in the context of an environmental program regulating—literally—the very breath of life. "You couldn't get bigger environmental law issues before the Court," said Richard Lazarus, an environmental law expert and director of Georgetown University Law Center's Supreme Court Institute.

The consolidated Trucking Association cases were among thirty-four disputes that the justices placed on the calendar for the coming term before they began their summer recess at the end of June. The Court added thirteen cases to its calendar in September before the opening of the new term—one case on September 8 and a dozen cases on September 26 after the justices' all-day conference the previous day to go over petitions that had accumulated over the summer. That brought the number of cases scheduled for argument as the Court began the new term to forty-seven—comparable to the number at the same time in the previous two years: forty-four in 1999 and forty-five in 1998.

The case list did not—indeed, could not—top the stunning collection of issues the Court ruled on in the 1999–2000 term. But it promised more than enough, even at an early date, to engage opposing interest groups, Court watchers, and the justices themselves.

Fresh from a new pair of federalism rulings limiting the powers of Congress, the Court took up new challenges to expansive federal authority. In one case, the Court agreed to decide whether state employees could sue state governments under the Americans with Disabilities Act, which prohibited discrimination against persons with disabilities. The federal appeals court in Atlanta allowed suits under the law by two Alabama state employees, but the state argued that the ruling conflicted with the Court's decision in January holding that states have immunity from similar suits under the federal age discrimination law.

In a second federalism case, the Court was to rule on the scope of the federal government's regulatory authority under the Clean Water Act over isolated wetlands. The constitutional issue turned on the unlikely question whether the use of small, scattered wet spots as habitat by migratory birds had a sufficient effect on interstate commerce to sustain Congress's regulatory power under the Commerce Clause. The federal appeals court in Chicago said yes, but the Court's recent decisions had been narrowing Congress's flexibility in defining the scope of its commerce power.

The Court also took on three seemingly unrelated cases dealing with drug issues. In one case, the justices agreed to decide whether police could set up "narcotics checkpoints" similar to drunken-driving roadblocks. In another, the Court was to rule on a policy adopted by a public hospital in Charleston, South Carolina, of testing pregnant women for drugs and turning the information over to law enforcement. And in a third case the Court agreed to decide whether companies can fire employees for a positive drug test even if a labor arbitrator disagrees.

In a politically contentious case, the Court agreed to decide whether Congress violated the Constitution when it prohibited federally funded legal aid lawyers from engaging in welfare reform litigation. The restriction, part of a 1996 funding measure, was struck down by the federal appeals court in New York.

The justices also said they would rule on the constitutionality of laws passed by congressional term limit supporters in nine states that called for specifying congressional candidates' position on the issue on the Election Day ballot. And the Court took up—for the fourth time—a claim by white voters that North Carolina legislators had improperly considered race in drawing lines for one of the state's congressional districts.

Among criminal law cases, the justices agreed to decide an issue that could affect anyone who drives an automobile: whether police can arrest someone for a minor traffic violation. The federal appeals court in New Orleans, ruling in a case of a Texas woman arrested for not wearing a seat belt, said yes.

In business-related cases, the Court agreed to rule on the increasingly common practice among employers of requiring prospective employees to sign arbitration agreements relinquishing their right to go to court with any employment-related disputes. The justices also took up an important telecommunications issue: an appeal by a local telephone company challenging the way the Federal Communications Commission (FCC) calculated subsidies for providing service in high-cost areas.

Of the cases added in September, the one attracting most attention was a disability rights dispute between the Professional Golfers' Association (PGA) and the golfer Casey Martin, who was limited in his ability to walk because of a painful circulatory condition in his leg. Martin sued the PGA in 1997 under the Americans with Disabilities Act to force the association to grant him a waiver from its general rule prohibiting the use of golf carts during tournaments. The federal appeals court in San Francisco ruled in Martin's favor. It agreed that the waiver was a "reasonable accommodation" required under the disability rights law and rejected the PGA's argument that the waiver would give Martin an unfair advantage over other golfers. The federal appeals court in Chicago ruled the opposite way in another case, however, and the Court took up Martin's case to settle the issue. *(PGA Tour, Inc. v. Martin)*

The Court also added to its list of search-and-seizure cases by agreeing to decide whether law enforcement officers need a search warrant to use a thermal imaging device that helps police locate the high-intensity lights used in marijuana-growing operations. A convicted marijuana offender, Danny Lee Kyllo, was challenging a ruling by the federal appeals court in San Francisco that the use of the device did not constitute a search *(Kyllo v. United States)*. In another significant case, the Court agreed to decide whether private individuals can sue to enforce the Civil Rights Act provision that prohibits discrimination on the basis of race or national origin in state and local programs that receive federal money. The state of Alabama was appealing a ruling by the federal appeals court in Atlanta that allowed a private suit to challenge English-only driver's license tests. *(Alexander v. Sandoval)*

In the most eagerly awaited decision of the summer, however, the Court refused to expedite a ruling in the federal government's antitrust suit against the computer and software giant, Microsoft Corporation. The government had won a ruling from a federal judge in Washington in April requiring the partial breakup of the company because of a pattern of anti-competitive business practices. Microsoft appealed the ruling to the U.S. Court of Appeals for the District of Columbia Circuit. But the government invoked a law allowing the Court to take up direct appeals in antitrust cases of special importance rather than wait for rulings by the intermediate appeals courts.

The Court rejected the government's plea in a two-sentence order without explanation. Although the justices did not announce their vote, Breyer issued a brief dissent saying he would hear the appeal. "Speed in reaching a final decision may help create legal certainty," Breyer wrote. Observers generally viewed the Court's action delaying a final resolution of the case as a setback for the government. Nonetheless, the D.C. Circuit promptly said it would set an accelerated briefing schedule for the appeal.

Even with the new cases, the Court's calendar seemed less weighty than in some previous years. "So far the docket is missing the sort of lightning rod emotional issues that the last term ended with," commented Stephen Wermeil, director of the law and policy program at American University's Washington College of Law. "But in other respects the docket does reflect the themes that we know to be major points of interest for the Rehnquist Court—for example, more federalism issues and a fair amount of criminal procedure and civil rights fine-tuning."

Wermeil, who covered the Court for the *Wall Street Journal* for several years, noted that some of the other cases "are not as easy to pigeonhole," such as the disputes over drug roadblocks or restrictions on legal aid lawyers. "We're seeing a set of cases that are derivative of other recent cases," Wermeil said. "They're a little more complicated. They have variables that make them difficult to predict."

Smog and Soot Standards

The challenge to the EPA's smog and soot regulation involved what one environmental lawyer called "the heart and the soul" of the Clean Air Act: two provisions, sections 108 and 109, that authorized the agency to set maximum permissible levels for specified pollutants in the outside or "ambient" air.

Environmentalists contended that the 1970 act compared favorably to other regulatory statutes in specifying procedures and substantive criteria for the EPA to follow in administering the law. The act directed the EPA's

Haze obscures Philadephia's cityscape. The Supreme Court agreed to hear an industry challenge to new rules by the Environmental Protection Agency aimed at reducing ground-level smog and soot.

administrator to promulgate "national ambient air quality standards"—or NAAQS in bureaucratese—for any pollutant that "may reasonably be anticipated to endanger public health or welfare." The law required "primary" standards be set at levels that, "in the judgment of the administrator . . . and allowing an adequate margin of safety, are requisite to protect the public health." It specified secondary standards to be set at levels "requisite to protect the public welfare from any known or anticipated adverse effects."

The law required the administrator to rely on "air quality criteria" that "accurately reflect the latest scientific knowledge. . . ." Toward that end, the statute required the appointment of a seven-member advisory committee to recommend new standards or revision of existing ones. The administrator was to explain any departure from the committee's recommendation. In addition, the standards were to be reviewed at least at five-year intervals.

Once the EPA established an air quality standard for a particular pollutant, it was to designate parts of the country that had attained that standard and the "nonattainment" areas where the standard was not met. Each state was responsible for developing an "implementation plan" to meet the specified standard within its border.

Through the 1970s, the EPA established standards for six pollutants: sulfur dioxide, carbon monoxide, nitrogen oxide, lead, ozone, and particulate matter. By the 1990s, environmental experts agreed that the standards had contributed to dramatic progress in cleaning up the nation's air. In particular, airborne lead—which can cause mental retardation and other brain damage in young children—had been virtually eliminated.

Ozone had also been substantially reduced following the adoption of a standard in 1979 that prescribed no more than 120 parts per billion of ozone in the air as averaged over a one-hour period. As of the mid-1990s, however, more than 100 million people lived in areas, mostly cities, where the ozone standard had not been met. In addition, the EPA had evidence of serious health effects from soot at concentrations below those set in the 1987 standard for particulate matter.

Each of the EPA's rulemakings was long and hard. None was harder than the decade-long fight over the lead standard. That battle climaxed in 1980 with a decision in the EPA's favor by the U.S. Court of Appeals for the District of Columbia Circuit. Ruling in the so-called *Lead Industries Association* case, the appeals court upheld the EPA's standard and, significantly for future cases, rejected the industry's effort to require the agency to consider costs in setting standards. The Supreme Court refused to review the decision.

The Court itself in the same year turned aside an effort to require cost-benefit analyses in the setting of workplace safety standards by the federal Occupational Safety and Health Administration (OSHA). The justices voted 5–4 in *Industrial Union Department v. American Petroleum Institute* to strike down the benzene standard as arbitrary, but only one of the justices—Lewis F. Powell Jr.—voted in a separate concurrence to incorporate cost-benefit calculations in the decisionmaking process.

Rehnquist, then an associate justice, also concurred separately in an opinion that called for a revival of the nondelegation doctrine. Acknowledging that the theory had fallen into disfavor since the New Deal, Rehnquist nonetheless used it as his rationale for striking down OSHA's benzene standard. "We ought not to shy away from our judicial duty to invalidate unconstitutional delegations of legislative authority solely out of concern that we should thereby reinvigorate discredited constitutional doctrine of the pre–New Deal era," Rehnquist wrote.

Through the 1980s and 1990s, Congress considered a host of regulatory reform proposals, including a variety of bills to require agencies to use cost-benefit analyses in adopting new rules. But no omnibus cost-benefit requirement was enacted. Congress amended the Clean Air Act several times, including a major overhaul in 1990, but industry groups failed to persuade lawmakers to attach a cost-benefit calculus to the air quality standards sections.

As for the nondelegation doctrine, it showed no sign of life. Congress gave some lip service to the need to give better guidance to regulatory agencies, but the goal typically gave way to the need for compromise in the legislative process and the need for agency discretion in the administrative process. The Court itself evinced no interest. In one notable case, the Court in 1989 unanimously rejected an argument that Congress had violated the doctrine in setting up the federal Sentencing Commission. Scalia, who dissented on another ground, all but buried the doctrine, at least as a judicial remedy: "[W]e have almost never felt qualified to second-guess Congress regarding the permissible degree of policy judgment that can be left to those executing or applying the law."

As EPA administrator since the start of the Clinton administration in 1993, Browner had plenty of problems on her plate without worrying about arcane legal theories. The career environmentalist, who worked for Gore in the Senate in the 1980s, gained a reputation for fearlessness as she presided over an agency with a formidable list of political opponents and a daunting set of organizational and managerial challenges.

The revisions of the smog and soot standards that got under way in 1996 were long overdue. Ozone had not been reviewed since 1979, particulate matter not since 1987. The rules that emerged after a ferocious fight included two major changes. The new ozone regulation set a more stringent standard of 80 parts per billion, averaged over an eight-hour period, replacing the standard of 120 parts per million over a one-hour period. On smog, the new rule tightened the standard for so-called "coarse particulate matter"—measuring 10 micrometers in diameter or PM_{10}—and for the first time included a standard for so-called "fine particles"—measuring 2.5 micrometers in diameter ($PM_{2.5}$).

Browner described the new rules as "a major step forward" that would provide new health protections to 125 million Americans, including 35 million children. Environmental organizations praised the new rules, but an industry coalition said they amounted to a "crushing blow" to the economy. Business groups mounted a full-scale legal attack on the rules before the U.S. Court of Appeals for the District of Columbia Circuit, the designated forum for hearing challenges to the EPA's air quality standards.

In sending the standards back to the EPA for reconsideration, the appeals court majority said that the agency had failed to explain how it had decided what level of ozone or particulate matter would be tolerated.

"EPA's formulation of its policy judgment leaves it free to pick any point between zero and a hair below the concentration yielding London's Killer Fog," the court wrote, referring to a 1952 air pollution incident that left some 4,000 people dead.

In its petition for Supreme Court review, the solicitor general's office called the appeals court decision "a radical departure from settled law respecting the nondelegation doctrine." It warned that the court's approach "would unjustifiably expand the role of the courts in reviewing agency action."

The business groups followed with a cross-petition urging the Court to consider the doctrine of the *Lead Industries* decision that the EPA was barred from making cost-benefit calculations in setting air quality standards. Cost factors "*must* be considered at the outset, in standard-setting," the business groups contended.

As the opposing lawyers and interest groups worked on their legal briefs, the lead attorney for the business groups appeared to be soft-pedaling the nondelegation doctrine somewhat and instead emphasizing the cost-benefit issue. "Fundamentally, the case is about the Supreme Court's opportunity to correct what's been a twenty-year error by the Court of Appeals in interpreting the Clean Air Act in a one-sided way which doesn't consider any of the common sense factors that have to weigh in the balance in setting standards," said Edward Warren, a lawyer with a Washington firm who had successfully represented the business groups that challenged the benzene standards in 1980.

As for the nondelegation doctrine, Warren said, "I would certainly urge the Court to address the statutory issues because, if they do, the constitutional issues don't have to be addressed squarely."

For their part, environmental and public health advocates insisted that business groups were wrong on both issues. Howard Fox, managing attorney with Earthjustice Legal Defense Fund, who was representing the American Lung Association in the case, said that Congress had deliberately decided in 1970 to omit any requirement for the EPA to consider costs in setting national air quality standards. "Congress wanted the standards to be an accurate picture of what the public health requires," Fox said. "At that point, the attention turns to how to clean up the air to that level of pollution. At that point, the states can consider those costs."

As for the nondelegation doctrine, Fox said the business groups "want to throw out fifty to sixty years of Supreme Court precedents that say Congress doesn't have to stand behind the EPA's administrator and use its congressional hand to guide the administrator's hand to a specific number. Congress can leave the agency with sufficient room to make a policy judgment."

In handicapping the case, Professor Lazarus said that he expected the government to prevail on the nondelegation issue. "One has to assume that there are four pretty solid votes not to buy into resurrecting the delegation doctrine," Lazarus said, referring to the bloc of four liberal justices: Stevens, Souter, Ginsburg, and Breyer. He said that O'Connor and Kennedy also seemed likely to shy away from the issue for fear of raising constitutional doubts about "a whole host of other, settled federal statutory schemes."

The cost-benefit issue might be more problematic for the government, Lazarus said, in part because of views that Breyer expressed before his appointment to the Court. Breyer "has long expressed skepticism of the environmental statutes and the extent to which they do not allow for consideration of costs," Lazarus explained. "The question becomes to what extent his stated views on policy will influence his decision on statutory construction." Without Breyer's vote, Lazarus concluded, "[i]t's hard to imagine the government winning."

The briefing schedule in the consolidated cases was complicated. Lawyers filed their briefs on the nondelegation issue in late July; briefs on the cost-benefit issue were filed in early September, and the last of the reply briefs in the first week of October, shortly after the opening of the new term. Arguments were scheduled for November 7—coincidentally, Election Day.

Following are some of the other major cases on the Supreme Court's calendar as it began its 2000–2001 term:

Criminal Law and Procedure

Drug Roadblocks. The city of Indianapolis asked the Court to allow it to resume a practice of using police roadblocks and drug-sniffing dogs to try to catch motorists carrying illegal narcotics in their vehicles.

The city operated the "narcotics checkpoint" program between August and November 1998, stopped some 1,100 motorists, and arrested fifty-five persons for drug charges and forty-nine for other offenses. Two motorists who were stopped but not charged challenged the program in federal court as a violation of the Fourth Amendment's prohibition against "unreasonable" seizures. A lower federal court judge ruled the program legal, likening it to drunken-driving roadblocks that had been upheld by the Supreme Court. In a 2–1 decision, however, the Seventh U.S. Circuit Court of Appeals ruled the program illegal, calling it "a pretext for a dragnet search for criminals."

In asking the Court to reverse the decision, lawyers for the city said the government's interests in battling illegal drugs outweighed what they called the "minimal intrusions on motorists." But lawyers for the American Civil Liberties Union, representing the plaintiffs, said the city was seeking "to create a new exception to the Fourth Amendment." *(City of Indianapolis v. Edmond)*

Traffic Arrests. The Court agreed to decide whether the Fourth Amendment prohibits police from arresting a motorist for a minor traffic offense.

Gail Atwater raised the issue after a Lago Vista, Texas, officer placed her under arrest on March 26, 1997, for violating the city's ordinance requiring motorists to wear seat belts. Atwater was handcuffed in view of her children, who also were not wearing seat belts; taken to the police station; fingerprinted and booked; and held in jail for an hour before being taken before a magistrate. Later, she pleaded no contest to the offense and paid the maximum fine of $50.

Atwater filed a federal civil rights suit, contending that the arrest violated the Fourth Amendment's prohibition against unreasonable seizures. The suit was rejected by a lower-court judge, reinstated by a three-judge appeals court panel, and then rejected again by the full Fifth U.S. Circuit Court of Appeals in an 11–6 decision.

In appealing the decision, Atwater's lawyers argued that the "millions of licensed drivers do not expect to be placed under custodial arrest for traffic offenses punished only by fines." But lawyers for the city said Atwater's Fourth Amendment rights were not violated. "Her arrest was effected in a public place, with probable cause, and without the use of excessive physical force," the city's lawyers said. *(Atwater v. Lago Vista)*

Home Search. The Court agreed to decide whether police can prevent a resident from entering his home for the time needed to obtain a search warrant.

Police in Sullivan, Illinois, following up information that Charles McArthur had marijuana inside his trailer home, kept McArthur on the porch for a little over two hours while getting a search warrant after McArthur refused to consent to a search. In seeking to suppress the drugs found in the search, McArthur contended that the officers violated his

Fourth Amendment rights by preventing him from going inside, even though he acknowledged that he would have destroyed the drugs if allowed into the trailer. The trial judge and the Illinois Appellate Court both agreed that the officers' action amounted to an "unconstitutional seizure" of the premises.

The case posed a question left open by the Court's splintered decision in 1984 holding that police could secure a house from the inside. In urging the Court to hear the case, the Illinois attorney general's office argued that the "external impoundment" was justified because of the "very limited" nature of the seizure and the state's "compelling" interest in preventing the destruction of evidence. But McArthur's attorneys argued that police should be barred from "warrantless . . . seizures" of a home in cases of misdemeanors or petty offenses. *(Illinois v. McArthur)*

Election Law

Term Limits. The state of Missouri asked the Court to reinstate a voter initiative requiring that that congressional candidates' position on the issue of term limits be listed beside their names on the general election ballot.

Missouri was one of nine states that adopted so-called "informed voter" provisions following the Court's 1995 decisions that term limits could be imposed on members of Congress only by a constitutional amendment proposed by Congress and then approved by three-fourths of the states. The initiative included a provision ostensibly instructing members of the state's congressional delegation to vote for a term limits amendment. It went on to provide that any representative or senator who failed to vote for term limits would be identified on the next ballot by the designation, "Disregarded voters' instructions on term limits." Nonincumbent candidates would be asked to pledge to vote for term limits and those who declined to make the pledge would be identified on the ballot by a similar designation.

Donald Gralike, a candidate for the House in the 1998, challenged the initiative on several federal constitutional grounds. A lower federal court ruled the measure invalid for three reasons. First, the court held, the measure added a qualification for election to Congress, in violation of the so-called "Qualifications Clause" in Article I of the Constitution. Second, the provision was held to violate the free speech rights of congressional candidates. And third, the provision "usurped" Congress's role to amend the Constitution by allowing the people to propose a constitutional amendment. The Eighth U.S. Circuit Court of Appeals upheld the lower court's reasoning on all three grounds and added a fourth. It said the initiative violated the so-called "Speech and Debate Clause" by allowing the citizenry to comment on the official acts of members of Congress.

In seeking Court review, the Missouri attorney general's office denied that the initiative added a new qualification for election to Congress, intruded on Congress's powers, or unconstitutionally infringed on candidates' free speech rights. "[T]he people's fundamental interest in preserving their voice in government," the state's lawyers wrote, "outweighs any slight effect [the initiative] may have on the free speech rights of candidates for Congress." But lawyers for Gralike and a second congressional candidate who intervened after Gralike withdrew his candidacy countered that the initiative was "a patently unconstitutional effort . . . to circumvent [the Court's term limits ruling] by dictating that all candidates for Congress support a constitutional term limits amendment . . . and by attaching pejorative ballot labels next to the names of those candidates who hold different views." *(Cook v. Gralike)*

Racial Redistricting. The Court agreed to take up for the fourth time a decade-long redistricting dispute over the shape and racial makeup of a North Carolina congressional district.

The dispute involved North Carolina's new twelfth congressional district, which was created because of population increases after the 1990 census and originally drawn to include a majority African American population. The Court in 1992 allowed white voters to challenge the oddly shaped district as a racial gerrymander and in 1996—following a lower court ruling—ruled the plan unconstitutional because race had been the predominant factor in drawing the district.

In the new appeal, the state of North Carolina and the NAACP Legal Defense and Educational Fund asked the Court to uphold a 1997 redistricting plan that redrew the district to be somewhat more compact and to include about a 46 percent African American population. A three-judge federal court ruled the district unconstitutional because it too closely resembled the original, invalid district.

Attorneys for the state insisted that North Carolina legislators drew up the new plan in order to create a safe Democratic district in the center of the state. The lower court, the state's lawyers argued, "wrongly equated mere consideration of race with racial gerrymandering." Lawyers for the white voters challenging the plan countered that the high percentage of African Americans included in the district "was designed to ensure that the vast majority of those voting in the Democratic primary would be African-

American and to make sure that an African-American Democratic nominee would win the seat." *(Hunt v. Cromartie; Smallwood v. Cromartie)*

Environmental Law

Wetlands. The Court agreed to decide whether the federal government can use the Clean Water Act to regulate the filling of small, isolated wetlands solely because they provide habitat to migratory birds.

The case stemmed from an effort by the regional Solid Waste Agency of Northern Cook County (Chicago) dating from 1985 to find a new landfill site. The 17.6 acre forested site it located included seasonally wet depressions left from a previous strip mining operation. The Clean Water Act prohibits discharging "dredged or fill material" into "waters of the United States," which are defined by regulation to include any wetlands "the use, degradation or destruction of which could affect interstate commerce." The Army Corps of Engineers, applying that definition, denied the permit to fill the site because breaking up the forest would cause "unmitigable" impacts to "area sensitive birds." The agency appealed the decision to federal court. It contended that the wetlands regulation went beyond the statutory definition or, alternatively, that Congress had no power under the Commerce Clause to regulate individual wetlands solely because of effects on migratory birds. A lower court and the Seventh U.S. Circuit Court of Appeals both upheld the Corps' decision.

In its appeal, the agency argued that the Corps' interpretation of its jurisdiction was too broad. "Virtually any water body is or could be used as a feeding or resting place by some of the five billion birds that migrate over the continental United States each year," lawyers for the agency wrote. But the government contended that the Corps' migratory bird rule "fits comfortably within Congress's commerce power" and would not "impermissibly impinge on the authority of state and local governments." *(Solid Waste Agency of Northern Cook County v. U.S. Army Corps of Engineers)*

Federal Government

Telephone Rates. The local telephone company GTE Corp. asked the Court to set aside an FCC rule limiting subsidies for providing universal telephone service in high-cost areas.

The rule stemmed from provisions in the Telecommunications Act of 1996, which opened local telephone service to competition. The law directed the FCC to establish a universal service fund to ensure continuing subsidies for service in remote rural areas. All providers of telecommunications services were to contribute to the fund, and the proceeds were to go to local telephone companies that serve high-cost areas. In establishing the fund, the FCC decided to base the subsidy not on the telephone companies' cost of setting up their networks but on the anticipated lower costs of providing services in the future. The Fifth U.S. Circuit Court of Appeals upheld that part of the FCC's order.

In appealing the decision, lawyers for GTE argued that the FCC rule amounted to an uncompensated taking of its property in violation of the so-called "Takings Clause" of the Fifth Amendment. The FCC's rule, the lawyers wrote, "understates the costs that real-world carriers actually face in operating their networks and thus fails to provide sufficient compensation." But the government disagreed: "There is no reason to assume that the FCC's forward-looking cost methodology will produce confiscatory results in any context." (*GTE Service Corp. v. Federal Communications Commission*)

Medical Devices. The Court agreed to decide whether federal law regulating medical devices preempts product liability suits in state courts for fraud on the Food and Drug Administration (FDA) in obtaining approval to market a new device.

The issue stemmed from a consolidated case involving more than 2,300 claims against the Buckman Company, a regulatory consultant firm, for alleged fraud in obtaining the FDA's approval for the marketing of a surgical screw. The FDA barred initial applications for use of the screw with spinal implants, but approved a later application to market the device for use in arm and leg bones. Many orthopedic surgeons legally used the screw for spinal implants—a so-called "off-label use." Patients who claimed injuries from the operations sued Buckman for fraud in state courts. A lower federal court ruled that the Medical Device Amendments to the FDA's charter preempted the suits, but the Third U.S. Circuit Court of Appeals disagreed.

In appealing the decision, lawyers for the company argued, "The FDA, not the courts, is the appropriate forum for considering such claims." The plaintiffs' lawyers countered, "[N]othing in federal law . . . precluded plaintiffs from seeking damages for injuries proximately caused for fraud on the FDA. . . ." (*Buckman Company v. Plaintiffs Legal Committee*)

First Amendment

Legal Aid Lawyers. The Court agreed to decide whether Congress violated free speech principles in 1996 when it barred federally funded legal aid lawyers from engaging in welfare reform litigation.

The limitation was one of an array of restrictions that Congress included in the 1996 appropriations measure for the Legal Services Corporation (LSC), the quasi-independent body that funnels federal funds to state and local organizations providing legal aid for the poor. The provision barred the use of any LSC funds by any lawyer in connection with "litigation, lobbying, or rulemaking, involving an effort to reform a Federal or State welfare system." But it did allow lawyers to represent "an individual eligible client who is seeking specific relief from a welfare agency if such relief does not involve an effort to amend or otherwise challenge existing law. . . ."

The provisions were challenged in federal court in New York City by a variety of plaintiffs, including legal aid clients, lawyers, donors, and organizations. Carmen Velazquez, the lead plaintiff, was a welfare recipient who—because of the restriction—was unable to challenge a state regulation that prevented her from contesting a termination of welfare benefits. A federal district court judge upheld the regulations. On appeal, the Second U.S. Circuit Court of Appeals upheld all but one of the restrictions. But, by a 2–1 vote, the appeals court held that the so-called "suit for benefits" limitation amounted to unconstitutional viewpoint discrimination in a government subsidy program in violation of the First Amendment. In a separate case, the Ninth U.S. Circuit Court of Appeals had upheld all the restrictions.

In urging the Court to uphold the restriction, both the Legal Services Corporation and the Justice Department argued that Congress was not required—as the LSC brief put it—"to subsidize the attempted overhaul of its welfare system." But attorneys from the Brennan Center for Justice at New York University Law School, representing the challengers, argued that Congress "may not selectively allocate speech subsidies in a viewpoint-discriminatory manner, especially when . . . Congress is attempting to shield the government's own viewpoint from effective challenge." (*Legal Services Corp. v. Velazquez; United States v. Velazquez*)

Judicial Review. An adult bookstore in Waukesha, Wisconsin, challenged a local licensing ordinance because it allowed the city to revoke its license and close the business without prior judicial review.

The dispute arose after the Waukesha Common Council refused in December 1995 to renew the annual license of an adult bookstore, City News and Novelty, located in the city's downtown. The council found the store had violated provisions aimed at curbing illicit sex by requiring viewing booths to be open to public view. Attorneys for the store challenged the ordinance on a variety of constitutional grounds, including the failure to provide for preserving the status quo during judicial review of a license denial. Wisconsin courts upheld the ordinance, noting that the city council could not dictate a schedule for state courts in such cases.

In asking the Court to review the decision, attorneys for the bookstore argued that the ordinance "has the potential for long-term suppression of expression prior to any type of judicial review." But the city attorney countered by noting the city's inability to set a deadline for courts to act: "Preserving the status quo throughout the judicial process would do absolutely nothing to hasten review." (*City News and Novelty, Inc. v. Waukesha*)

Individual Rights

Drug Testing. A group of women from Charleston, South Carolina, asked the Court to reinstate their challenge to a public hospital's discontinued policy of testing pregnant women for drugs in order to provide the results to police for arrest and prosecution.

The ten women sued Charleston and state officials for damages and injunctive relief over a drug testing policy in effect from 1989 to 1993 at a city hospital with a predominantly African American patient population. The policy called for drug testing of urine samples taken from women with specified indications of possible cocaine use. Positive results were turned over to Charleston police, who had helped set up the program with the hospital staff and the city solicitor's office. Some 259 women tested positive under the policy before its suspension because of litigation; thirty were arrested, including nine of the plaintiffs.

The women claimed the policy was illegal on a variety of grounds, including as a violation of the Fourth Amendment's prohibition against "unreasonable" searches. A federal court jury rejected the women's suit after finding that they consented to the search. On appeal, the Fourth U.S. Circuit Court of Appeals—without reaching the consent issue—ruled, 2–1, that the hospital policy was justified by a so-called "special needs" exception to the Fourth Amendment, permitting searches that serve important governmental purposes other than law enforcement. The full appeals court refused to rehear the case on an 8–5 vote.

In seeking Court review, attorneys for the Center for Reproductive Law and Policy argued that Fourth Amendment protections "would disappear" under the appeals court's decision. "Women seeking medical care at public hospitals . . . have, if anything, a *heightened* expectation of privacy with respect to their medical care and records," the attorneys wrote. But attorneys for the city argued that the "minimal intrusion" on the women's privacy was justified by the need to deal with what they called "an epidemic of cocaine use among [the hospital's] maternity patient base and the serious consequent health problems and associated fiscal costs." *(Ferguson v. City of Charleston)*

Wiretapping Suit. The Court agreed to decide whether someone can be punished under antiwiretapping laws for disclosing the contents of an illegally intercepted telephone call if he or she had nothing to do with the original interception.

The important, unsettled privacy issue stemmed from a suit by two Pennsylvania teachers union officials, Gloria Bartnicki and Anthony Kane, against a rival union leader and a radio talk show host for airing a surreptitiously recorded cell phone conversation. Kane, president of the Wyoming Valley teachers union, was heard in the recording making threatening comments about the local school board over wage negotiations. The recording was given anonymously to Jack Yocum, president of a rival teachers union, who gave it to a radio talk show host, Frederick Vopper, who in turn aired it on his program.

Bartnicki, the Pennsylvania State Education Association's liaison to local unions, and Kane sued Yocum, Vopper, and the two radio stations that carried Vopper's program for violating the federal and state antiwiretapping laws. Both laws provided for civil damages against anyone who—in the federal statute's words—"intentionally discloses" the contents of an illegally intercepted telephone conversation "knowing or having reason to know" that the information was obtained illegally. The Third U.S. Circuit Court of Appeals, however, ruled that the First Amendment prohibited punishing anyone who was not personally involved in violating the law.

In urging the Court to hear the case, lawyers for Bartnicki and Kane argued that broader liability was necessary because of "the ease with which electronic communications and the harm that is caused when . . . intercepted communications are disclosed. . . ." But lawyers for the defendants countered that someone who disclosed "information of significant public concern" should not be punished if he "played no role" in violating wire-tapping laws. *(Bartnicki v. Vopper, United States v. Vopper)*

Labor Law

Arbitration. A West Virginia coal company asked the Court to set aside a labor arbitrator's decision so that it could fire a truck driver who had twice tested positive for use of marijuana.

Eastern Associated Coal Corporation was appealing a decision by the Fourth U.S. Circuit Court of Appeals upholding an arbitrator's ruling in a union grievance proceeding to reinstate the driver, James Smith. Smith tested positive for marijuana in March 1996 when he first moved into the driver's position and again in a random drug test in June 1997. The company twice sought to fire Smith, but an arbitrator reinstated him both times. The company filed suit in federal court after the second decision, arguing that it violated public policy. But the lower court and the Fourth Circuit both upheld the arbitrator's decision, saying that public policy did not require automatic discharge for a positive drug test.

In seeking review, the company argued, "Reinstatement of a commercial driver who has twice failed a drug test within 15 months violates . . . clear public policy." But lawyers for the United Mine Workers, representing Smith, argued the court's ruling "goes too far toward undermining the finality of arbitration awards and toward permitting the courts to substitute their resolution of a collective bargaining issue for the resolution provided by the parties" in the contract. *(Eastern Associated Coal Corp. v. United Mine Workers, District 17)*

In a second arbitration case, the Court agreed to decide whether federal law allows businesses to enforce agreements that require employees to use arbitration rather than filing lawsuits over employment-related disputes.

Circuit City Stores, a national electronics retailer, asked the Court to block Saint Clair Adams, an employee in its Santa Rosa, California, store, from suing the company in state court for sexual harassment claims. The company had required Adams to sign a pre-employment agreement requiring arbitration for all employment-related claims. The Federal Arbitration Act, passed in 1925, generally provides for court enforcement of arbitration agreements, but excludes "contracts of employment of seamen, railroad employees, or any other class of workers engaged in foreign or interstate commerce." The Ninth U.S. Circuit Court of Appeals ruled that the exclusion applied to Adams's agreement and allowed him to proceed with his state court suit.

In seeking to overturn the decision, Circuit City contended that the exclusion applied only to the specific groups of transportation workers named, not to all employees generally. But lawyers for Adams disagreed, noting that the act was passed at a time when Congress was thought to have only limited power over employment relations. *(Circuit City Stores, Inc. v. Adams)*

States

Workers with Disabilities. The state of Alabama asked the Court to overturn a federal appeals court decision that allowed state employees to sue the state for damages for claimed violations of the Americans with Disabilities Act (ADA).

In one of the cases, Patricia Garrett, a nurse at the University of Alabama Hospital in Birmingham, claimed that she was demoted after she returned to work following chemotherapy for breast cancer. In the other case, Milton Ash, a security officer at a youth correctional facility, claimed that managers failed to make reasonable accommodations—as required by the law—for several chronic physical conditions, including asthma and sleep apnea. The Eleventh U.S. Circuit Court of Appeals rejected the state's argument that the suits were barred by sovereign immunity.

In its appeal, the state contended that Congress had no power under the Fourteenth Amendment to authorize employee suits against state governments under the disability rights law because there was no evidence of unconstitutional discrimination by the states against disabled workers. "Congress did not identify any pattern or practice of unconstitutional State action," lawyers for the state wrote. They emphasized the Court's ruling earlier in the year in *Kimel v. Florida Board of Regents* that barred state employees from suing state governments for violations of the federal Age Discrimination in Employment Act.

On the other side, lawyers for the two employees and for the Justice Department urged the Court to allow the suits to proceed. The law "falls squarely within Congress's comprehensive legislative power under Section 5 of the Fourteenth Amendment to prohibit, remedy, and prevent violations of the rights secured by that Amendment," the government said in its brief.

The case also attracted an unusual brief by former president George Bush, who signed the ADA into law in 1990, in support of the two employees. "Given the pervasive nature of discrimination faced by individuals with disabilities. . . ," Bush's lawyers wrote, "it was critical that the legislation be comprehensive and cover both public and private entities." *(University of Alabama Board of Trustees v. Garrett)*

Appendix

Opinion Excerpts

Following are excerpts from some of the most important rulings of the Supreme Court's 1999–2000 term. They appear in the order in which they were announced. Footnotes and legal citations are omitted.

Nos. 98-791 and 98-796

J. Daniel Kimel, Jr., et al., Petitioners v. Florida Board of Regents et al.
United States, Petitioner v. Florida Board of Regents et al.

On writs of certiorari to the United States Court of Appeals for the Eleventh Circuit

[January 11, 2000]

JUSTICE O'CONNOR delivered the opinion of the Court.

The Age Discrimination in Employment Act of 1967 (ADEA or Act), as amended, 29 U.S.C. §621 *et seq.*, makes it unlawful for an employer, including a State, "to fail or refuse to hire or to discharge any individual or otherwise discriminate against any individual . . . because of such individual's age." 29 U.S.C. §623(a)(1). In these cases, three sets of plaintiffs filed suit under the Act, seeking money damages for their state employers' alleged discrimination on the basis of age. In each case, the state employer moved to dismiss the suit on the basis of its Eleventh Amendment immunity. The District Court in one case granted the motion to dismiss, while in each of the remaining cases the District Court denied the motion. Appeals in the three cases were consolidated before the Court of Appeals for the Eleventh Circuit, which held that the ADEA does not validly abrogate the States' Eleventh Amendment immunity. In these cases, we are asked to consider whether the ADEA contains a clear statement of Congress' intent to abrogate the States' Eleventh Amendment immunity and, if so, whether the ADEA is a proper exercise of Congress' constitutional authority. We conclude that the ADEA does contain a clear statement of Congress' intent to abrogate the States' immunity, but that the abrogation exceeded Congress' authority under §5 of the Fourteenth Amendment.

I

A

The ADEA makes it unlawful for an employer "to fail or refuse to hire or to discharge any individual or otherwise discriminate against any individual with respect to his compensation, terms, conditions, or privileges of employment, because of such individual's age." 29 U.S.C. §623(a)(1). The Act also provides several exceptions to this broad prohibition. . . . Although the Act's prohibitions originally applied only to individuals "at least forty years of age but less than sixty-five years of age," Congress subsequently removed the upper age limit, and the Act now covers individuals age 40 and over. Any person aggrieved by an employer's violation of the Act "may bring a civil action in any court of competent jurisdiction" for legal or equitable relief. §626(c)(1). Section 626(b) also permits aggrieved employees to enforce the Act through certain provisions of the Fair Labor Standards Act of 1938 (FLSA), and the ADEA specifically incorporates §16(b) of the FLSA, 29 U.S.C. §216(b).

Since its enactment, the ADEA's scope of coverage has been expanded by amendment. Of particular importance to these cases is the Act's treatment of state employers and employees. When first passed in 1967, the ADEA applied only to private employers. . . . In 1974, in a statute consisting primarily of amendments to the FLSA, Congress extended application of the ADEA's substantive requirements to the States. Fair Labor Standards Amendments of 1974 (1974 Act), §28. Congress accomplished that expansion in scope by a simple amendment to the definition of "employer" contained in 29 U.S.C. §630(b): "The term [employer] also means . . . a State or political subdivision of a State and any agency or instrumentality of a State or a political subdivision of a State. . . ." Congress also amended the ADEA's definition of "employee," still defining the term to mean "an individual employed by any employer," but excluding elected officials and appointed policymakers at the state and local levels. §630(f). In the same 1974 Act, Congress amended 29 U.S.C. §216(b), the FLSA enforcement provision incorporated by reference into the ADEA. Section 216(b) now permits an individual to bring a civil action "against any employer (including a public agency) in any Federal or State court of competent jurisdiction." Section 203(x) defines "[p]ublic agency" to include "the Government of a State or political subdivision thereof," and "any agency of . . . a State, or a political subdivision of a State." Finally, in the 1974 Act, Congress added a provision prohibiting age discrimination generally in employment at the Federal Government. 29 U.S.C. §633a. Under the current ADEA, mandatory age limits for law enforcement officers and firefighters—at federal, state, and local levels—are exempted from the statute's coverage.

B

In December 1994, Roderick MacPherson and Marvin Narz, ages 57 and 58 at the time, filed suit under the ADEA against their employer, the University of Montevallo, in the United States District Court for the Northern District of Alabama.

In their complaint, they alleged that the university had discriminated against them on the basis of their age, that it had retaliated against them for filing discrimination charges with the Equal Employment Opportunity Commission (EEOC), and that its College of Business, at which they were associate professors, employed an evaluation system that had a disparate impact on older faculty members. MacPherson and Narz sought declaratory and injunctive relief, backpay, promotions to full professor, and compensatory and punitive damages. The University of Montevallo moved to dismiss the suit for lack of subject matter jurisdiction, contending it was barred by the Eleventh Amendment. No party disputes the District Court's holding that the University is an instrumentality of the State of Alabama. On September 9, 1996, the District Court granted the University's motion. The court determined that, although the ADEA contains a clear statement of Congress' intent to abrogate the States' Eleventh Amendment immunity, Congress did not enact or extend the ADEA under its Fourteenth Amendment §5 enforcement power. The District Court therefore held that the ADEA did not abrogate the States' Eleventh Amendment immunity.

In April 1995, a group of current and former faculty and librarians of Florida State University, including J. Daniel Kimel, Jr., the named petitioner in one of today's cases, filed suit against the Florida Board of Regents in the United States District Court for the Northern District of Florida. The complaint was subsequently amended to add as plaintiffs current and former faculty and librarians of Florida International University. The plaintiffs, all over age 40, alleged that the Florida Board of Regents refused to require the two state universities to allocate funds to provide previously agreed upon market adjustments to the salaries of eligible university employees. The plaintiffs contended that the failure to allocate the funds violated both the ADEA and the Florida Civil Rights Act of 1992 because it had a disparate impact on the base pay of employees with a longer record of service, most of whom were older employees. The plaintiffs sought backpay, liquidated damages, and permanent salary adjustments as relief. The Florida Board of Regents moved to dismiss the suit on the grounds of Eleventh Amendment immunity. On May 17, 1996, the District Court denied the motion, holding that Congress expressed its intent to abrogate the States' Eleventh Amendment immunity in the ADEA, and that the ADEA is a proper exercise of congressional authority under the Fourteenth Amendment.

In May 1996, Wellington Dickson filed suit against his employer, the Florida Department of Corrections, in the United States District Court for the Northern District of Florida. Dickson alleged that the state employer failed to promote him because of his age and because he had filed grievances with respect to the alleged acts of age discrimination. Dickson sought injunctive relief, backpay, and compensatory and punitive damages. The Florida Department of Corrections moved to dismiss the suit on the grounds that it was barred by the Eleventh Amendment. The District Court denied that motion on November 5, 1996, holding that Congress unequivocally expressed its intent to abrogate the States' Eleventh Amendment immunity in the ADEA, and that Congress had authority to do so under §5 of the Fourteenth Amendment.

The plaintiffs in the MacPherson case, and the state defendants in the Kimel and Dickson cases, appealed to the Court of Appeals for the Eleventh Circuit. The

United States also intervened in all three cases to defend the ADEA's abrogation of the States' Eleventh Amendment immunity. The Court of Appeals consolidated the appeals and, in a divided panel opinion, held that the ADEA does not abrogate the States' Eleventh Amendment immunity. (1998). Judge Edmondson . . . rested his opinion on the ADEA's lack of unmistakably clear language evidencing Congress' intent to abrogate the States' sovereign immunity. . . . Judge Cox, however, chose not to address "the thorny issue of Congress's intent," but instead found that Congress lacks the power under §5 of the Fourteenth Amendment to abrogate the States' Eleventh Amendment immunity under the ADEA. . . . Chief Judge Hatchett dissented from both grounds.

We granted certiorari (1999) to resolve a conflict among the Federal Courts of Appeals on the question whether the ADEA validly abrogates the States' Eleventh Amendment immunity. . . .

II

The Eleventh Amendment states:

> "The Judicial power of the United States shall not be construed to extend to any suit in law or equity, commenced or prosecuted against one of the United States by Citizens of another State, or by Citizens or Subjects of any Foreign State."

Although today's cases concern suits brought by citizens against their own States, this Court has long "understood the Eleventh Amendment to stand not so much for what it says, but for the presupposition . . . which it confirms." *Seminole Tribe of Fla. v. Florida* (1996). Accordingly, for over a century now, we have made clear that the Constitution does not provide for federal jurisdiction over suits against nonconsenting States. *College Savings Bank v. Florida Prepaid Postsecondary Ed. Expense Bd.* (1999); *Seminole Tribe;* see *Hans v. Louisiana* (1890). Petitioners nevertheless contend that the States of Alabama and Florida must defend the present suits on the merits because Congress abrogated their Eleventh Amendment immunity in the ADEA. To determine whether petitioners are correct, we must resolve two predicate questions: first, whether Congress unequivocally expressed its intent to abrogate that immunity; and second, if it did, whether Congress acted pursuant to a valid grant of constitutional authority.

III

To determine whether a federal statute properly subjects States to suits by individuals, we apply a "simple but stringent test: 'Congress may abrogate the States' constitutionally secured immunity from suit in federal court only by making its intention unmistakably clear in the language of the statute.'" *Dellmuth v. Muth* (1989) (quoting *Atascadero State Hospital v. Scanlon* (1985)). We agree with petitioners that the ADEA satisfies that test. The ADEA states that its provisions "shall be enforced in accordance with the powers, remedies, and procedures provided in sections 211(b), 216 (except for subsection (a) thereof), and 217 of this title, and subsection (c) of this section." 29 U.S.C. §626(b). Section 216(b), in turn, clearly provides for suits by individuals against States. That provision authorizes employees to maintain actions for backpay "against any employer (including a public agency) in any Federal or State court of competent jurisdiction. . . ." Any doubt concerning the identity of the "public agency" defendant named in §216(b) is dispelled by looking to §203(x), which defines the term to include "the government of a State or political subdivision thereof," and "any agency of . . . a State, or a political subdivision of a State." Read as a whole, the plain language of these provisions clearly demonstrates Congress' intent to subject the States to suit for money damages at the hands of individual employees. [Remainder of section omitted; six other justices concurred in this section: Rehnquist, Stevens, Scalia, Souter, Ginsburg, and Breyer; Justices Thomas and Kennedy dissented from this part of the Court's opinion, but joined in the remainder.]

IV

A

This is not the first time we have considered the constitutional validity of the 1974 extension of the ADEA to state and local governments. In *EEOC v. Wyoming* (1983), we held that the ADEA constitutes a valid exercise of Congress' power "[t]o regulate Commerce . . . among the several States," and that the Act did not transgress any external restraints imposed on the commerce power by the Tenth Amendment. Because we found the ADEA valid under Congress' Commerce Clause power, we concluded that it was unnecessary to determine whether the Act also could be supported by Congress' power under §5 of the Fourteenth Amendment. Resolution of today's cases requires us to decide that question.

In *Seminole Tribe*, we held that Congress lacks power under Article I to abrogate the States' sovereign immunity. . . . Last Term, in a series of three decisions, we reaffirmed that central holding of *Seminole Tribe*. See *College Savings Bank; Florida Prepaid Postsecondary Ed. Expense Bd. v. College Savings Bank* (1999); *Alden v. Maine* (1999). . . . Under our firmly established precedent then, if the ADEA rests solely on Congress' Article I commerce power, the private petitioners in today's cases cannot maintain their suits against their state employers.

JUSTICE STEVENS disputes that well-established precedent again. [Citation to dissenting opinions in prior cases omitted.] . . . For purposes of today's decision, it is sufficient to note that we have on more than one occasion explained the substantial reasons for adhering to that constitutional design. . . . Indeed, the present dissenters' refusal to accept the validity and natural import of decisions like *Hans*, rendered over a full century ago by this Court, makes it difficult to engage in additional meaningful debate on the place of state sovereign immunity in the Constitution. Today we adhere to our holding in *Seminole Tribe:* Congress' powers under Article I of the Constitution do not include the power to subject States to suit at the hands of private individuals.

Section 5 of the Fourteenth Amendment, however, does grant Congress the authority to abrogate the States' sovereign immunity. In *Fitzpatrick v. Bitzer* (1976), we recognized that "the Eleventh Amendment, and the principle of state sovereignty which it embodies, are necessarily limited by the enforcement provisions of

§5 of the Fourteenth Amendment." Since our decision in *Fitzpatrick*, we have reaffirmed the validity of that congressional power on numerous occasions. . . . Accordingly, the private petitioners in these cases may maintain their ADEA suits against the States of Alabama and Florida if, and only if, the ADEA is appropriate legislation under §5.

B

The Fourteenth Amendment provides, in relevant part:

> "Section 1. . . . No State shall make or enforce any law which shall abridge the privileges or immunities of citizens of the United States; nor shall any State deprive any person of life, liberty, or property, without due process of law; nor deny to any person within its jurisdiction the equal protection of the laws."

> . . . .

> "Section 5. The Congress shall have power to enforce, by appropriate legislation, the provisions of this article."

As we recognized most recently in *City of Boerne v. Flores* (1997), §5 is an affirmative grant of power to Congress. . . . Congress' §5 power is not confined to the enactment of legislation that merely parrots the precise wording of the Fourteenth Amendment. Rather, Congress' power "to enforce" the Amendment includes the authority both to remedy and to deter violation of rights guaranteed thereunder by prohibiting a somewhat broader swath of conduct, including that which is not itself forbidden by the Amendment's text.

Nevertheless, we have also recognized that the same language that serves as the basis for the affirmative grant of congressional power also serves to limit that power. For example, Congress cannot "decree the *substance* of the Fourteenth Amendment's restrictions on the States. . . . It has been given the power 'to enforce,' not the power to determine *what constitutes* a constitutional violation." [*City of Boerne*] (emphases added). The ultimate interpretation and determination of the Fourteenth Amendment's substantive meaning remains the province of the Judicial Branch. In *City of Boerne*, we noted that the determination whether purportedly prophylactic legislation constitutes appropriate remedial legislation, or instead effects a substantive redefinition of the Fourteenth Amendment right at issue, is often difficult. The line between the two is a fine one. Accordingly, recognizing that "Congress must have wide latitude in determining where [that line] lies," we held that "[t]here must be a congruence and proportionality between the injury to be prevented or remedied and the means adopted to that end." . . .

C

Applying the same "congruence and proportionality" test in these cases, we conclude that the ADEA is not "appropriate legislation" under §5 of the Fourteenth Amendment. Initially, the substantive requirements the ADEA imposes on state and local governments are disproportionate to any unconstitutional conduct that conceivably could be targeted by the Act. We have considered claims of unconstitutional age discrimination under the Equal Protection Clause three times. See *Gregory v. Ashcroft* (1991); *Vance v. Bradley* (1979); *Massachusetts Bd. of Retirement v. Murgia*, 427 U.S. 307 (1976). In all three cases, we held that the age classifications at issue did not violate the Equal Protection Clause. Age classifications, unlike governmental conduct based on race or gender, cannot be characterized as "so seldom relevant to the achievement of any legitimate state interest that laws grounded in such considerations are deemed to reflect prejudice and antipathy." *Cleburne v. Cleburne Living Center, Inc.* (1985). Older persons, again, unlike those who suffer discrimination on the basis of race or gender, have not been subjected to a "history of purposeful unequal treatment." *Murgia.* Old age also does not define a discrete and insular minority because all persons, if they live out their normal life spans, will experience it. Accordingly, as we recognized in *Murgia, Bradley*, and *Gregory*, age is not a suspect classification under the Equal Protection Clause.

States may discriminate on the basis of age without offending the Fourteenth Amendment if the age classification in question is rationally related to a legitimate state interest. The rationality commanded by the Equal Protection Clause does not require States to match age distinctions and the legitimate interests they serve with razorlike precision. . . . In contrast, when a State discriminates on the basis of race or gender, we require a tighter fit between the discriminatory means and the legitimate ends they serve. . . . Under the Fourteenth Amendment, a State may rely on age as a proxy for other qualities, abilities, or characteristics that are relevant to the State's legitimate interests. The Constitution does not preclude reliance on such generalizations. That age proves to be an inaccurate proxy in any individual case is irrelevant. . . . Finally, because an age classification is presumptively rational, the individual challenging its constitutionality bears the burden of proving that the "facts on which the classification is apparently based could not reasonably be conceived to be true by the governmental decisionmaker." *Bradley.*

Our decisions in *Murgia, Bradley*, and *Gregory* illustrate these principles. In all three cases, we held that the States' reliance on broad generalizations with respect to age did not violate the Equal Protection Clause. In *Murgia*, we upheld against an equal protection challenge a Massachusetts statute requiring state police officers to retire at age 50. . . . In *Bradley*, we considered an equal protection challenge to a federal statute requiring Foreign Service officers to retire at age 60. [O'Connor quoted from the opinion rejecting the challenge.] Finally, in *Gregory*, we upheld a provision of the Missouri Constitution that required judges to retire at age 70. . . . These decisions thus demonstrate that the constitutionality of state classifications on the basis of age cannot be determined on a person-by-person basis. Our Constitution permits States to draw lines on the basis of age when they have a rational basis for doing so at a class-based level, even if it "is probably not true" that those reasons are valid in the majority of cases.

Judged against the backdrop of our equal protection jurisprudence, it is clear that the ADEA is "so out of proportion to a supposed remedial or preventive object that it cannot be understood as responsive to, or designed to prevent, unconstitutional behavior." *City of Boerne.* The Act, through its broad restriction on the use of age as a discriminating factor, prohibits substantially more state employment decisions and practices than would likely be held unconstitutional under the applicable equal protection, rational basis standard. The ADEA makes unlawful, in the employment context, all "discriminat[ion] against any individual . . . because of such individual's age." 29 U.S.C. §623(a)(1). Petitioners, relying on the Act's exceptions, dispute the extent to which the ADEA erects protections beyond the Constitution's requirements. They contend that the Act's prohibition, considered together with its exceptions, applies only to arbitrary age discrimination, which in the majority of cases corresponds to conduct that violates the Equal Protection Clause. We disagree.

Petitioners stake their claim on §623(f)(1). That section permits employers to rely on age when it "is a bona fide occupational qualification reasonably necessary to the normal operation of the particular business." Petitioners' reliance on the "bona fide occupational qualification" (BFOQ) defense is misplaced. . . .

Under the ADEA, even with its BFOQ defense, the State's use of age is prima facie unlawful. . . . Application of the Act therefore starts with a presumption in favor of requiring the employer to make an individualized determination. . . . Measured against the rational basis standard of our equal protection jurisprudence, the ADEA plainly imposes substantially higher burdens on state employers. Thus, although it is true that the existence of the BFOQ defense makes the ADEA's prohibition of age discrimination less than absolute, the Act's substantive requirements nevertheless remain at a level akin to our heightened scrutiny cases under the Equal Protection Clause.

Petitioners also place some reliance on the next clause in §623(f)(1), which permits employers to engage in conduct otherwise prohibited by the Act "where the differentiation is based on reasonable factors other than age." This exception confirms, however, rather than disproves, the conclusion that the ADEA's protection extends beyond the requirements of the Equal Protection Clause. . . .

That the ADEA prohibits very little conduct likely to be held unconstitutional, while significant, does not alone provide the answer to our §5 inquiry. Difficult and intractable problems often require powerful remedies, and we have never held that §5 precludes Congress from enacting reasonably prophylactic legislation. Our task is to determine whether the ADEA is in fact just such an appropriate remedy or, instead, merely an attempt to substantively redefine the States' legal obligations with respect to age discrimination. One means by which we have made such a determination in the past is by examining the legislative record containing the reasons for Congress' action. . . .

Our examination of the ADEA's legislative record confirms that Congress' 1974 extension of the Act to the States was an unwarranted response to a perhaps inconsequential problem. Congress never identified any pattern of age discrimination by the States, much less any discrimination whatsoever that rose to the level of constitutional violation. The evidence compiled by petitioners to demonstrate such attention by Congress to age discrimination by the States falls well short of the mark. That evidence consists almost entirely of isolated sentences clipped from floor debates and legislative reports. . . .

Petitioners place additional reliance on Congress' consideration of a 1966 report prepared by the State of California on age discrimination in its public agencies. . . . Like the assorted sentences petitioners cobble together from a decade's worth of congressional reports and floor debates, the California study does not indicate that the State had engaged in any unconstitutional age discrimination. . . .

Finally, the United States' argument that Congress found substantial age discrimination in the private sector is beside the point. Congress made no such findings with respect to the States. Although we also have doubts whether the findings Congress did make with respect to the private sector could be extrapolated to support a finding of *unconstitutional* age discrimination in the public sector, it is sufficient for these cases to note that Congress failed to identify a widespread pattern of age discrimination by the States.

A review of the ADEA's legislative record as a whole, then, reveals that Congress had virtually no reason to believe that state and local governments were unconstitutionally discriminating against their employees on the basis of age. Although that lack of support is not determinative of the §5 inquiry, Congress' failure to uncover any significant pattern of unconstitutional discrimination here confirms that Congress had no reason to believe that broad prophylactic legislation was necessary in this field. In light of the indiscriminate scope of the Act's substantive requirements, and the lack of evidence of widespread and unconstitutional age discrimination by the States, we hold that the ADEA is not a valid exercise of Congress' power under §5 of the Fourteenth Amendment. The ADEA's purported abrogation of the States' sovereign immunity is accordingly invalid.

D

Our decision today does not signal the end of the line for employees who find themselves subject to age discrimination at the hands of their state employers. We hold only that, in the ADEA, Congress did not validly abrogate the States' sovereign immunity to suits by private individuals. State employees are protected by state age discrimination statutes, and may recover money damages from their state employers, in almost every State of the Union. Those avenues of relief remain available today, just as they were before this decision.

Because the ADEA does not validly abrogate the States' sovereign immunity, however, the present suits must be dismissed. Accordingly, the judgment of the Court of Appeals is affirmed.

It is so ordered.

JUSTICE STEVENS, with whom JUSTICE SOUTER, JUSTICE GINS-BURG, and JUSTICE BREYER join, dissenting in part and concurring in part.

Congress' power to regulate the American economy includes the power to regulate both the public and the private sectors of the labor market. Federal rules outlawing discrimination in the workplace, like the regulation of wages and hours or health and safety standards, may be enforced against public as well as private employers. In my opinion, Congress' power to authorize federal remedies against state agencies that violate federal statutory obligations is coextensive with its power to impose those obligations on the States in the first place. Neither the Eleventh Amendment nor the doctrine of sovereign immunity places any limit on that power. See *Seminole Tribe of Fla. v. Florida* (1996) (SOUTER, J., dissenting); *EEOC v. Wyoming* (1983) (STEVENS, J., concurring).

The application of the ancient judge-made doctrine of sovereign immunity in cases like these is supposedly justified as a freestanding limit on congressional authority, a limit necessary to protect States' "dignity and respect" from impairment by the National Government. The Framers did not, however, select the Judicial Branch as the constitutional guardian of those state interests. Rather, the Framers designed important structural safeguards to ensure that when the National Government enacted substantive law (and provided for its enforcement), the normal operation of the legislative process itself would adequately defend state interests from undue infringement. . . .

It is the Framers' compromise giving each State equal representation in the Senate that provides the principal structural protection for the sovereignty of the several States. The composition of the Senate was originally determined by the legislatures of the States, which would guarantee that their interests could not be ignored by Congress. The Framers also directed that the House be composed of Representatives selected by voters in the several States. . . .

Whenever Congress passes a statute, it does so against the background of state law already in place; the propriety of taking national action is thus measured by the metric of the existing state norms that Congress seeks to supplement or supplant. The persuasiveness of any justification for overcoming legislative inertia and taking national action, either creating new federal obligations or providing for their enforcement, must necessarily be judged in reference to state interests, as expressed in existing state laws. The precise scope of federal laws, of course, can be shaped with nuanced attention to state interests. The Congress also has the authority to grant or withhold jurisdiction in lower federal courts. The burden of being haled into a federal forum for the enforcement of federal law, thus, can be expanded or contracted as Congress deems proper, which decision, like all other legislative acts, necessarily contemplates state interests. Thus, Congress can use its broad range of flexible legislative tools to approach the delicate issue of how to balance local and national interests in the most responsive and careful manner. It is quite evident, therefore, that the Framers did not view this Court as the ultimate guardian of the States' interest in protecting their own sovereignty from impairment by "burdensome" federal laws.

Federalism concerns do make it appropriate for Congress to speak clearly when it regulates state action. But when it does so, as it has in these cases, we can safely presume that the burdens the statute imposes on the sovereignty of the several States were taken into account during the deliberative process leading to the enactment of the measure. Those burdens necessarily include the cost of defending against enforcement proceedings and paying whatever penalties might be incurred for violating the statute. In my judgment, the question whether those enforcement proceedings should be conducted exclusively by federal agencies, or may be brought by private parties as well, is a matter of policy for Congress to decide. In either event, once Congress has made its policy choice, the sovereignty concerns of the several States are satisfied, and the federal interest in evenhanded enforcement of federal law, explicitly endorsed in Article VI of the Constitution, does not countenance further limitations. There is not a word in the text of the Constitution supporting the Court's conclusion that the judge-made doctrine of sovereign immunity limits Congress' power to authorize private parties, as well as federal agencies, to enforce federal law against the States. The importance of respecting the Framers' decision to assign the business of lawmaking to the Congress dictates firm resistance to the present majority's repeated substitution of its own views of federalism for those expressed in statutes enacted by the Congress and signed by the President.

The Eleventh Amendment simply does not support the Court's view. . . . [T]he Amendment only places a textual limitation on the diversity jurisdiction of the federal courts. . . . Here, however, private petitioners did not invoke the federal courts' diversity jurisdiction; they are citizens of the same State as the defendants and they are asserting claims that arise under federal law. Thus, today's decision (relying as it does on *Seminole Tribe*) rests entirely on a novel judicial interpretation of the doctrine of sovereign immunity, which the Court treats as though it were a constitutional precept. It is nevertheless clear to me that if Congress has the power to create the federal rights that these petitioners are asserting, it must also have the power to give the federal courts jurisdiction to remedy violations of those rights. . . .

. . . Despite my respect for *stare decisis*, I am unwilling to accept *Seminole Tribe* as controlling precedent. First and foremost, the reasoning of that opinion is so profoundly mistaken and so fundamentally inconsistent with the Framers' conception of the constitutional order that it has forsaken any claim to the usual deference or respect owed to decisions of this Court. *Stare decisis*, furthermore, has less force in the area of constitutional law. . . . And in this instance, it is but a hollow pretense for any State to seek refuge in *stare decisis'* protection of reliance interests. It cannot be credibly maintained that a State's ordering of its affairs with respect to potential liability under federal law requires adherence to *Seminole Tribe*, as that decision leaves open a State's liability upon enforcement of federal law by federal agencies. Nor can a State find solace in the *stare decisis* interest of promoting "the evenhanded . . . and consistent development of legal principles." That principle is perverted when invoked to rely on sovereign immunity as a defense to deliberate violations of settled federal law. Further, *Seminole Tribe* is a case that will unquestionably have serious ramifications in future cases; indeed, it has already had such an effect, as in the Court's decision today and in the equally misguided opinion of *Alden v. Maine* (1999). Further still, the *Seminole Tribe* decision unnecessarily forces the Court to resolve vexing questions of constitutional law respecting Congress' §5 authority. Finally, by its own repeated overruling of earlier precedent, the majority has itself discounted the importance of *stare decisis* in this area of the law. The kind of judicial activism manifested in cases like *Seminole Tribe, Alden v. Maine, Florida Prepaid Postsecondary Ed. Expense Bd. v. College Savings Bank*, (1999), and *College Savings Bank v. Florida Prepaid Postsecondary Ed. Expense Bd.* (1999) represents such a radical departure from the proper role of this Court that it should be opposed whenever the opportunity arises.

Accordingly, I respectfully dissent.

JUSTICE THOMAS, with whom JUSTICE KENNEDY joins, concurring in part and dissenting in part.

In *Atascadero State Hospital v. Scanlon* (1985), this Court, cognizant of the impact of an abrogation of the States' Eleventh Amendment immunity from suit in federal court on "the usual constitutional balance between the States and the Federal Government," reaffirmed that "Congress may abrogate . . . only by making its intention unmistakably clear in the language of the statute." This rule "assures that the legislature has in fact faced, and intended to bring into issue, the critical matters involved in the judicial decision." *Will v. Michigan Dept. of State Police* (1989). And it is especially applicable when this Court deals with a statute like the Age Discrimination in Employment Act of 1967 (ADEA), whose substantive mandates extend to "elevator operators, janitors, charwomen, security guards, secretaries, and the like in every office building in a State's governmental hierarchy." Employees of Dept. of Public Health and Welfare of Mo. v. Department of Public Health and Welfare of Mo. (1973). Because I think that Congress has not made its intention to abrogate "unmistakably clear" in the text of the ADEA, I respectfully dissent from Part III of the Court's opinion. [Thomas noted in a footnote that he concurred in Parts I, II, and IV of the Court's opinion "because I agree that the purported abrogation of the States' Eleventh Amendment immunity in the ADEA falls outside Congress' §5 enforcement power." Remainder of opinion deleted.]

No. 98-963

Jeremiah W. (Jay) Nixon, Attorney General of Missouri, Petitioners v. Shrink Missouri Government PAC et al.

On writ of certiorari to the United States Court of Appeals for the Eighth Circuit

[January 24, 2000]

JUSTICE SOUTER delivered the opinion of the Court.

The principal issues in this case are whether *Buckley v. Valeo* (1976) is authority for state limits on contributions to state political candidates and whether the federal limits approved in *Buckley*, with or without adjustment for inflation, define the scope of permissible state limitations today. We hold *Buckley* to be authority for comparable state regulation, which need not be pegged to *Buckley*'s dollars.

I

In 1994, the Legislature of Missouri enacted Senate Bill 650 (SB650) to restrict the permissible amounts of contributions to candidates for state office. Mo. Rev. Stat. §130.032 (1994). Before the statute became effective, however, Missouri voters approved a ballot initiative with even stricter contribution limits, effective immediately. The United States Court of Appeals for the Eighth Circuit then held the initiative's contribution limits unconstitutional under the First Amendment, *Carver v. Nixon* (1995), cert. denied (1996), with the upshot that the previously dormant 1994 statute took effect. As amended in 1997, that statute imposes contribution limits ranging from $250 to a $1,000, depending on specified state office or size of constituency. The particular provision challenged here reads that

> "[t]o elect an individual to the office of governor, lieutenant governor, secretary of state, state treasurer, state auditor or attorney general, [(t)he amount of contributions made by or accepted from any person other than the candidate in any one election shall not exceed] one thousand dollars."

The statutory dollar amounts are baselines for an adjustment each even-numbered year, to be made "by multiplying the base year amount by the cumulative consumer price index . . . and rounded to the nearest twenty-five-dollar amount, for all years since January 1, 1995." When this suit was filed, the limits ranged from a high of $1,075 for contributions to candidates for statewide office (including state auditor) and for any office where the population exceeded 250,000, down to $275 for contributions to candidates for state representative or for any office for which there were fewer than 100,000 people represented.

Respondents Shrink Missouri Government PAC, a political action committee, and Zev David Fredman, a candidate for the 1998 Republican nomination for state auditor, sought to enjoin enforcement of the contribution statute as violating their First and Fourteenth Amendment rights (presumably those of free speech, association, and equal protection, although the complaint did not so state). Shrink Missouri gave $1,025 to Fredman's candidate committee in 1997, and another $50 in 1998. Shrink Missouri represented that, without the limitation, it would contribute more to the Fredman campaign. Fredman alleged he could campaign effectively only with more generous contributions than §130.032.1 allowed. On cross-motions for summary judgment, the District Court sustained the statute. . . .

The Court of Appeals for the Eighth Circuit nonetheless enjoined enforcement of the law pending appeal, and ultimately reversed the District Court. [*Shrink Missouri Government PAC v. Adams* (1998).] . . .

Given the large number of States that limit political contributions, we granted certiorari to review the congruence of the Eighth Circuit's decision with *Buckley* (1999). We reverse.

II

The matters raised in *Buckley v. Valeo* included claims that federal campaign finance legislation infringed speech and association guarantees of the First Amendment and the Equal Protection Clause of the Fourteenth. The Federal Election Campaign Act of 1971, as amended by the Federal Election Campaign Act Amendments of 1974, limited (and still limits) contributions by individuals to any single candidate for federal office to $1,000 per election. 18 U.S.C. §608(b)(1), (3). Until *Buckley* struck it down, the law also placed a $1,000 annual ceiling on independent expenditures linked to specific candidates. 18 U.S.C. §608(e). We found violations of the First Amendment in the expenditure regulations, but held the contribution restrictions constitutional.

A

Precision about the relative rigor of the standard to review contribution limits was not a pretense of the *Buckley per curiam* opinion. . . . [W]e explicitly rejected both *O'Brien* intermediate scrutiny for communicative action, see *United States v. O'Brien* (1968), and the similar standard applicable to merely time, place, and manner restrictions. . . . In distinguishing these tests, the discussion referred generally to "the exacting scrutiny required by the First Amendment," and added that "the constitutional guarantee has its fullest and most urgent application precisely to the conduct of campaigns for political office."

We then, however, drew a line between expenditures and contributions, treating expenditure restrictions as direct restraints on speech, which nonetheless suffered little direct effect from contribution limits. [Excerpt from *Buckley* opinion omitted.] We thus said, in effect, that limiting contributions left communication significantly unimpaired.

We flagged a similar difference between expenditure and contribution limitations in their impacts on the association right. While an expenditure limit "precludes most associations from effectively amplifying the voice of their adherents" . . . the contribution limits "leave the contributor free to become a member of any political association and to assist personally in the association's efforts on behalf of candidates." . . . It has . . . been plain ever since *Buckley* that contribution limits would more readily clear the hurdles before them [than expenditure limits]. . . .

[Souter noted that the *Buckley* decision recognized "the prevention of corruption and the appearance of corruption" to be a "constitutionally sufficient justification" for enactment of campaign contribution limits. He continued:]

In speaking of "improper influence" and "opportunities for abuse" in addition to "*quid pro quo* arrangements," we recognized a concern not confined to bribery of public officials, but extending to the broader threat from politicians too compliant with the wishes of large contributors. These were the obvious points behind our recognition that the Congress could constitutionally address the power of money "to influence governmental action" in ways less "blatant and specific" than bribery.

B

In defending its own statute, Missouri espouses those same interests of preventing corruption and the appearance of it that flows from munificent campaign contributions. . . . [W]e spoke in *Buckley* of the perception of corruption "inherent in a regime of large individual financial contributions" to candidates for public office as a source of concern "almost equal" to *quid pro quo* improbity. The public interest in countering that perception was, indeed, the entire answer to the overbreadth claim raised in the *Buckley* case. This made perfect sense. Leave the perception of impropriety unanswered, and the cynical assumption that large donors call the tune could jeopardize the willingness of voters to take part in democratic governance. . . .

Although respondents neither challenge the legitimacy of these objectives nor call for any reconsideration of *Buckley*, they take the State to task, as the Court of Appeals did, for failing to justify the invocation of those interests with empirical evidence of actually corrupt practices or of a perception among Missouri voters that unrestricted contributions must have been exerting a covertly corrosive influence. The state statute is not void, however, for want of evidence.

The quantum of empirical evidence needed to satisfy heightened judicial scrutiny of legislative judgments will vary up or down with the novelty and plausibility of the justification raised. *Buckley* demonstrates that the dangers of large, corrupt contributions and the suspicion that large contributions are corrupt are neither novel nor implausible. . . .

While *Buckley*'s evidentiary showing exemplifies a sufficient justification for contribution limits, it does not speak to what may be necessary as a minimum. As to that, respondents are wrong in arguing that in the years since *Buckley* came down we have "supplemented" its holding with a new requirement that governments enacting contribution limits must "demonstrate that the recited harms are real, not merely conjectural." . . .

In any event, this case does not present a close call requiring further definition of whatever the State's evidentiary obligation may be. While the record does not show that the Missouri Legislature relied on the evidence and findings accepted in *Buckley*, the evidence introduced into the record by respondents or cited by the lower courts in this action and the action regarding Proposition A is enough to show that the substantiation of the congressional concerns reflected in *Buckley* has its counterpart supporting the Missouri law. Although Missouri does not preserve legislative history, the State presented an affidavit from State Senator Wayne Goode, the co-chair of the state legislature's Interim Joint Committee on Campaign Finance Reform at the time the State enacted the contribution limits, who stated that large contributions have "the real potential to buy votes." The District Court cited newspaper accounts of large contributions supporting inferences of impropriety. One report questioned the state treasurer's decision to use a certain bank for most of Missouri's banking business after that institution contributed $20,000 to the treasurer's campaign. Another made much of the receipt by a candidate for state auditor of a $40,000 contribution from a brewery and one for $20,000 from a bank. In *Carver v. Nixon* (1995), the Eighth Circuit itself, while invalidating the limits Proposition A imposed, identified a $420,000 contribution to candidates in northern Missouri from a political action committee linked to an investment bank, and three scandals, including one in which a state representative was "accused of sponsoring legislation in exchange for kickbacks," and another in which Missouri's former attorney general pleaded guilty to charges of conspiracy to misuse state property after being indicted for using a state workers' compensation fund to benefit campaign contributors. And although majority votes do not, as such, defeat First Amendment protections, the statewide vote on Proposition A certainly attested to the perception relied upon here: "[A]n overwhelming 74 percent of the voters of Missouri determined that contribution limits are necessary to combat corruption and the appearance thereof." [Quoting district court's opinion in *Carver v. Nixon*.]

There might, of course, be need for a more extensive evidentiary documentation if petitioners had made any showing of their own to cast doubt on the apparent implications of *Buckley*'s evidence and the record here, but the closest respondents come to challenging these conclusions is their invocation of academic studies said to indicate that large contributions to public officials or candidates do not actually result in changes in candidates' positions. [Citation to several law journal articles omitted.] Other studies, however, point the other way. [Citations omitted.] Given the conflict among these publications, and the absence of any reason to think that public perception has been influenced by the studies cited by respondents, there is little reason to doubt that sometimes large contributions will work actual corruption of our political system, and no reason to question the existence of a corresponding suspicion among voters.

C

Nor do we see any support for respondents' various arguments that in spite of their striking resemblance to the limitations sustained in *Buckley*, those in Missouri are so different in kind as to raise essentially a new issue about the adequacy of the

Missouri statute's tailoring to serve its purposes. Here, as in *Buckley*, "[t]here is no indication . . . that the contribution limitations imposed by the [law] would have any dramatic[ally] adverse effect on the funding of campaigns and political associations," and thus no showing that "the limitations prevented the candidates and political committees from amassing the resources necessary for effective advocacy." The District Court found here that in the period since the Missouri limits became effective, "candidates for state elected office [have been] quite able to raise funds sufficient to run effective campaigns," and that "candidates for political office in the state are still able to amass impressive campaign war chests." The plausibility of these conclusions is buttressed by petitioners' evidence that in the 1994 Missouri elections (before any relevant state limitations went into effect), 97.62 percent of all contributors to candidates for state auditor made contributions of $2,000 or less. Even if we were to assume that the contribution limits affected respondent Fredman's ability to wage a competitive campaign (no small assumption given that Fredman only identified one contributor, Shrink Missouri, that would have given him more than $1,075 per election), a showing of one affected individual does not point up a system of suppressed political advocacy that would be unconstitutional under *Buckley*.

These conclusions of the District Court and the supporting evidence also suffice to answer respondents' variant claim that the Missouri limits today differ in kind from *Buckley*'s owing to inflation since 1976. Respondents seem to assume that *Buckley* set a minimum constitutional threshold for contribution limits, which in dollars adjusted for loss of purchasing power are now well above the lines drawn by Missouri. But this assumption is a fundamental misunderstanding of what we held.

In *Buckley*, we specifically rejected the contention that $1,000, or any other amount, was a constitutional minimum below which legislatures could not regulate. . . . [W]e referred instead to the outer limits of contribution regulation by asking whether there was any showing that the limits were so low as to impede the ability of candidates to "amas[s] the resources necessary for effective advocacy." We asked, in other words, whether the contribution limitation was so radical in effect as to render political association ineffective, drive the sound of a candidate's voice below the level of notice, and render contributions pointless. Such being the test, the issue in later cases cannot be truncated to a narrow question about the power of the dollar, but must go to the power to mount a campaign with all the dollars likely to be forthcoming. As Judge Gibson put it, the dictates of the First Amendment are not mere functions of the Consumer Price Index [dissenting opinion in the Court of Appeals].

D

The dissenters in this case think our reasoning evades the real issue. JUSTICE THOMAS chides us for "hiding behind" *Buckley*, and JUSTICE KENNEDY faults us for seeing this case as "a routine application of our analysis" in *Buckley* instead of facing up to what he describes as the consequences of *Buckley*. Each dissenter would overrule *Buckley* and thinks we should do the same.

The answer is that we are supposed to decide this case. Shrink and Fredman did not request that *Buckley* be overruled; the furthest reach of their arguments about the law was that subsequent decisions already on the books had enhanced the State's burden of justification beyond what *Buckley* required, a proposition we have rejected as mistaken.

III

There is no reason in logic or evidence to doubt the sufficiency of *Buckley* to govern this case in support of the Missouri statute. The judgment of the Court of Appeals is, accordingly, reversed, and the case is remanded for proceedings consistent with this opinion.

It is so ordered.

JUSTICE STEVENS, concurring.

JUSTICE KENNEDY suggests that the misuse of soft money tolerated by this Court's misguided decision in *Colorado Republican Federal Campaign Comm. v. Federal Election Comm'n* (1996) demonstrates the need for a fresh examination of the constitutional issues raised by Congress' enactment of the Federal Election Campaign Acts of 1971 and 1974 and this Court's resolution of those issues in *Buckley v. Valeo*. In response to his call for a new beginning, therefore, I make one simple point. Money is property; it is not speech.

Speech has the power to inspire volunteers to perform a multitude of tasks on a campaign trail, on a battleground, or even on a football field. Money, meanwhile, has the power to pay hired laborers to perform the same tasks. It does not follow, however, that the First Amendment provides the same measure of protection to the use of money to accomplish such goals as it provides to the use of ideas to achieve the same results.

. . . The right to use one's own money to hire gladiators, or to fund "speech by proxy," certainly merits significant constitutional protection. These property rights, however, are not entitled to the same protection as the right to say what one pleases.

JUSTICE BREYER, with whom JUSTICE GINSBURG joins, concurring.

The dissenters accuse the Court of weakening the First Amendment. They believe that failing to adopt a "strict scrutiny" standard "balance[s] away First Amendment freedoms." But the principal dissent oversimplifies the problem faced in the campaign finance context. It takes a difficult constitutional problem and turns it into a lopsided dispute between political expression and government censorship. Under the cover of this fiction and its accompanying formula, the dissent would make the Court absolute arbiter of a difficult question best left, in the main, to the political branches. I write separately to address the critical question of how the Court ought to review this kind of problem, and to explain why I believe the Court's choice here is correct. . . .

On the one hand, a decision to contribute money to a campaign is a matter of First Amendment concern—not because money *is* speech (it is not); but because it *enables* speech. . . .

On the other hand, restrictions upon the amount any one individual can contribute to a particular candidate seek to protect the integrity of the electoral process. . . . Moreover, by limiting the size of the largest contributions, such restrictions aim to democratize the influence that money itself may bring to bear upon the electoral process. . . .

In service of these objectives, the statute imposes restrictions of degree. It does not deny the contributor the opportunity to associate with the candidate through a contribution, though it limits a contribution's size. Nor does it prevent the contributor from using money (alone or with others) to pay for the expression of the same views in other ways. Instead, it permits all supporters to contribute the same amount of money, in an attempt to make the process fairer and more democratic.

Under these circumstances, a presumption against constitutionality is out of place. . . .

In such circumstances—where a law significantly implicates competing constitutionally protected interests in complex ways—the Court has closely scrutinized the statute's impact on those interests, but refrained from employing a simple test that effectively presumes unconstitutionality. Rather, it has balanced interests. . . . And in practice that has meant asking whether the statute burdens any one such interest in a manner out of proportion to the statute's salutary effects upon the others (perhaps, but not necessarily, because of the existence of a clearly superior, less restrictive alternative). Where a legislature has significantly greater institutional expertise, . . . the Court in practice defers to empirical legislative judgments. . . . For the dissenters to call the approach "*sui generis*" overstates their case.

Applying this approach to the present case, I would uphold the statute essentially for the reasons stated by the Court. I agree that the legislature understands the problem . . . better than do we. We should defer to its political judgment that unlimited spending threatens the integrity of the electoral process. But we should not defer in respect to whether its solution, by imposing too low a contribution limit, significantly increases the reputation-related or media-related advantages of incumbency and thereby insulates legislators from effective electoral challenge. The statutory limit here, $1,075 (or 378, 1976 dollars) is low enough to raise such a question. But given the empirical information presented—the type of election at issue; the record of adequate candidate financing post-reform; and the fact that the statute indexes the amount for inflation—I agree with the Court that the statute does not work disproportionate harm. . . .

The approach I have outlined here is consistent with the approach this Court has taken in many complex First Amendment cases. The *Buckley* decision, as well, might be interpreted as embodying sufficient flexibility for the problem at hand. After all, *Buckley*'s holding seems to leave the political branches broad authority to enact laws regulating contributions that take the form of "soft money." . . . Alternatively, it might prove possible to reinterpret aspects of *Buckley* in light of the post-*Buckley* experience stressed by JUSTICE KENNEDY, making less absolute the contribution/expenditure line, particularly in respect to independently wealthy candidates, whose expenditures might be considered contributions to their own campaigns.

But what if I am wrong about *Buckley*? Suppose *Buckley* denies the political branches sufficient leeway to enact comprehensive solutions to the problems posed by campaign finance. If so, like JUSTICE KENNEDY, I believe the Constitution would require us to reconsider *Buckley*.

With that understanding I join the Court's opinion.

JUSTICE KENNEDY, dissenting.

The Court's decision has lasting consequences for political speech in the course of elections, the speech upon which democracy depends. Yet in defining the controlling standard of review and applying it to the urgent claim presented, the Court seems almost indifferent. . . .

It would be no answer to say that this is a routine application of our analysis in *Buckley v. Valeo* (1976) to a similar set of facts, so that a cavalier dismissal of the petitioners' claim is appropriate. The justifications for the case system and *stare decisis* must rest upon the Court's capacity, and responsibility, to acknowledge its missteps. It is our duty to face up to adverse, unintended consequences flowing from our own prior decisions. With all respect, I submit the Court does not accept this obligation in the case before us. Instead, it perpetuates and compounds a serious distortion of the First Amendment resulting from our own intervention in *Buckley*. . . .

I

. . . [T]he compromise the Court invented in *Buckley* set the stage for a new kind of speech to enter the political system. It is covert speech. The Court has forced a substantial amount of political speech underground, as contributors and candidates devise ever more elaborate methods of avoiding contribution limits, limits which take no account of rising campaign costs. The preferred method has been to conceal the real purpose of the speech. Soft money may be contributed to political parties in unlimited amounts, and is used often to fund so-called issue advocacy, advertisements that promote or attack a candidate's positions without specifically urging his or her election or defeat. Issue advocacy, like soft money, is unrestricted, while straightforward speech in the form of financial contributions paid to a candidate, speech subject to full disclosure and prompt evaluation by the public, is not. . . . This mocks the First Amendment. The current system would be unfortunate, and suspect under the First Amendment, had it evolved from a deliberate legislative choice; but its unhappy origins are in our earlier decree in *Buckley*, which by accepting half of what Congress did (limiting contributions) but rejecting the other (limiting expenditures) created a misshapen system, one which distorts the meaning of speech. . . .

II

. . . I would overrule *Buckley* and then free Congress or state legislatures to attempt some new reform, if, based upon their own considered view of the First Amendment, it is possible to do so. Until any reexamination takes place, however, the existing distortion of speech caused by the half-way house we created in *Buckley* ought to be eliminated. The First Amendment ought to be allowed to take its own course without further obstruction from the artificial system we have imposed. It suffices here to say that the law in question does not come even close to passing any serious scrutiny. . . .

JUSTICE THOMAS with whom JUSTICE SCALIA, joins, dissenting.

In the process of ratifying Missouri's sweeping repression of political speech, the Court today adopts the analytic fallacies of our flawed decision in *Buckley v. Valeo* (1976). Unfortunately, the Court is not content to merely adhere to erroneous precedent. Under the guise of applying *Buckley*, the Court proceeds to weaken the already enfeebled constitutional protection that *Buckley* afforded campaign contributions. In the end, the Court employs a *sui generis* test to balance away First Amendment freedoms.

Because the Court errs with each step it takes, I dissent. As I indicated in *Colorado Republican Federal Campaign Comm. v. Federal Election Comm'n* (1996) (opinion concurring in judgment and dissenting in part), our decision in *Buckley* was in error, and I would overrule it. I would subject campaign contribution limitations to strict scrutiny, under which Missouri's contribution limits are patently unconstitutional.

I

I begin with a proposition that ought to be unassailable: Political speech is the primary object of First Amendment protection. [Citations omitted.] The Founders sought to protect the rights of individuals to engage in political speech because a self-governing people depends upon the free exchange of political information. And that free exchange should receive the most protection when it matters the most—during campaigns for elective office. . . .

I do not start with these foundational principles because the Court openly disagrees with them—it could not, for they are solidly embedded in our precedents. . . . Instead, I start with them because the Court today abandons them. . . . [T]he majority today, rather than going out of its way to *protect* political speech, goes out of its way to *avoid* protecting it. . . . [C]ontributions to political campaigns generate essential political speech. And contribution caps, which place a direct and substantial limit on core speech, should be met with the utmost skepticism and should receive the strictest scrutiny.

II

At bottom, the majority's refusal to apply strict scrutiny to contribution limits rests upon *Buckley*'s discounting of the First Amendment interests at stake. The analytic foundation of *Buckley*, however, was tenuous from the very beginning and has only continued to erode in the intervening years. What remains of *Buckley* fails to provide an adequate justification for limiting individual contributions to political candidates.

A

[In this part, Thomas criticized the rationales the Court in *Buckley* used to justify upholding contribution limitations while striking down expenditure limitations. In particular, he criticized the Court's statement that "the transformation of contributions into political debate involves speech by someone other than the contributor"—what Thomas called the "speech by proxy" argument. He wrote: ". . . [T]his was a faulty distinction *ab initio* because it ignored the reality of how speech of all kinds is disseminated."]

Without the assistance of the speech-by-proxy argument, the remainder of *Buckley*'s rationales founder.... These contentions simply ignore that a contribution, by amplifying the voice of the candidate, helps to ensure the dissemination of the messages that the contributor wishes to convey....

... The result is simply the suppression of political speech. By depriving donors of their right to speak through the candidate, contribution limits relegate donors' points of view to less effective modes of communication. Additionally, limiting contributions curtails individual participation.... *Buckley* completely failed in its attempt to provide a basis for permitting government to second-guess the individual choices of citizens partaking in quintessentially democratic activities....

B

The Court in *Buckley* denigrated the speech interests not only of contributors, but also of candidates.... The Court did not even attempt to claim that contribution limits do not suppress the speech of political candidates.... Instead, the Court abstracted from a candidate's individual right to speak and focused exclusively on aggregate campaign funding. [Quoting from *Buckley:* "There is no indication ... that the contribution limitations imposed by the Act would have any dramatic adverse effect on the funding of campaigns."] ...

The Court's flawed and unsupported aggregate approach ignores both the rights and value of individual candidates.... [T]he right to free speech is a right held by each American, not by Americans en masse. The Court in *Buckley* provided no basis for suppressing the speech of an individual candidate simply because other candidates (or candidates in the aggregate) may succeed in reaching the voting public.... In the case at hand, the Missouri scheme has a clear and detrimental effect on a candidate such as petitioner Fredman, who lacks the advantages of incumbency, name recognition, or substantial personal wealth, but who has managed to attract the support of a relatively small number of dedicated supporters: It forbids his message from reaching the voters. And the silencing of a candidate has consequences for political debate and competition overall....

III

Today, the majority blindly adopts *Buckley*'s flawed reasoning without so much as pausing to consider the collapse of the speech-by-proxy argument or the reality that *Buckley*'s remaining premises fall when deprived of that support.

After ignoring these shortcomings, the Court proceeds to apply something less—much less—than strict scrutiny. Just how much less the majority never says. The Court in *Buckley* at least purported to employ a test of "closest scrutiny." ... The Court today abandons even that pretense and reviews contributions under the *sui generis* "*Buckley*'s standard of scrutiny," which fails to obscure the Court's ad hoc balancing away of First Amendment rights....

Unfortunately, the majority does not stop with a revision of *Buckley*'s labels.... [T]he Court proceeds to significantly extend the holding in that case. The Court's substantive departure from *Buckley* begins with a revision of our compelling-interest jurisprudence. In *Buckley*, the Court indicated that the only interest that could qualify as "compelling" in this area was the government's interest in reducing actual and apparent corruption. And the Court repeatedly used the word "corruption" in the *narrow quid pro quo* sense. . . .

The majority today, by contrast, separates "corruption" from its *quid pro quo* roots and gives it a new, far-reaching (and speech-suppressing) definition, something like "[t]he perversion of anything from an original state of purity." [Quoting Oxford English Dictionary.] . . . [W]ithout bothering to offer any elaboration, much less justification, the majority permits vague and unenumerated harms to suffice as a compelling reason for the government to smother political speech.

. . . [T]he Court then goes on to weaken the requisite precision in tailoring. . . . [T]he majority ratifies a law with a much broader sweep than that approved in *Buckley*. In *Buckley*, the Court upheld contribution limits of $1,000 on individuals and $5,000 on political committees (in 1976 dollars). Here, by contrast, the Court approves much more restrictive contribution limitations, ranging from $250 to $1,000 (in 1995 dollars) for both individuals and political committees. The disparity between Missouri's caps and those upheld in *Buckley* is more pronounced when one takes into account some measure of inflation. . . . Yet the Court's opinion gives not a single indication that the two laws may differ in their tailoring. . . . I cannot fathom how a $251 contribution could pose a substantial risk of "secur[ing] a political *quid pro quo*." Thus, contribution caps set at such levels could never be "closely drawn" to preventing *quid pro quo* corruption. . . .

The Court also reworks *Buckley*'s aggregate approach to the free speech rights of candidates. . . . [T]he Court . . . deviates from *Buckley*, persuading itself that Missouri's limits do not suppress political speech because, prior to the enactment of contribution limits, "97.62 percent of all contributors to candidates for state auditor made contributions of $2,000 or less." . . . [T]he statistic provides no assurance that Missouri's law has not reduced the resources supporting political speech, since the largest contributors provide a disproportionate amount of funds. The majority conspicuously offers no data revealing the percentage of funds provided by large contributors. . . . But whatever the data would reveal, the Court's position would remain indefensible. If the majority's assumption is incorrect—*i.e.*, if Missouri's contribution limits actually do significantly reduce campaign speech—then the majority's calm assurance that political speech remains unaffected collapses. If the majority's assumption is correct—*i.e.*, if large contributions provide very little assistance to a candidate seeking to get out his message (and thus will not be missed when capped)—then the majority's reasoning still falters. For if large contributions offer as little help to a candidate as the Court maintains, then the Court fails to explain why a candidate would engage in "corruption" for such a meager benefit. . . .

IV

In light of the importance of political speech to republican government, Missouri's substantial restriction of speech warrants strict scrutiny, which requires that contribution limits be narrowly tailored to a compelling governmental interest.

Missouri does assert that its contribution caps are aimed at preventing actual and apparent corruption. . . . But the State's contribution limits are not narrowly tailored to that harm. The limits directly suppress the political speech of both contributors and candidates, and only clumsily further the governmental interests that they allegedly serve. They are crudely tailored because they are massively overinclusive, prohibiting all donors who wish to contribute in excess of the cap from doing so and restricting donations without regard to whether the donors pose any real corruption risk. . . . Moreover, the government has less restrictive means of addressing its interest in curtailing corruption. Bribery laws bar precisely the *quid pro quo* arrangements that are targeted here. And disclosure laws "deter actual corruption and avoid the appearance of corruption by exposing large contributions and expenditures to the light of publicity." [Quoting brief by American Constitutional Law Foundation.] In fact, Missouri has enacted strict disclosure laws. [Citing statutes.]

In the end, contribution limitations find support only in the proposition that other means will not be as effective at rooting out corruption. But when it comes to a significant infringement on our fundamental liberties, that some undesirable conduct may not be deterred is an insufficient justification to sweep in vast amounts of protected political speech. . . .

The same principles apply here, and dictate a result contrary to the one the majority reaches. States are free to enact laws that directly punish those engaged in corruption and require the disclosure of large contributions, but they are not free to enact generalized laws that suppress a tremendous amount of protected speech along with the targeted corruption.

V

Because the Court unjustifiably discounts the First Amendment interests of citizens and candidates, and consequently fails to strictly scrutinize the inhibition of political speech and competition, I respectfully dissent.

No. 98-1152

Food and Drug Administration, et al., Petitioners, v. Brown & Williamson Tobacco Corporation et al.

On writ of certiorari to the United States Court of Appeals for the Fourth Circuit

[March 21, 2000]

JUSTICE O'CONNOR delivered the opinion of the Court.

This case involves one of the most troubling public health problems facing our Nation today: the thousands of premature deaths that occur each year because of tobacco use. In 1996, the Food and Drug Administration (FDA), after having expressly disavowed any such authority since its inception, asserted jurisdiction to regulate tobacco products. See 61 Fed. Reg. 44619-45318. The FDA concluded that nicotine is a "drug" within the meaning of the Food, Drug, and Cosmetic Act (FDCA or Act), 21 U.S.C. §301 *et seq.*, and that cigarettes and smokeless tobacco are "combination products" that deliver nicotine to the body. Pursuant to this authority, it promulgated regulations intended to reduce tobacco consumption among children and adolescents. The agency believed that, because most tobacco consumers begin their use before reaching the age of 18, curbing tobacco use by minors could substantially reduce the prevalence of addiction in future generations and thus the incidence of tobacco-related death and disease.

Regardless of how serious the problem an administrative agency seeks to address, however, it may not exercise its authority "in a manner that is inconsistent with the administrative structure that Congress enacted into law." [Citation omitted.] And although agencies are generally entitled to deference in the interpretation of statutes that they administer, a reviewing "court, as well as the agency, must give effect to the unambiguously expressed intent of Congress." *Chevron U. S. A. Inc. v. Natural Resources Defense Council, Inc.* (1984). In this case, we believe that Congress has clearly precluded the FDA from asserting jurisdiction to regulate tobacco products. Such authority is inconsistent with the intent that Congress has expressed in the FDCA's overall regulatory scheme and in the tobacco-specific legislation that it has enacted subsequent to the FDCA. In light of this clear intent, the FDA's assertion of jurisdiction is impermissible.

I

The FDCA grants the FDA, as the designee of the Secretary of Health and Human Services, the authority to regulate, among other items, "drugs" and "devices." See 21 U.S.C. §§321(g)-(h), 393.

The Act defines "drug" to include "articles (other than food) intended to affect the structure or any function of the body." 21 U.S.C. §321(g)(1)(C). It defines "device," in part, as "an instrument, apparatus, implement, machine, contrivance, . . . or other similar or related article, including any component, part, or accessory, which is . . . intended to affect the structure or any function of the body." §321(h). The Act also grants the FDA the authority to regulate so-called "combination products," which "constitute a combination of a drug, device, or biologic product." §353(g)(1). The FDA has construed this provision as giving it the discretion to regulate combination products as drugs, as devices, or as both.

On August 11, 1995, the FDA published a proposed rule concerning the sale of cigarettes and smokeless tobacco to children and adolescents. The rule, which included several restrictions on the sale, distribution, and advertisement of tobacco products, was designed to reduce the availability and attractiveness of tobacco products to young people. A public comment period followed, during which the FDA received over 700,000 submissions, more than "at any other time in its history on any other subject."

On August 28, 1996, the FDA issued a final rule entitled "Regulations Restricting the Sale and Distribution of Cigarettes and Smokeless Tobacco to Protect Children and Adolescents." The FDA determined that nicotine is a "drug" and that cigarettes and smokeless tobacco are "drug delivery devices," and therefore it had jurisdiction under the FDCA to regulate tobacco products as customarily marketed—that is, without manufacturer claims of therapeutic benefit. First, the FDA found that tobacco products "affect the structure or any function of the body" because nicotine "has significant pharmacological effects." Specifically, nicotine "exerts psychoactive, or mood-altering, effects on the brain" that cause and sustain addiction, have both tranquilizing and stimulating effects, and control weight. Second, the FDA determined that these effects were "intended" under the FDCA because they "are so widely known and foreseeable that [they] may be deemed to have been intended by the manufacturers," consumers use tobacco products "predominantly or nearly exclusively" to obtain these effects, and the statements, research, and actions of manufacturers revealed that they "have 'designed' cigarettes to provide pharmacologically active doses of nicotine to consumers." Finally, the agency concluded that cigarettes and smokeless tobacco are "combination products" because, in addition to containing nicotine, they include device components that deliver a controlled amount of nicotine to the body.

Having resolved the jurisdictional question, the FDA next explained the policy justifications for its regulations, detailing the deleterious health effects associated with tobacco use. It found that tobacco consumption was "the single leading cause of preventable death in the United States." According to the FDA, "[m]ore than 400,000 people die each year from tobacco-related illnesses, such as cancer, respiratory illnesses, and heart disease." The agency also determined that the only way to reduce the amount of tobacco-related illness and mortality was to reduce the level of addiction, a goal that could be accomplished only by preventing children and adolescents from starting to use tobacco. . . .

Based on these findings, the FDA promulgated regulations concerning tobacco products' promotion, labeling, and accessibility to children and adolescents. The access regulations prohibit the sale of cigarettes or smokeless tobacco to persons younger than 18; require retailers to verify through photo identification the age of all purchasers younger than 27; prohibit the sale of cigarettes in quantities smaller than 20; prohibit the distribution of free samples; and prohibit sales through self-service displays and vending machines except in adult-only locations. The promotion regulations require that any print advertising appear in a black-and-white, text-only format unless the publication in which it appears is read almost exclusively by adults; prohibit outdoor advertising within 1,000 feet of any public playground or school; prohibit the distribution of any promotional items, such as T-shirts or hats, bearing the manufacturer's brand name; and prohibit a manufacturer from sponsoring any athletic, musical, artistic, or other social or cultural event using its brand name. The labeling regulation requires that the statement, "A Nicotine-Delivery Device for Persons 18 or Older," appear on all tobacco product packages.

The FDA promulgated these regulations pursuant to its authority to regulate "restricted devices." . . . Under 21 U.S.C. §360j(e), the agency may "require that a device be restricted to sale, distribution, or use . . . upon such other conditions as [the FDA] may prescribe in such regulation, if, because of its potentiality for harmful effect or the collateral measures necessary to its use, [the FDA] determines that there cannot otherwise be reasonable assurance of its safety and effectiveness." . . .

Respondents, a group of tobacco manufacturers, retailers, and advertisers, filed suit in United States District Court for the Middle District of North Carolina challenging the regulations. They moved for summary judgment on the grounds that the FDA lacked jurisdiction to regulate tobacco products as customarily marketed, the regulations exceeded the FDA's authority under 21 U.S.C. §360j(e), and the advertising restrictions violated the First Amendment. The District Court granted respondents' motion in part and denied it in part. [*Coyne Beahm, Inc. v. FDA* (1997).] The court held that the FDCA authorizes the FDA to regulate tobacco products as customarily marketed and that the FDA's access and labeling regulations are permissible, but it also found that the agency's advertising and promotion restrictions exceed its authority under §360j(e). . . .

The Court of Appeals for the Fourth Circuit reversed, holding that Congress has not granted the FDA jurisdiction to regulate tobacco products (1998). [Discussion of appeals court opinion omitted.]

We granted the Government's petition for certiorari (1999) to determine whether the FDA has authority under the FDCA to regulate tobacco products as customarily marketed.

II

The FDA's assertion of jurisdiction to regulate tobacco products is founded on its conclusions that nicotine is a "drug" and that cigarettes and smokeless tobacco are "drug delivery devices." . . .

A threshold issue is the appropriate framework for analyzing the FDA's assertion of authority to regulate tobacco products. Because this case involves an administrative agency's construction of a statute that it administers, our analysis is governed by *Chevron U.S.A. Inc. v. Natural Resources Defense Council, Inc.* (1984). Under *Chevron*, a reviewing court must first ask "whether Congress has directly spoken to the precise question at issue." If Congress has done so, the inquiry is at an end; the court "must give effect to the unambiguously expressed intent of Congress." But if Congress has not specifically addressed the question, a reviewing court must respect the agency's construction of the statute so long as it is permissible. . . .

In determining whether Congress has specifically addressed the question at issue, a reviewing court should not confine itself to examining a particular statutory provision in isolation. The meaning—or ambiguity—of certain words or phrases may only become evident when placed in context. . . . Similarly, the meaning of one statute may be affected by other Acts, particularly where Congress has spoken subsequently and more specifically to the topic at hand. In addition, we must be guided to a degree by common sense as to the manner in which Congress is likely to delegate a policy decision of such economic and political magnitude to an administrative agency. . . .

With these principles in mind, we find that Congress has directly spoken to the issue here and precluded the FDA's jurisdiction to regulate tobacco products.

A

Viewing the FDCA as a whole, it is evident that one of the Act's core objectives is to ensure that any product regulated by the FDA is "safe" and "effective" for its intended use. . . . This essential purpose pervades the FDCA. . . .

In its rulemaking proceeding, the FDA quite exhaustively documented that "to-bacco products are unsafe," "dangerous," and "cause great pain and suffering from illness." . . .

These findings logically imply that, if tobacco products were "devices" under the FDCA, the FDA would be required to remove them from the market. [Citing provisions of the FDCA, O'Connor said that cigarettes and smokeless tobacco would be considered "misbranded" because they are "dangerous to health" when used in the manner prescribed and because it would be impossible to include in the labeling "adequate directions for use . . . as are necessary for the protections of users."] Thus, were tobacco products within the FDA's jurisdiction, the Act would deem them misbranded devices that could not be introduced into interstate commerce. Contrary to the dissent's contention, the Act admits no remedial discretion once it is evident that the device is misbranded.

Second, the FDCA requires the FDA to place all devices that it regulates into one of three classifications. [O'Connor said the FDA would be required to classify cigarettes and smokeless tobacco as Class III devices, which cannot be marketed without "a showing of reasonable assurance of" safety when used in the prescribed manner.] In view of the FDA's conclusions regarding the health effects of tobacco use, the agency would have no basis for finding any such reasonable assurance of safety. Thus, once the FDA fulfilled its statutory obligation to classify tobacco products, it could not allow them to be marketed.

The FDCA's misbranding and device classification provisions therefore make evident that were the FDA to regulate cigarettes and smokeless tobacco, the Act would require the agency to ban them. . . .

Congress, however, has foreclosed the removal of tobacco products from the market. . . . Congress has directly addressed the problem of tobacco and health through legislation on six occasions since 1965. See Federal Cigarette Labeling and Advertising Act (FCLAA); Public Health Cigarette Smoking Act of 1969; Alcohol and Drug Abuse Amendments of 1983; Comprehensive Smoking Education Act; Comprehensive Smokeless Tobacco Health Education Act of 1986 [CSTHEA]; Alcohol, Drug Abuse, and Mental Health Administration Reorganization Act. When Congress enacted these statutes, the adverse health consequences of tobacco use were well known, as were nicotine's pharmacological effects. . . . Nonetheless, Congress stopped well short of ordering a ban. Instead, it has generally regulated the labeling and advertisement of tobacco products. . . . Congress' decisions to regulate labeling and advertising and to adopt the express policy of protecting "commerce and the national economy . . . to the maximum extent" reveal its intent that tobacco products remain on the market. . . . A ban of tobacco products by the FDA would therefore plainly contradict congressional policy.

The FDA apparently recognized this dilemma and concluded, somewhat ironically, that tobacco products are actually "safe" within the meaning of the FDCA. . . . [T]he FDA reasoned that, in determining whether a device is safe under the Act, it must consider "not only the risks presented by a product but also any of the countervailing effects of use of that product, including the consequences of not permitting the product to be marketed." Applying this standard, the FDA found that, because of the high level of addiction among tobacco users, a ban would likely be "dangerous." In particular, current tobacco users could suffer from extreme withdrawal, the health care system and available pharmaceuticals might not be able to meet the treatment demands of those suffering from withdrawal, and a black market offering cigarettes even more dangerous than those currently sold legally would likely develop. . . .

. . . [T]he FDA's judgment that leaving tobacco products on the market "is more effective in achieving public health goals than a ban" is no substitute for the specific safety determinations required by the FDCA's various operative provisions. . . .

The FDA's conception of safety is also incompatible with the FDCA's misbranding provision. . . .

. . . [I]f tobacco products were within the FDA's jurisdiction, the Act would require the FDA to remove them from the market entirely. But a ban would contradict Congress' clear intent as expressed in its more recent, tobacco-specific legislation. The inescapable conclusion is that there is no room for tobacco products within the FDCA's regulatory scheme. If they cannot be used safely for any therapeutic purpose, and yet they cannot be banned, they simply do not fit.

B

In determining whether Congress has spoken directly to the FDA's authority to regulate tobacco, we must also consider in greater detail the tobacco-specific legislation that Congress has enacted over the past 35 years. . . .

Congress has enacted six separate pieces of legislation since 1965 addressing the problem of tobacco use and human health. Those statutes, among other things, require that health warnings appear on all packaging and in all print and outdoor advertisements, see 15 U.S.C. §§1331, 1333, 4402; prohibit the advertisement of tobacco products through "any medium of electronic communication" subject to regulation by the Federal Communications Commission (FCC), see §§1335, 4402(f); require the Secretary of Health and Human Services (HHS) to report every three years to Congress on research findings concerning "the addictive property of tobacco," 42 U.S.C. §290aa-2(b)(2); and make States' receipt of certain federal block grants contingent on their making it unlawful "for any manufacturer, retailer, or distributor of tobacco products to sell or distribute any such product to any individual under the age of 18," §300x-26(a)(1).

In adopting each statute, Congress has acted against the backdrop of the FDA's consistent and repeated statements that it lacked authority under the FDCA to regulate tobacco absent claims of therapeutic benefit by the manufacturer. In fact, on several occasions over this period, and after the health consequences of tobacco use and nicotine's pharmacological effects had become well known, Congress considered and rejected bills that would have granted the FDA such jurisdiction. Under these circumstances, it is evident that Congress' tobacco-specific statutes have effectively ratified the FDA's long-held position that it lacks jurisdiction under the FDCA to regulate tobacco products. Congress has created a distinct regulatory scheme to address the problem of tobacco and health, and that scheme, as presently constructed, precludes any role for the FDA. [Detailed history omitted.]

Taken together, these actions by Congress over the past 35 years preclude an interpretation of the FDCA that grants the FDA jurisdiction to regulate tobacco products. . . . [T]his is not a case of simple inaction by Congress that purportedly represents its acquiescence in an agency's position. To the contrary, Congress has enacted several statutes addressing the particular subject of tobacco and health, creating a distinct regulatory scheme for cigarettes and smokeless tobacco. In doing so, Congress has been aware of tobacco's health hazards and its pharmacological effects. It has also enacted this legislation against the background of the FDA repeatedly and consistently asserting that it lacks jurisdiction under the FDCA to regulate tobacco products as customarily marketed. Further, Congress has persistently acted to preclude a meaningful role for any administrative agency in making policy on the subject of tobacco and health. Moreover, the substance of Congress' regulatory scheme is, in an important respect, incompatible with FDA jurisdiction. Although the supervision of product labeling to protect consumer health is a substantial component of the FDA's regulation of drugs and devices, the FCLAA and the CSTHEA explicitly prohibit any federal agency from imposing any health-related labeling requirements on cigarettes or smokeless tobacco products, see 15 U.S.C. §§1334(a), 4406(a).

Under these circumstances, it is clear that Congress' tobacco-specific legislation has effectively ratified the FDA's previous position that it lacks jurisdiction to regulate tobacco. . . . Congress has affirmatively acted to address the issue of tobacco and health, relying on the representations of the FDA that it had no authority to regulate tobacco. It has created a distinct scheme to regulate the sale of tobacco products, focused on labeling and advertising, and premised on the belief that the FDA lacks such jurisdiction under the FDCA. As a result, Congress' tobacco-specific statutes preclude the FDA from regulating tobacco products as customarily marketed. . . .

C

Finally, our inquiry into whether Congress has directly spoken to the precise question at issue is shaped, at least in some measure, by the nature of the question presented. Deference under *Chevron* to an agency's construction of a statute that it administers is premised on the theory that a statute's ambiguity constitutes an implicit delegation from Congress to the agency to fill in the statutory gaps. In extraordinary cases, however, there may be reason to hesitate before concluding that Congress has intended such an implicit delegation. . . .

This is hardly an ordinary case. Contrary to its representations to Congress since 1914, the FDA has now asserted jurisdiction to regulate an industry constituting a significant portion of the American economy. In fact, the FDA contends that, were it to determine that tobacco products provide no "reasonable assurance of safety," it would have the authority to ban cigarettes and smokeless tobacco entirely. Owing to its unique place in American history and society, tobacco has its own unique political history. Congress, for better or for worse, has created a distinct regulatory scheme for tobacco products, squarely rejected proposals to give the FDA jurisdiction over tobacco, and repeatedly acted to preclude any agency from exercising significant policymaking authority in the area. Given this history and the breadth of the authority that the FDA has asserted, we are obliged to defer not to the agency's expansive construction of the statute, but to Congress' consistent judgment to deny the FDA this power. . . .

* * *

By no means do we question the seriousness of the problem that the FDA has sought to address. The agency has amply demonstrated that tobacco use, particularly among children and adolescents, poses perhaps the single most significant threat to public health in the United States. Nonetheless, no matter how "important, conspicuous, and controversial" the issue, and regardless of how likely the public is to hold the Executive Branch politically accountable, an administrative agency's power to regulate in the public interest must always be grounded in a valid grant of authority from Congress. . . . Reading the FDCA as a whole, as well as in conjunction with Congress' subsequent tobacco-specific legislation, it is plain that Congress has not given the FDA the authority that it seeks to exercise here. For these reasons, the judgment of the Court of Appeals for the Fourth Circuit is affirmed.

It is so ordered.

JUSTICE BREYER, with whom JUSTICE STEVENS, JUSTICE SOUTER, and JUSTICE GINSBURG join, dissenting.

The Food and Drug Administration (FDA) has the authority to regulate "articles (other than food) intended to affect the structure or any function of the body. . . ." Federal Food, Drug and Cosmetic Act (FDCA), 21 U.S.C. §321(g)(1)(C). Unlike the majority, I believe that tobacco products fit within this statutory language.

In its own interpretation, the majority nowhere denies the following two salient points. First, tobacco products (including cigarettes) fall within the scope of this statutory definition, read literally. Cigarettes achieve their mood-stabilizing effects through the interaction of the chemical nicotine and the cells of the central nervous system. Both cigarette manufacturers and smokers alike know of, and desire, that chemically induced result. Hence, cigarettes are "intended to affect" the body's "structure" and "function," in the literal sense of these words.

Second, the statute's basic purpose—the protection of public health—supports the inclusion of cigarettes within its scope. . . .

Unregulated tobacco use causes "[m]ore than 400,000 people [to] die each year from tobacco-related illnesses, such as cancer, respiratory illnesses, and heart disease." [Quoting Federal Register's publication of FDA regulation, 1996.] Indeed, tobacco products kill more people in this country every year "than . . . AIDS, car accidents, alcohol, homicides, illegal drugs, suicides, and fires, *combined*" (emphasis added).

Despite the FDCA's literal language and general purpose (both of which support the FDA's finding that cigarettes come within its statutory authority), the majority nonetheless reads the statute as excluding tobacco products for two basic reasons:

> (1) the FDCA does not "fit" the case of tobacco because the statute requires the FDA to prohibit dangerous drugs or devices (like cigarettes) outright, and the agency concedes that simply banning the sale of cigarettes is not a proper remedy; and
> 2) Congress has enacted other statutes, which, when viewed in light of the FDA's long history of denying tobacco-related jurisdiction and considered together with Congress' failure explicitly to grant the agency

> tobacco-specific authority, demonstrate that Congress did not intend for
> the FDA to exercise jurisdiction over tobacco.

In my view, neither of these propositions is valid. Rather, the FDCA does not significantly limit the FDA's remedial alternatives. And the later statutes do not tell the FDA it cannot exercise jurisdiction, but simply leave FDA jurisdictional law where Congress found it. . . .

The bulk of the opinion that follows will explain the basis for these latter conclusions. In short, I believe that the most important indicia of statutory meaning—language and purpose—along with the FDCA's legislative history (described briefly in Part I) are sufficient to establish that the FDA has authority to regulate tobacco. The statute-specific arguments against jurisdiction that the tobacco companies and the majority rely upon (discussed in Part II) are based on erroneous assumptions and, thus, do not defeat the jurisdiction-supporting thrust of the FDCA's language and purpose. The inferences that the majority draws from later legislative history are not persuasive, since (as I point out in Part III) one can just as easily infer from the later laws that Congress did not intend to affect the FDA's tobacco-related authority at all. And the fact that the FDA changed its mind about the scope of its own jurisdiction is legally insignificant because (as Part IV establishes) the agency's reasons for changing course are fully justified. Finally, as I explain in Part V, the degree of accountability that likely will attach to the FDA's action in this case should alleviate any concern that Congress, rather than an administrative agency, ought to make this important regulatory decision.

I

Before 1938, the federal Pure Food and Drug Act contained only two jurisdictional definitions of "drug":

> "[1] medicines and preparations recognized in the United States Pharmacopoeia or National Formulary . . . and [2] any substance or mixture of substances intended to be used for the cure, mitigation, or prevention of disease."

In 1938, Congress added a third definition, relevant here:

> "(3) articles (other than food) intended to affect the structure or any function of the body. . . ." (codified at 21 U.S.C. §321(g)(1)(C)).

It also added a similar definition in respect to a "device" (codified at 21 U.S.C. §321(h)). . . . [T]he literal language of the third definition and the FDCA's general purpose both strongly support a projurisdiction reading of the statute.

The statute's history offers further support. The FDA drafted the new language, and it testified before Congress that the third definition would expand the FDCA's jurisdictional scope significantly. . . . While the drafters focused specifically upon the need to give the FDA jurisdiction over "slenderizing" products such as "antifat remedies," they were aware that, in doing so, they had created what was "admittedly an inclusive, a wide definition." And that broad language was included *deliberately*, so that jurisdiction could be had over "*all* substances and preparations, other than food, and *all* devices intended to affect the structure or any function of the body. . . ." (emphasis added). . . .

II

A

The tobacco companies contend that the FDCA's words cannot possibly be read to mean what they literally say. The statute defines "device," for example, as "an instrument, apparatus, implement, machine, contrivance, implant, in vitro reagent, or other similar or related article . . . intended to affect the structure or any function of the body. . . ." Taken literally, this definition might include everything from room air conditioners to thermal pajamas. The companies argue that, to avoid such a result, the meaning of "drug" or "device" should be confined to medical or therapeutic products, narrowly defined.

The companies may well be right that the statute should not be read to cover room air conditioners and winter underwear. But . . . I do not agree that we must accept their proposed limitation. For one thing, such a cramped reading contravenes the established purpose of the statutory language. . . .

Most importantly, the statute's language itself supplies a different, more suitable, limitation: that a "drug" must be a *chemical* agent. The FDCA's "device" definition states that an article which affects the structure or function of the body is a "device" only if it "does *not* achieve its primary intended purposes through chemical action within . . . the body," and "is *not* dependent upon being metabolized for the achievement of its primary intended purposes." §321(h) (emphasis added). One can readily infer from this language that at least an article that *does* achieve its primary purpose through chemical action within the body and that is dependent upon being metabolized is a "drug," provided that it otherwise falls within the scope of the "drug" definition. And one need not hypothesize about air conditioners or thermal pajamas to recognize that the chemical nicotine, an important tobacco ingredient, meets this test. . . .

[Breyer described the chemical effects of nicotine on the body. Nicotine, he said, "stabilizes mood, suppresses appetite, tranquilizes, and satisfies a physical craving that nicotine itself has helped to create—all through chemical action within the body after being metabolized."]

. . . [F]or present purposes, that chemistry demonstrates that nicotine affects the "structure" and "function" of the body in a manner that is quite similar to the effects of other regulated substances. . . . And, since the nicotine in cigarettes plainly is not a "food," its chemical effects suffice to establish that it is as a "drug" (and the cigarette that delivers it a drug-delivery "device") for the purpose of the FDCA.

B, C [OMITTED]

III

In the majority's view, laws enacted since 1965 require us to deny jurisdiction, whatever the FDCA might mean in their absence. But why? Do those laws contain language barring FDA jurisdiction? The majority must concede that they do not. Do they contain provisions that are inconsistent with the FDA's exercise of jurisdiction? With one exception [preemption provision of the 1965 Federal Cigarette Labeling and Advertising Act], the majority points to no such provision. Do they somehow repeal the principles of law . . . that otherwise would lead to the conclusion that the FDA has jurisdiction in this area? The companies themselves deny making any such claim. Perhaps the later laws "shape" and "focus" what the 1938 Congress meant a generation earlier. But this Court has warned against using the views of a later Congress to construe a statute enacted many years before. . . . And, while the majority suggests that the subsequent history "control[s] our construction" of the FDCA, this Court expressly has held that such subsequent views are not "controlling." . . .

Regardless, the later statutes do not support the majority's conclusion. That is because, whatever individual Members of Congress after 1964 may have assumed about the FDA's jurisdiction, the laws they enacted did not embody any such "no jurisdiction" assumption. And one cannot automatically infer an antijurisdiction intent, as the majority does, for the later statutes are both (and similarly) consistent with quite a different congressional desire, namely, the intent to proceed without interfering with whatever authority the FDA otherwise may have possessed. [Remainder of section omitted.]

IV

I now turn to the final historical fact that the majority views as a factor in its interpretation of the subsequent legislative history: the FDA's former denials of its tobacco-related authority.

Until the early 1990's, the FDA expressly maintained that the 1938 statute did not give it the power that it now seeks to assert. It then changed its mind. . . . In my view, the FDA's change of policy, like the subsequent statutes themselves, does nothing to advance the majority's position.

When it denied jurisdiction to regulate cigarettes, the FDA consistently stated why that was so. In 1963, for example, FDA administrators wrote that cigarettes did not satisfy the relevant FDCA definitions—in particular, the "intent" requirement—because cigarette makers did not sell their product with accompanying "therapeutic claims." And subsequent FDA Commissioners made roughly the same assertion. . . .

What changed? For one thing, the FDA obtained evidence sufficient to prove the necessary "intent" despite the absence of specific "claims." This evidence, which first became available in the early 1990's, permitted the agency to demonstrate that the tobacco companies knew nicotine achieved appetite-suppressing, mood-stabilizing, and habituating effects through chemical (not psychological) means, even at a time when the companies were publicly denying such knowledge.

Moreover, scientific evidence of adverse health effects mounted, until, in the late 1980's, a consensus on the seriousness of the matter became firm. . . .

Finally, administration policy changed. Earlier administrations may have hesitated to assert jurisdiction for the reasons prior Commissioners expressed. Commissioners of the current administration simply took a different regulatory attitude.

Nothing in the law prevents the FDA from changing its policy for such reasons. By the mid-1990's, the evidence needed to prove objective intent—even without an express claim—had been found. The emerging scientific consensus about tobacco's adverse, chemically induced, health effects may have convinced the agency that it should spend its resources on this important regulatory effort. . . .

V [OMITTED]

* * *

According to the FDA, only 2.5% of smokers successfully stop smoking each year, even though 70% say they want to quit and 34% actually make an attempt to do so. The fact that only a handful of those who try to quit smoking actually succeed illustrates a certain reality—the reality that the nicotine in cigarettes creates a powerful physiological addiction flowing from chemically induced changes in the brain. The FDA has found that the makers of cigarettes "intend" these physical effects. Hence, nicotine is a "drug"; the cigarette that delivers nicotine to the body is a "device"; and the FDCA's language, read in light of its basic purpose, permits the FDA to assert the disease-preventing jurisdiction that the agency now claims.

The majority finds that cigarettes are so dangerous that the FDCA would require them to be banned (a result the majority believes Congress would not have desired); thus, it concludes that the FDA has no tobacco-related authority. I disagree that the statute would require a cigarette ban. But even if I am wrong about the ban, the statute would restrict only the agency's choice of remedies, not its jurisdiction.

The majority also believes that subsequently enacted statutes deprive the FDA of jurisdiction. But the later laws say next to nothing about the FDA's tobacco-related authority. Previous FDA disclaimers of jurisdiction may have helped to form the legislative atmosphere out of which Congress' own tobacco-specific statutes emerged. But a legislative atmosphere is not a law, unless it is embodied in a statutory word or phrase. And the relevant words and phrases here reveal nothing more than an intent not to change the jurisdictional status quo.

The upshot is that the Court today holds that a regulatory statute aimed at unsafe drugs and devices does not authorize regulation of a drug (nicotine) and a device (a cigarette) that the Court itself finds unsafe. Far more than most, this particular drug and device risks the life-threatening harms that administrative regulation seeks to rectify. The majority's conclusion is counter-intuitive. And, for the reasons set forth, I believe that the law does not require it.

Consequently, I dissent.

Nos. 99-5 and 99-29

United States, Petitioner v. Antonio J. Morrison
Christy Brzonkala, Petitioner v. Antonio J. Morrison

On writs of certiorari to the United States Court of Appeals
for the Fourth Circuit

[May 15, 2000]

CHIEF JUSTICE REHNQUIST delivered the opinion of the Court.
In these cases we consider the constitutionality of 42 U.S.C. §13981, which provides a federal civil remedy for the victims of gender-motivated violence. The
United States Court of Appeals for the Fourth Circuit, sitting en banc, struck down
§13981 because it concluded that Congress lacked constitutional authority to enact the section's civil remedy. Believing that these cases are controlled by our decisions in *United States v. Lopez* (1995), *United States v. Harris* (1883), and the *Civil
Rights Cases* (1883), we affirm.

I

Petitioner Christy Brzonkala enrolled at Virginia Polytechnic Institute (Virginia
Tech) in the fall of 1994. In September of that year, Brzonkala met respondents Antonio Morrison and James Crawford, who were both students at Virginia Tech and
members of its varsity football team. Brzonkala alleges that, within 30 minutes of
meeting Morrison and Crawford, they assaulted and repeatedly raped her. After the
attack, Morrison allegedly told Brzonkala, "You better not have any . . . diseases."
In the months following the rape, Morrison also allegedly announced in the dormitory's dining room that he "like[d] to get girls drunk and. . . ." The omitted portions, quoted verbatim in the briefs on file with this Court, consist of boasting, de-
based remarks about what Morrison would do to women, vulgar remarks that
cannot fail to shock and offend.
Brzonkala alleges that this attack caused her to become severely emotionally dis-
turbed and depressed. She sought assistance from a university psychiatrist, who
prescribed antidepressant medication. Shortly after the rape Brzonkala stopped attending classes and withdrew from the university.
In early 1995, Brzonkala filed a complaint against respondents under Virginia
Tech's Sexual Assault Policy. During the school-conducted hearing on her complaint, Morrison admitted having sexual contact with her despite the fact that
she had twice told him "no." After the hearing, Virginia Tech's Judicial Committee found insufficient evidence to punish Crawford, but found Morrison guilty of
sexual assault and sentenced him to immediate suspension for two semesters.
Virginia Tech's dean of students upheld the judicial committee's sentence. However, in July 1995, Virginia Tech informed Brzonkala that Morrison intended to
initiate a court challenge to his conviction under the Sexual Assault Policy. Uni-

versity officials told her that a second hearing would be necessary to remedy the school's error in prosecuting her complaint under that policy, which had not been widely circulated to students. The university therefore conducted a second hearing under its Abusive Conduct Policy, which was in force prior to the dissemination of the Sexual Assault Policy. Following this second hearing the Judicial Committee again found Morrison guilty and sentenced him to an identical 2-semester suspension. This time, however, the description of Morrison's offense was, without explanation, changed from "sexual assault" to "using abusive language."

Morrison appealed his second conviction through the university's administrative system. On August 21, 1995, Virginia Tech's senior vice president and provost set aside Morrison's punishment. She concluded that it was "excessive when compared with other cases where there has been a finding of violation of the Abusive Conduct Policy." Virginia Tech did not inform Brzonkala of this decision. After learning from a newspaper that Morrison would be returning to Virginia Tech for the fall 1995 semester, she dropped out of the university.

In December 1995, Brzonkala sued Morrison, Crawford, and Virginia Tech in the United States District Court for the Western District of Virginia. Her complaint alleged that Morrison's and Crawford's attack violated §13981 and that Virginia Tech's handling of her complaint violated Title IX of the Education Amendments of 1972. Morrison and Crawford moved to dismiss this complaint on the grounds that it failed to state a claim and that §13981's civil remedy is unconstitutional. The United States intervened to defend §13981's constitutionality.

The District Court dismissed Brzonkala's Title IX claims against Virginia Tech for failure to state a claim upon which relief can be granted. (1996). It then held that Brzonkala's complaint stated a claim against Morrison and Crawford under §13981, but dismissed the complaint because it concluded that Congress lacked authority to enact the section under either the Commerce Clause or §5 of the Fourteenth Amendment. (1996).

A divided panel of the Court of Appeals reversed the District Court, reinstating Brzonkala's §13981 claim and her Title IX hostile environment claim. (1997). The full Court of Appeals vacated the panel's opinion and reheard the case en banc. The en banc court then issued an opinion affirming the District Court's conclusion that Brzonkala stated a claim under §13981 because her complaint alleged a crime of violence and the allegations of Morrison's crude and derogatory statements regarding his treatment of women sufficiently indicated that his crime was motivated by gender animus. Nevertheless, the court by a divided vote affirmed the District Court's conclusion that Congress lacked constitutional authority to enact §13981's civil remedy. (1999). Because the Court of Appeals invalidated a federal statute on constitutional grounds, we granted certiorari.

Section 13981 was part of the Violence Against Women Act of 1994. It states that "[a]ll persons within the United States shall have the right to be free from crimes of violence motivated by gender." 42 U.S.C. §13981(b). To enforce that right, subsection (c) declares:

> "A person (including a person who acts under color of any statute, ordinance, regulation, custom, or usage of any State) who commits a crime of violence motivated by gender and thus deprives another of the right declared in subsection (b) of this section shall be liable to the party injured,

in an action for the recovery of compensatory and punitive damages, injunctive and declaratory relief, and such other relief as a court may deem appropriate."

Section 13981 defines a "crim[e] of violence motivated by gender" as "a crime of violence committed because of gender or on the basis of gender, and due, at least in part, to an animus based on the victim's gender." §13981(d)(1). . . .

. . . [S]ubsection (e)(2) states that "[n]othing in this section requires a prior criminal complaint, prosecution, or conviction to establish the elements of a cause of action under subsection (c) of this section." And subsection (e)(3) provides a §13981 litigant with a choice of forums: Federal and state courts "shall have concurrent jurisdiction" over complaints brought under the section. . . .

Every law enacted by Congress must be based on one or more of its powers enumerated in the Constitution. . . . Congress explicitly identified the sources of federal authority on which it relied in enacting §13981. It said that a "federal civil rights cause of action" is established "[p]ursuant to the affirmative power of Congress . . . under section 5 of the Fourteenth Amendment to the Constitution, as well as under section 8 of Article I of the Constitution." 42 U.S.C. §13981(a). We address Congress' authority to enact this remedy under each of these constitutional provisions in turn.

II

Due respect for the decisions of a coordinate branch of Government demands that we invalidate a congressional enactment only upon a plain showing that Congress has exceeded its constitutional bounds. With this presumption of constitutionality in mind, we turn to the question whether §13981 falls within Congress' power under Article I, §8, of the Constitution. Brzonkala and the United States rely upon the third clause of the Article, which gives Congress power "[t]o regulate Commerce with foreign Nations, and among the several States, and with the Indian Tribes." . . .

Lopez emphasized . . . that even under our modern, expansive interpretation of the Commerce Clause, Congress' regulatory authority is not without effective bounds. [Quote from *Lopez* omitted.]

As we observed in *Lopez*, modern Commerce Clause jurisprudence has "identified three broad categories of activity that Congress may regulate under its commerce power." "First, Congress may regulate the use of the channels of interstate commerce." "Second, Congress is empowered to regulate and protect the instrumentalities of interstate commerce, or persons or things in interstate commerce, even though the threat may come only from intrastate activities." "Finally, Congress' commerce authority includes the power to regulate those activities having a substantial relation to interstate commerce, . . . *i.e.*, those activities that substantially affect interstate commerce."

Petitioners . . . seek to sustain §13981 as a regulation of activity that substantially affects interstate commerce. Given §13981's focus on gender-motivated violence wherever it occurs (rather than violence directed at the instrumentalities of interstate commerce, interstate markets, or things or persons in interstate commerce), we agree that this is the proper inquiry.

. . . In *Lopez*, we held that the Gun-Free School Zones Act of 1990, 18 U.S.C. §922(q)(1)(A), which made it a federal crime to knowingly possess a firearm in a school zone, exceeded Congress' authority under the Commerce Clause. Several significant considerations contributed to our decision.

First, we observed that §922(q) was "a criminal statute that by its terms has nothing to do with 'commerce' or any sort of economic enterprise, however broadly one might define those terms." . . .

. . . [A] fair reading of *Lopez* shows that the noneconomic, criminal nature of the conduct at issue was central to our decision in that case. [Several quotations from *Lopez* omitted.] *Lopez*'s review of Commerce Clause case law demonstrates that in those cases where we have sustained federal regulation of intrastate activity based upon the activity's substantial effects on interstate commerce, the activity in question has been some sort of economic endeavor.

The second consideration that we found important in analyzing §922(q) was that the statute contained "no express jurisdictional element which might limit its reach to a discrete set of firearm possessions that additionally have an explicit connection with or effect on interstate commerce." Such a jurisdictional element may establish that the enactment is in pursuance of Congress' regulation of interstate commerce.

Third, we noted that neither §922(q) "nor its legislative history contain[s] express congressional findings regarding the effects upon interstate commerce of gun possession in a school zone." While "Congress normally is not required to make formal findings as to the substantial burdens that an activity has on interstate commerce," the existence of such findings may "enable us to evaluate the legislative judgment that the activity in question substantially affect[s] interstate commerce, even though no such substantial effect [is] visible to the naked eye."

Finally, our decision in *Lopez* rested in part on the fact that the link between gun possession and a substantial effect on interstate commerce was attenuated. The United States argued that the possession of guns may lead to violent crime, and that violent crime "can be expected to affect the functioning of the national economy in two ways. First, the costs of violent crime are substantial, and, through the mechanism of insurance, those costs are spread throughout the population. Second, violent crime reduces the willingness of individuals to travel to areas within the country that are perceived to be unsafe." The Government also argued that the presence of guns at schools poses a threat to the educational process, which in turn threatens to produce a less efficient and productive workforce, which will negatively affect national productivity and thus interstate commerce.

We rejected these "costs of crime" and "national productivity" arguments because they would permit Congress to "regulate not only all violent crime, but all activities that might lead to violent crime, regardless of how tenuously they relate to interstate commerce." [Quotation from *Lopez* omitted.]

With these principles underlying our Commerce Clause jurisprudence as reference points, the proper resolution of the present cases is clear. Gender-motivated crimes of violence are not, in any sense of the phrase, economic activity. While we need not adopt a categorical rule against aggregating the effects of any noneconomic activity in order to decide these cases, thus far in our Nation's history our cases have upheld Commerce Clause regulation of intrastate activity only where that activity is economic in nature.

Like the Gun-Free School Zones Act at issue in *Lopez*, §13981 contains no jurisdictional element establishing that the federal cause of action is in pursuance of
Congress' power to regulate interstate commerce. Although *Lopez* makes clear that
such a jurisdictional element would lend support to the argument that §13981
is sufficiently tied to interstate commerce, Congress elected to cast §13981's
remedy over a wider, and more purely intrastate, body of violent crime. In contrast with the lack of congressional findings that we faced in *Lopez*, §13981 *is* supported by numerous findings regarding the serious impact that gender-motivated
violence has on victims and their families. But the existence of congressional findings is not sufficient, by itself, to sustain the constitutionality of Commerce Clause
legislation. . . .

In these cases, Congress' findings are substantially weakened by the fact that they
rely so heavily on a method of reasoning that we have already rejected as unworkable if we are to maintain the Constitution's enumeration of powers. . . . The reasoning that petitioners advance seeks to follow the but-for causal chain from the
initial occurrence of violent crime (the suppression of which has always been the
prime object of the States' police power) to every attenuated effect upon interstate
commerce. If accepted, petitioners' reasoning would allow Congress to regulate
any crime as long as the nationwide, aggregated impact of that crime has substantial effects on employment, production, transit, or consumption. Indeed, if Congress may regulate gender-motivated violence, it would be able to regulate murder
or any other type of violence since gender-motivated violence, as a subset of all violent crime, is certain to have lesser economic impacts than the larger class of which
it is a part.

Petitioners' reasoning, moreover, will not limit Congress to regulating violence
but may . . . be applied equally as well to family law and other areas of traditional
state regulation since the aggregate effect of marriage, divorce, and childrearing on
the national economy is undoubtedly significant. Congress may have recognized
this specter when it expressly precluded §13981 from being used in the family law
context. Under our written Constitution, however, the limitation of congressional
authority is not solely a matter of legislative grace.

We accordingly reject the argument that Congress may regulate noneconomic,
violent criminal conduct based solely on that conduct's aggregate effect on interstate commerce. The Constitution requires a distinction between what is truly national and what is truly local. In recognizing this fact we preserve one of the few
principles that has been consistent since the Clause was adopted. The regulation
and punishment of intrastate violence that is not directed at the instrumentalities,
channels, or goods involved in interstate commerce has always been the province of
the States. . . . Indeed, we can think of no better example of the police power, which
the Founders denied the National Government and reposed in the States, than the
suppression of violent crime and vindication of its victims. . . .

III

Because we conclude that the Commerce Clause does not provide Congress with
authority to enact §13981, we address petitioners' alternative argument that the
section's civil remedy should be upheld as an exercise of Congress' remedial power

under §5 of the Fourteenth Amendment. As noted above, Congress expressly invoked the Fourteenth Amendment as a source of authority to enact §13981.

The principles governing an analysis of congressional legislation under §5 are well settled. Section 5 states that Congress may "'enforce,' by 'appropriate legislation' the constitutional guarantee that no State shall deprive any person of 'life, liberty or property, without due process of law,' nor deny any person 'equal protection of the laws.'" *City of Boerne v. Flores* (1997). Section 5 is "a positive grant of legislative power," *Katzenbach v. Morgan* (1966), that includes authority to "prohibit conduct which is not itself unconstitutional and [to] intrud[e] into legislative spheres of autonomy previously reserved to the States." *Flores.* However, "[a]s broad as the congressional enforcement power is, it is not unlimited." *Oregon v. Mitchell* (1970). In fact, as we discuss in detail below, several limitations inherent in §5's text and constitutional context have been recognized since the Fourteenth Amendment was adopted.

Petitioners' §5 argument is founded on an assertion that there is pervasive bias in various state justice systems against victims of gender-motivated violence. This assertion is supported by a voluminous congressional record. Specifically, Congress received evidence that many participants in state justice systems are perpetuating an array of erroneous stereotypes and assumptions. Congress concluded that these discriminatory stereotypes often result in insufficient investigation and prosecution of gender-motivated crime, inappropriate focus on the behavior and credibility of the victims of that crime, and unacceptably lenient punishments for those who are actually convicted of gender-motivated violence. Petitioners contend that this bias denies victims of gender-motivated violence the equal protection of the laws and that Congress therefore acted appropriately in enacting a private civil remedy against the perpetrators of gender-motivated violence to both remedy the States' bias and deter future instances of discrimination in the state courts.

. . . [S]tate-sponsored gender discrimination violates equal protection unless it "serves important governmental objectives and . . . the discriminatory means employed are substantially related to the achievement of those objectives." [Citation omitted.] However, the language and purpose of the Fourteenth Amendment place certain limitations on the manner in which Congress may attack discriminatory conduct. These limitations are necessary to prevent the Fourteenth Amendment from obliterating the Framers' carefully crafted balance of power between the States and the National Government. . . . Foremost among these limitations is the time-honored principle that the Fourteenth Amendment, by its very terms, prohibits only state action. . . .

Shortly after the Fourteenth Amendment was adopted, we decided two cases interpreting the Amendment's provisions, *United States v. Harris* (1883) and the *Civil Rights Cases* (1883). In *Harris*, the Court considered a challenge to §2 of the Civil Rights Act of 1871. That section sought to punish "private persons" for "conspiring to deprive any one of the equal protection of the laws enacted by the State." We concluded that this law exceeded Congress' §5 power because the law was "directed exclusively against the action of private persons, without reference to the laws of the State, or their administration by her officers." . . .

We reached a similar conclusion in the *Civil Rights Cases.* In those consolidated cases, we held that the public accommodation provisions of the Civil Rights Act of

1875, which applied to purely private conduct, were beyond the scope of the §5 enforcement power.

The force of the doctrine of *stare decisis* behind these decisions stems not only from the length of time they have been on the books, but also from the insight attributable to the Members of the Court at that time. Every Member had been appointed by President Lincoln, Grant, Hayes, Garfield, or Arthur—and each of their judicial appointees obviously had intimate knowledge and familiarity with the events surrounding the adoption of the Fourteenth Amendment.

Petitioners contend that two more recent decisions have in effect overruled this longstanding limitation on Congress' §5 authority. [Rehnquist noted two cases in which justices had questioned the rule laid down in the *Civil Rights Cases—United States v. Guest* (1966) and *District of Columbia v. Carter* (1973)—but said that neither case had specifically dealt with the issue or expressly overruled the earlier decision.]

Petitioners alternatively argue that, unlike the situation in the *Civil Rights Cases*, here there has been gender-based disparate treatment by state authorities, whereas in those cases there was no indication of such state action. There is abundant evidence, however, to show that the Congresses that enacted the Civil Rights Acts of 1871 and 1875 had a purpose similar to that of Congress in enacting §13981: There were state laws on the books bespeaking equality of treatment, but in the administration of these laws there was discrimination against newly freed slaves. . . .

But even if that distinction were valid, we do not believe it would save §13981's civil remedy. For the remedy is simply not "corrective in its character, adapted to counteract and redress the operation of such prohibited [s]tate laws or proceedings of [s]tate officers." *Civil Rights Cases.* Or, as we have phrased it in more recent cases, prophylactic legislation under §5 must have a "congruence and proportionality between the injury to be prevented or remedied and the means adopted to that end." *Florida Prepaid Postsecondary Ed. Expense Bd. v. College Savings Bank* (1999); *Flores.* Section 13981 is not aimed at proscribing discrimination by officials which the Fourteenth Amendment might not itself proscribe; it is directed not at any State or state actor, but at individuals who have committed criminal acts motivated by gender bias.

In the present cases, for example, §13981 visits no consequence whatever on any Virginia public official involved in investigating or prosecuting Brzonkala's assault. The section is, therefore, unlike any of the §5 remedies that we have previously upheld. [Rehnquist noted the Court's decisions in *Katzenbach v. Morgan* (1966) and *South Carolina v. Katzenbach* (1966) upholding provisions of the Voting Rights Act of 1965 based on evidence of states' discriminating against Spanish-speaking people and blacks.] . . .

Section 13981 is also different from these previously upheld remedies in that it applies uniformly throughout the Nation. Congress' findings indicate that the problem of discrimination against the victims of gender-motivated crimes does not exist in all States, or even most States. By contrast, the §5 remedy upheld in *Katzenbach v. Morgan* was directed only to the State where the evil found by Congress existed, and in *South Carolina v. Katzenbach* the remedy was directed only to those States in which Congress found that there had been discrimination.

For these reasons, we conclude that Congress' power under §5 does not extend to the enactment of §13981.

IV

Petitioner Brzonkala's complaint alleges that she was the victim of a brutal assault. But Congress' effort in §13981 to provide a federal civil remedy can be sustained neither under the Commerce Clause nor under §5 of the Fourteenth Amendment. If the allegations here are true, no civilized system of justice could fail to provide her a remedy for the conduct of respondent Morrison. But under our federal system that remedy must be provided by the Commonwealth of Virginia, and not by the United States. The judgment of the Court of Appeals is

Affirmed.

JUSTICE THOMAS, concurring.

The majority opinion correctly applies our decision in *United States v. Lopez* (1995), and I join it in full. I write separately only to express my view that the very notion of a "substantial effects" test under the Commerce Clause is inconsistent with the original understanding of Congress' powers and with this Court's early Commerce Clause cases. By continuing to apply this rootless and malleable standard, however circumscribed, the Court has encouraged the Federal Government to persist in its view that the Commerce Clause has virtually no limits. Until this Court replaces its existing Commerce Clause jurisprudence with a standard more consistent with the original understanding, we will continue to see Congress appropriating state police powers under the guise of regulating commerce.

JUSTICE SOUTER, with whom JUSTICE STEVENS, JUSTICE GINS-BURG, and JUSTICE BREYER join, dissenting.

The Court says both that it leaves Commerce Clause precedent undisturbed and that the Civil Rights Remedy of the Violence Against Women Act of 1994, 42 U.S.C. §13981, exceeds Congress's power under that Clause. I find the claims irreconcilable and respectfully dissent.

I

Our cases, which remain at least nominally undisturbed, stand for the following propositions. Congress has the power to legislate with regard to activity that, in the aggregate, has a substantial effect on interstate commerce. [Citations omitted.] The fact of such a substantial effect is not an issue for the courts in the first instance, but for the Congress. . . By passing legislation, Congress indicates its conclusion, whether explicitly or not, that facts support its exercise of the commerce power. The business of the courts is to review the congressional assessment, not for soundness but simply for the rationality of concluding that a jurisdictional basis exists in fact. Any explicit findings that Congress chooses to make, though not dispositive of the question of rationality, may advance judicial review by identifying factual authority on which Congress relied. Applying those propositions in these cases can lead to only one conclusion.

. . . Passage of the Act in 1994 was preceded by four years of hearings, which included testimony from physicians and law professors; from survivors of rape and domestic violence; and from representatives of state law enforcement and private business. The record includes reports on gender bias from task forces in 21 States,

and we have the benefit of specific factual findings in the eight separate Reports issued by Congress and its committees over the long course leading to enactment.
[Lengthy summary of congressional findings omitted.]

Based on the data thus partially summarized, Congress found that

> "crimes of violence motivated by gender have a substantial adverse effect
> on interstate commerce, by deterring potential victims from traveling in-
> terstate, from engaging in employment in interstate business, and from
> transacting with business, and in places involved, in interstate com-
> merce. . . [,] by diminishing national productivity, increasing medical and
> other costs, and decreasing the supply of and the demand for interstate
> products. . . ." [Quoting conference report.]

Congress thereby explicitly stated the predicate for the exercise of its Commerce
Clause power. . . . [T]he sufficiency of the evidence before Congress to provide a
rational basis for the finding cannot seriously be questioned. . . .

II

The Act would have passed muster at any time between *Wickard [v. Filburn]* in
1942 and *[United States v.] Lopez* in 1995, a period in which the law enjoyed a stable
understanding that congressional power under the Commerce Clause, comple-
mented by the authority of the Necessary and Proper Clause, Art. I. §8 cl. 18, extended to all activity that, when aggregated, has a substantial effect on interstate
commerce. . . .

The fact that the Act does not pass muster before the Court today is therefore
proof . . . that the Court's nominal adherence to the substantial effects test is merely
that. . . . [I]t is clear that some congressional conclusions about obviously substantial, cumulative effects on commerce are being assigned lesser values than the once-
stable doctrine would assign them. These devaluations are accomplished . . . by supplanting rational basis scrutiny with a new criterion of review.

Thus the elusive heart of the majority's analysis in these cases is its statement that
Congress's findings of fact are "weakened" by the presence of a disfavored "method
of reasoning." This seems to suggest that the "substantial effects" analysis is not a
factual enquiry, for Congress in the first instance with subsequent judicial review
looking only to the rationality of the congressional conclusion, but one of a rather
different sort, dependent upon a uniquely judicial competence.

This new characterization of substantial effects has no support in our cases. . . .

A

. . . [F]or significant periods of our history, the Court has defined the commerce
power as plenary, unsusceptible to categorical exclusions, and this was the view expressed throughout the latter part of the 20th century in the substantial effects
test. . . .

. . . [T]oday's attempt to distinguish between primary activities affecting commerce in terms of the relatively commercial or noncommercial character of the primary conduct proscribed comes with the pedigree of near-tragedy. . . . In the half
century following the modern activation of the commerce power with passage
of the Interstate Commerce Act in 1887, this Court from time to time created

categorical enclaves beyond congressional reach by declaring such activities as "mining," "production," "manufacturing," and union membership to be outside the definition of "commerce" and by limiting application of the effects test to "direct" rather than "indirect" commercial consequences. [Lengthy citation of cases omitted.]

. . . [A]dherence to these formalistically contrived confines of commerce power in large measure provoked the judicial crisis of 1937 . . . And yet today's decision can only be seen as a step toward recapturing the prior mistakes. Its revival of a distinction between commercial and noncommercial conduct is at odds with *Wickard*, which repudiated that analysis, and the enquiry into commercial purpose, first intimated by the *Lopez* concurrence [citing opinion by Kennedy], is cousin to the intent-based analysis . . . rejected for Commerce Clause purposes in *Heart of Atlanta* [*Motel, Inc. v. United States* (1964) (upholding Title II of Civil Rights Act of 1964)].

Why is the majority tempted to reject the lesson so painfully learned in 1937? [Souter contrasted the ruling in *Wickard* with the Court's decision in *Carter v. Carter Coal. Co.* (1936), which he said "held mining regulation beyond the national commerce power." The reason for the decision, Souter continued, "was laissez-faire economics, the point of which was to keep government interference to a minimum."] The Court in *Carter Coal* was still trying to create a laissez-faire world out of the 20th-century economy, and formalistic commercial distinctions were thought to be useful instruments in achieving that object. . . .

. . . [I]n the minds of the majority there is a new animating theory that makes categorical formalism seem useful again. Just as the old formalism had value in the service of an economic conception, the new one is useful in serving a conception of federalism. It is the instrument by which assertions of national power are to be limited in favor of preserving a supposedly discernible, proper sphere of state autonomy to legislate or refrain from legislating as the individual States see fit. . . . The essential issue is . . . the strength of the majority's claim to have a constitutional warrant for its current conception of a federal relationship enforceable by this Court through limits on otherwise plenary commerce power. . . .

B

The Court finds it relevant that the statute addresses conduct traditionally subject to state prohibition under domestic criminal law. . . . [T]he theory of traditional state concern as grounding a limiting principle has been rejected previously, and more than once. [Citation and discussion of cases omitted.]

The objection to reviving traditional state spheres of action as a consideration in commerce analysis . . . is compounded by a further defect. . . . The defect, in essence, is the majority's rejection of the Founders' considered judgment that politics, not judicial review, should mediate between state and national interests as the strength and legislative jurisdiction of the National Government inevitably increased through the expected growth of the national economy. . . .

C

. . . Today's majority . . . finds no significance whatever in the state support for the Act based upon the States' acknowledged failure to deal adequately with gender-based violence in state courts, and the belief of their own law enforcement agencies that national action is essential. . . .

The collective opinion of state officials that the Act was needed continues virtually unchanged, and when the Civil Rights Remedy was challenged in court, the States came to its defense. Thirty-six of them and the Commonwealth of Puerto Rico have filed an *amicus* brief in support of petitioners in these cases, and only one State has taken respondents' side. It is, then, not the least irony of these cases that the States will be forced to enjoy the new federalism whether they want it or not. . . .

III

All of this convinces me that today's ebb of the commerce power rests on error, and at the same time leads me to doubt that the majority's view will prove to be enduring law. . . . The facts that cannot be ignored today are the facts of integrated national commerce and a political relationship between States and Nation much affected by their respective treasuries and constitutional modifications adopted by the people. The federalism of some earlier time is no more adequate to account for those facts today than the theory of laissez-faire was able to govern the national economy 70 years ago.

JUSTICE BREYER, with whom JUSTICE STEVENS joins, and with whom JUSTICE SOUTER and JUSTICE GINSBURG join as to Part I-A, dissenting.

. . .

I

The majority holds that the federal commerce power does not extend to such "noneconomic" activities as "noneconomic, violent criminal conduct" that significantly affects interstate commerce only if we "aggregate" the interstate "effect[s]" of individual instances. . . . [T]he majority's holding illustrates the difficulty of finding a workable judicial Commerce Clause touchstone—a set of comprehensible interpretive rules that courts might use to impose some meaningful limit, but not too great a limit, upon the scope of the legislative authority that the Commerce Clause delegates to Congress.

A

Consider the problems. The "economic/noneconomic" distinction is not easy to apply. Does the local street corner mugger engage in "economic" activity or "noneconomic" activity when he mugs for money? . . . Would evidence that desire for economic domination underlies many brutal crimes against women save the present statute? . . .

More important, why should we give critical constitutional importance to the economic, or noneconomic, nature of an interstate-commerce-affecting *cause?* If chemical emanations through indirect environmental change cause identical, severe commercial harm outside a State, why should it matter whether local factories or home fireplaces release them? . . .

Most important, the Court's complex rules seem unlikely to help secure the very object that they seek, namely, the protection of "areas of traditional state regulation" from federal intrusion. . . . [T]he Court reaffirms, as it should, Congress' well-established and frequently exercised power to enact laws that satisfy a commerce-related jurisdictional prerequisite—for example, that some item relevant to the federally regulated activity has at some time crossed a state line. . . .

And in a world where most everyday products or their component parts cross interstate boundaries, Congress will frequently find it possible to redraft a statute using language that ties the regulation to the interstate movement of some relevant object. . . . [T]his possibility . . . means that any substantive limitation will apply randomly in terms of the interests the majority seeks to protect. . . .

B

I would also note that Congress, when it enacted the statute, followed procedures that help to protect the federalism values at stake. It provided adequate notice to the States of its intent to legislate in an "are[a] of traditional state regulation." And in response, attorneys general in the overwhelming majority of States (38) supported congressional legislation. . . . [Remainder of section omitted.]

II

Given my conclusion on the Commerce Clause question, I need not consider Congress' authority under §5 of the Fourteenth Amendment. Nonetheless, I doubt the Court's reasoning rejecting that source of authority. [Remainder of section omitted.]

No. 99-138

Jenifer Troxel, et vir., Petitioners v. Tommie Granville
On writ of certiorari to the Supreme Court of Washington

[June 5, 2000]

JUSTICE O'CONNOR announced the judgment of the Court and delivered an opinion, in which THE CHIEF JUSTICE, JUSTICE GINSBURG, and JUSTICE BREYER join.

Section 26.10.160(3) of the Revised Code of Washington permits "[a]ny person" to petition a superior court for visitation rights "at any time," and authorizes that court to grant such visitation rights whenever "visitation may serve the best interest of the child." Petitioners Jenifer and Gary Troxel petitioned a Washington Superior Court for the right to visit their grandchildren, Isabelle and Natalie Troxel. Respondent Tommie Granville, the mother of Isabelle and Natalie, opposed the petition. The case ultimately reached the Washington Supreme Court, which held that §26.10.160(3) unconstitutionally interferes with the fundamental right of parents to rear their children.

I

Tommie Granville and Brad Troxel shared a relationship that ended in June 1991. The two never married, but they had two daughters, Isabelle and Natalie. Jenifer and Gary Troxel are Brad's parents, and thus the paternal grandparents of Isabelle and Natalie. After Tommie and Brad separated in 1991, Brad lived with his parents and regularly brought his daughters to his parents' home for weekend visitation. Brad committed suicide in May 1993. Although the Troxels at first continued to see Isabelle and Natalie on a regular basis after their son's death, Tommie Granville informed the Troxels in October 1993 that she wished to limit their visitation with her daughters to one short visit per month.

In December 1993, the Troxels commenced the present action by filing, in the Washington Superior Court for Skagit County, a petition to obtain visitation rights with Isabelle and Natalie. The Troxels filed their petition under two Washington statutes, Wash. Rev. Code §§26.09.240 and 26.10.160(3). Only the latter statute is at issue in this case. Section 26.10.160(3) provides: "Any person may petition the court for visitation rights at any time including, but not limited to, custody proceedings. The court may order visitation rights for any person when visitation may serve the best interest of the child whether or not there has been any change of circumstances." At trial, the Troxels requested two weekends of overnight visitation per month and two weeks of visitation each summer. Granville did not oppose visitation altogether, but instead asked the court to order one day of visitation per month with no overnight stay. In 1995, the Superior Court issued an oral ruling and entered a visitation decree ordering visitation one weekend per month, one week during the summer, and four hours on both of the petitioning grandparents' birthdays.

Granville appealed, during which time she married Kelly Wynn. Before addressing the merits of Granville's appeal, the Washington Court of Appeals remanded the case to the Superior Court for entry of written findings of fact and conclusions of law. On remand, the Superior Court found that visitation was in Isabelle and Natalie's best interests. [Excerpt from opinion omitted.] Approximately nine months after the Superior Court entered its order on remand, Granville's husband formally adopted Isabelle and Natalie.

The Washington Court of Appeals reversed the lower court's visitation order and dismissed the Troxels' petition for visitation, holding that nonparents lack standing to seek visitation under §26.10.160(3) unless a custody action is pending. [*In re Troxel* (1997).] In the Court of Appeals' view, that limitation on nonparental visitation actions was "consistent with the constitutional restrictions on state interference with parents' fundamental liberty interest in the care, custody, and management of their children." Having resolved the case on the statutory ground, however, the Court of Appeals did not expressly pass on Granville's constitutional challenge to the visitation statute.

The Washington Supreme Court granted the Troxels' petition for review and, after consolidating their case with two other visitation cases, affirmed. [*In re Smith* (1998).] The court disagreed with the Court of Appeals' decision on the statutory issue and found that the plain language of §26.10.160(3) gave the Troxels standing to seek visitation, irrespective of whether a custody action was pending. The Washington Supreme Court nevertheless agreed with the Court of Appeals' ultimate conclusion that the Troxels could not obtain visitation of Isabelle and Natalie pursuant to §26.10.160(3). The court rested its decision on the Federal Constitution, holding that §26.10.160(3) unconstitutionally infringes on the fundamental right of parents to rear their children. In the court's view, there were at least two problems with the nonparental visitation statute. First, according to the Washington Supreme Court, the Constitution permits a State to interfere with the right of parents to rear their children only to prevent harm or potential harm to a child. Section 26.10.160(3) fails that standard because it requires no threshold showing of harm. Second, by allowing "'any person' to petition for forced visitation of a child at 'any time' with the only requirement being that the visitation serve the best interest of the child," the Washington visitation statute sweeps too broadly. . . . Four justices dissented from the Washington Supreme Court's holding on the constitutionality of the statute.

We granted certiorari (1999), and now affirm the judgment.

II

The demographic changes of the past century make it difficult to speak of an average American family. The composition of families varies greatly from household to household. While many children may have two married parents and grandparents who visit regularly, many other children are raised in single-parent households. In 1996, children living with only one parent accounted for 28 percent of all children under age 18 in the United States. Understandably, in these single-parent households, persons outside the nuclear family are called upon with increasing frequency to assist in the everyday tasks of child rearing. In many cases, grandparents play an important role. For example, in 1998, approximately 4 million children—or 5.6 percent of all children under age 18—lived in the household of their grandparents.

The nationwide enactment of nonparental visitation statutes is assuredly due, in some part, to the States' recognition of these changing realities of the American family. Because grandparents and other relatives undertake duties of a parental nature in many households, States have sought to ensure the welfare of the children therein by protecting the relationships those children form with such third parties. The States' nonparental visitation statutes are further supported by a recognition, which varies from State to State, that children should have the opportunity to benefit from relationships with statutorily specified persons—for example, their grandparents. The extension of statutory rights in this area to persons other than a child's parents, however, comes with an obvious cost. For example, the State's recognition of an independent third-party interest in a child can place a substantial burden on the traditional parent-child relationship. Contrary to JUSTICE STEVENS' accusation, our description of state nonparental visitation statutes in these terms, of course, is not meant to suggest that "children are so much chattel." Rather, our terminology is intended to highlight the fact that these statutes can present questions of constitutional import. In this case, we are presented with just such a question. Specifically, we are asked to decide whether §26.10.160(3), as applied to Tommie Granville and her family, violates the Federal Constitution.

The Fourteenth Amendment provides that no State shall "deprive any person of life, liberty, or property, without due process of law." We have long recognized that the Amendment's Due Process Clause, like its Fifth Amendment counterpart, "guarantees more than fair process." The Clause also includes a substantive component that "provides heightened protection against government interference with certain fundamental rights and liberty interests." [*Washington v. Glucksberg* (1997).]

The liberty interest at issue in this case—the interest of parents in the care, custody, and control of their children—is perhaps the oldest of the fundamental liberty interests recognized by this Court. More than 75 years ago, in *Meyer v. Nebraska* (1923), we held that the "liberty" protected by the Due Process Clause includes the right of parents to "establish a home and bring up children" and "to control the education of their own." Two years later, in *Pierce v. Society of Sisters* (1925), we again held that the "liberty of parents and guardians" includes the right "to direct the upbringing and education of children under their control." . . .

In subsequent cases also, we have recognized the fundamental right of parents to make decisions concerning the care, custody, and control of their children. [Citations omitted.] In light of this extensive precedent, it cannot now be doubted that the Due Process Clause of the Fourteenth Amendment protects the fundamental right of parents to make decisions concerning the care, custody, and control of their children.

Section 26.10.160(3), as applied to Granville and her family in this case, unconstitutionally infringes on that fundamental parental right. The Washington nonparental visitation statute is breathtakingly broad. According to the statute's text, "*[a]ny* person may petition the court for visitation rights at *any time*," and the court may grant such visitation rights whenever "visitation may serve *the best interest of the child*." §26.10.160(3) (emphases added). That language effectively permits any third party seeking visitation to subject any decision by a parent concerning visitation of the parent's children to state-court review. Once the visitation petition has been filed in court and the matter is placed before a judge, a parent's decision that visitation would not be in the child's best interest is accorded no deference. Section 26.10.160(3) contains no requirement that a court accord the parent's decision any presumption of validity or any weight whatsoever. Instead, the Washington statute places the best-interest determination solely in the hands of the judge. Should the judge disagree with the parent's estimation of the child's best interests, the judge's view necessarily prevails. Thus, in practical effect, in the State of Washington a court can disregard and overturn any decision by a fit custodial parent concerning visitation whenever a third party affected by the decision files a visitation petition, based solely on the judge's determination of the child's best interests. The Washington Supreme Court had the opportunity to give §26.10.160(3) a narrower reading, but it declined to do so. . . .

Turning to the facts of this case, the record reveals that the Superior Court's order was based on precisely the type of mere disagreement we have just described and nothing more. The Superior Court's order was not founded on any special factors that might justify the State's interference with Granville's fundamental right to make decisions concerning the rearing of her two daughters. To be sure, this case involves a visitation petition filed by grandparents soon after the death of their son—the father of Isabelle and Natalie—but the combination of several factors here compels our conclusion that §26.10.160(3), as applied, exceeded the bounds of the Due Process Clause.

First, the Troxels did not allege, and no court has found, that Granville was an unfit parent. That aspect of the case is important, for there is a presumption that fit parents act in the best interests of their children. . . . Accordingly, so long as a parent adequately cares for his or her children (*i.e.*, is fit), there will normally be no reason for the State to inject itself into the private realm of the family to further question the ability of that parent to make the best decisions concerning the rearing of that parent's children.

The problem here is not that the Washington Superior Court intervened, but that when it did so, it gave no special weight at all to Granville's determination of her daughters' best interests. More importantly, it appears that the Superior Court applied exactly the opposite presumption. In reciting its oral ruling after the conclusion of closing arguments, the Superior Court judge explained:

> "The burden is to show that it is in the best interest of the children to have
> some visitation and some quality time with their grandparents. I think in
> most situations a commonsensical approach [is that] it is normally in the
> best interest of the children to spend quality time with the grandparent,
> unless the grandparent, [*sic*] there are some issues or problems involved
> wherein the grandparents, their lifestyles are going to impact adversely
> upon the children. That certainly isn't the case here from what I can tell."

The judge's comments suggest that he presumed the grandparents' request should be granted unless the children would be "impact[ed] adversely." In effect, the judge placed on Granville, the fit custodial parent, the burden of disproving that visitation would be in the best interest of her daughters. The judge reiterated moments later: "I think [visitation with the Troxels] would be in the best interest of the children and I haven't been shown it is not in [the] best interest of the children."

The decisional framework employed by the Superior Court directly contravened the traditional presumption that a fit parent will act in the best interest of his or her child. In that respect, the court's presumption failed to provide any protection for Granville's fundamental constitutional right to make decisions concerning the rearing of her own daughters. . . . In an ideal world, parents might always seek to cultivate the bonds between grandparents and their grandchildren. Needless to say, however, our world is far from perfect, and in it the decision whether such an intergenerational relationship would be beneficial in any specific case is for the parent to make in the first instance. And, if a fit parent's decision of the kind at issue here becomes subject to judicial review, the court must accord at least some special weight to the parent's own determination.

Finally, we note that there is no allegation that Granville ever sought to cut off visitation entirely. Rather, the present dispute originated when Granville informed the Troxels that she would prefer to restrict their visitation with Isabelle and Natalie to one short visit per month and special holidays. In the Superior Court proceedings Granville did not oppose visitation but instead asked that the duration of any visitation order be shorter than that requested by the Troxels. While the Troxels requested two weekends per month and two full weeks in the summer, Granville asked the Superior Court to order only one day of visitation per month (with no overnight stay) and participation in the Granville family's holiday celebrations. . . . The Superior Court gave no weight to Granville's having assented to visitation even before the filing of any visitation petition or subsequent court intervention.

The court instead rejected Granville's proposal and settled on a middle ground, ordering one weekend of visitation per month, one week in the summer, and time on both of the petitioning grandparents' birthdays. Significantly, many other States expressly provide by statute that courts may not award visitation unless a parent has denied (or unreasonably denied) visitation to the concerned third party. [Citing Mississippi, Oregon, and Rhode Island statutes.]

Considered together with the Superior Court's reasons for awarding visitation to the Troxels, the combination of these factors demonstrates that the visitation order in this case was an unconstitutional infringement on Granville's fundamental right to make decisions concerning the care, custody, and control of her two daughters. The Washington Superior Court failed to accord the determination of Granville, a fit custodial parent, any material weight. In fact, the Superior Court made only two formal findings in support of its visitation order. First, the Troxels "are part of a large, central, loving family, all located in this area, and the [Troxels] can provide opportunities for the children in the areas of cousins and music." Second, "[t]he children would be benefitted from spending quality time with the [Troxels], provided that that time is balanced with time with the childrens' [*sic*] nuclear family." These slender findings, in combination with the court's announced presumption in favor of grandparent visitation and its failure to accord significant weight to Granville's already having offered meaningful visitation to the Troxels, show that this case involves nothing more than a simple disagreement between the Washington Superior Court and Granville concerning her children's best interests. The Superior Court's announced reason for ordering one week of visitation in the summer demonstrates our conclusion as well: "I look back on some personal experiences. . . . We always spen[t] as kids a week with one set of grandparents and another set of grandparents, [and] it happened to work out in our family that [it] turned out to be an enjoyable experience. Maybe that can, in this family, if that is how it works out." As we have explained, the Due Process Clause does not permit a State to infringe on the fundamental right of parents to make childrearing decisions simply because a state judge believes a "better" decision could be made. Neither the Washington nonparental visitation statute generally—which places no limits on either the persons who may petition for visitation or the circumstances in which such a petition may be granted—nor the Superior Court in this specific case required anything more. Accordingly, we hold that §26.10.160(3), as applied in this case, is unconstitutional.

Because we rest our decision on the sweeping breadth of §26.10.160(3) and the application of that broad, unlimited power in this case, we do not consider the primary constitutional question passed on by the Washington Supreme Court— whether the Due Process Clause requires all nonparental visitation statutes to include a showing of harm or potential harm to the child as a condition precedent to granting visitation. We do not, and need not, define today the precise scope of the parental due process right in the visitation context. In this respect, we agree with JUSTICE KENNEDY that the constitutionality of any standard for awarding visitation turns on the specific manner in which that standard is applied and that the constitutional protections in this area are best "elaborated with care." Because much state-court adjudication in this context occurs on a case-by-case basis, we would be hesitant to hold that specific nonparental visitation statutes violate the Due Process Clause as a *per se* matter. . . .

JUSTICE STEVENS criticizes our reliance on what he characterizes as merely "a guess" about the Washington courts' interpretation of §26.10.160(3). JUSTICE KENNEDY likewise states that "[m]ore specific guidance should await a case in which a State's highest court has considered all of the facts in the course of elaborating the protection afforded to parents by the laws of the State and by the Constitution itself." We respectfully disagree. There is no need to hypothesize about how the Washington courts might apply §26.10.160(3) because the Washington Superior Court did apply the statute in this very case. Like the Washington Supreme Court, then, we are presented with an actual visitation order and the reasons why the Superior Court believed entry of the order was appropriate in this case. Faced with the Superior Court's application of §26.10.160(3) to Granville and her family, the Washington Supreme Court chose not to give the statute a narrower construction. Rather, that court gave §26.10.160(3) a literal and expansive interpretation. As we have explained, that broad construction plainly encompassed the Superior Court's application of the statute.

There is thus no reason to remand the case for further proceedings in the Washington Supreme Court. As JUSTICE KENNEDY recognizes, the burden of litigating a domestic relations proceeding can itself be "so disruptive of the parent-child relationship that the constitutional right of a custodial parent to make certain basic determinations for the child's welfare becomes implicated." In this case, the litigation costs incurred by Granville on her trip through the Washington court system and to this Court are without a doubt already substantial. As we have explained, it is apparent that the entry of the visitation order in this case violated the Constitution. We should say so now, without forcing the parties into additional litigation that would further burden Granville's parental right. We therefore hold that the application of §26.10.160(3) to Granville and her family violated her due process right to make decisions concerning the care, custody, and control of her daughters.

Accordingly, the judgment of the Washington Supreme Court is affirmed.

It is so ordered.

JUSTICE SOUTER, concurring in the judgment.

I concur in the judgment affirming the decision of the Supreme Court of Washington, whose facial invalidation of its own state statute is consistent with this Court's prior cases addressing the substantive interests at stake. I would say no more. The issues that might well be presented by reviewing a decision addressing the specific application of the state statute by the trial court are not before us and do not call for turning any fresh furrows in the "treacherous field" of substantive due process.

The Supreme Court of Washington invalidated its state statute based on the text of the statute alone, not its application to any particular case. Its ruling rested on two independently sufficient grounds: the failure of the statute to require harm to the child to justify a disputed visitation order and the statute's authorization of "any person" at "any time" to petition and to receive visitation rights subject only to a free-ranging best-interests-of-the-child standard. I see no error in the second reason, that because the state statute authorizes any person at any time to request (and a judge to award) visitation rights, subject only to the State's particular best-interests standard, the state statute sweeps too broadly and is unconstitutional on its face. Consequently, there is no need to decide whether harm is required or to consider the precise scope of the parent's right or its necessary protections. . . .

JUSTICE THOMAS, concurring in the judgment.

. . . [N]either party has argued that our substantive due process cases were wrongly decided and that the original understanding of the Due Process Clause precludes judicial enforcement of unenumerated rights under that constitutional provision. As a result, I express no view on the merits of this matter. . . .

Consequently, I agree with the plurality that this Court's recognition of a fundamental right of parents to direct the upbringing of their children resolves this case. Our decision in *Pierce v. Society of Sisters* (1925) holds that parents have a fundamental constitutional right to rear their children, including the right to determine who shall educate and socialize them. The opinions of the plurality, JUSTICE KENNEDY, and JUSTICE SOUTER recognize such a right, but curiously none of them articulates the appropriate standard of review. I would apply strict scrutiny to infringements of fundamental rights. Here, the State of Washington lacks even a legitimate governmental interest—to say nothing of a compelling one—in second-guessing a fit parent's decision regarding visitation with third parties. On this basis, I would affirm the judgment below.

JUSTICE STEVENS, dissenting.

The Court today wisely declines to endorse either the holding or the reasoning of the Supreme Court of Washington. In my opinion, the Court would have been even wiser to deny certiorari. Given the problematic character of the trial court's decision and the uniqueness of the Washington statute, there was no pressing need to review a State Supreme Court decision that merely requires the state legislature to draft a better statute.

Having decided to address the merits, however, the Court should begin by recognizing that the State Supreme Court rendered a federal constitutional judgment holding a state law invalid on its face. In light of that judgment, I believe that we should confront the federal questions presented directly. For the Washington statute is not made facially invalid either because it may be invoked by too many hypothetical plaintiffs, or because it leaves open the possibility that someone may be permitted to sustain a relationship with a child without having to prove that serious harm to the child would otherwise result.

I

In response to Tommie Granville's federal constitutional challenge, the State Supreme Court broadly held that Wash. Rev. Code §26.10.160(3) was invalid on its face under the Federal Constitution.

Despite the nature of this judgment, JUSTICE O'CONNOR would hold that the Washington visitation statute violated the Due Process Clause of the Fourteenth Amendment only as applied. I agree with JUSTICE SOUTER that this approach is untenable.

. . . I believe the Court should identify and correct the two flaws in the reasoning of the state court's majority opinion, and remand for further review of the trial court's disposition of this specific case.

II

In my view, the State Supreme Court erred in its federal constitutional analysis because neither the provision granting "any person" the right to petition the court for visitation nor the absence of a provision requiring a "threshold . . . finding of harm to the child" provides a sufficient basis for holding that the statute is invalid in all its applications. . . . Under the Washington statute, there are plainly any number of cases . . . in which the "person" among "any" seeking visitation is a once-custodial caregiver, an intimate relation, or even a genetic parent. Even the Court would seem to agree that in many circumstances, it would be constitutionally permissible for a court to award some visitation of a child to a parent or previous caregiver in cases of parental separation or divorce, cases of disputed custody, cases involving temporary foster care or guardianship, and so forth. . . . [T]he State Supreme Court majority incorrectly concluded that a statute authorizing "any person" to file a petition seeking visitation privileges would invariably run afoul of the Fourteenth Amendment.

The second key aspect of the Washington Supreme Court's holding—that the Federal Constitution requires a showing of actual or potential "harm" to the child before a court may order visitation continued over a parent's objections—finds no support in this Court's case law. While . . . the Federal Constitution certainly protects the parent-child relationship from arbitrary impairment by the State, we have never held that the parent's liberty interest in this relationship is so inflexible as to establish a rigid constitutional shield, protecting every arbitrary parental decision from any challenge absent a threshold finding of harm. . . . [E]ven a fit parent is capable of treating a child like a mere possession.

Cases like this do not present a bipolar struggle between the parents and the State over who has final authority to determine what is in a child's best interests. There is at a minimum a third individual, whose interests are implicated in every case to which the statute applies—the child. . . .

A parent's rights with respect to her child have . . . never been regarded as absolute, but rather are limited by the existence of an actual, developed relationship with a child, and are tied to the presence or absence of some embodiment of family. These limitations have arisen, not simply out of the definition of parenthood itself, but because of this Court's assumption that a parent's interests in a child must be balanced against the State's long-recognized interests as parens patriae, and, critically, the child's own complementary interest in preserving relationships that serve her welfare and protection.

. . . [I]it seems to me extremely likely that, to the extent parents and families have fundamental liberty interests in preserving such intimate relationships, so, too, do children have these interests, and so, too, must their interests be balanced in the equation. . . . The constitutional protection against arbitrary state interference with parental rights should not be extended to prevent the States from protecting children against the arbitrary exercise of parental authority that is not in fact motivated by an interest in the welfare of the child.

. . . [W]e should recognize that there may be circumstances in which a child has a stronger interest at stake than mere protection from serious harm caused by the termination of visitation by a "person" other than a parent. The almost infinite variety of family relationships that pervade our ever-changing society strongly counsel against the creation by this Court of a constitutional rule that treats a biological parent's liberty interest in the care and supervision of her child as an isolated right that may be exercised arbitrarily. It is indisputably the business of the States, rather than a federal court employing a national standard, to assess in the first instance the relative importance of the conflicting interests that give rise to disputes such as this. Far from guaranteeing that parents' interests will be trammeled in the sweep of cases arising under the statute, the Washington law merely gives an individual—with whom a child may have an established relationship—the procedural right to ask the State to act as arbiter, through the entirely well-known best-interests standard, between the parent's protected interests and the child's. It seems clear to me that the Due Process Clause of the Fourteenth Amendment leaves room for States to consider the impact on a child of possibly arbitrary parental decisions that neither serve nor are motivated by the best interests of the child.

Accordingly, I respectfully dissent.

JUSTICE SCALIA, dissenting.

In my view, a right of parents to direct the upbringing of their children is among the "unalienable Rights" with which the Declaration of Independence proclaims "all Men . . . are endowed by their Creator." And in my view that right is also among the "othe[r] [rights] retained by the people" which the Ninth Amendment says the Constitution's enumeration of rights "shall not be construed to deny or disparage." The Declaration of Independence, however, is not a legal prescription conferring powers upon the courts; and the Constitution's refusal to "deny or disparage" other rights is far removed from affirming any one of them, and even farther removed from authorizing judges to identify what they might be, and to enforce the judges' list against laws duly enacted by the people. Consequently, while I would think it entirely compatible with the commitment to representative democracy set forth in the founding documents to argue, in legislative chambers or in electoral campaigns, that the state has no power to interfere with parents' authority over the rearing of their children, I do not believe that the power which the Constitution confers upon me as a judge entitles me to deny legal effect to laws that (in my view) infringe upon what is (in my view) that unenumerated right.

Only three holdings of this Court rest in whole or in part upon a substantive constitutional right of parents to direct the upbringing of their children—two of them from an era rich in substantive due process holdings that have since been repudiated. See *Meyer v. Nebraska* (1923); *Pierce v. Society of Sisters* (1925); *Wisconsin v. Yoder* (1972). . . . The sheer diversity of today's opinions persuades me that the theory of unenumerated parental rights underlying these three cases has small claim to *stare decisis* protection. . . . While I would not now overrule those earlier cases . . . , neither would I extend the theory upon which they rested to this new context.

Judicial vindication of "parental rights" under a Constitution that does not even mention them requires . . . not only a judicially crafted definition of parents, but also—unless, as no one believes, the parental rights are to be absolute—judicially approved assessments of "harm to the child" and judicially defined gradations of other persons (grandparents, extended family, adoptive family in an adoption later found to be invalid, long-term guardians, etc.) who may have some claim against the wishes of the parents. If we embrace this unenumerated right, I think it obvious . . . that we will be ushering in a new regime of judicially prescribed, and federally prescribed, family law. I have no reason to believe that federal judges will be better at this than state legislatures; and state legislatures have the great advantages of doing harm in a more circumscribed area, of being able to correct their mistakes in a flash, and of being removable by the people.

For these reasons, I would reverse the judgment below.

JUSTICE KENNEDY, dissenting.

The Supreme Court of Washington has determined that petitioners Jenifer and Gary Troxel have standing under state law to seek court-ordered visitation with their grandchildren, notwithstanding the objections of the children's parent, respondent Tommie Granville. . . .

After acknowledging this statutory right to sue for visitation, the State Supreme Court invalidated the statute as violative of the United States Constitution, because it interfered with a parent's right to raise his or her child free from unwarranted interference. . . .

The first flaw the State Supreme Court found in the statute is that it allows an award of visitation to a non-parent without a finding that harm to the child would result if visitation were withheld; and the second is that the statute allows any person to seek visitation at any time. In my view the first theory is too broad to be correct, as it appears to contemplate that the best interests of the child standard may not be applied in any visitation case. . . .

Given the error I see in the State Supreme Court's central conclusion. . . , that court should have the first opportunity to reconsider this case. I would remand the case to the state court for further proceedings. . . .

My principal concern is that the holding seems to proceed from the assumption that the parent or parents who resist visitation have always been the child's primary caregivers and that the third parties who seek visitation have no legitimate and established relationship with the child. That idea, in turn, appears influenced by the concept that the conventional nuclear family ought to establish the visitation standard for every domestic relations case. As we all know, this is simply not the structure or prevailing condition in many households. . . .

Cases are sure to arise—perhaps a substantial number of cases—in which a third party, by acting in a caregiving role over a significant period of time, has developed a relationship with a child which is not necessarily subject to absolute parental veto. . . . Some pre-existing relationships, then, serve to identify persons who have a strong attachment to the child with the concomitant motivation to act in a responsible way to ensure the child's welfare. . . . In the design and elaboration of their visitation laws, States may be entitled to consider that certain relationships are such that to avoid the risk of harm, a best interests standard can be employed by their domestic relations courts in some circumstances.

Indeed, contemporary practice should give us some pause before rejecting the best interests of the child standard in all third-party visitation cases. . . . The standard has been recognized for many years as a basic tool of domestic relations law in visitation proceedings. Since 1965 all 50 States have enacted a third-party visitation statute of some sort. Each of these statutes, save one, permits a court order to issue in certain cases if visitation is found to be in the best interests of the child. . . . [T]he statutes also include a variety of methods for limiting parents' exposure to third-party visitation petitions and for ensuring parental decisions are given respect. Many States limit the identity of permissible petitioners by restricting visitation petitions to grandparents, or by requiring petitioners to show a substantial relationship with a child, or both. . . . The statutes vary in other respects—for instance, some permit visitation petitions when there has been a change in circumstances such as divorce or death of a parent, and some apply a presumption that parental decisions should control. Georgia's is the sole State Legislature to have adopted a general harm to the child standard, and it did so only after the Georgia Supreme Court held the State's prior visitation statute invalid under the Federal and Georgia Constitutions.

. . . In my view, it would be more appropriate to conclude that the constitutionality of the application of the best interests standard depends on more specific factors. In short, a fit parent's right vis-à-vis a complete stranger is one thing; her right vis-à-vis another parent or a *de facto* parent may be another. The protection the Constitution requires, then, must be elaborated with care, using the discipline and instruction of the case law system. We must keep in mind that family courts in the 50 States confront these factual variations each day, and are best situated to consider the unpredictable, yet inevitable, issues that arise.

It must be recognized, of course, that a domestic relations proceeding in and of itself can constitute state intervention that is so disruptive of the parent-child relationship that the constitutional right of a custodial parent to make certain basic determinations for the child's welfare becomes implicated. . . . If a single parent who is struggling to raise a child is faced with visitation demands from a third party, the attorney's fees alone might destroy her hopes and plans for the child's future. Our system must confront more often the reality that litigation can itself be so disruptive that constitutional protection may be required; and I do not discount the possibility that in some instances the best interests of the child standard may provide insufficient protection to the parent-child relationship. We owe it to the Nation's domestic relations legal structure, however, to proceed with caution. . . .

No. 99-62

Santa Fe Independent School District, Petitioner v. Jane Doe, individually and as next friend for her minor children, Jane and John Doe et al.

On writ of certiorari to the United States Court of Appeals for the Fifth Circuit

[June 19, 2000]

JUSTICE STEVENS delivered the opinion of the Court.

Prior to 1995, the Santa Fe High School student who occupied the school's elective office of student council chaplain delivered a prayer over the public address system before each varsity football game for the entire season. This practice, along with others, was challenged in District Court as a violation of the Establishment Clause of the First Amendment. While these proceedings were pending in the District Court, the school district adopted a different policy that permits, but does not require, prayer initiated and led by a student at all home games. The District Court entered an order modifying that policy to permit only nonsectarian, nonproselytizing prayer. The Court of Appeals held that, even as modified by the District Court, the football prayer policy was invalid. We granted the school district's petition for certiorari to review that holding.

I

The Santa Fe Independent School District (District) is a political subdivision of the State of Texas, responsible for the education of more than 4,000 students in a small community in the southern part of the State. The District includes the Santa Fe High School, two primary schools, an intermediate school and the junior high school. Respondents are two sets of current or former students and their respective mothers. One family is Mormon and the other is Catholic. The District Court permitted respondents (Does) to litigate anonymously to protect them from intimidation or harassment.

Respondents commenced this action in April 1995 and moved for a temporary restraining order to prevent the District from violating the Establishment Clause at the imminent graduation exercises. In their complaint the Does alleged that the District had engaged in several proselytizing practices, such as promoting attendance at a Baptist revival meeting, encouraging membership in religious clubs, chastising children who held minority religious beliefs, and distributing Gideon Bibles on school premises. They also alleged that the District allowed students to read Christian invocations and benedictions from the stage at graduation ceremonies, and to deliver overtly Christian prayers over the public address system at home football games.

On May 10, 1995, the District Court entered an interim order addressing a number of different issues. With respect to the impending graduation, the order provided that "non-denominational prayer" consisting of "an invocation and/or benediction" could be presented by a senior student or students selected by members of the graduating class. The text of the prayer was to be determined by the students, without scrutiny or preapproval by school officials. References to particular religious figures "such as Mohammed, Jesus, Buddha, or the like" would be permitted "as long as the general thrust of the prayer is non-proselytizing."

In response to that portion of the order, the District adopted a series of policies over several months dealing with prayer at school functions. The policies enacted in May and July for graduation ceremonies provided the format for the August and October policies for football games. The May policy provided:

> "The board has chosen to permit the graduating senior class, with the advice and counsel of the senior class principal or designee, to elect by secret ballot to choose whether an invocation and benediction shall be part of the graduation exercise. If so chosen the class shall elect by secret ballot, from a list of student volunteers, students to deliver nonsectarian, nonproselytizing invocations and benedictions for the purpose of solemnizing their graduation ceremonies."

The parties stipulated that after this policy was adopted, "the senior class held an election to determine whether to have an invocation and benediction at the commencement [and that the] class voted, by secret ballot, to include prayer at the high school graduation." In a second vote the class elected two seniors to deliver the invocation and benediction.

In July, the District enacted another policy eliminating the requirement that invocations and benedictions be "nonsectarian and nonproselytising," but also providing that if the District were to be enjoined from enforcing that policy, the May policy would automatically become effective.

The August policy, which was titled "Prayer at Football Games," was similar to the July policy for graduations. It also authorized two student elections, the first to determine whether "invocations" should be delivered, and the second to select the spokesperson to deliver them. Like the July policy, it contained two parts, an initial statement that omitted any requirement that the content of the invocation be "nonsectarian and nonproselytising," and a fallback provision that automatically added that limitation if the preferred policy should be enjoined. On August 31, 1995, according to the parties' stipulation, "the district's high school students voted to determine whether a student would deliver prayer at varsity football games. . . . The students chose to allow a student to say a prayer at football games." A week later, in a separate election, they selected a student "to deliver the prayer at varsity football games."

The final policy (October policy) is essentially the same as the August policy, though it omits the word "prayer" from its title, and refers to "messages" and "statements" as well as "invocations." It is the validity of that policy that is before us.

The District Court did enter an order precluding enforcement of the first, open-ended policy. Relying on our decision in *Lee v. Weisman* (1992), it held that the school's "action must not 'coerce anyone to support or participate in' a religious exercise." Applying that test, it concluded that the graduation prayers appealed "to distinctively Christian beliefs," and that delivering a prayer "over the school's public address system prior to each football and baseball game coerces student participation in religious events." Both parties appealed, the District contending that the enjoined portion of the October policy was permissible and the Does contending that both alternatives violated the Establishment Clause. The Court of Appeals majority agreed with the Does.

The decision of the Court of Appeals followed Fifth Circuit precedent that had announced two rules. In *Jones v. Clear Creek Independent School Dist.* (1992), that court held that student-led prayer that was approved by a vote of the students and was nonsectarian and nonproselytizing was permissible at high school graduation ceremonies. On the other hand, in later cases the Fifth Circuit made it clear that the Clear Creek rule applied only to high school graduations and that school-encouraged prayer was constitutionally impermissible at school-related sporting events. . . .

We granted the District's petition for certiorari, limited to the following question: "Whether petitioner's policy permitting student-led, student-initiated prayer at football games violates the Establishment Clause." (1999). We conclude, as did the Court of Appeals, that it does.

II

The first Clause in the First Amendment to the Federal Constitution provides that "Congress shall make no law respecting an establishment of religion, or prohibiting the free exercise thereof." The Fourteenth Amendment imposes those substantive limitations on the legislative power of the States and their political subdivisions. In *Lee v. Weisman* (1992), we held that a prayer delivered by a rabbi at a middle school graduation ceremony violated that Clause. . . .

As we held in that case:

> "The principle that government may accommodate the free exercise of religion does not supersede the fundamental limitations imposed by the Establishment Clause. It is beyond dispute that, at a minimum, the Constitution guarantees that government may not coerce anyone to support or participate in religion or its exercise, or otherwise act in a way which 'establishes a [state] religion or religious faith, or tends to do so.'"

In this case the District first argues that this principle is inapplicable to its October policy because the messages are private student speech, not public speech. . . . [W]e are not persuaded that the pregame invocations should be regarded as "private speech."

These invocations are authorized by a government policy and take place on government property at government-sponsored school-related events. . . . [T]he school allows only one student, the same student for the entire season, to give the invocation. The statement or invocation, moreover, is subject to particular regulations that confine the content and topic of the student's message. . . .

Granting only one student access to the stage at a time does not, of course, necessarily preclude a finding that a school has created a limited public forum. Here, however, Santa Fe's student election system ensures that only those messages deemed "appropriate" under the District's policy may be delivered. That is, the majoritarian process implemented by the District guarantees, by definition, that minority candidates will never prevail and that their views will be effectively silenced.

In *Lee*, the school district made the related argument that its policy of endorsing only "civic or nonsectarian" prayer was acceptable because it minimized the intrusion on the audience as a whole. We rejected that claim by explaining that such a majoritarian policy "does not lessen the offense or isolation to the objectors. At best it narrows their number, at worst increases their sense of isolation and affront." Similarly, while Santa Fe's majoritarian election might ensure that most of the students are represented, it does nothing to protect the minority; indeed, it likely serves to intensify their offense.

Moreover, the District has failed to divorce itself from the religious content in the invocations. . . . Contrary to the District's repeated assertions that it has adopted a "hands-off" approach to the pregame invocation, the realities of the situation plainly reveal that its policy involves both perceived and actual endorsement of religion. In this case, as we found in *Lee*, the "degree of school involvement" makes it clear that the pregame prayers bear "the imprint of the State and thus put school-age children who objected in an untenable position."

The District has attempted to disentangle itself from the religious messages by developing the two-step student election process. The text of the October policy, however, exposes the extent of the school's entanglement. . . . Even though the particular words used by the speaker are not determined by those votes, the policy mandates that the "statement or invocation" be "consistent with the goals and purposes of this policy," which are "to solemnize the event, to promote good sportsmanship and student safety, and to establish the appropriate environment for the competition."

In addition to involving the school in the selection of the speaker, the policy, by its terms, invites and encourages religious messages. The policy itself states that the purpose of the message is "to solemnize the event." A religious message is the most obvious method of solemnizing an event. Moreover, the requirements that the message "promote good citizenship" and "establish the appropriate environment for competition" further narrow the types of message deemed appropriate. . . . Thus, the expressed purposes of the policy encourage the selection of a religious message, and that is precisely how the students understand the policy. . . . We recognize the important role that public worship plays in many communities, as well as the sincere desire to include public prayer as a part of various occasions so as to mark those occasions' significance. But such religious activity in public schools, as elsewhere, must comport with the First Amendment.

The actual or perceived endorsement of the message, moreover, is established by factors beyond just the text of the policy. Once the student speaker is selected and the message composed, the invocation is then delivered to a large audience assembled as part of a regularly scheduled, school-sponsored function conducted on school property. The message is broadcast over the school's public address system, which remains subject to the control of school officials. It is fair to assume that the pregame ceremony is clothed in the traditional indicia of school sporting events, which generally include not just the team, but also cheerleaders and band members dressed in uniforms sporting the school name and mascot. The school's name is likely written in large print across the field and on banners and flags. The crowd will certainly include many who display the school colors and insignia on their school T-shirts, jackets, or hats and who may also be waving signs displaying the school name. It is in a setting such as this that "[t]he board has chosen to permit" the elected student to rise and give the "statement or invocation."

In this context the members of the listening audience must perceive the pregame message as a public expression of the views of the majority of the student body delivered with the approval of the school administration. . . . Regardless of the listener's support for, or objection to, the message, an objective Santa Fe High School student will unquestionably perceive the inevitable pregame prayer as stamped with her school's seal of approval.

The text and history of this policy, moreover, reinforce our objective student's perception that the prayer is, in actuality, encouraged by the school. . . .

According to the District, the secular purposes of the policy are to "foste[r] free expression of private persons . . . as well [as to] solemniz[e] sporting events, promot[e] good sportsmanship and student safety, and establis[h] an appropriate environment for competition." We note, however, that the District's approval of only one specific kind of message, an "invocation," is not necessary to further any of these purposes. Additionally, the fact that only one student is permitted to give a content-limited message suggests that this policy does little to "foste[r] free expression." Furthermore, regardless of whether one considers a sporting event an appropriate occasion for solemnity, the use of an invocation to foster such solemnity is impermissible when, in actuality, it constitutes prayer sponsored by the school. And it is unclear what type of message would be both appropriately "solemnizing" under the District's policy and yet non-religious.

Most striking to us is the evolution of the current policy from the long-sanctioned office of "Student Chaplain" to the candidly titled "Prayer at Football Games" regulation. This history indicates that the District intended to preserve the practice of prayer before football games. The conclusion that the District viewed the October policy simply as a continuation of the previous policies is dramatically illustrated by the fact that the school did not conduct a new election, pursuant to the current policy, to replace the results of the previous election, which occurred under the former policy. Given these observations, and in light of the school's history of regular delivery of a student-led prayer at athletic events, it is reasonable to infer that the specific purpose of the policy was to preserve a popular "state-sponsored religious practice."

School sponsorship of a religious message is impermissible because it sends the ancillary message to members of the audience who are nonadherents "that they are outsiders, not full members of the political community, and an accompanying message to adherents that they are insiders, favored members of the political community." The delivery of such a message—over the school's public address system, by a speaker representing the student body, under the supervision of school faculty, and pursuant to a school policy that explicitly and implicitly encourages public prayer—is not properly characterized as "private" speech.

III

The District next argues that its football policy is distinguishable from the graduation prayer in *Lee* because it does not coerce students to participate in religious observances. Its argument has two parts: first, that there is no impermissible government coercion because the pregame messages are the product of student choices; and second, that there is really no coercion at all because attendance at an extracurricular event, unlike a graduation ceremony, is voluntary.

The reasons just discussed explaining why the alleged "circuit-breaker" mechanism of the dual elections and student speaker do not turn public speech into private speech also demonstrate why these mechanisms do not insulate the school from the coercive element of the final message. In fact, this aspect of the District's argument exposes anew the concerns that are created by the majoritarian election system. The parties' stipulation clearly states that the issue resolved in the first election was "whether a student would deliver prayer at varsity football games," and the controversy in this case demonstrates that the views of the students are not unanimous on that issue.

One of the purposes served by the Establishment Clause is to remove debate over this kind of issue from governmental supervision or control. . . . The two student elections authorized by the policy, coupled with the debates that presumably must precede each, impermissibly invade that private sphere. The election mechanism, when considered in light of the history in which the policy in question evolved, reflects a device the District put in place that determines whether religious messages will be delivered at home football games. The mechanism encourages divisiveness along religious lines in a public school setting, a result at odds with the Establishment Clause. Although it is true that the ultimate choice of student speaker is "attributable to the students," the District's decision to hold the constitutionally problematic election is clearly "a choice attributable to the State."

The District further argues that attendance at the commencement ceremonies at issue in *Lee* "differs dramatically" from attendance at high school football games, which it contends "are of no more than passing interest to many students" and are "decidedly extracurricular," thus dissipating any coercion. Attendance at a high school football game, unlike showing up for class, is certainly not required in order to receive a diploma. Moreover, we may assume that the District is correct in arguing that the informal pressure to attend an athletic event is not as strong as a senior's desire to attend her own graduation ceremony.

There are some students, however, such as cheerleaders, members of the band, and, of course, the team members themselves, for whom seasonal commitments mandate their attendance, sometimes for class credit. The District also minimizes the importance to many students of attending and participating in extracurricular activities as part of a complete educational experience. . . . High school home football games are traditional gatherings of a school community; they bring together students and faculty as well as friends and family from years present and past to root for a common cause. Undoubtedly, the games are not important to some students, and they voluntarily choose not to attend. For many others, however, the choice between whether to attend these games or to risk facing a personally offensive religious ritual is in no practical sense an easy one. The Constitution, moreover, demands that the school may not force this difficult choice upon these students. . . .

Even if we regard every high school student's decision to attend a home football game as purely voluntary, we are nevertheless persuaded that the delivery of a pregame prayer has the improper effect of coercing those present to participate in an act of religious worship. . . . As in *Lee*, "[w]hat to most believers may seem nothing more than a reasonable request that the nonbeliever respect their religious practices, in a school context may appear to the nonbeliever or dissenter to be an attempt to employ the machinery of the State to enforce a religious orthodoxy." The constitutional command will not permit the District "to exact religious conformity from a student as the price" of joining her classmates at a varsity football game.

The Religion Clauses of the First Amendment prevent the government from making any law respecting the establishment of religion or prohibiting the free exercise thereof. By no means do these commands impose a prohibition on all religious activity in our public schools. [Citation of cases omitted.] . . . [N]othing in the Constitution as interpreted by this Court prohibits any public school student from voluntarily praying at any time before, during, or after the schoolday. But the religious liberty protected by the Constitution is abridged when the State affirmatively sponsors the particular religious practice of prayer.

IV

Finally, the District argues repeatedly that the Does have made a premature facial challenge to the October policy that necessarily must fail. The District emphasizes, quite correctly, that until a student actually delivers a solemnizing message under the latest version of the policy, there can be no certainty that any of the statements or invocations will be religious. Thus, it concludes, the October policy necessarily survives a facial challenge.

This argument, however, assumes that we are concerned only with the serious constitutional injury that occurs when a student is forced to participate in an act of religious worship because she chooses to attend a school event. But the Constitution also requires that we keep in mind "the myriad, subtle ways in which Establishment Clause values can be eroded," and that we guard against other different, yet equally important, constitutional injuries. One is the mere passage by the District of a policy that has the purpose and perception of government establishment of religion. Another is the implementation of a governmental electoral process that subjects the issue of prayer to a majoritarian vote.

. . . [T]he text of the October policy alone reveals that it has an unconstitutional purpose. The plain language of the policy clearly spells out the extent of school involvement in both the election of the speaker and the content of the message. Additionally, the text of the October policy specifies only one, clearly preferred message—that of Santa Fe's traditional religious "invocation." Finally, the extremely selective access of the policy and other content restrictions confirm that it is not a content-neutral regulation that creates a limited public forum for the expression of student speech.

. . . [T]he simple enactment of this policy, with the purpose and perception of school endorsement of student prayer, was a constitutional violation. We need not wait for the inevitable to confirm and magnify the constitutional injury. . . . [E]ven if no Santa Fe High School student were ever to offer a religious message, the October policy fails a facial challenge because the attempt by the District to encourage prayer is also at issue. Government efforts to endorse religion cannot evade constitutional reproach based solely on the remote possibility that those attempts may fail.

This policy likewise does not survive a facial challenge because it impermissibly imposes upon the student body a majoritarian election on the issue of prayer. Through its election scheme, the District has established a governmental electoral mechanism that turns the school into a forum for religious debate. It further empowers the student body majority with the authority to subject students of minority views to constitutionally improper messages. . . . Such a system encourages divisiveness along religious lines and threatens the imposition of coercion upon those students not desiring to participate in a religious exercise. Simply by establishing this school-related procedure, which entrusts the inherently nongovernmental subject of religion to a majoritarian vote, a constitutional violation has occurred. . . .

. . . [T]his policy does not provide the District with the constitutional safe harbor it sought. The policy is invalid on its face because it establishes an improper majoritarian election on religion, and unquestionably has the purpose and creates the perception of encouraging the delivery of prayer at a series of important school events.

The judgment of the Court of Appeals is, accordingly, affirmed.

It is so ordered.

CHIEF JUSTICE REHNQUIST, with whom JUSTICE SCALIA and JUSTICE THOMAS join, dissenting.

The Court distorts existing precedent to conclude that the school district's student-message program is invalid on its face under the Establishment Clause. But even more disturbing than its holding is the tone of the Court's opinion; it bristles with hostility to all things religious in public life. Neither the holding nor the tone of the opinion is faithful to the meaning of the Establishment Clause, when it is recalled that George Washington himself, at the request of the very Congress which passed the Bill of Rights, proclaimed a day of "public thanksgiving and prayer, to be observed by acknowledging with grateful hearts the many and signal favors of Almighty God."

We do not learn until late in the Court's opinion that respondents in this case challenged the district's student-message program at football games before it had been put into practice. . . . No speech will be "chilled" by the existence of a government policy that might unconstitutionally endorse religion over nonreligion.

Therefore, the question is not whether the district's policy may be applied in violation of the Establishment Clause, but whether it inevitably will be.

The Court, venturing into the realm of prophesy, decides that it "need not wait for the inevitable" and invalidates the district's policy on its face. To do so, it applies the most rigid version of the oft-criticized test of *Lemon v. Kurtzman* (1971).

Lemon has had a checkered career in the decisional law of this Court. [Opinions criticizing *Lemon* test omitted.] We have even gone so far as to state that it has never been binding on us. . . . Indeed, in *Lee v. Weisman* (1992), an opinion upon which the Court relies heavily today, we mentioned but did not feel compelled to apply the *Lemon* test. . . .

Even if it were appropriate to apply the *Lemon* test here, the district's student-message policy should not be invalidated on its face. The Court applies *Lemon* and holds that the "policy is invalid on its face because it establishes an improper majoritarian election on religion, and unquestionably has the purpose and creates the perception of encouraging the delivery of prayer at a series of important school events." The Court's reliance on each of these conclusions misses the mark.

First, the Court misconstrues the nature of the "majoritarian election" permitted by the policy as being an election on "prayer" and "religion." To the contrary, the election permitted by the policy is a two-fold process whereby students vote first on whether to have a student speaker before football games at all, and second, if the students vote to have such a speaker, on who that speaker will be. It is conceivable that the election could become one in which student candidates campaign on platforms that focus on whether or not they will pray if elected. It is also conceivable that the election could lead to a Christian prayer before 90 percent of the football games. If, upon implementation, the policy operated in this fashion, we would have a record before us to review whether the policy, as applied, violated the Establishment Clause or unduly suppressed minority viewpoints. But it is possible that the students might vote not to have a pregame speaker, in which case there would be no threat of a constitutional violation. It is also possible that the election would not focus on prayer, but on public speaking ability or social popularity. And if student campaigning did begin to focus on prayer, the school might decide to implement reasonable campaign restrictions.

But the Court ignores these possibilities by holding that merely granting the student body the power to elect a speaker that may choose to pray, "regardless of the students' ultimate use of it, is not acceptable." The Court so holds despite that any speech that may occur as a result of the election process here would be private, not government, speech. The elected student, not the government, would choose what to say. Support for the Court's holding cannot be found in any of our cases. And it essentially invalidates all student elections. A newly elected student body president, or even a newly elected prom king or queen, could use opportunities for public speaking to say prayers. Under the Court's view, the mere grant of power to the students to vote for such offices, in light of the fear that those elected might publicly pray, violates the Establishment Clause.

Second, with respect to the policy's purpose, the Court holds that "the simple enactment of this policy, with the purpose and perception of school endorsement of student prayer, was a constitutional violation." But the policy itself has plausible secular purposes: "[T]o solemnize the event, to promote good sportsmanship and student safety, and to establish the appropriate environment for the competition." . . . The Court grants no deference to—and appears openly hostile toward—the policy's stated purposes, and wastes no time in concluding that they are a sham.

For example, the Court dismisses the secular purpose of solemnization by claiming that it "invites and encourages religious messages." . . . The Court so concludes based on its rather strange view that a "religious message is the most obvious means of solemnizing an event." But it is easy to think of solemn messages that are not religious in nature, for example urging that a game be fought fairly. And sporting events often begin with a solemn rendition of our national anthem, with its concluding verse "And this be our motto: 'In God is our trust.'" Under the Court's logic, a public school that sponsors the singing of the national anthem before football games violates the Establishment Clause. Although the Court apparently believes that solemnizing football games is an illegitimate purpose, the voters in the school district seem to disagree. Nothing in the Establishment Clause prevents them from making this choice.

The Court bases its conclusion that the true purpose of the policy is to endorse student prayer on its view of the school district's history of Establishment Clause violations and the context in which the policy was written, that is, as "the latest step in developing litigation brought as a challenge to institutional practices that unquestionably violated the Establishment Clause." But the context—attempted compliance with a District Court order—actually demonstrates that the school district was acting diligently to come within the governing constitutional law. The District Court ordered the school district to formulate a policy consistent with Fifth Circuit precedent, which permitted a school district to have a prayer-only policy. But the school district went further than required by the District Court order and eventually settled on a policy that gave the student speaker a choice to deliver either an invocation or a message. In so doing, the school district exhibited a willingness to comply with, and exceed, Establishment Clause restrictions. Thus, the policy cannot be viewed as having a sectarian purpose.

The Court also relies on our decision in *Lee v. Weisman* to support its conclusion. In *Lee*, we concluded that the content of the speech at issue, a graduation prayer given by a rabbi, was "directed and controlled" by a school official. In other words, at issue in *Lee* was *government* speech. Here, by contrast, the potential speech at issue, if the policy had been allowed to proceed, would be a message or invocation selected or created by a student. That is, if there were speech at issue here, it would be *private* speech. . . .

Had the policy been put into practice, the students may have chosen a speaker according to wholly secular criteria—like good public speaking skills or social popularity—and the student speaker may have chosen, on her own accord, to deliver a religious message. Such an application of the policy would likely pass constitutional muster. . . .

Finally, the Court seems to demand that a government policy be completely neutral as to content or be considered one that endorses religion. This is undoubtedly a new requirement, as our Establishment Clause jurisprudence simply does not mandate "content neutrality." That concept is found in our First Amendment speech cases and is used as a guide for determining when we apply strict scrutiny. . . .

But even our speech jurisprudence would not require that all public school actions with respect to student speech be content neutral. . . . Schools do not violate the First Amendment every time they restrict student speech to certain categories. But under the Court's view, a school policy under which the student body president is to solemnize the graduation ceremony by giving a favorable introduction to the guest speaker would be facially unconstitutional. Solemnization "invites and encourages" prayer and the policy's content limitations prohibit the student body president from giving a solemn, yet non-religious, message like "commentary on United States foreign policy."

The policy at issue here may be applied in an unconstitutional manner, but it will be time enough to invalidate it if that is found to be the case. I would reverse the judgment of the Court of Appeals.

No. 99-5525

Charles Thomas Dickerson, Petitioner v. United States

On writ of certiorari to the United States Court of Appeals for the Fourth Circuit

[June 26, 2000]

CHIEF JUSTICE REHNQUIST delivered the opinion of the Court.

In *Miranda v. Arizona* (1966), we held that certain warnings must be given before a suspect's statement made during custodial interrogation could be admitted in evidence. In the wake of that decision, Congress enacted 18 U.S.C. §3501, which in essence laid down a rule that the admissibility of such statements should turn only on whether or not they were voluntarily made. We hold that *Miranda*, being a constitutional decision of this Court, may not be in effect overruled by an Act of Congress, and we decline to overrule *Miranda* ourselves. We therefore hold that *Miranda* and its progeny in this Court govern the admissibility of statements made during custodial interrogation in both state and federal courts.

Petitioner Dickerson was indicted for bank robbery, conspiracy to commit bank robbery, and using a firearm in the course of committing a crime of violence, all in violation of the applicable provisions of Title 18 of the United States Code. Before trial, Dickerson moved to suppress a statement he had made at a Federal Bureau of Investigation field office, on the grounds that he had not received "*Miranda* warnings" before being interrogated. The District Court granted his motion to suppress, and the Government took an interlocutory appeal to the United States Court of Appeals for the Fourth Circuit. That court, by a divided vote, reversed the District Court's suppression order. It agreed with the District Court's conclusion that petitioner had not received *Miranda* warnings before making his statement. But it went on to hold that §3501, which in effect makes the admissibility of statements such as Dickerson's turn solely on whether they were made voluntarily, was satisfied in this case. It then concluded that our decision in *Miranda* was not a constitutional holding, and that therefore Congress could by statute have the final say on the question of admissibility. (1999).

Because of the importance of the questions raised by the Court of Appeals' decision, we granted certiorari (1999), and now reverse.

We begin with a brief historical account of the law governing the admission of confessions. Prior to *Miranda*, we evaluated the admissibility of a suspect's confession under a voluntariness test. The roots of this test developed in the common law, as the courts of England and then the United States recognized that coerced confessions are inherently untrustworthy. [Citation of cases omitted.] Over time, our cases recognized two constitutional bases for the requirement that a confession be voluntary to be admitted into evidence: the Fifth Amendment right against self-incrimination and the Due Process Clause of the Fourteenth Amendment. See, *e.g.*, *Bram v. United States* (1897) (stating that the voluntariness test "is controlled by that portion of the Fifth Amendment . . . commanding that no person 'shall be compelled in any criminal case to be a witness against himself'"); *Brown v. Mississippi* (1936) (reversing a criminal conviction under the Due Process Clause because it was based on a confession obtained by physical coercion).

While *Bram* was decided before *Brown* and its progeny, for the middle third of the 20th century our cases based the rule against admitting coerced confessions primarily, if not exclusively, on notions of due process. We applied the due process voluntariness test in "some 30 different cases decided during the era that intervened between *Brown* and *Escobedo v. Illinois* [(1964)]." *Schneckcloth v. Bustamonte* (1973). [Examples omitted.] Those cases refined the test into an inquiry that examines "whether a defendant's will was overborne" by the circumstances surrounding the giving of a confession. *Schneckcloth.* The due process test takes into consideration "the totality of all the surrounding circumstances—both the characteristics of the accused and the details of the interrogation." . . .

We have never abandoned this due process jurisprudence, and thus continue to exclude confessions that were obtained involuntarily. But our decisions in *Malloy v. Hogan* (1964) and *Miranda* changed the focus of much of the inquiry in determining the admissibility of suspects' incriminating statements. In *Malloy*, we held that the Fifth Amendment's Self-Incrimination Clause is incorporated in the Due Process Clause of the Fourteenth Amendment and thus applies to the States. We decided *Miranda* on the heels of *Malloy*.

In *Miranda*, we noted that the advent of modern custodial police interrogation brought with it an increased concern about confessions obtained by coercion. Because custodial police interrogation, by its very nature, isolates and pressures the individual, we stated that "[e]ven without employing brutality, the 'third degree' or [other] specific stratagems, . . . custodial interrogation exacts a heavy toll on individual liberty and trades on the weakness of individuals." We concluded that the coercion inherent in custodial interrogation blurs the line between voluntary and involuntary statements, and thus heightens the risk that an individual will not be "accorded his privilege under the Fifth Amendment . . . not to be compelled to incriminate himself." Accordingly, we laid down "concrete constitutional guidelines for law enforcement agencies and courts to follow." Those guidelines established that the admissibility in evidence of any statement given during custodial interrogation of a suspect would depend on whether the police provided the suspect with four warnings. These warnings (which have come to be known colloquially as "*Miranda* rights") are: a suspect "has the right to remain silent, that anything he says can be used against him in a court of law, that he has the right to the presence of an attorney, and that if he cannot afford an attorney one will be appointed for him prior to any questioning if he so desires."

Two years after *Miranda* was decided, Congress enacted §3501. That section provides, in relevant part:

> "(a) In any criminal prosecution brought by the United States or by the District of Columbia, a confession . . . shall be admissible in evidence if it is voluntarily given. Before such confession is received in evidence, the trial judge shall, out of the presence of the jury, determine any issue as to voluntariness. If the trial judge determines that the confession was voluntarily made it shall be admitted in evidence and the trial judge shall permit the jury to hear relevant evidence on the issue of voluntariness and shall instruct the jury to give such weight to the confession as the jury feels it deserves under all the circumstances.
>
> "(b) The trial judge in determining the issue of voluntariness shall take into consideration all the circumstances surrounding the giving of the confession, including (1) the time elapsing between arrest and arraign-

ment of the defendant making the confession, if it was made after arrest and before arraignment, (2) whether such defendant knew the nature of the offense with which he was charged or of which he was suspected at the time of making the confession, (3) whether or not such defendant was advised or knew that he was not required to make any statement and that any such statement could be used against him, (4) whether or not such defendant had been advised prior to questioning of his right to the assistance of counsel; and (5) whether or not such defendant was without the assistance of counsel when questioned and when giving such confession.

"The presence or absence of any of the above-mentioned factors to be taken into consideration by the judge need not be conclusive on the issue of voluntariness of the confession."

Given §3501's express designation of voluntariness as the touchstone of admissibility, its omission of any warning requirement, and the instruction for trial courts to consider a nonexclusive list of factors relevant to the circumstances of a confession, we agree with the Court of Appeals that Congress intended by its enactment to overrule *Miranda*. . . . Because of the obvious conflict between our decision in *Miranda* and §3501, we must address whether Congress has constitutional authority to thus supersede *Miranda*. If Congress has such authority, §3501's totality-of-the-circumstances approach must prevail over *Miranda*'s requirement of warnings; if not, that section must yield to *Miranda*'s more specific requirements.

The law in this area is clear. This Court has supervisory authority over the federal courts, and we may use that authority to prescribe rules of evidence and procedure that are binding in those tribunals. However, the power to judicially create and enforce nonconstitutional "rules of procedure and evidence for the federal courts exists only in the absence of a relevant Act of Congress." [Citations omitted.] Congress retains the ultimate authority to modify or set aside any judicially created rules of evidence and procedure that are not required by the Constitution.

But Congress may not legislatively supersede our decisions interpreting and applying the Constitution. This case therefore turns on whether the *Miranda* Court announced a constitutional rule or merely exercised its supervisory authority to regulate evidence in the absence of congressional direction. Recognizing this point, the Court of Appeals surveyed *Miranda* and its progeny to determine the constitutional status of the *Miranda* decision. Relying on the fact that we have created several exceptions to *Miranda*'s warnings requirement and that we have repeatedly referred to the *Miranda* warnings as "prophylactic," *New York v. Quarles* (1984), and "not themselves rights protected by the Constitution," *Michigan v. Tucker* (1974), the Court of Appeals concluded that the protections announced in *Miranda* are not constitutionally required.

We disagree with the Court of Appeals' conclusion, although we concede that there is language in some of our opinions that supports the view taken by that court. But first and foremost of the factors on the other side—that *Miranda* is a constitutional decision—is that both *Miranda* and two of its companion cases applied the rule to proceedings in state courts—to wit, Arizona, California, and New York. Since that time, we have consistently applied *Miranda*'s rule to prosecutions arising in state courts. It is beyond dispute that we do not hold a supervisory power over the courts of the several States. . . . With respect to proceedings in state courts, our "authority is limited to enforcing the commands of the United States Constitution." . . .

The *Miranda* opinion itself begins by stating that the Court granted certiorari "to explore some facets of the problems . . . of applying the privilege against self-incrimination to in-custody interrogation, *and to give concrete constitutional guidelines for law enforcement agencies and courts to follow*" (emphasis added). In fact, the majority opinion is replete with statements indicating that the majority thought it was announcing a constitutional rule. Indeed, the Court's ultimate conclusion was that the unwarned confessions obtained in the four cases before the Court in *Miranda* "were obtained from the defendant under circumstances that did not meet constitutional standards for protection of the privilege."

Additional support for our conclusion that *Miranda* is constitutionally based is found in the *Miranda* Court's invitation for legislative action to protect the constitutional right against coerced self-incrimination. After discussing the "compelling pressures" inherent in custodial police interrogation, the *Miranda* Court concluded that, "[i]n order to combat these pressures and to permit a full opportunity to exercise the privilege against self-incrimination, the accused must be adequately and effectively appraised of his rights and the exercise of those rights must be fully honored." However, the Court emphasized that it could not foresee "the potential alternatives for protecting the privilege which might be devised by Congress or the States," and it accordingly opined that the Constitution would not preclude legislative solutions that differed from the prescribed *Miranda* warnings but which were "at least as effective in apprising accused persons of their right of silence and in assuring a continuous opportunity to exercise it."

The Court of Appeals also relied on the fact that we have, after our *Miranda* decision, made exceptions from its rule in cases such as *New York v. Quarles* and *Harris v. New York* (1971). But we have also broadened the application of the *Miranda* doctrine in cases such as *Doyle v. Ohio* (1976) and *Arizona v. Roberson* (1988). These decisions illustrate the principle—not that *Miranda* is not a constitutional rule—but that no constitutional rule is immutable. No court laying down a general rule can possibly foresee the various circumstances in which counsel will seek to apply it, and the sort of modifications represented by these cases are as much a normal part of constitutional law as the original decision.

The Court of Appeals also noted that in *Oregon v. Elstad* (1985), we stated that "'[t]he *Miranda* exclusionary rule . . . serves the Fifth Amendment and sweeps more broadly than the Fifth Amendment itself.'" Our decision in that case—refusing to apply the traditional "fruits" doctrine developed in Fourth Amendment cases—does not prove that *Miranda* is a nonconstitutional decision, but simply recognizes the fact that unreasonable searches under the Fourth Amendment are different from unwarned interrogation under the Fifth Amendment.

As an alternative argument for sustaining the Court of Appeals' decision, the court-invited *amicus curiae* contends that the section complies with the requirement that a legislative alternative to *Miranda* be equally as effective in preventing coerced confessions. We agree with the *amicus'* contention that there are more remedies available for abusive police conduct than there were at the time *Miranda* was decided. . . . But we do not agree that these additional measures supplement §3501's protections sufficiently to meet the constitutional minimum. *Miranda* requires procedures that will warn a suspect in custody of his right to remain silent and which will assure the suspect that the exercise of that right will be honored. As discussed above, §3501 explicitly eschews a requirement of pre-interrogation warnings in favor of an approach that looks to the administration of such warnings as only one factor in determining the voluntariness of a suspect's confession. The additional remedies cited by *amicus* do not, in our view, render them, together with §3501 an adequate substitute for the warnings required by *Miranda*.

The dissent argues that it is judicial overreaching for this Court to hold §3501 unconstitutional unless we hold that the *Miranda* warnings are required by the Constitution, in the sense that nothing else will suffice to satisfy constitutional requirements. But we need not go farther than *Miranda* to decide this case. In *Miranda*, the Court noted that reliance on the traditional totality-of-the-circumstances test raised a risk of overlooking an involuntary custodial confession, a risk that the Court found unacceptably great when the confession is offered in the case in chief to prove guilt. The Court therefore concluded that something more than the totality test was necessary. As discussed above, §3501 reinstates the totality test as sufficient. Section 3501 therefore cannot be sustained if *Miranda* is to remain the law.

Whether or not we would agree with *Miranda*'s reasoning and its resulting rule, were we addressing the issue in the first instance, the principles of *stare decisis* weigh heavily against overruling it now.... While "'*stare decisis* is not an inexorable command'" [citation omitted], particularly when we are interpreting the Constitution, "even in constitutional cases, the doctrine carries such persuasive force that we have always required a departure from precedent to be supported by some 'special justification.'" [Citation omitted.]

We do not think there is such justification for overruling *Miranda*. *Miranda* has become embedded in routine police practice to the point where the warnings have become part of our national culture.... While we have overruled our precedents when subsequent cases have undermined their doctrinal underpinnings, we do not believe that this has happened to the *Miranda* decision. If anything, our subsequent cases have reduced the impact of the *Miranda* rule on legitimate law enforcement while reaffirming the decision's core ruling that unwarned statements may not be used as evidence in the prosecution's case in chief.

The disadvantage of the *Miranda* rule is that statements which may be by no means involuntary, made by a defendant who is aware of his "rights," may nonetheless be excluded and a guilty defendant go free as a result. But experience suggests that the totality-of-the-circumstances test which §3501 seeks to revive is more difficult than *Miranda* for law enforcement officers to conform to, and for courts to apply in a consistent manner.... The requirement that *Miranda* warnings be given does not, of course, dispense with the voluntariness inquiry. But as we said in *Berkemer v. McCarty* (1984), "[c]ases in which a defendant can make a colorable argument that a self-incriminating statement was 'compelled' despite the fact that the law enforcement authorities adhered to the dictates of *Miranda* are rare."

In sum, we conclude that *Miranda* announced a constitutional rule that Congress may not supersede legislatively. Following the rule of *stare decisis*, we decline to overrule *Miranda* ourselves. The judgment of the Court of Appeals is therefore

Reversed.

JUSTICE SCALIA, with whom JUSTICE THOMAS joins, dissenting.

. . . [A]n Act of Congress will not be enforced by the courts if what it prescribes violates the Constitution of the United States. That was the basis on which *Miranda* [*v. Arizona* (1966)] was decided. One will search today's opinion in vain, however, for a statement . . . that what 18 U.S.C. §3501 prescribes—the use at trial of a voluntary confession, even when a *Miranda* warning or its equivalent has failed to be given—violates the Constitution. The reason the statement does not appear is not only (and perhaps not so much) that it would be absurd, inasmuch as §3501 excludes from trial precisely what the Constitution excludes from trial, viz., compelled confessions; but also that Justices whose votes are needed to compose today's majority are on record as believing that a violation of *Miranda* is not a violation of the Constitution. [See *Davis v. United States* (1994) (opinion of the Court, in which KENNEDY, J., joined); *Duckworth v. Eagan* (1989) (opinion of the Court, in which KENNEDY, J., joined); *Oregon v. Elstad* (1985) (opinion of the Court by O'CONNOR, J.); *New York v. Quarles* (1984) (opinion of the Court by REHNQUIST, J.)] And so, to justify today's agreed-upon result, the Court must adopt a significant new, if not entirely comprehensible, principle of constitutional law. As the Court chooses to describe that principle, statutes of Congress can be disregarded, not only when what they prescribe violates the Constitution, but when what they prescribe contradicts a decision of this Court that "announced a constitutional rule." . . . [T]he only thing that can possibly mean in the context of this case is that this Court has the power, not merely to apply the Constitution but to expand it, imposing what it regards as useful "prophylactic" restrictions upon Congress and the States. That is an immense and frightening antidemocratic power, and it does not exist.

It takes only a small step to bring today's opinion out of the realm of power-judging and into the mainstream of legal reasoning: The Court need only go beyond its carefully couched iterations that "*Miranda* is a constitutional decision," that "*Miranda* is constitutionally based," that *Miranda* has "constitutional underpinnings," and come out and say quite clearly: "We reaffirm today that custodial interrogation that is not preceded by *Miranda* warnings or their equivalent violates the Constitution of the United States." It cannot say that, because a majority of the Court does not believe it. The Court therefore acts in plain violation of the Constitution when it denies effect to this Act of Congress.

I

. . . It was once possible to characterize the so-called *Miranda* rule as resting (however implausibly) upon the proposition that what the statute here before us permits—the admission at trial of un-*Mirandized* confessions—violates the Constitution. That is the fairest reading of the *Miranda* case itself. The Court began by announcing that the Fifth Amendment privilege against self-incrimination applied in the context of extrajudicial custodial interrogation. . . . Having extended the privilege into the confines of the station house, the Court liberally sprinkled throughout its sprawling 60-page opinion suggestions that, because of the compulsion inherent in custodial interrogation, the privilege was violated by any statement thus obtained that did not conform to the rules set forth in *Miranda*, or some functional equivalent. . . .

So understood, *Miranda* was objectionable for innumerable reasons, not least the fact that cases spanning more than 70 years had rejected its core premise that, absent the warnings and an effective waiver of the right to remain silent and of the (thitherto unknown) right to have an attorney present, a statement obtained pursuant to custodial interrogation was necessarily the product of compulsion. . . . Moreover, history and precedent aside, the decision in *Miranda*, if read as an explication of what the Constitution requires, is preposterous. There is, for example, simply no basis in reason for concluding that a response to the very first question asked, by a suspect who already knows all of the rights described in the *Miranda* warning, is anything other than a volitional act. And even if one assumes that the elimination of compulsion absolutely requires informing even the most knowledgeable suspect of his right to remain silent, it cannot conceivably require the right to have counsel present. There is a world of difference, which the Court recognized under the traditional voluntariness test but ignored in *Miranda*, between compelling a suspect to incriminate himself and preventing him from foolishly doing so of his own accord. Only the latter (which is not required by the Constitution) could explain the Court's inclusion of a right to counsel and the requirement that it, too, be knowingly and intelligently waived. Counsel's presence is not required to tell the suspect that he need not speak; the interrogators can do that. The only good reason for having counsel there is that he can be counted on to advise the suspect that he should not speak. . . .

Preventing foolish (rather than compelled) confessions is likewise the only conceivable basis for the rules . . . that courts must exclude any confession elicited by questioning conducted, without interruption, after the suspect has indicated a desire to stand on his right to remain silent, see *Michigan v. Mosley* (1975), or initiated by police after the suspect has expressed a desire to have counsel present, see *Edwards v. Arizona* (1981). Nonthreatening attempts to persuade the suspect to reconsider that initial decision are not, without more, enough to render a change of heart the product of anything other than the suspect's free will. Thus, what is most remarkable about the *Miranda* decision—and what made it unacceptable as a matter of straightforward constitutional interpretation . . . —is its palpable hostility toward the act of confession *per se*, rather than toward what the Constitution abhors, *compelled* confession. . . .

For these reasons, and others more than adequately developed in the *Miranda* dissents and in the subsequent works of the decision's many critics, any conclusion that a violation of the *Miranda* rules necessarily amounts to a violation of the privilege against compelled self-incrimination can claim no support in history, precedent, or common sense, and as a result would at least presumptively be worth reconsidering even at this late date. But that is unnecessary, since the Court has (thankfully) long since abandoned the notion that failure to comply with *Miranda*'s rules is itself a violation of the Constitution.

II

As the Court today acknowledges, since *Miranda* we have explicitly, and repeatedly, interpreted that decision as having announced, not the circumstances in which custodial interrogation runs afoul of the Fifth or Fourteenth Amendment, but rather only "prophylactic" rules that go beyond the right against compelled self-incrimination. Of course the seeds of this "prophylactic" interpretation of *Miranda* were present in the decision itself. [Excerpts from *Miranda* omitted.] In subsequent cases, the seeds have sprouted and borne fruit: The Court has squarely concluded that it is possible—indeed not uncommon—for the police to violate *Miranda* without also violating the Constitution.

Michigan v. Tucker (1974), an opinion for the Court written by then-JUSTICE REHNQUIST, rejected the . . . failure-to-warn-as-constitutional-violation interpretation of *Miranda*. It held that exclusion of the "fruits" of a *Miranda* violation— the statement of a witness whose identity the defendant had revealed while in custody—was not required. . . . The "procedural safeguards" adopted in *Miranda*, the Court said, "were not themselves rights protected by the Constitution but were instead measures to insure that the right against compulsory self-incrimination was protected," and to "provide practical reinforcement for the right." . . .

The next year, in *Oregon v. Hass* (1975), the Court held that a defendant's statement taken in violation of *Miranda* that was nonetheless voluntary could be used at trial for impeachment purposes. This holding turned upon the recognition that violation of *Miranda* is not unconstitutional compulsion, since statements obtained in actual violation of the privilege against compelled self-incrimination, "as opposed to . . . taken in violation of *Miranda*," quite simply "may not be put to any testimonial use whatever against [the defendant] in a criminal trial," including as impeachment evidence. [Citation omitted.]

Nearly a decade later, in *New York v. Quarles* (1984), the Court relied upon the fact that "[t]he prophylactic *Miranda* warnings . . . are not themselves rights protected by the Constitution," to create a "public safety" exception. In that case, police apprehended, after a chase in a grocery store, a rape suspect known to be carrying a gun. After handcuffing and searching him (and finding no gun)—but before reading him his *Miranda* warnings—the police demanded to know where the gun was. The defendant nodded in the direction of some empty cartons and responded that "the gun is over there." The Court held that both the unwarned statement—"the gun is over there"—and the recovered weapon were admissible in the prosecution's case in chief under a "public safety exception" to the "prophylactic rules enunciated in *Miranda*." It explicitly acknowledged that if the *Miranda* warnings were an imperative of the Fifth Amendment itself, such an exigency exception would be impossible, since the Fifth Amendment's bar on compelled self-incrimination is absolute. . . .

The next year, the Court again declined to apply the "fruit of the poisonous tree" doctrine to a *Miranda* violation, this time allowing the admission of a suspect's properly warned statement even though it had been preceded (and, arguably, induced) by an earlier inculpatory statement taken in violation of *Miranda*. *Oregon v. Elstad* (1985). As in *Tucker*, the Court distinguished the case from those holding that a confession obtained as a result of an unconstitutional search is inadmissible, on the ground that the violation of *Miranda* does not involve an "actual infringement of the suspect's constitutional rights." . . .

In light of these cases, and our statements to the same effect in others, it is simply no longer possible for the Court to conclude . . . that a violation of *Miranda*'s rules is a violation of the Constitution. But . . . that is what is required before the Court may disregard a law of Congress governing the admissibility of evidence in federal court. . . . By disregarding congressional action that concededly does not violate the Constitution, the Court flagrantly offends fundamental principles of separation of powers, and arrogates to itself prerogatives reserved to the representatives of the people.

The Court seeks to avoid this conclusion in two ways: First, by misdescribing these post-*Miranda* cases as mere dicta. The Court concedes only "that there is language in some of our opinions that supports the view" that *Miranda*'s protections are not "constitutionally required." It is not a matter of *language;* it is a matter of *holdings.* The proposition that failure to comply with *Miranda*'s rules does not establish a constitutional violation was central to the *holdings* of *Tucker, Hass, Quarles,* and *Elstad.*

The second way the Court seeks to avoid the impact of these cases is simply to disclaim responsibility for reasoned decisionmaking. [Scalia quotes the passage from Rehnquist's opinion declaring that "no constitutional rule is immutable."] The issue, however, is not whether court rules are "mutable"; they assuredly are. It is not whether, in the light of "various circumstances," they can be "modifi[ed]"; they assuredly can. The issue is whether, as mutated and modified, they must make sense. The requirement that they do so is the only thing that prevents this Court from being some sort of nine-headed Caesar, giving thumbs-up or thumbs-down to whatever outcome, case by case, suits or offends its collective fancy. And if confessions procured in violation of *Miranda* are confessions "compelled" in violation of the Constitution, the post-*Miranda* decisions I have discussed do not make sense. The only reasoned basis for their outcome was that a violation of *Miranda* is not a violation of the Constitution. . . .

Finally, the Court asserts that *Miranda* must be a "constitutional decision" announcing a "constitutional rule," and thus immune to congressional modification, because we have since its inception applied it to the States. . . . In my view, our continued application of the *Miranda* code to the States despite our consistent statements that running afoul of its dictates does not necessarily—or even usually—result in an actual constitutional violation, represents not the source of *Miranda*'s salvation but rather evidence of its ultimate illegitimacy. . . .

III, IV [OMITTED]

* * *

Today's judgment converts *Miranda* from a milestone of judicial overreaching into the very Cheops' Pyramid (or perhaps the Sphinx would be a better analogue) of judicial arrogance. In imposing its Court-made code upon the States, the original opinion at least *asserted* that it was demanded by the Constitution. Today's decision does not pretend that it is—and yet *still* asserts the right to impose it against the will of the people's representatives in Congress. Far from believing that *stare decisis* compels this result, I believe we cannot allow to remain on the books even a celebrated decision—*especially* a celebrated decision—that has come to stand for the proposition that the Supreme Court has power to impose extraconstitutional constraints upon Congress and the States. This is not the system that was established by the Framers, or that would be established by any sane supporter of government by the people.

I dissent from today's decision, and, until §3501 is repealed, will continue to apply it in all cases where there has been a sustainable finding that the defendant's confession was voluntary.

No. 99-830

Don Stenberg, Attorney General of Nebraska, et al., Petitioners v. Leroy Carhart

On writ of certiorari to the United States Court of Appeals for the Eighth Circuit

[June 28, 2000]

JUSTICE BREYER delivered the opinion of the Court.

We again consider the right to an abortion. We understand the controversial nature of the problem. Millions of Americans believe that life begins at conception and consequently that an abortion is akin to causing the death of an innocent child; they recoil at the thought of a law that would permit it. Other millions fear that a law that forbids abortion would condemn many American women to lives that lack dignity, depriving them of equal liberty and leading those with least resources to undergo illegal abortions with the attendant risks of death and suffering. Taking account of these virtually irreconcilable points of view, aware that constitutional law must govern a society whose different members sincerely hold directly opposing views, and considering the matter in light of the Constitution's guarantees of fundamental individual liberty, this Court, in the course of a generation, has determined and then redetermined that the Constitution offers basic protection to the woman's right to choose. *Roe v. Wade* (1973); *Planned Parenthood of Southeastern Pa. v. Casey* (1992). We shall not revisit those legal principles. Rather, we apply them to the circumstances of this case.

Three established principles determine the issue before us. We shall set them forth in the language of the joint opinion in *Casey*. [Joint opinion of O'CONNOR, KENNEDY, and SOUTER, JJ.] First, before "viability . . . the woman has a right to choose to terminate her pregnancy."

Second, "a law designed to further the State's interest in fetal life which imposes an undue burden on the woman's decision before fetal viability" is unconstitutional. An "undue burden is . . . shorthand for the conclusion that a state regulation has the purpose or effect of placing a substantial obstacle in the path of a woman seeking an abortion of a nonviable fetus."

Third, "'subsequent to viability, the State in promoting its interest in the potentiality of human life may, if it chooses, regulate, and even proscribe, abortion except where it is necessary, in appropriate medical judgment, for the preservation of the life or health of the mother.'" [Quoting *Roe v. Wade*.]

We apply these principles to a Nebraska law banning "partial birth abortion." The statute reads as follows:

> "No partial birth abortion shall be performed in this state, unless such procedure is necessary to save the life of the mother whose life is endangered by a physical disorder, physical illness, or physical injury, including a life-endangering physical condition caused by or arising from the pregnancy itself." Neb. Rev. Stat. Ann. §28-328(1)

The statute defines "partial birth abortion" as:

> "an abortion procedure in which the person performing the abortion partially delivers vaginally a living unborn child before killing the unborn child and completing the delivery." §28-326(9).

It further defines "partially delivers vaginally a living unborn child before killing the unborn child" to mean

> "deliberately and intentionally delivering into the vagina a living unborn child, or a substantial portion thereof, for the purpose of performing a procedure that the person performing such procedure knows will kill the unborn child and does kill the unborn child."

The law classifies violation of the statute as a "Class III felony" carrying a prison term of up to 20 years, and a fine of up to $25,000. §§28-328(2), 28-105. It also provides for the automatic revocation of a doctor's license to practice medicine in Nebraska. §28-328(4).

We hold that this statute violates the Constitution.

I

A

Dr. Leroy Carhart is a Nebraska physician who performs abortions in a clinical setting. He brought this lawsuit in Federal District Court seeking a declaration that the Nebraska statute violates the Federal Constitution, and asking for an injunction forbidding its enforcement. After a trial on the merits, during which both sides presented several expert witnesses, the District Court held the statute unconstitutional (1998). On appeal, the Eighth Circuit affirmed (1999). . . . We granted certiorari to consider the matter.

B

Because Nebraska law seeks to ban one method of aborting a pregnancy, we must describe and then discuss several different abortion procedures. Considering the fact that those procedures seek to terminate a potential human life, our discussion may seem clinically cold or callous to some, perhaps horrifying to others. There is no alternative way, however, to acquaint the reader with the technical distinctions among different abortion methods and related factual matters, upon which the outcome of this case depends. . . .

1. About 90% of all abortions performed in the United States take place during the first trimester of pregnancy, before 12 weeks of gestational age. During the first trimester, the predominant abortion method is "vacuum aspiration," which involves insertion of a vacuum tube (cannula) into the uterus to evacuate the contents. Such an abortion is typically performed on an outpatient basis under local anesthesia. Vacuum aspiration is considered particularly safe. . . . As the fetus grows in size, however, the vacuum aspiration method becomes increasingly difficult to use.

2. Approximately 10% of all abortions are performed during the second tri-mester of pregnancy (12 to 24 weeks). In the early 1970's, inducing labor through the injection of saline into the uterus was the predominant method of second tri-mester abortion. Today, however, the medical profession has switched from medi-cal induction of labor to surgical procedures for most second trimester abortions. The most commonly used procedure is called "dilation and evacuation" (D&E). That procedure (together with a modified form of vacuum aspiration used in the early second trimester) accounts for about 95% of all abortions performed from 12 to 20 weeks of gestational age.

3. D&E "refers generically to transcervical procedures performed at 13 weeks gestation or later." [Detailed description of procedure as performed at 13–15 weeks of gestation, after 15 weeks, and after 20 weeks omitted.]

There are variations in D&E operative strategy. . . . However, the common points are that D&E involves (1) dilation of the cervix; (2) removal of at least some fetal tissue using nonvacuum instruments; and (3) (after the 15th week) the poten-tial need for instrumental disarticulation or dismemberment of the fetus or the col-lapse of fetal parts to facilitate evacuation from the uterus.

4. When instrumental disarticulation incident to D&E is necessary, it typically occurs as the doctor pulls a portion of the fetus through the cervix into the birth canal. [Quoting excerpts from Dr. Carhart's testimony at trial; in one answer, Carhart stated: "I don't know of any way that one could go in and intentionally dis-member the fetus in the uterus."] Dr. Carhart's specification of the location of fe-tal disarticulation is consistent with other sources. . . .

5. The D&E procedure carries certain risks. The use of instruments within the uterus creates a danger of accidental perforation and damage to neighboring or-gans. Sharp fetal bone fragments create similar dangers. And fetal tissue acciden-tally left behind can cause infection and various other complications. Nonetheless, studies show that the risks of mortality and complication that accompany the D&E procedure between the 12th and 20th weeks of gestation are significantly lower than those accompanying induced labor procedures. . . .

6. At trial, Dr. Carhart and Dr. [Philip] Stubblefield described a variation of the D&E procedure, which they referred to as an "intact D&E." Like other versions of the D&E technique, it begins with induced dilation of the cervix. The procedure then involves removing the fetus from the uterus through the cervix "intact," *i.e.*, in one pass, rather than in several passes. It is used after 16 weeks at the earliest, as vac-uum aspiration becomes ineffective and the fetal skull becomes too large to pass through the cervix. The intact D&E proceeds in one of two ways, depending on the presentation of the fetus. If the fetus presents head first (a vertex presentation), the doctor collapses the skull; and the doctor then extracts the entire fetus through the cervix. If the fetus presents feet first (a breech presentation), the doctor pulls the fetal body through the cervix, collapses the skull, and extracts the fetus through the cervix. The breech extraction version of the intact D&E is also known commonly as "dilation and extraction," or D&X. In the late second trimester, vertex, breech, and traverse/compound (sideways) presentations occur in roughly similar proportions.

7. The intact D&E procedure can also be found described in certain obstetric and abortion clinical textbooks, where two variations are recognized. The first, as just described, calls for the physician to adapt his method for extracting the intact fetus depending on fetal presentation. This is the method used by Dr. Carhart. A

slightly different version of the intact D&E procedure, associated with Dr. Martin Haskell, calls for conversion to a breech presentation in all cases.

8. The American College of Obstetricians and Gynecologists describes the D&X procedure in a manner corresponding to a breech-conversion intact D&E, including the following steps:

"1. deliberate dilatation of the cervix, usually over a sequence of days;

"2. instrumental conversion of the fetus to a footling breech;

"3. breech extraction of the body excepting the head; and

"4. partial evacuation of the intracranial contents of a living fetus to effect vaginal delivery of a dead but otherwise intact fetus." American College of Obstetricians and Gynecologists Executive Board, Statement on Intact Dilation and Extraction (Jan. 12, 1997) (hereinafter ACOG Statement).

Despite the technical differences we have just described, intact D&E and D&X are sufficiently similar for us to use the terms interchangeably.

9. Dr. Carhart testified he attempts to use the intact D&E procedure during weeks 16 to 20 because (1) it reduces the dangers from sharp bone fragments passing through the cervix, (2) minimizes the number of instrument passes needed for extraction and lessens the likelihood of uterine perforations caused by those instruments, (3) reduces the likelihood of leaving infection-causing fetal and placental tissue in the uterus, and (4) could help to prevent potentially fatal absorption of fetal tissue into the maternal circulation. The District Court made no findings about the D&X procedure's overall safety. The District Court concluded, however, that "the evidence is both clear and convincing that Carhart's D&X procedure is superior to, and safer than, the . . . other abortion procedures used during the relevant gestational period in the 10 to 20 cases a year that present to Dr. Carhart."

10. The materials presented at trial referred to the potential benefits of the D&X procedure in circumstances involving nonviable fetuses, such as fetuses with abnormal fluid accumulation in the brain (hydrocephaly). . . . Others have emphasized its potential for women with prior uterine scars, or for women for whom induction of labor would be particularly dangerous. . . .

11. There are no reliable data on the number of D&X abortions performed annually. Estimates have ranged between 640 and 5,000 per year. . . .

II

The question before us is whether Nebraska's statute, making criminal the performance of a "partial birth abortion," violates the Federal Constitution, as interpreted in *Planned Parenthood of Southeastern Pa. v. Casey* (1992) and *Roe v. Wade* (1973). We conclude that it does for at least two independent reasons. First, the law lacks any exception "for the preservation of the . . . health of the mother." Second, it "imposes an undue burden on a woman's ability" to choose a D&E abortion, thereby unduly burdening the right to choose abortion itself. . . .

A

The *Casey* joint opinion reiterated what the Court held in Roe; that "subsequent to viability, the State in promoting its interest in the potentiality of human life may, if it chooses, regulate, and even proscribe, abortion *except where it is necessary, in ap-*

propriate medical judgment, for the preservation of the life or health of the mother" (emphasis added).

The fact that Nebraska's law applies both pre- and postviability aggravates the constitutional problem presented. The State's interest in regulating abortion previability is considerably weaker than postviability. Since the law requires a health exception in order to validate even a postviability abortion regulation, it at a minimum requires the same in respect to previability regulation. . . .

The quoted standard also depends on the state regulations "promoting [the State's] interest in the potentiality of human life." The Nebraska law, of course, does not directly further an interest "in the potentiality of human life" by saving the fetus in question from destruction, as it regulates only a method of performing abortion. Nebraska describes its interests differently. It says the law "show[s] concern for the life of the unborn," "prevent[s] cruelty to partially born children," and "preserve[s] the integrity of the medical profession." But we cannot see how the interest-related differences could make any difference to the question at hand, namely, the application of the "health" requirement.

Consequently, the governing standard requires an exception "where it is necessary, in appropriate medical judgment for the preservation of the life or health of the mother," *Casey*, for this Court has made clear that a State may promote but not endanger a woman's health when it regulates the methods of abortion. [Citations to four previous cases omitted.]

JUSTICE THOMAS says that the cases just cited limit this principle to situations where the pregnancy itself creates a threat to health. He is wrong. The cited cases, reaffirmed in *Casey*, recognize that a State cannot subject women's health to significant risks both in that context, and also where state regulations force women to use riskier methods of abortion. Our cases have repeatedly invalidated statutes that in the process of regulating the methods of abortion, imposed significant health risks. They make clear that a risk to a woman's health is the same whether it happens to arise from regulating a particular method of abortion, or from barring abortion entirely. . . .

1

Nebraska responds that the law does not require a health exception unless there is a need for such an exception. And here there is no such need, it says. It argues that "safe alternatives remain available" and "a ban on partial-birth abortion/D&X would create no risk to the health of women." The problem for Nebraska is that the parties strongly contested this factual question in the trial court below; and the findings and evidence support Dr. Carhart. The State fails to demonstrate that banning D&X without a health exception may not create significant health risks for women, because the record shows that significant medical authority supports the proposition that in some circumstances, D&X would be the safest procedure. [Summary of district court's findings omitted.]

2

Nebraska, along with supporting *amici*, replies that these findings are irrelevant, wrong, or applicable only in a tiny number of instances. It says (1) that the D&X procedure is "little-used," (2) by only "a handful of doctors." It argues (3) that D&E

and labor induction are at all times "safe alternative procedures." It refers to the testimony of petitioners' medical expert, who testified (4) that the ban would not increase a woman's risk of several rare abortion complications (disseminated intravascular coagulopathy and amniotic fluid embolus).

The Association of American Physicians and Surgeons et al., *amici* supporting Nebraska, argue (5) that elements of the D&X procedure may create special risks, including cervical incompetence caused by overdilitation, injury caused by conversion of the fetal presentation, and dangers arising from the "blind" use of instrumentation to pierce the fetal skull while lodged in the birth canal.

Nebraska further emphasizes (6) that there are no medical studies "establishing the safety of the partial-birth abortion/D&X procedure," and "no medical studies comparing the safety of partial-birth abortion/D&X to other abortion procedures." It points to (7) an American Medical Association policy statement [from 1997] that "there does not appear to be any identified situation in which intact D&X is the only appropriate procedure to induce abortion." And it points out (8) that the American College of Obstetricians and Gynecologists qualified its statement that D&X "may be the best or most appropriate procedure," by adding that the panel "could identify no circumstances under which [the D&X] procedure . . . would be the only option to save the life or preserve the health of the woman."

3

We find these eight arguments insufficient to demonstrate that Nebraska's law needs no health exception. For one thing, certain of the arguments are beside the point. The D&X procedure's relative rarity (argument (1)) is not highly relevant. The D&X is an infrequently used abortion procedure; but the health exception question is whether protecting women's health requires an exception for those infrequent occasions. . . . Nor can we know whether the fact that only a "handful" of doctors use the procedure (argument (2)) reflects the comparative rarity of late second term abortions, the procedure's recent development, the controversy surrounding it, or, as Nebraska suggests, the procedure's lack of utility.

For another thing, the record responds to Nebraska's (and *amici*'s) medically based arguments. In respect to argument (3), for example, the District Court agreed that alternatives, such as D&E and induced labor, are "safe" but found that the D&X method was significantly safer in certain circumstances. In respect to argument (4), the District Court simply relied on different expert testimony—testimony stating that "[a]nother advantage of the Intact D&E is that it eliminates the risk of embolism of cerebral tissue into the woman's blood stream." [Quoting statement by W. Hern before Senate Judiciary Committee, 1995.]

In response to *amici*'s argument (5), the American College of Obstetricians and Gynecologists, in its own *amici* brief, denies that D&X generally poses risks greater than the alternatives. It says that the suggested alternative procedures involve similar or greater risks of cervical and uterine injury. . . .

We do not quarrel with Nebraska's argument (6), for Nebraska is right. There are no general medical studies documenting comparative safety. Neither do we deny the import of the American Medical Association's statement (argument (7))—

even though the State does omit the remainder of that statement: "The AMA recommends that the procedure not be used *unless alternative procedures pose materially greater risk to the woman.*" (emphasis added).

We cannot, however, read the American College of Obstetricians and Gynecologists panel's qualification (that it could not "identify" a circumstance where D&X was the "only" life- or health-preserving option) as if, according to Nebraska's argument (8), it denied the potential health-related need for D&X. That is because the College writes the following in its *amici* brief: [Breyer quoted a lengthy excerpt from the ACOG brief that said the D&X procedure "involves less risk of uterine perforation or cervical laceration" than the D&E procedure and "reduces the risk of retained fetal tissue" or other complications. The excerpt concluded: "Especially for women with particular health conditions, there is medical evidence that D&X may be safer than available alternatives."]

4

The upshot is a District Court finding that D&X significantly obviates health risks in certain circumstances, a highly plausible record-based explanation of why that might be so, a division of opinion among some medical experts over whether D&X is generally safer, and an absence of controlled medical studies that would help answer these medical questions. Given these medically related evidentiary circumstances, we believe the law requires a health exception.

The word "necessary" in *Casey*'s phrase "necessary, in appropriate medical judgment, for the preservation of the life or health of the mother" cannot refer to an absolute necessity or to absolute proof. Medical treatments and procedures are often considered appropriate (or inappropriate) in light of estimated comparative health risks (and health benefits) in particular cases. Neither can that phrase require unanimity of medical opinion. Doctors often differ in their estimation of comparative health risks and appropriate treatment. And *Casey*'s words "appropriate medical judgment" must embody the judicial need to tolerate responsible differences of medical opinion. . . .

For another thing, the division of medical opinion about the matter at most means uncertainty, a factor that signals the presence of risk, not its absence. . . . [T]he uncertainty means a significant likelihood that those who believe that D&X is a safer abortion method in certain circumstances may turn out to be right. If so, then the absence of a health exception will place women at an unnecessary risk of tragic health consequences. If they are wrong, the exception will simply turn out to have been unnecessary.

In sum, Nebraska has not convinced us that a health exception is "never necessary to preserve the health of women." Rather, a statute that altogether forbids D&X creates a significant health risk. The statute consequently must contain a health exception. This is not to say, as JUSTICE THOMAS and JUSTICE KENNEDY claim, that a State is prohibited from proscribing an abortion procedure whenever a particular physician deems the procedure preferable. . . . [W]here substantial medical authority supports the proposition that banning a particular abortion procedure could endanger women's health, *Casey* requires the statute to include a health exception. . . .

B

The Eighth Circuit found the Nebraska statute unconstitutional because, in *Casey*'s words, it has the "effect of placing a substantial obstacle in the path of a woman seeking an abortion of a nonviable fetus." It thereby places an "undue burden" upon a woman's right to terminate her pregnancy before viability. Nebraska does not deny that the statute imposes an "undue burden" if it applies to the more commonly used D&E procedure as well as to D&X. And we agree with the Eighth Circuit that it does so apply.

Our earlier discussion of the D&E procedure shows that it falls within the statutory prohibition. The statute forbids "deliberately and intentionally delivering into the vagina a living unborn child, or a substantial portion thereof, for the purpose of performing a procedure that the person performing such procedure knows will kill the unborn child." We do not understand how one could distinguish, using this language, between D&E (where a foot or arm is drawn through the cervix) and D&X (where the body up to the head is drawn through the cervix). . . .

Even if the statute's basic aim is to ban D&X, its language makes clear that it also covers a much broader category of procedures. The language does not track the medical differences between D&E and D&X—though it would have been a simple matter, for example, to provide an exception for the performance of D&E and other abortion procedures. [Citing Kansas statute.] Nor does the statute anywhere suggest that its application turns on whether a portion of the fetus' body is drawn into the vagina as part of a process to extract an intact fetus after collapsing the head as opposed to a process that would dismember the fetus. Thus, the dissenters' argument that the law was generally intended to bar D&X can be both correct and irrelevant. The relevant question is not whether the legislature wanted to ban D&X; it is whether the law was intended to apply *only* to D&X. The plain language covers both procedures. . . .

The Nebraska State Attorney General argues that the statute does differentiate between the two procedures. He says that the statutory words "substantial portion" mean "the child up to the head." He consequently denies the statute's application where the physician introduces into the birth canal a fetal arm or leg or anything less than the entire fetal body. He argues further that we must defer to his views about the meaning of the state statute.

We cannot accept the Attorney General's narrowing interpretation of the Nebraska statute. This Court's case law makes clear that we are not to give the Attorney General's interpretative views controlling weight. For one thing, this Court normally follows lower federal-court interpretations of state law. . . . In this case, the two lower courts have both rejected the Attorney General's narrowing interpretation.

For another, our precedent warns against accepting as "authoritative" an Attorney General's interpretation of state law when "the Attorney General does not bind the state courts or local law enforcement authorities." . . .

Nor can we say that the lower courts used the wrong legal standard in assessing the Attorney General's interpretation.

Regardless, even were we to grant the Attorney General's views "substantial weight," we still have to reject his interpretation, for it conflicts with the statutory language. . . .

We are aware that adopting the Attorney General's interpretation might avoid the constitutional problem discussed in this section. But we are "without power to adopt a narrowing construction of a state statute unless such a construction is reasonable and readily apparent." [Citation omitted.] For the reasons stated, it is not reasonable to replace the term "substantial portion" with the Attorney General's phrase "body up to the head." . . .

In sum, using this law some present prosecutors and future Attorneys General may choose to pursue physicians who use D&E procedures, the most commonly used method for performing previability second trimester abortions. All those who perform abortion procedures using that method must fear prosecution, conviction, and imprisonment. The result is an undue burden upon a woman's right to make an abortion decision. We must consequently find the statute unconstitutional.

The judgment of the Court of Appeals is

Affirmed.

JUSTICE STEVENS, with whom JUSTICE GINSBURG joins, concurring.

Although much ink is spilled today describing the gruesome nature of late-term abortion procedures, that rhetoric does not provide me a reason to believe that the procedure Nebraska here claims it seeks to ban is more brutal, more gruesome, or less respectful of "potential life" than the equally gruesome procedure Nebraska claims it still allows. . . . [T]he notion that either of these two equally gruesome procedures performed at this late stage of gestation is more akin to infanticide than the other, or that the State furthers any legitimate interest by banning the one but not the other, is simply irrational.

JUSTICE O'CONNOR, concurring.

. . . I agree that Nebraska's statute cannot be reconciled with our decision in *Planned Parenthood of Southeastern Pa. v. Casey* (1992) and is therefore unconstitutional. . . .

. . . [U]nlike Nebraska, some other States have enacted statutes more narrowly tailored to proscribing the D&X procedure alone. Some of those statutes have done so by specifically excluding from their coverage the most common methods of abortion, such as the D&E and vacuum aspiration procedures. [Citing Kansas, Utah, and Montana statutes.]

If Nebraska's statute limited its application to the D&X procedure and included an exception for the life and health of the mother, the question presented would be quite different than the one we face today. . . . [A] ban on partial-birth abortion that only proscribed the D&X method of abortion and that included an exception to preserve the life and health of the mother would be constitutional in my view. . . .

JUSTICE GINSBURG, with whom JUSTICE STEVENS joins, concurring.

I write separately only to stress that amidst all the emotional uproar caused by an abortion case, we should not lose sight of the character of Nebraska's "partial birth abortion" law. As the Court observes, this law does not save any fetus from destruction, for it targets only "a method of performing abortion." Nor does the statute seek to protect the lives or health of pregnant women. Moreover, as JUSTICE STEVENS points out, the most common method of performing previability second trimester abortions is no less distressing or susceptible to gruesome description. . . .

CHIEF JUSTICE REHNQUIST, dissenting.

I did not join the joint opinion in *Planned Parenthood of Southeastern Pa. v. Casey* (1992) and continue to believe that case is wrongly decided. Despite my disagreement with the opinion, . . . the *Casey* joint opinion represents the holding of the Court in that case. I believe JUSTICE KENNEDY and JUSTICE THOMAS have correctly applied *Casey's* principles and join their dissenting opinions.

JUSTICE SCALIA, dissenting.

I am optimistic enough to believe that, one day, *Stenberg v. Carhart* will be assigned its rightful place in the history of this Court's jurisprudence beside *Korematsu* and *Dred Scott*. The method of killing a human child—one cannot even accurately say an entirely unborn human child—proscribed by this statute is so horrible that the most clinical description of it evokes a shudder of revulsion. And the Court must know (as most state legislatures banning this procedure have concluded) that demanding a "health exception"—which requires the abortionist to assure himself that, in his expert medical judgment, this method is, in the case at hand, marginally safer than others (how can one prove the contrary beyond a reasonable doubt?)—is to give live-birth abortion free rein. . . .

[In the remainder of his opinion, Scalia sharply criticized the *Casey* decision and its "undue burden" standard, which he had described in dissent in that case as "unprincipled in origin" and "hopelessly unworkable in practice." He concluded: "*Casey* must be overruled."]

JUSTICE KENNEDY, with whom THE CHIEF JUSTICE joins, dissenting.

. . . When the Court reaffirmed the essential holding of *Roe* [*v. Wade* (1973)], a central premise was that the States retain a critical and legitimate role in legislating on the subject of abortion, as limited by the woman's right the Court restated and again guaranteed. *Planned Parenthood of Southeastern Pa. v. Casey* (1992). The political processes of the State are not to be foreclosed from enacting laws to promote the life of the unborn and to ensure respect for all human life and its potential. [Citing joint opinion of O'CONNOR, KENNEDY, and SOUTER, JJ.] . . .

The Court's decision today, in my submission, repudiates this understanding by invalidating a statute advancing critical state interests, even though the law denies no woman the right to choose an abortion and places no undue burden upon the right. The legislation is well within the State's competence to enact. Having concluded Nebraska's law survives the scrutiny dictated by a proper understanding of *Casey*, I dissent from the judgment invalidating it.

I

The Court's failure to accord any weight to Nebraska's interest in prohibiting partial-birth abortion is erroneous and undermines its discussion and holding. . . . The majority views the procedures from the perspective of the abortionist, rather than from the perspective of a society shocked when confronted with a new method of ending human life. . . .

. . . The State's brief describes its interests as including concern for the life of the unborn and "for the partially-born," in preserving the integrity of the medical profession, and in "erecting a barrier to infanticide." A review of *Casey* demonstrates the legitimacy of these policies. The Court should say so.

States may take sides in the abortion debate and come down on the side of life, even life in the unborn. . . .

States also have an interest in forbidding medical procedures which, in the State's reasonable determination, might cause the medical profession or society as a whole to become insensitive, even disdainful, to life, including life in the human fetus. . . .

A State may take measures to ensure the medical profession and its members are viewed as healers, sustained by a compassionate and rigorous ethic and cognizant of the dignity and value of human life, even life which cannot survive without the assistance of others.

. . . It is argued, however, that a ban on the D&X does not further these interests. This is because, the reasoning continues, the D&E method, which Nebraska claims to be beyond its intent to regulate, can still be used to abort a fetus and is no less dehumanizing than the D&X method. . . . The issue is not whether members of the judiciary can see a difference between the two procedures. It is whether Nebraska can. The Court's refusal to recognize Nebraska's right to declare a moral difference between the procedure is a dispiriting disclosure of the illogic and illegitimacy of the Court's approach to the entire case. . . .

II

Demonstrating a further and basic misunderstanding of *Casey*, the Court holds the ban on the D&X procedure fails because it does not include an exception permitting an abortionist to perform a D&X whenever he believes it will best preserve the health of the woman. Casting aside the views of distinguished physicians and the statements of leading medical organizations, the Court awards each physician a veto power over the State's judgment that the procedures should not be performed. Dr. Carhart has made the medical judgment to use the D&X procedure in every case, regardless of indications, after 15 weeks gestation. Requiring Nebraska to defer to Dr. Carhart's judgment is no different than forbidding Nebraska from enacting a ban at all; for it is now Dr. Leroy Carhart who sets abortion policy for the State of Nebraska, not the legislature or the people. *Casey* does not give precedence to the views of a single physician or a group of physicians regarding the relative safety of a particular procedure. [Remainder of section omitted.]

III

The Court's next holding is that Nebraska's ban forbids both the D&X procedure and the more common D&E procedure. In so ruling the Court misapplies settled doctrines of statutory construction and contradicts *Casey*'s premise that the States have a vital constitutional position in the abortion debate. . . . Like the ruling requiring a physician veto, requiring a State to meet unattainable standards of statutory draftsmanship in order to have its voice heard on this grave and difficult subject is no different from foreclosing state participation altogether. [Remainder of section omitted.]

IV

Ignoring substantial medical and ethical opinion, the Court substitutes its own judgment for the judgment of Nebraska and some 30 other States and sweeps the law away. The Court's holding stems from misunderstanding the record, misinterpretation of *Casey*, outright refusal to respect the law of a State, and statutory construction in conflict with settled rules. The decision nullifies a law expressing the will of the people of Nebraska that medical procedures must be governed by moral principles having their foundation in the intrinsic value of human life, including life of the unborn. Through their law the people of Nebraska were forthright in confronting an issue of immense moral consequence. The State chose to forbid a procedure many decent and civilized people find so abhorrent as to be among the most serious of crimes against human life, while the State still protected the woman's autonomous right of choice as reaffirmed in *Casey*. The Court closes its eyes to these profound concerns.

From the decision, the reasoning, and the judgment, I dissent.

JUSTICE THOMAS, with whom THE CHIEF JUSTICE and JUSTICE SCALIA join, dissenting.

In 1973, this Court struck down an Act of the Texas Legislature that had been in effect since 1857, thereby rendering unconstitutional abortion statutes in dozens of States. *Roe v. Wade*. . . . [T]hat decision was grievously wrong. . . . Abortion is a unique act, in which a woman's exercise of control over her own body ends, depending on one's view, human life or potential human life. Nothing in our Federal Constitution deprives the people of this country of the right to determine whether the consequences of abortion to the fetus and to society outweigh the burden of an unwanted pregnancy on the mother. Although a State *may* permit abortion, nothing in the Constitution dictates that a State *must* do so.

In the years following *Roe*, this Court applied, and, worse, extended, that decision to strike down numerous state statutes that purportedly threatened a woman's ability to obtain an abortion. . . .

It appeared that this era of Court-mandated abortion on demand had come to an end, first with our decision in *Webster v. Reproductive Health Services* (1989), . . . and then finally (or so we were told) in our decision in *Planned Parenthood of Southeastern Pa. v. Casey* (1992). . . . The joint opinion authored by JUSTICES O'CONNOR, KENNEDY, and SOUTER concluded that prior case law "went too far" in "undervalu[ing] the State's interest in potential life" and in "striking down . . . some abortion regulations which in no real sense deprived women of the ultimate decision." *Roe* and subsequent cases, according to the joint opinion, had wrongly "treat[ed] all governmental attempts to influence a woman's decision on behalf of the potential life within her as unwarranted," a treatment that was "incompatible with the recognition that there is a substantial state interest in potential life throughout pregnancy." Accordingly, the joint opinion held that so long as state regulation of abortion furthers legitimate interests—that is, interests not designed to strike at the right itself—the regulation is invalid only if it imposes an undue burden on a woman's ability to obtain an abortion, meaning that it places a *substantial obstacle* in the woman's path.

. . . Even assuming . . . that *Casey*'s fabricated undue-burden standard merits adherence (which it does not), today's decision is extraordinary. Today, the Court inexplicably holds that the States cannot constitutionally prohibit a method of abortion that millions find hard to distinguish from infanticide and that the Court hesitates even to describe. This holding cannot be reconciled with *Casey*'s undue-burden standard, as that standard was explained to us by the authors of the joint opinion, and the majority hardly pretends otherwise. In striking down this statute—which expresses a profound and legitimate respect for fetal life and which leaves unimpeded several other safe forms of abortion—the majority opinion gives the lie to the promise of *Casey* that regulations that do no more than "express profound respect for the life of the unborn are permitted, if they are not a substantial obstacle to the woman's exercise of the right to choose" whether or not to have an abortion. Today's decision is so obviously irreconcilable with *Casey*'s explication of what its undue-burden standard requires, let alone the Constitution, that it should be seen for what it is, a reinstitution of the pre-*Webster* abortion-on-demand era in which the mere invocation of "abortion rights" trumps any contrary societal interest. If this statute is unconstitutional under *Casey*, then *Casey* meant nothing at all, and the Court should candidly admit it.

To reach its decision, the majority must take a series of indefensible steps. The majority must first disregard the principles that this Court follows in every context but abortion: We interpret statutes according to their plain meaning and we do not strike down statutes susceptible of a narrowing construction. The majority also must disregard the very constitutional standard it purports to employ, and then displace the considered judgment of the people of Nebraska and 29 other States. The majority's decision is lamentable, because of the result the majority reaches, the illogical steps the majority takes to reach it, and because it portends a return to an era I had thought we had at last abandoned.

I

. . . From reading the majority's sanitized description, one would think that this case involves state regulation of a widely accepted routine medical procedure. Nothing could be further from the truth. The most widely used method of abortion during this stage of pregnancy is so gruesome that its use can be traumatic even for the physicians and medical staff who perform it. . . .

[Thomas gave a detailed clinical description of abortion by "dilation and evacuation" (D&E) and a brief description of abortion by induction using a saline solution. He then continued:]

3. A third form of abortion for use during or after 16 weeks' gestation is referred to by some medical professionals as "intact D&E." There are two variations of this method, both of which require the physician to dilate the woman's cervix. The first variation is used only in vertex presentations, that is, when the fetal head is presented first. To perform a vertex-presentation intact D&E, the doctor will insert an instrument into the fetus' skull while the fetus is still in utero and remove the brain and other intracranial contents. When the fetal skull collapses, the physician will remove the fetus.

The second variation of intact D&X is the procedure commonly known as "partial birth abortion." This procedure, which is used only rarely, is performed on mid- to late-second-trimester (and sometimes third-trimester) fetuses. Although there are variations, it is generally performed as follows: After dilating the cervix, the physician will grab the fetus by its feet and pull the fetal body out of the uterus into the vaginal cavity. At this stage of development, the head is the largest part of the body. Assuming the physician has performed the dilation procedure correctly, the head will be held inside the uterus by the woman's cervix. While the fetus is stuck in this position, dangling partly out of the woman's body, and just a few inches from a completed birth, the physician uses an instrument such as a pair of scissors to tear or perforate the skull. The physician will then either crush the skull or will use a vacuum to remove the brain and other intracranial contents from the fetal skull, collapse the fetus' head, and pull the fetus from the uterus. . . .

II

Nebraska, along with 29 other States, has attempted to ban the partial birth abortion procedure. Although the Nebraska statute purports to prohibit only "partial birth abortion," a phrase which is commonly used . . . to refer to the breech extraction version of intact D&E, the majority concludes that this statute could also be read in some future case to prohibit ordinary D&E. . . . According to the majority, such an application would pose a substantial obstacle to some women seeking abortions and, therefore, the statute is unconstitutional. The majority errs with its very first step. I think it is clear that the Nebraska statute does not prohibit the D&E procedure. [Excerpts from statute, including definition of "partial-birth abortion" omitted. See majority opinion.]

A

Starting with the statutory definition of "partial birth abortion," I think it highly doubtful that the statute could be applied to ordinary D&E. First, the Nebraska statute applies only if the physician "partially *delivers* vaginally a living unborn child," which phrase is defined to mean "deliberately and intentionally *delivering* into the vagina a living unborn child, or a substantial portion thereof." (emphases added). When read in context, the term "partially delivers" cannot be fairly interpreted to include removing pieces of an unborn child from the uterus one at a time. [Remainder of section omitted.]

B

Although I think that the text of §28-326(9) forecloses any application of the Nebraska statute to the D procedure, even if there were any ambiguity, the ambiguity would be conclusively resolved by reading the definition in light of the fact that the Nebraska statute, by its own terms, applies only to "partial birth abortion." §28-328(1). By ordinary rules of statutory interpretation, we should resolve any ambiguity in the specific statutory definition to comport with the common understanding of "partial birth abortion," for that term itself, no less than the specific definition, is part of the statute. [Discussion of use of "partial-birth abortion" by medical authorities, courts, and Congress and state legislatures omitted.]

C

Were there any doubt remaining whether the statute could apply to a D&E procedure, that doubt is no ground for invalidating the statute. Rather, we are bound to first consider whether a construction of the statute is fairly possible that would avoid the constitutional question. . . . Although our interpretation of a Nebraska law is of course not binding on Nebraska courts, it is clear . . . that, absent a conflicting interpretation by Nebraska (and there is none here), we should, if the text permits, adopt such a construction. [Remainder of section omitted.]

III

[In Part III, Thomas criticized the majority for its methodology in interpreting the Nebraska statute. He said the majority was wrong in faulting the Nebraska legislature for failing to use terminology accepted by the medical community, in deferring to the lower federal courts' interpretation of the statute, and in refusing to defer to the attorney general's interpretation of the law.]

IV

Having resolved that Nebraska's partial birth abortion statute permits doctors to perform D&E abortions, the question remains whether a State can constitutionally prohibit the partial birth abortion procedure without a health exception. Although the majority and JUSTICE O'CONNOR purport to rely on the standard articulated in the *Casey* joint opinion in concluding that a State may not, they in fact disregard it entirely.

A [OMITTED]

B

There is no question that the State of Nebraska has a valid interest—one not designed to strike at the right itself—in prohibiting partial birth abortion. *Casey* itself noted that States may "express profound respect for the life of the unborn." States may, without a doubt, express this profound respect by prohibiting a procedure that approaches infanticide, and thereby dehumanizes the fetus and trivializes human life. The [American Medical Association] has recognized that this procedure is "ethically different from other destructive abortion techniques because the fetus, normally twenty weeks or longer in gestation, is killed outside the womb. The 'partial birth' gives the fetus an autonomy which separates it from the right of the woman to choose treatments for her own body." AMA Board of Trustees Factsheet on H. R. 1122 (June 1997). Thirty States have concurred with this view. . . .

C

The next question, therefore, is whether the Nebraska statute is unconstitutional because it does not contain an exception that would allow use of the procedure whenever "necessary in appropriate medical judgment, for the preservation of the . . . health of the mother." . . .

The majority and JUSTICE O'CONNOR suggest that their rule is dictated by a straightforward application of *Roe* and *Casey*. But that is simply not true. . . . These cases addressed only the situation in which a woman must obtain an abortion because of some threat to her health from continued pregnancy. But *Roe* and *Casey* say nothing at all about cases in which a physician considers one prohibited method of abortion to be preferable to permissible methods. . . .

. . . [T]he majority expands the health exception rule . . . in one additional and equally pernicious way. Although *Roe* and *Casey* mandated a health exception for cases in which abortion is "necessary" for a woman's health, the majority concludes that a procedure is "necessary" if it has any comparative health benefits. . . . But such a health exception requirement eviscerates *Casey*'s undue burden standard and imposes unfettered abortion-on-demand. The exception entirely swallows the rule. In effect, no regulation of abortion procedures is permitted because there will always be *some* support for a procedure and there will always be some doctors who conclude that the procedure is preferable. . . . JUSTICE O'CONNOR's assurance that the constitutional failings of Nebraska's statute can be easily fixed is illusory. The majority's insistence on a health exception is a fig leaf barely covering its hostility to any abortion regulation by the States. . . .

D

The majority assiduously avoids addressing the *actual* standard articulated in *Casey*—whether prohibiting partial birth abortion without a health exception poses a substantial obstacle to obtaining an abortion. And for good reason: Such an obstacle does not exist. There are two essential reasons why the Court cannot identify a substantial obstacle. First, the Court cannot identify any real, much less substantial, barrier to any woman's ability to obtain an abortion. And second, the Court cannot demonstrate that any such obstacle would affect a sufficient number of women to justify invalidating the statute on its face. [Remainder of section omitted.]

* * *

We were reassured repeatedly in *Casey* that not all regulations of abortion are unwarranted and that the States may express profound respect for fetal life. Under *Casey*, the regulation before us today should easily pass constitutional muster. But the Court's abortion jurisprudence is a particularly virulent strain of constitutional exegesis. And so today we are told that 30 States are prohibited from banning one rarely used form of abortion that they believe to border on infanticide. It is clear that the Constitution does not compel this result.

I respectfully dissent.

No. 98-1648

Guy Mitchell, et al., Petitioners v. Mary L. Helms et al.

On writ of certiorari to the United States Court of Appeals for the Fifth Circuit

[June 28, 2000]

JUSTICE THOMAS announced the judgment of the Court and delivered an opinion, in which THE CHIEF JUSTICE, JUSTICE SCALIA, and JUSTICE KENNEDY join.

As part of a longstanding school aid program known as Chapter 2, the Federal Government distributes funds to state and local governmental agencies, which in turn lend educational materials and equipment to public and private schools, with the enrollment of each participating school determining the amount of aid that it receives. The question is whether Chapter 2, as applied in Jefferson Parish, Louisiana, is a law respecting an establishment of religion, because many of the private schools receiving Chapter 2 aid in that parish are religiously affiliated. We hold that Chapter 2 is not such a law.

I

A

Chapter 2 of the Education Consolidation and Improvement Act of 1981, 20 U.S.C. §§7301-7373, has its origins in the Elementary and Secondary Education Act of 1965 (ESEA), and is a close cousin of the provision of the ESEA that we recently considered in *Agostini v. Felton* (1997). Like the provision at issue in *Agostini*, Chapter 2 channels federal funds to local educational agencies (LEA's), which are usually public school districts, via state educational agencies (SEA's), to implement programs to assist children in elementary and secondary schools. Among other things, Chapter 2 provides aid

> "for the acquisition and use of instructional and educational materials, including library services and materials (including media materials), assessments, reference materials, computer software and hardware for instructional use, and other curricular materials." 20 U.S.C. §7351(b)(2).

LEA's and SEA's must offer assistance to both public and private schools (although any private school must be nonprofit). Participating private schools receive Chapter 2 aid based on the number of children enrolled in each school, and allocations of Chapter 2 funds for those schools must generally be "equal (consistent with the number of children to be served) to expenditures for programs . . . for children enrolled in the public schools of the [LEA]." LEA's must in all cases "assure equitable participation" of the children of private schools "in the purposes and benefits" of Chapter 2. Further, Chapter 2 funds may only "supplement and, to the extent practical, increase the level of funds that would . . . be made available from non-Federal sources." LEA's and SEA's may not operate their programs "so as to supplant funds from non-Federal sources."

Several restrictions apply to aid to private schools. Most significantly, the "services, materials, and equipment" provided to private schools must be "secular, neutral, and nonideological." In addition, private schools may not acquire control of Chapter 2 funds or title to Chapter 2 materials, equipment, or property. . . .

In Jefferson Parish (the Louisiana governmental unit at issue in this case), as in Louisiana as a whole, private schools have primarily used their allocations for nonrecurring expenses, usually materials and equipment. In the 1986-1987 fiscal year, for example, 44% of the money budgeted for private schools in Jefferson Parish was spent by LEA's for acquiring library and media materials, and 48% for instructional equipment. Among the materials and equipment provided have been library books, computers, and computer software, and also slide and movie projectors, overhead projectors, television sets, tape recorders, VCR's, projection screens, laboratory equipment, maps, globes, filmstrips, slides, and cassette recordings.

It appears that, in an average year, about 30% of Chapter 2 funds spent in Jefferson Parish are allocated for private schools. For the 1985-1986 fiscal year, 41 private schools participated in Chapter 2. For the following year, 46 participated, and the participation level has remained relatively constant since then. Of these 46, 34 were Roman Catholic; 7 were otherwise religiously affiliated; and 5 were not religiously affiliated.

B

Respondents filed suit in December 1985, alleging, among other things, that Chapter 2, as applied in Jefferson Parish, violated the Establishment Clause of the First Amendment of the Federal Constitution. The case's tortuous history over the next 15 years indicates well the degree to which our Establishment Clause jurisprudence has shifted in recent times, while nevertheless retaining anomalies with which the lower courts have had to struggle.

In 1990, after extended discovery, Chief Judge Heebe of the District Court for the Eastern District of Louisiana granted summary judgment in favor of respondents. He held that Chapter 2 violated the Establishment Clause because, under the second part of our three-part test in *Lemon v. Kurtzman* (1971), the program had the primary effect of advancing religion. . . . Chief Judge Heebe relied primarily on Meek v. Pittenger (1975) and *Wolman v. Walter* (1977), in which we held unconstitutional programs that provided many of the same sorts of materials and equipment as does Chapter 2. In 1994, after having resolved the numerous other issues in the case, he issued an order permanently excluding pervasively sectarian schools in Jefferson Parish from receiving any Chapter 2 materials or equipment.

Two years later, Chief Judge Heebe having retired, Judge Livaudais received the case. Ruling in early 1997 on postjudgment motions, he reversed the decision of former Chief Judge Heebe and upheld Chapter 2, pointing to several significant changes in the legal landscape over the previous seven years. In particular, Judge Livaudais cited our 1993 decision in *Zobrest v. Catalina Foothills School Dist.* in which we held that a State could, as part of a federal program for the disabled, provide a sign-language interpreter to a deaf student at a Catholic high school.

Judge Livaudais also relied heavily on a 1995 decision of the Court of Appeals for the Ninth Circuit, *Walker v. San Francisco Unified School Dist.*, upholding Chapter 2 on facts that he found "virtually indistinguishable." . . .

Finally, . . . Judge Livaudais invoked *Rosenberger v. Rector and Visitors of Univ. of Va.* (1995), in which, a few months after *Walker*, we held that the Establishment Clause does not require a public university to exclude a student-run religious publication from assistance available to numerous other student-run publications.

Following Judge Livaudais's ruling, respondents appealed to the Court of Appeals for the Fifth Circuit. While that appeal was pending, we decided *Agostini*, in which we approved a program that, under Title I of the ESEA, provided public employees to teach remedial classes at private schools, including religious schools. In so holding, we overruled *Aguilar v. Felton* (1985), and partially overruled School Dist. of Grand Rapids v. Ball (1985), both of which had involved such a program.

The Fifth Circuit thus faced a dilemma between, on the one hand, the Ninth Circuit's holding and analysis in *Walker* and our subsequent decisions in *Rosenberger* and *Agostini*, and, on the other hand, our holdings in *Meek and Wolman*. . . . [T]hat court . . . concluded that *Agostini* had neither directly overruled *Meek* and *Wolman* nor rejected their distinction between textbooks and other in-kind aid. The Fifth Circuit therefore concluded that *Meek* and *Wolman* controlled, and thus it held Chapter 2 unconstitutional [1998]. We granted certiorari (1999).

II

The Establishment Clause of the First Amendment dictates that "Congress shall make no law respecting an establishment of religion." In the over 50 years since *Everson* [*v. Board of Education* (1947)], we have consistently struggled to apply these simple words in the context of governmental aid to religious schools. . . .

In *Agostini*, however, we brought some clarity to our case law, by overruling two anomalous precedents (one in whole, the other in part) and by consolidating some of our previously disparate considerations under a revised test. Whereas in *Lemon* we had considered whether a statute (1) has a secular purpose, (2) has a primary effect of advancing or inhibiting religion, or (3) creates an excessive entanglement between government and religion, in *Agostini* we modified *Lemon* for purposes of evaluating aid to schools and examined only the first and second factors. . . We then set out revised criteria for determining the effect of a statute:

> "To summarize, New York City's Title I program does not run afoul of any of three primary criteria we currently use to evaluate whether government aid has the effect of advancing religion: It does not result in governmental indoctrination; define its recipients by reference to religion; or create an excessive entanglement."

In this case, our inquiry under *Agostini*'s purpose and effect test is a narrow one. Because respondents do not challenge the District Court's holding that Chapter 2 has a secular purpose, and because the Fifth Circuit also did not question that holding, we will consider only Chapter 2's effect. Further, in determining that effect, we will consider only the first two *Agostini* criteria, since neither respondents nor the Fifth Circuit has questioned the District Court's holding that Chapter 2 does not create an excessive entanglement. Considering Chapter 2 in light of our more recent case law, we conclude that it neither results in religious indoctrination by the government nor defines its recipients by reference to religion. We therefore hold that Chapter 2 is not a "law respecting an establishment of religion." In so holding, we acknowledge what both the Ninth and Fifth Circuits saw was inescapable—

Meek and *Wolman* are anomalies in our case law. We therefore conclude that they are no longer good law.

A

... [T]he question whether governmental aid to religious schools results in governmental indoctrination is ultimately a question whether any religious indoctrination that occurs in those schools could reasonably be attributed to governmental action.... We have also indicated that the answer to the question of indoctrination will resolve the question whether a program of educational aid "subsidizes" religion, as our religion cases use that term.

In distinguishing between indoctrination that is attributable to the State and indoctrination that is not, we have consistently turned to the principle of neutrality, upholding aid that is offered to a broad range of groups or persons without regard to their religion. If the religious, irreligious, and areligious are all alike eligible for governmental aid, no one would conclude that any indoctrination that any particular recipient conducts has been done at the behest of the government.... To put the point differently, if the government, seeking to further some legitimate secular purpose, offers aid on the same terms, without regard to religion, to all who adequately further that purpose, ... then it is fair to say that any aid going to a religious recipient only has the effect of furthering that secular purpose....

As a way of assuring neutrality, we have repeatedly considered whether any governmental aid that goes to a religious institution does so "only as a result of the genuinely independent and private choices of individuals." *Agostini*.... For if numerous private choices, rather than the single choice of a government, determine the distribution of aid pursuant to neutral eligibility criteria, then a government cannot, or at least cannot easily, grant special favors that might lead to a religious establishment. Private choice also helps guarantee neutrality by mitigating the preference for pre-existing recipients that is arguably inherent in any governmental aid program, and that could lead to a program inadvertently favoring one religion or favoring religious private schools in general over nonreligious ones....

Agostini's second primary criterion for determining the effect of governmental aid is closely related to the first. The second criterion requires a court to consider whether an aid program "define[s] its recipients by reference to religion." ... This second criterion looks to the same set of facts as does our focus, under the first criterion, on neutrality, but the second criterion uses those facts to answer a somewhat different question—whether the criteria for allocating the aid "creat[e] a financial incentive to undertake religious indoctrination." In *Agostini* we set out the following rule for answering this question:

> "This incentive is not present, however, where the aid is allocated on the basis of neutral, secular criteria that neither favor nor disfavor religion, and is made available to both religious and secular beneficiaries on a nondiscriminatory basis. Under such circumstances, the aid is less likely to have the effect of advancing religion."

The cases on which *Agostini* relied for this rule, and *Agostini* itself, make clear the close relationship between this rule, incentives, and private choice. For to say that a program does not create an incentive to choose religious schools is to say that the private choice is truly "independent." ...

We hasten to add, what should be obvious from the rule itself, that simply because an aid program offers private schools, and thus religious schools, a benefit that they did not previously receive does not mean that the program, by reducing the cost of securing a religious education, creates, under *Agostini*'s second criterion, an "incentive" for parents to choose such an education for their children. For any aid will have some such effect.

B

Respondents inexplicably make no effort to address Chapter 2 under the *Agostini* test. Instead, dismissing *Agostini* as factually distinguishable, they offer two rules that they contend should govern our determination of whether Chapter 2 has the effect of advancing religion. They argue first, and chiefly, that "direct, nonincidental" aid to the primary educational mission of religious schools is always impermissible. Second, they argue that provision to religious schools of aid that is divertible to religious use is similarly impermissible. Respondents' arguments are inconsistent with our more recent case law, in particular *Agostini* and *Zobrest*, and we therefore reject them.

1

Although some of our earlier cases . . . did emphasize the distinction between direct and indirect aid, the purpose of this distinction was merely to prevent "subsidization" of religion. . . . [O]ur more recent cases address this purpose not through the direct/indirect distinction but rather through the principle of private choice, as incorporated in the first *Agostini* criterion (*i.e.*, whether any indoctrination could be attributed to the government). If aid to schools, even "direct aid," is neutrally available and, before reaching or benefiting any religious school, first passes through the hands (literally or figuratively) of numerous private citizens who are free to direct the aid elsewhere, the government has not provided any "support of religion." Although the presence of private choice is easier to see when aid literally passes through the hands of individuals. . . , there is no reason why the Establishment Clause requires such a form. . . .

2

Respondents also contend that the Establishment Clause requires that aid to religious schools not be impermissibly religious in nature or be divertible to religious use. We agree with the first part of this argument but not the second. Respondents' "no divertibility" rule is inconsistent with our more recent case law and is unworkable. So long as the governmental aid is not itself "unsuitable for use in the public schools because of religious content," *[Board of Ed. of Central School Dist. No. 1 v.] Allen* [(1968)], and eligibility for aid is determined in a constitutionally permissible manner, any use of that aid to indoctrinate cannot be attributed to the government and is thus not of constitutional concern. And, of course, the use to which the aid is put does not affect the criteria governing the aid's allocation and thus does not create any impermissible incentive under *Agostini*'s second criterion. . . .

The issue is not divertibility of aid but rather whether the aid itself has an impermissible content. Where the aid would be suitable for use in a public school, it is also suitable for use in any private school. Similarly, the prohibition against the government providing impermissible content resolves the Establishment Clause concerns that exist if aid is actually diverted to religious uses. . . .

A concern for divertibility, as opposed to improper content, is misplaced not only because it fails to explain why the sort of aid that we have allowed is permissible, but also because it is boundless—enveloping all aid, no matter how trivial. . . . Presumably, for example, government-provided lecterns, chalk, crayons, pens, paper, and paintbrushes would have to be excluded from religious schools under respondents' proposed rule. But we fail to see how indoctrination by means of (*i.e.,* diversion of) such aid could be attributed to the government. . . . Finally, any aid, with or without content, is "divertible" in the sense that it allows schools to "divert" resources. Yet we have "not accepted the recurrent argument that all aid is forbidden because aid to one aspect of an institution frees it to spend its other resources on religious ends." *[Committee for Public Ed. and Religious Liberty v.] Regan* [(1980)].

It is perhaps conceivable that courts could take upon themselves the task of distinguishing among the myriad kinds of possible aid based on the ease of diverting each kind. But it escapes us how a court might coherently draw any such line. It not only is far more workable, but also is actually related to real concerns about preventing advancement of religion by government, simply to require . . . that a program of aid to schools not provide improper content and that it determine eligibility and allocate the aid on a permissible basis.

C

The dissent serves up a smorgasbord of 11 factors that, depending on the facts of each case "in all its particularity" could be relevant to the constitutionality of a school-aid program. . . . [A]t least one additional factor is evident from the dissent itself: The dissent resurrects the concern for political divisiveness that once occupied the Court but that post-*Aguilar* cases have rightly disregarded. . . . While the dissent delights in the perverse chaos that all these factors produce, the Constitution becomes unnecessarily clouded, and legislators, litigants, and lower courts groan, as the history of this case amply demonstrates.

One of the dissent's factors deserves special mention: whether a school that receives aid (or whose students receive aid) is pervasively sectarian. The dissent is correct that there was a period when this factor mattered, particularly if the pervasively sectarian school was a primary or secondary school. But that period is one that the Court should regret, and it is thankfully long past.

There are numerous reasons to formally dispense with this factor.

First, its relevance in our precedents is in sharp decline. . . . [W]e have not struck down an aid program in reliance on this factor since 1985, in *Aguilar* and *Ball*. *Agostini* of course overruled *Aguilar* in full and *Ball* in part, and today JUSTICE O'CONNOR distances herself from the part of *Ball* with which she previously agreed, by rejecting the distinction between public and private employees that was so prominent in *Agostini*. . . .

Second, the religious nature of a recipient should not matter to the constitutional analysis, so long as the recipient adequately furthers the government's secular purpose. If a program offers permissible aid to the religious (including the pervasively sectarian), the areligious, and the irreligious, it is a mystery which view of religion the government has established, and thus a mystery what the constitutional violation would be. . . .

Third, the inquiry into the recipient's religious views required by a focus on whether a school is pervasively sectarian is not only unnecessary but also offensive. It is well established, in numerous other contexts, that courts should refrain from trolling through a person's or institution's religious beliefs. Yet that is just what this factor requires. . . .

Finally, hostility to aid to pervasively sectarian schools has a shameful pedigree that we do not hesitate to disavow. . . . Opposition to aid to "sectarian" schools acquired prominence in the 1870's with Congress's consideration (and near passage) of the Blaine Amendment, which would have amended the Constitution to bar any aid to sectarian institutions. Consideration of the amendment arose at a time of pervasive hostility to the Catholic Church and to Catholics in general, and it was an open secret that "sectarian" was code for "Catholic." Notwithstanding its history, of course, "sectarian" could, on its face, describe the school of any religious sect, but the Court eliminated this possibility of confusion when, in *Hunt v. McNair* [(1973)], it coined the term "pervasively sectarian"—a term which, at that time, could be applied almost exclusively to Catholic parochial schools and which even today's dissent exemplifies chiefly by reference to such schools.

In short, nothing in the Establishment Clause requires the exclusion of pervasively sectarian schools from otherwise permissible aid programs, and other doctrines of this Court bar it. This doctrine, born of bigotry, should be buried now.

III

Applying the two relevant *Agostini* criteria, we see no basis for concluding that Jefferson Parish's Chapter 2 program "has the effect of advancing religion." Chapter 2 does not result in governmental indoctrination, because it determines eligibility for aid neutrally, allocates that aid based on the private choices of the parents of schoolchildren, and does not provide aid that has an impermissible content. Nor does Chapter 2 define its recipients by reference to religion.

Taking the second criterion first, it is clear that Chapter 2 aid "is allocated on the basis of neutral, secular criteria that neither favor nor disfavor religion, and is made available to both religious and secular beneficiaries on a nondiscriminatory basis." . . .

Chapter 2 also satisfies the first *Agostini* criterion. The program makes a broad array of schools eligible for aid without regard to their religious affiliations or lack thereof. We therefore have no difficulty concluding that Chapter 2 is neutral with regard to religion. Chapter 2 aid also . . . reaches participating schools only "as a consequence of private decisionmaking." Private decisionmaking controls because of the per capita allocation scheme, and those decisions are independent because of the program's neutrality. It is the students and their parents—not the government—who, through their choice of school, determine who receives Chapter 2 funds. The aid follows the child.

Because Chapter 2 aid is provided pursuant to private choices, it is not problematic that one could fairly describe Chapter 2 as providing "direct" aid. . . . Nor . . . is it of constitutional significance that the schools themselves, rather than the students, are the bailees of the Chapter 2 aid. The ultimate beneficiaries of Chapter 2 aid are the students who attend the schools that receive that aid, and this is so regardless of whether individual students lug computers to school each day or, as Jefferson Parish has more sensibly provided, the schools receive the computers. . . .

Finally, Chapter 2 satisfies the first *Agostini* criterion because it does not provide to religious schools aid that has an impermissible content. The statute explicitly bars anything of the sort, . . . and nonideological," and the record indicates that the Louisiana SEA and the Jefferson Parish LEA have faithfully enforced this requirement. . . . The chief aid at issue is computers, computer software, and library books. The computers presumably have no pre-existing content, or at least none that would be impermissible for use in public schools. . . . Respondents also offer no evidence that religious schools have received software from the government that has an impermissible content.

There is evidence that equipment has been, or at least easily could be, diverted for use in religious classes. . . . [F]or reasons we discussed in Part II-B-2, the evidence of actual diversion and the weakness of the safeguards against actual diversion are not relevant to the constitutional inquiry, whatever relevance they may have under the statute and regulations.

Respondents do, however, point to some religious books that the LEA improperly allowed to be loaned to several religious schools, and they contend that the monitoring programs of the SEA and the Jefferson Parish LEA are insufficient to prevent such errors. The evidence, however, establishes just the opposite, for the improper lending of library books occurred—and was discovered and remedied—before this litigation began almost 15 years ago. In other words, the monitoring system worked. Further, the violation by the LEA and the private schools was minor and, in the view of the SEA's coordinator, inadvertent. . . .

IV

In short, Chapter 2 satisfies both the first and second primary criteria of *Agostini*. It therefore does not have the effect of advancing religion. For the same reason, Chapter 2 also "cannot reasonably be viewed as an endorsement of religion." Accordingly, we hold that Chapter 2 is not a law respecting an establishment of religion. Jefferson Parish need not exclude religious schools from its Chapter 2 program. To the extent that *Meek* and *Wolman* conflict with this holding, we overrule them. . . .

The judgment of the Fifth Circuit is reversed.

It is so ordered.

JUSTICE O'CONNOR, with whom JUSTICE BREYER joins, concurring in the judgment.

In 1965, Congress passed the Elementary and Secondary Education Act. Under Title I, Congress provided monetary grants to States to address the needs of educationally deprived children of low-income families. Under Title II, Congress provided further monetary grants to States for the acquisition of library resources, textbooks, and other instructional materials for use by children and teachers in public and private elementary and secondary schools. Since 1965, Congress has reauthorized the Title I and Title II programs several times. Three Terms ago, we held in *Agostini v. Felton* (1997) that Title I, as applied in New York City, did not violate the Establishment Clause. I believe that Agostini likewise controls the constitutional inquiry respecting Title II presented here, and requires the reversal of the Court of Appeals' judgment that the program is unconstitutional as applied in Jefferson Parish, Louisiana. To the extent our decisions in *Meek v. Pittenger* (1975) and *Wolman v. Walter* (1977), are inconsistent with the Court's judgment today, I agree that those decisions should be overruled. I therefore concur in the judgment.

I

I write separately because, in my view, the plurality announces a rule of unprecedented breadth for the evaluation of Establishment Clause challenges to government school-aid programs. Reduced to its essentials, the plurality's rule states that government aid to religious schools does not have the effect of advancing religion so long as the aid is offered on a neutral basis and the aid is secular in content. The plurality also rejects the distinction between direct and indirect aid, and holds that the actual diversion of secular aid by a religious school to the advancement of its religious mission is permissible. . . . [T]wo specific aspects of the opinion compel me to write separately. First, the plurality's treatment of neutrality comes close to assigning that factor singular importance in the future adjudication of Establishment Clause challenges to government school-aid programs. Second, the plurality's approval of actual diversion of government aid to religious indoctrination is in tension with our precedents and, in any event, unnecessary to decide the instant case. . . .

I do not quarrel with the plurality's recognition that neutrality is an important reason for upholding government-aid programs against Establishment Clause challenges. . . . Nevertheless, we have never held that a government-aid program passes constitutional muster solely because of the neutral criteria it employs as a basis for distributing aid. . . .

I also disagree with the plurality's conclusion that actual diversion of government aid to religious indoctrination is consistent with the Establishment Clause. . . . At least two of the decisions at the heart of today's case demonstrate that we have long been concerned that secular government aid not be diverted to the advancement of religion. In both *Agostini*, our most recent school-aid case, and *Board of Ed. of Central School Dist. No. 1 v. Allen* (1968), we rested our approval of the relevant programs in part on the fact that the aid had not been used to advance the religious missions of the recipient schools. . . .

Second, I believe the distinction between a per-capita school-aid program and a true private-choice program is significant for purposes of endorsement. In terms of public perception, a government program of direct aid to religious schools based on the number of students attending each school differs meaningfully from the government distributing aid directly to individual students who, in turn, decide to use the aid at the same religious schools. In the former example, if the religious school uses the aid to inculcate religion in its students, it is reasonable to say that the government has communicated a message of endorsement. . . . In contrast, when government aid supports a school's religious mission only because of independent decisions made by numerous individuals to guide their secular aid to that school, "[n]o reasonable observer is likely to draw from the facts . . . an inference that the State itself is endorsing a religious practice or belief." *Witters* [*v. Washington Dept. of Servs. for Blind* (1986)] (O'CONNOR, J., concurring in part and concurring in judgment). Rather, endorsement of the religious message is reasonably attributed to the individuals who select the path of the aid.

Finally, the distinction between a per-capita-aid program and a true private-choice program is important when considering aid that consists of direct monetary subsidies. . . . If, as the plurality contends, a per-capita-aid program is identical in relevant constitutional respects to a true private-choice program, then there is no reason that, under the plurality's reasoning, the government should be precluded from providing direct money payments to religious organizations (including churches) based on the number of persons belonging to each organization. And, because actual diversion is permissible under the plurality's holding, the participating religious organizations (including churches) could use that aid to support religious indoctrination. . . . In its logic—as well as its specific advisory language—the plurality opinion foreshadows the approval of direct monetary subsidies to religious organizations, even when they use the money to advance their religious objectives. . . .

II

[In Part II, O'Connor said that the Court had "articulated three primary criteria to guide the determination whether government aid impermissibly advances religion: (1) whether the aid results in governmental indoctrination, (2) whether the aid program defines its recipients by reference to religion, and (3) whether the aid creates an excessive entanglement between government and religion." The same criteria, she said, had been used "to determine whether a government-aid program constitutes an endorsement of religion."

[Because the respondents did not claim an excessive entanglement, O'Connor turned to the first two criteria. On the second, she said, "it is clear that Chapter 2 does not define aid recipients by reference to religion." As to indoctrination, she cited three factors in finding no Establishment Clause violation: "First, . . . Chapter 2 aid is distributed on the basis of neutral, secular criteria. . . . Second, the statute requires participating [school systems] to use and allocate Chapter 2 funds only to supplement the funds otherwise available to a religious school. . . . Third, no Chapter 2 funds ever reach the coffers of a religious school."]

III

[In Part III, O'Connor rejected the respondents' argument that the case should be controlled not by *Agostini* but by the earlier decisions, *Meek* and *Wolman*, which both held unconstitutional programs that used federal funds to pay for instructional materials and equipment provided to religious schools. She said those rulings "created an inexplicable rift" with the earlier decision, *Allen*, which upheld the lending of textbooks to students attending religious schools. She rejected the respondents' argument that the distinction was logical because instructional materials and equipment were more easily "divertible" to religious use. "An educator can use virtually any instructional tool . . . to teach a religious message," O'Connor wrote.]

IV

Because divertibility fails to explain the distinction our cases have drawn between textbooks and instructional materials and equipment, there remains the question of which of the two irreconcilable strands of our Establishment Clause jurisprudence we should now follow. Between the two, I would adhere to the rule that we have applied in the context of textbook lending programs: To establish a First Amendment violation, plaintiffs must prove that the aid in question actually is, or has been, used for religious purposes. . . , I would now hold that *Agostini* and the cases on which it relied have undermined the assumptions underlying *Meek* and *Wolman*. [Remainder of section omitted.]

V

[In Part V, O'Connor rejected the respondents' contention that the actual administration of Chapter 2 in Jefferson Parish violated the Establishment Clause because of evidence of diversion and lack of adequate safeguards against diversion. She called "the limited evidence" of diversion "at best *de minimis*" and said there was "no constitutional need for pervasive monitoring under the Chapter 2 program."]

* * *

Given the important similarities between the Chapter 2 program here and the Title I program at issue in *Agostini*, respondents' Establishment Clause challenge must fail. As in *Agostini*, the Chapter 2 aid is allocated on the basis of neutral, secular criteria; the aid must be supplementary and cannot supplant non-Federal funds; no Chapter 2 funds ever reach the coffers of religious schools; the aid must be secular; any evidence of actual diversion is *de minimis*; and the program includes adequate safeguards. Regardless of whether these factors are constitutional requirements, they are surely sufficient to find that the program at issue here does not have the impermissible effect of advancing religion. For the same reasons, "this carefully constrained program also cannot reasonably be viewed as an endorsement of religion." *Agostini*. Accordingly, I concur in the judgment.

JUSTICE SOUTER, with whom JUSTICE STEVENS and JUSTICE GINSBURG join, dissenting.

The First Amendment's Establishment Clause prohibits Congress (and, by incorporation, the States) from making any law respecting an establishment of religion. It has been held to prohibit not only the institution of an official church, but any government act favoring religion, a particular religion, or for that matter irreligion. Thus it bars the use of public funds for religious aid.

. . . [A] few fundamental generalizations are . . . possible. There may be no aid supporting a sectarian school's religious exercise or the discharge of its religious mission, while aid of a secular character with no discernible benefit to such a sectarian objective is allowable. Because the religious and secular spheres largely overlap in the life of many such schools, the Court has tried to identify some facts likely to reveal the relative religious or secular intent or effect of the government benefits in particular circumstances. We have asked whether the government is acting neutrally in distributing its money, and about the form of the aid itself, its path from government to religious institution, its divertibility to religious nurture, its potential for reducing traditional expenditures of religious institutions, and its relative importance to the recipient, among other things.

. . . [T]his case comes at a time when our judgment requires perspective on how the Establishment Clause has come to be understood and applied. It is not just that a majority today mistakes the significance of facts that have led to conclusions of unconstitutionality in earlier cases, though I believe the Court commits error in failing to recognize the divertibility of funds to the service of religious objectives. What is more important is the view revealed in the plurality opinion, which espouses a new conception of neutrality as a practically sufficient test of constitutionality that would, if adopted by the Court, eliminate enquiry into a law's effects. The plurality position breaks fundamentally with Establishment Clause principle, and with the methodology painstakingly worked out in support of it. . . . From that new view of the law, and from a majority's mistaken application of the old, I respectfully dissent.

I

The prohibition that "Congress shall make no law respecting an establishment of religion" eludes elegant conceptualization simply because the prohibition applies to such distinct phenomena as state churches and aid to religious schools, and as applied to school aid has prompted challenges to programs ranging from construction subsidies to hearing aids to textbook loans. . . .

A

At least three concerns have been expressed since the founding and run throughout our First Amendment jurisprudence. First, compelling an individual to support religion violates the fundamental principle of freedom of conscience. . . .

Second, government aid corrupts religion. . . .

Third, government establishment of religion is inextricably linked with conflict. . . .

B

These concerns are reflected in the Court's classic summation delivered in *Everson v. Board of Education* [(1947)], its first opinion directly addressing standards governing aid to religious schools [Excerpt from opinion omitted.] The most directly pertinent doctrinal statements here are these: no government "can pass laws which aid one religion [or] all religions. . . . No tax in any amount . . . can be levied to support any religious activities or institutions . . . whatever form they may adopt to teach . . . religion." Thus, the principle of "no aid," with which no one in *Everson* disagreed. . . .

Today, the substantive principle of no aid to religious mission remains the governing understanding of the Establishment Clause as applied to public benefits inuring to religious schools. . . . The Court's decisions demonstrate its repeated attempts to isolate considerations relevant in classifying particular benefits as between those that do not discernibly support or threaten support of a school's religious mission, and those that cross or threaten to cross the line into support for religion.

II

A

The most deceptively familiar of those considerations is "neutrality." . . . [W]e have used the term in at least three ways in our cases. . . . "Neutrality" has been employed as a term to describe the requisite state of government equipoise between the forbidden encouragement and discouragement of religion; to characterize a benefit or aid as secular; and to indicate evenhandedness in distributing it. . . .

In the days when "neutral" was used in *Everson*'s sense of equipoise, neutrality was tantamount to constitutionality. . . . This is not so at all, however, under the most recent use of "neutrality" to refer to generality or evenhandedness of distribution. This kind of neutrality is relevant in judging whether a benefit scheme . . . should be seen as aiding a sectarian school's religious mission, but this neutrality is not alone sufficient to qualify the aid as constitutional. It is to be considered only along with other characteristics of aid, its administration, its recipients, or its potential . . . as indicators of just how religious the intent and effect of a given aid scheme really is.

B

The insufficiency of evenhandedness neutrality as a stand-alone criterion of constitutional intent or effect has been clear from the beginning of our interpretative efforts, for an obvious reason. Evenhandedness in distributing a benefit approaches the equivalence of constitutionality in this area only when the term refers to such universality of distribution that it makes no sense to think of the benefit as going to any discrete group. Conversely, when evenhandedness refers to distribution to limited groups within society, like groups of schools or schoolchildren, it does make sense to regard the benefit as aid to the recipients. . . .

Hence, if we looked no further than evenhandedness, . . . religious schools could be blessed with government funding as massive as expenditures made for the benefit of their public school counterparts, and religious missions would thrive on public money. . . .

At least three main lines of enquiry addressed particularly to school aid have emerged to complement evenhandedness neutrality. First, we have noted that two types of aid recipients heighten Establishment Clause concern: pervasively religious schools and primary and secondary religious schools. Second, we have identified two important characteristics of the method of distributing aid: directness or indirectness of distribution and distribution by genuinely independent choice. Third, we have found relevance in at least five characteristics of the aid itself: its religious content; its cash form; its divertibility or actually diversion to religious support; its supplantation of traditional items of religious school expense; and its substantiality. [Detailed discussion of factors omitted.]

III

A

. . . [T]he plurality's new criterion . . . appears to take evenhandedness neutrality and in practical terms promote it to a single and sufficient test for the establishment constitutionality of school aid. . . . [A]ttention to at least three of its mistaken assumptions will show the degree to which the plurality's proposal would replace the principle of no aid with a formula for generous religious support.

First, the plurality treats an external observer's attribution of religious support to the government as the sole impermissible effect of a government aid scheme. . . .

Second, the plurality apparently assumes as a fact that equal amounts of aid to religious and nonreligious schools will have exclusively secular and equal effects, on both external perception and on incentives to attend different schools. . . .

Third, the plurality assumes that per capita distribution rules safeguard the same principles as independent, private choices. But that is clearly not so. . . .

. . . Under the plurality's regime, little would be left of the right of conscience against compelled support for religion; the more massive the aid the more potent would be the influence of the government on the teaching mission; the more generous the support, the more divisive would be the resentments of those resisting religious support, and those religions without school systems ready to claim their fair share.

B

The plurality's conception of evenhandedness does not, however, control the case, whose disposition turns on the misapplication of accepted categories of school aid analysis. The facts most obviously relevant to the Chapter 2 scheme in Jefferson Parish are those showing divertibility and actual diversion in the circumstance of pervasively sectarian religious schools. The type of aid, the structure of the program, and the lack of effective safeguards clearly demonstrate the divertibility of the aid. While little is known about its use, owing to the anemic enforcement system in the parish, even the thin record before us reveals that actual diversion occurred. [Remainder of section omitted.]

IV

. . . [T]he plurality's notion of evenhandedness neutrality as a practical guarantee of the validity of aid to sectarian schools would be the end of the principle of no aid to the schools' religious mission. And if that were not so obvious it would become so after reflecting on the plurality's thoughts about diversion and about giving attention to the pervasiveness of a school's sectarian teaching.

The plurality is candid in pointing out the extent of actual diversion of Chapter 2 aid to religious use in the case before us, and equally candid in saying it does not matter. . . .

And if this were not enough to prove that no aid in religious school aid is dead under the plurality's First Amendment, the point is nailed down in the plurality's attack on the legitimacy of considering a school's pervasively sectarian character when judging whether aid to the school is likely to aid its religious mission. The relevance of this consideration is simply a matter of common sense: where religious indoctrination pervades school activities of children and adolescents, it takes great care to be able to aid the school without supporting the doctrinal effort. This is obvious. The plurality nonetheless condemns any enquiry into the pervasiveness of doctrinal content as a remnant of anti-Catholic bigotry. . . , and it equates a refusal to aid religious schools with hostility to religion. . . .

[T]he plurality's choice to employ imputations of bigotry and irreligion as terms in the Court's debate makes one point clear: that in rejecting the principle of no aid to a school's religious mission the plurality is attacking the most fundamental assumption underlying the Establishment Clause, that government can in fact operate with neutrality in its relation to religion. I believe that it can, and so respectfully dissent.

No. 99-699

Boy Scouts of America and Monmouth Council, et al., Petitioners v. James Dale

On writ of certiorari to the Supreme Court of New Jersey

[June 28, 2000]

CHIEF JUSTICE REHNQUIST delivered the opinion of the Court.

Petitioners are the Boy Scouts of America and the Monmouth Council, a division of the Boy Scouts of America (collectively, Boy Scouts). The Boy Scouts is a private, not-for-profit organization engaged in instilling its system of values in young people. The Boy Scouts asserts that homosexual conduct is inconsistent with the values it seeks to instill. Respondent is James Dale, a former Eagle Scout whose adult membership in the Boy Scouts was revoked when the Boy Scouts learned that he is an avowed homosexual and gay rights activist. The New Jersey Supreme Court held that New Jersey's public accommodations law requires that the Boy Scouts admit Dale. This case presents the question whether applying New Jersey's public accommodations law in this way violates the Boy Scouts' First Amendment right of expressive association. We hold that it does.

I

James Dale entered scouting in 1978 at the age of eight by joining Monmouth Council's Cub Scout Pack 142. Dale became a Boy Scout in 1981 and remained a Scout until he turned 18. By all accounts, Dale was an exemplary Scout. In 1988, he achieved the rank of Eagle Scout, one of Scouting's highest honors.

Dale applied for adult membership in the Boy Scouts in 1989. The Boy Scouts approved his application for the position of assistant scoutmaster of Troop 73. Around the same time, Dale left home to attend Rutgers University. After arriving at Rutgers, Dale first acknowledged to himself and others that he is gay. He quickly became involved with, and eventually became the copresident of, the Rutgers University Lesbian/Gay Alliance. In 1990, Dale attended a seminar addressing the psychological and health needs of lesbian and gay teenagers. A newspaper covering the event interviewed Dale about his advocacy of homosexual teenagers' need for gay role models. In early July 1990, the newspaper published the interview and Dale's photograph over a caption identifying him as the copresident of the Lesbian/Gay Alliance.

Later that month, Dale received a letter from Monmouth Council Executive James Kay revoking his adult membership. Dale wrote to Kay requesting the reason for Monmouth Council's decision. Kay responded by letter that the Boy Scouts "specifically forbid membership to homosexuals."

In 1992, Dale filed a complaint against the Boy Scouts in the New Jersey Superior Court. The complaint alleged that the Boy Scouts had violated New Jersey's public accommodations statute and its common law by revoking Dale's membership based solely on his sexual orientation. New Jersey's public accommodations statute prohibits, among other things, discrimination on the basis of sexual orientation in places of public accommodation.

The New Jersey Superior Court's Chancery Division granted summary judgment in favor of the Boy Scouts. The court held that New Jersey's public accommodations law was inapplicable because the Boy Scouts was not a place of public accommodation, and that, alternatively, the Boy Scouts is a distinctly private group exempted from coverage under New Jersey's law. The court rejected Dale's common-law claim holding that New Jersey's policy is embodied in the public accommodations law. The court also concluded that the Boy Scouts' position in respect of active homosexuality was clear and held that the First Amendment freedom of expressive association prevented the government from forcing the Boy Scouts to accept Dale as an adult leader.

The New Jersey Superior Court's Appellate Division affirmed the dismissal of Dale's common-law claim, but otherwise reversed and remanded for further proceedings (1998). It held that New Jersey's public accommodations law applied to the Boy Scouts and that the Boy Scouts violated it. The Appellate Division rejected the Boy Scouts' federal constitutional claims.

The New Jersey Supreme Court affirmed the judgment of the Appellate Division [1999]. It held that the Boy Scouts was a place of public accommodation subject to the public accommodations law, that the organization was not exempt from the law under any of its express exceptions, and that the Boy Scouts violated the law by revoking Dale's membership based on his avowed homosexuality. After considering the state-law issues, the court addressed the Boy Scouts' claims that application of the public accommodations law in this case violated its federal constitutional rights "to enter into and maintain . . . intimate or private relationships . . . [and] to associate for the purpose of engaging in protected speech." [Detailed summary of New Jersey court's reasoning in rejecting those claims omitted.]

We granted the Boy Scouts' petition for certiorari to determine whether the application of New Jersey's public accommodations law violated the First Amendment (2000).

II

In *Roberts v. United States Jaycees* (1984), we observed that "implicit in the right to engage in activities protected by the First Amendment" is "a corresponding right to associate with others in pursuit of a wide variety of political, social, economic, educational, religious, and cultural ends." This right is crucial in preventing the majority from imposing its views on groups that would rather express other, perhaps unpopular, ideas. . . . Government actions that may unconstitutionally burden this freedom may take many forms, one of which is "intrusion into the internal structure or affairs of an association" like a "regulation that forces the group to accept members it does not desire." Forcing a group to accept certain members may impair the ability of the group to express those views, and only those views, that it intends to express. . . .

The forced inclusion of an unwanted person in a group infringes the group's freedom of expressive association if the presence of that person affects in a significant way the group's ability to advocate public or private viewpoints. *New York State Club Assn., Inc. v. City of New York* (1988). But the freedom of expressive association, like many freedoms, is not absolute. We have held that the freedom could be overridden "by regulations adopted to serve compelling state interests, unrelated to the suppression of ideas, that cannot be achieved through means significantly less restrictive of associational freedoms." *Roberts.*

To determine whether a group is protected by the First Amendment's expressive associational right, we must determine whether the group engages in "expressive association." The First Amendment's protection of expressive association is not reserved for advocacy groups. But to come within its ambit, a group must engage in some form of expression, whether it be public or private.

Because this is a First Amendment case where the ultimate conclusions of law are virtually inseparable from findings of fact, we are obligated to independently review the factual record to ensure that the state court's judgment does not unlawfully intrude on free expression. The record reveals the following. The Boy Scouts is a private, nonprofit organization. According to its mission statement:

> "It is the mission of the Boy Scouts of America to serve others by helping to instill values in young people and, in other ways, to prepare them to make ethical choices over their lifetime in achieving their full potential.
>
> "The values we strive to instill are based on those found in the Scout Oath and Law:

"Scout Oath

> "On my honor I will do my best
> To do my duty to God and my country
> and to obey the Scout Law;
> To help other people at all times;
> To keep myself physically strong,
> mentally awake, and morally straight.

"Scout Law

> "A Scout is:
>
> | "Trustworthy | Obedient |
> | Loyal | Cheerful |
> | Helpful | Thrifty |
> | Friendly | Brave |
> | Courteous | Clean |
> | Kind | Reverent." |

Thus, the general mission of the Boy Scouts is clear: "[T]o instill values in young people." The Boy Scouts seeks to instill these values by having its adult leaders spend time with the youth members, instructing and engaging them in activities like camping, archery, and fishing. During the time spent with the youth members, the scoutmasters and assistant scoutmasters inculcate them with the Boy Scouts' values—both expressly and by example. It seems indisputable that an association that seeks to transmit such a system of values engages in expressive activity. . . .

Given that the Boy Scouts engages in expressive activity, we must determine whether the forced inclusion of Dale as an assistant scoutmaster would significantly affect the Boy Scouts' ability to advocate public or private viewpoints. This inquiry necessarily requires us first to explore, to a limited extent, the nature of the Boy Scouts' view of homosexuality.

The values the Boy Scouts seeks to instill are "based on" those listed in the Scout Oath and Law. . . . The Boy Scouts asserts that homosexual conduct is inconsistent with the values embodied in the Scout Oath and Law, particularly with the values represented by the terms "morally straight" and "clean."

Obviously, the Scout Oath and Law do not expressly mention sexuality or sexual orientation. And the terms "morally straight" and "clean" are by no means self-defining. Different people would attribute to those terms very different meanings. . . .

The New Jersey Supreme Court analyzed the Boy Scouts' beliefs and found that the "exclusion of members solely on the basis of their sexual orientation is inconsistent with Boy Scouts' commitment to a diverse and 'representative' membership . . . [and] contradicts Boy Scouts' overarching objective to reach 'all eligible youth.'" The court concluded that the exclusion of members like Dale "appears antithetical to the organization's goals and philosophy." But our cases reject this sort of inquiry; it is not the role of the courts to reject a group's expressed values because they disagree with those values or find them internally inconsistent. . . .

The Boy Scouts asserts that it "teach[es] that homosexual conduct is not morally straight," and that it does "not want to promote homosexual conduct as a legitimate form of behavior." We accept the Boy Scouts' assertion. We need not inquire further to determine the nature of the Boy Scouts' expression with respect to homosexuality. But because the record before us contains written evidence of the Boy Scouts' viewpoint, we look to it as instructive, if only on the question of the sincerity of the professed beliefs.

A 1978 position statement to the Boy Scouts' Executive Committee, signed by Downing B. Jenks, the President of the Boy Scouts, and Harvey L. Price, the Chief Scout Executive, expresses the Boy Scouts' "official position" with regard to "homosexuality and Scouting":

> "Q. May an individual who openly declares himself to be a homosexual be a volunteer Scout leader?
> "A. No. The Boy Scouts of America is a private, membership organization and leadership therein is a privilege and not a right. We do not believe that homosexuality and leadership in Scouting are appropriate. We will continue to select only those who in our judgment meet our standards and qualifications for leadership."

Thus, at least as of 1978—the year James Dale entered Scouting—the official position of the Boy Scouts was that avowed homosexuals were not to be Scout leaders.

A position statement promulgated by the Boy Scouts in 1991 (after Dale's membership was revoked but before this litigation was filed) also supports its current view:

> "We believe that homosexual conduct is inconsistent with the require-
> ment in the Scout Oath that a Scout be morally straight and in the Scout
> Law that a Scout be clean in word and deed, and that homosexuals do not
> provide a desirable role model for Scouts."

This position statement was redrafted numerous times but its core message remained consistent. For example, a 1993 position statement, the most recent in the
record, reads, in part:

> "The Boy Scouts of America has always reflected the expectations that
> Scouting families have had for the organization. We do not believe that
> homosexuals provide a role model consistent with these expectations. Ac-
> cordingly, we do not allow for the registration of avowed homosexuals as
> members or as leaders of the BSA."

The Boy Scouts publicly expressed its views with respect to homosexual conduct by its assertions in prior litigation. For example, throughout a California case
with similar facts filed in the early 1980's, the Boy Scouts consistently asserted
the same position with respect to homosexuality that it asserts today. [Citations
to California case omitted.] We cannot doubt that the Boy Scouts sincerely holds
this view.

We must then determine whether Dale's presence as an assistant scoutmaster
would significantly burden the Boy Scouts' desire to not "promote homosexual
conduct as a legitimate form of behavior." As we give deference to an association's
assertions regarding the nature of its expression, we must also give deference to an
association's view of what would impair its expression. . . . That is not to say that an
expressive association can erect a shield against antidiscrimination laws simply by
asserting that mere acceptance of a member from a particular group would impair
its message. But here Dale, by his own admission, is one of a group of gay Scouts
who have "become leaders in their community and are open and honest about their
sexual orientation." Dale was the copresident of a gay and lesbian organization at
college and remains a gay rights activist. Dale's presence in the Boy Scouts would,
at the very least, force the organization to send a message, both to the youth members and the world, that the Boy Scouts accepts homosexual conduct as a legitimate
form of behavior.

Hurley [*v. Irish-American Gay, Lesbian and Bisexual Group of Boston, Inc.* (1995)]
is illustrative on this point. There we considered whether the application of Massachusetts' public accommodations law to require the organizers of a private
St. Patrick's Day parade to include among the marchers an Irish-American gay, lesbian, and bisexual group, GLIB, violated the parade organizers' First Amendment
rights. We noted that the parade organizers did not wish to exclude the GLIB
members because of their sexual orientations, but because they wanted to march
behind a GLIB banner. We observed:

> "[A] contingent marching behind the organization's banner would at least
> bear witness to the fact that some Irish are gay, lesbian, or bisexual, and
> the presence of the organized marchers would suggest their view that
> people of their sexual orientations have as much claim to unqualified so-
> cial acceptance as heterosexuals . . . The parade's organizers may not be-
> lieve these facts about Irish sexuality to be so, or they may object to un-
> qualified social acceptance of gays and lesbians or have some other reason

for wishing to keep GLIB's message out of the parade. But whatever the reason, it boils down to the choice of a speaker not to propound a particular point of view, and that choice is presumed to lie beyond the government's power to control."

Here, we have found that the Boy Scouts believes that homosexual conduct is inconsistent with the values it seeks to instill in its youth members; it will not "promote homosexual conduct as a legitimate form of behavior." As the presence of GLIB in Boston's St. Patrick's Day parade would have interfered with the parade organizers' choice not to propound a particular point of view, the presence of Dale as an assistant scoutmaster would just as surely interfere with the Boy Scout's choice not to propound a point of view contrary to its beliefs.

The New Jersey Supreme Court determined that the Boy Scouts' ability to disseminate its message was not significantly affected by the forced inclusion of Dale as an assistant scoutmaster because of the following findings:

> "Boy Scout members do not associate for the purpose of disseminating the belief that homosexuality is immoral; Boy Scouts discourages its leaders from disseminating any views on sexual issues; and Boy Scouts includes sponsors and members who subscribe to different views in respect of homosexuality."

We disagree with the New Jersey Supreme Court's conclusion drawn from these findings.

First, associations do not have to associate for the "purpose" of disseminating a certain message in order to be entitled to the protections of the First Amendment. An association must merely engage in expressive activity that could be impaired in order to be entitled to protection. For example, the purpose of the St. Patrick's Day parade in *Hurley* was not to espouse any views about sexual orientation, but we held that the parade organizers had a right to exclude certain participants nonetheless.

Second, even if the Boy Scouts discourages Scout leaders from disseminating views on sexual issues—a fact that the Boy Scouts disputes with contrary evidence—the First Amendment protects the Boy Scouts' method of expression. If the Boy Scouts wishes Scout leaders to avoid questions of sexuality and teach only by example, this fact does not negate the sincerity of its belief discussed above.

Third, the First Amendment simply does not require that every member of a group agree on every issue in order for the group's policy to be "expressive association." The Boy Scouts takes an official position with respect to homosexual conduct, and that is sufficient for First Amendment purposes. In this same vein, Dale makes much of the claim that the Boy Scouts does not revoke the membership of heterosexual Scout leaders that openly disagree with the Boy Scouts' policy on sexual orientation. But if this is true, it is irrelevant. The presence of an avowed homosexual and gay rights activist in an assistant scoutmaster's uniform sends a distinctly different message from the presence of a heterosexual assistant scoutmaster who is on record as disagreeing with Boy Scouts policy. The Boy Scouts has a First Amendment right to choose to send one message but not the other. The fact that the organization does not trumpet its views from the housetops, or that it tolerates dissent within its ranks, does not mean that its views receive no First Amendment protection.

Having determined that the Boy Scouts is an expressive association and that the forced inclusion of Dale would significantly affect its expression, we inquire whether the application of New Jersey's public accommodations law to require that the Boy Scouts accept Dale as an assistant scoutmaster runs afoul of the Scouts' freedom of expressive association. We conclude that it does.

State public accommodations laws were originally enacted to prevent discrimination in traditional places of public accommodation—like inns and trains. . . . New Jersey's statutory definition of "[a] place of public accommodation" is extremely broad. The term is said to "include, but not be limited to," a list of over 50 types of places. Many on the list are what one would expect to be places where the public is invited. . . . But the statute also includes places that often may not carry with them open invitations to the public, like summer camps and roof gardens. In this case, the New Jersey Supreme Court went a step further and applied its public accommodations law to a private entity without even attempting to tie the term "place" to a physical location. As the definition of "public accommodation" has expanded from clearly commercial entities, such as restaurants, bars, and hotels, to membership organizations such as the Boy Scouts, the potential for conflict between state public accommodations laws and the First Amendment rights of organizations has increased.

We recognized in cases such as *Roberts* and *[Board of Directors of Rotary Int'l v. Rotary Club of] Duarte* [(1987)] that States have a compelling interest in eliminating discrimination against women in public accommodations. But in each of these cases we went on to conclude that the enforcement of these statutes would not materially interfere with the ideas that the organization sought to express. [Excerpts from opinions omitted.] . . .

Dale contends that we should apply the intermediate standard of review enunciated in *United States v. O'Brien* (1968) to evaluate the competing interests. There the Court enunciated a four-part test for review of a governmental regulation that has only an incidental effect on protected speech—in that case the symbolic burning of a draft card. A law prohibiting the destruction of draft cards only incidentally affects the free speech rights of those who happen to use a violation of that law as a symbol of protest. But New Jersey's public accommodations law directly and immediately affects associational rights, in this case associational rights that enjoy First Amendment protection. Thus, *O'Brien* is inapplicable.

In *Hurley*, we applied traditional First Amendment analysis to hold that the application of the Massachusetts public accommodations law to a parade violated the First Amendment rights of the parade organizers.

Although we did not explicitly deem the parade in *Hurley* an expressive association, the analysis we applied there is similar to the analysis we apply here. We have already concluded that a state requirement that the Boy Scouts retain Dale as an assistant scoutmaster would significantly burden the organization's right to oppose or disfavor homosexual conduct. The state interests embodied in New Jersey's public accommodations law do not justify such a severe intrusion on the Boy Scouts' rights to freedom of expressive association. That being the case, we hold that the First Amendment prohibits the State from imposing such a requirement through the application of its public accommodations law.

JUSTICE STEVENS' dissent makes much of its observation that the public perception of homosexuality in this country has changed. Indeed, it appears that homosexuality has gained greater societal acceptance. But this is scarcely an argument for denying First Amendment protection to those who refuse to accept these views. The First Amendment protects expression, be it of the popular variety or not. . . . And the fact that an idea may be embraced and advocated by increasing numbers of people is all the more reason to protect the First Amendment rights of those who wish to voice a different view. . . .

We are not, as we must not be, guided by our views of whether the Boy Scouts' teachings with respect to homosexual conduct are right or wrong; public or judicial disapproval of a tenet of an organization's expression does not justify the State's effort to compel the organization to accept members where such acceptance would derogate from the organization's expressive message. "While the law is free to promote all sorts of conduct in place of harmful behavior, it is not free to interfere with speech for no better reason than promoting an approved message or discouraging a disfavored one, however enlightened either purpose may strike the government." *Hurley.*

The judgment of the New Jersey Supreme Court is reversed, and the cause remanded for further proceedings not inconsistent with this opinion.

It is so ordered.

JUSTICE STEVENS, with whom JUSTICE SOUTER, JUSTICE GINS-BURG and JUSTICE BREYER join, dissenting.

New Jersey "prides itself on judging each individual by his or her merits" and on being "in the vanguard in the fight to eradicate the cancer of unlawful discrimination of all types from our society." [Quoting New Jersey Supreme Court decision in 1978.] Since 1945, it has had a law against discrimination. The law broadly protects the opportunity of all persons to obtain the advantages and privileges "of any place of public accommodation." The New Jersey Supreme Court's construction of the statutory definition of a "place of public accommodation" has given its statute a more expansive coverage than most similar state statutes. And as amended in 1991, the law prohibits discrimination on the basis of nine different traits including an individual's "sexual orientation." The question in this case is whether that expansive construction trenches on the federal constitutional rights of the Boy Scouts of America (BSA). . . .

The majority holds that New Jersey's law violates BSA's right to associate and its right to free speech. But that law does not "impos[e] any serious burdens" on BSA's "collective effort on behalf of [its] shared goals," *Roberts v. United States Jaycees* (1984), nor does it force BSA to communicate any message that it does not wish to endorse. New Jersey's law, therefore, abridges no constitutional right of the Boy Scouts.

I

[James Dale's background in scouting and the revocation of his membership in Boy Scouts on the basis of his homosexuality omitted.]

In this case, Boy Scouts of America contends that it teaches the young boys who are Scouts that homosexuality is immoral. Consequently, it argues, it would violate its right to associate to force it to admit homosexuals as members, as doing so would be at odds with its own shared goals and values. This contention, quite plainly, requires us to look at what, exactly, are the values that BSA actually teaches.

BSA's mission statement reads as follows: "It is the mission of the Boy Scouts of America to serve others by helping to instill values in young people and, in other ways, to prepare them to make ethical choices over their lifetime in achieving their full potential." . . . BSA describes itself as having a "representative membership," which it defines as "boy membership [that] reflects proportionately the characteristics of the boy population of its service area." In particular, the group emphasizes that "[n]either the charter nor the bylaws of the Boy Scouts of America permits the exclusion of any boy. . . ."

To bolster its claim that its shared goals include teaching that homosexuality is wrong, BSA directs our attention to two terms appearing in the Scout Oath and Law. The first is the phrase "morally straight," which appears in the Oath ("On my honor I will do my best . . . To keep myself . . . morally straight"); the second term is the word "clean," which appears in a list of 12 characteristics together comprising the Scout Law.

The Boy Scout Handbook defines "morally straight," as such:

> "To be a person of strong character, guide your life with honesty, purity, and justice. Respect and defend the rights of all people. Your relationships with others should be honest and open. Be clean in your speech and actions, and faithful in your religious beliefs. The values you follow as a Scout will help you become virtuous and self-reliant."

The Scoutmaster Handbook emphasizes these points about being "morally straight":

> "In any consideration of moral fitness, a key word has to be 'courage.' A boy's courage to do what his head and his heart tell him is right. And the courage to refuse to do what his heart and his head say is wrong. Moral fitness, like emotional fitness, will clearly present opportunities for wise guidance by an alert Scoutmaster."

As for the term "clean," the Boy Scout Handbook offers the following:

> "A Scout is CLEAN. *A Scout keeps his body and mind fit and clean. He chooses the company of those who live by these same ideals. He helps keep his home and community clean.*
> "You never need to be ashamed of dirt that will wash off. If you play hard and work hard you can't help getting dirty. But when the game is over or the work is done, that kind of dirt disappears with soap and water.
> "There's another kind of dirt that won't come off by washing. It is the kind that shows up in foul language and harmful thoughts.
> "Swear words, profanity, and dirty stories are weapons that ridicule other people and hurt their feelings. The same is true of racial slurs and jokes making fun of ethnic groups or people with physical or mental limitations. A Scout knows there is no kindness or honor in such mean-spirited behavior. He avoids it in his own words and deeds. He defends those who are targets of insults." (emphasis in original).

It is plain as the light of day that neither one of these principles—"morally straight" and "clean"—says the slightest thing about homosexuality. Indeed, neither term in the Boy Scouts' Law and Oath expresses any position whatsoever on sexual matters.

BSA's published guidance on that topic underscores this point. Scouts, for example, are directed to receive their sex education at home or in school, but not from the organization: "Your parents or guardian or a sex education teacher should give you the facts about sex that you must know." Boy Scout Handbook (1992). To be sure, Scouts are not forbidden from asking their Scoutmaster about issues of a sexual nature, but Scoutmasters are, literally, the last person Scouts are encouraged to ask: "If you have questions about growing up, about relationships, sex, or making good decisions, ask. Talk with your parents, religious leaders, teachers, or Scoutmaster." . . .

In light of BSA's self-proclaimed ecumenism, furthermore, it is even more difficult to discern any shared goals or common moral stance on homosexuality. Insofar as religious matters are concerned, BSA's bylaws state that it is "absolutely nonsectarian in its attitude toward . . . religious training." . . . In fact, many diverse religious organizations sponsor local Boy Scout troops. Because a number of religious groups do not view homosexuality as immoral or wrong and reject discrimination against homosexuals, it is exceedingly difficult to believe that BSA nonetheless adopts a single particular religious or moral philosophy when it comes to sexual orientation. . . .

II

The Court seeks to fill the void by pointing to a statement of "policies and procedures relating to homosexuality and Scouting" signed by BSA's President and Chief Scout Executive in 1978 and addressed to the members of the Executive Committee of the national organization. The letter says that the BSA does "not believe that homosexuality and leadership in Scouting are appropriate." But when the entire 1978 letter is read, BSA's position is far more equivocal [Quotation from letter omitted.]

Four aspects of the 1978 policy statement are relevant to the proper disposition of this case. First, at most this letter simply adopts an exclusionary membership policy. But simply adopting such a policy has never been considered sufficient, by itself, to prevail on a right to associate claim.

Second, the 1978 policy was never publicly expressed. . . . It was an internal memorandum, never circulated beyond the few members of BSA's Executive Committee. It remained, in effect, a secret Boy Scouts policy. . . .

Third, it is apparent that the draftsmen of the policy statement foresaw the possibility that laws against discrimination might one day be amended to protect homosexuals from employment discrimination. Their statement clearly provided that, in the event such a law conflicted with their policy, a Scout's duty to be "obedient" and "obe[y] the laws," even if "he thinks [the laws] are unfair," would prevail in such a contingency. . . .

Fourth, the 1978 statement simply says that homosexuality is not "appropriate." It makes no effort to connect that statement to a shared goal or expressive activity of the Boy Scouts. . . .

The majority also relies on four other policy statements that were issued between 1991 and 1993. All of them were written and issued after BSA revoked Dale's membership. Accordingly, they have little, if any, relevance to the legal question before this Court. In any event, they do not bolster BSA's claim. [Discussion omitted.]

III

BSA's claim finds no support in our cases. [Background on *Roberts v. United States Jaycees* (1984) and *Board of Directors of Rotary Int'l v. Rotary Club of Duarte* (1987) omitted.]

Several principles are made perfectly clear by *Jaycees* and *Rotary Club*. First, to prevail on a claim of expressive association in the face of a State's antidiscrimination law, it is not enough simply to engage in some kind of expressive activity. Both the Jaycees and the Rotary Club engaged in expressive activity protected by the First Amendment, yet that fact was not dispositive. Second, it is not enough to adopt an openly avowed exclusionary membership policy. Both the Jaycees and the Rotary Club did that as well. Third, it is not sufficient merely to articulate *some* connection between the group's expressive activities and its exclusionary policy. . . .

. . . The relevant question is whether the mere inclusion of the person at issue would "impose any serious burden," "affect in any significant way," or be "a substantial restraint upon" the organization's "shared goals," "basic goals," or "collective effort to foster beliefs." Accordingly, it is necessary to examine what, exactly, are BSA's shared goals and the degree to which its expressive activities would be burdened, affected, or restrained by including homosexuals.

The evidence before this Court makes it exceptionally clear that BSA has, at most, simply adopted an exclusionary membership policy and has no shared goal of disapproving of homosexuality. . . . Boy Scouts of America is simply silent on homosexuality. There is no shared goal or collective effort to foster a belief about homosexuality at all—let alone one that is significantly burdened by admitting homosexuals. . . .

Equally important is BSA's failure to adopt any clear position on homosexuality. . . . [N]othing in our cases suggests that a group can prevail on a right to expressive association if it, effectively, speaks out of both sides of its mouth. A State's antidiscrimination law does not impose a "serious burden" or a "substantial restraint" upon the group's "shared goals" if the group itself is unable to identify its own stance with any clarity.

IV

[Stevens criticized the majority for deferring to the Boy Scouts' assertions regarding the nature of its expression on the issue of homosexuality. He concluded: "[U]nless one is prepared to turn the right to associate into a free pass out of antidiscrimination laws, an independent inquiry is a necessity."]

V

[Stevens contended that there was "no evidence" that Dale would have violated the Boy Scouts' rule that sexual issues are not a "proper area" for adult leaders. He further contended that Dale's inclusion in the Boy Scouts "sends no cognizable message to the Scouts or to the world." Stevens concluded:]

"The only apparent explanation for the majority's holding, then, is that homosexuals are simply so different from the rest of society that their presence alone—unlike any other individual's—should be singled out for special First Amendment treatment. Under the majority's reasoning, an openly gay male is irreversibly affixed with the label 'homosexual.' That label, even though unseen, communicates a message that permits his exclusion wherever he goes. His openness is the sole and sufficient justification for his ostracism. Though unintended, reliance on such a justification is tantamount to a constitutionally prescribed symbol of inferiority. . . .

VI

Unfavorable opinions about homosexuals "have ancient roots." *Bowers v. Hardwick* (1986). Like equally atavistic opinions about certain racial groups, those roots have been nourished by sectarian doctrine. . . . Over the years, however, interaction with real people, rather than mere adherence to traditional ways of thinking about members of unfamiliar classes, have modified those opinions. . . .

That such prejudices are still prevalent and that they have caused serious and tangible harm to countless members of the class New Jersey seeks to protect are established matters of fact that neither the Boy Scouts nor the Court disputes. That harm can only be aggravated by the creation of a constitutional shield for a policy that is itself the product of a habitual way of thinking about strangers. . . .

If we would guide by the light of reason, we must let our minds be bold. I respectfully dissent.

JUSTICE SOUTER, with whom JUSTICE GINSBURG and JUSTICE BREYER join, dissenting.

I join JUSTICE STEVENS's dissent but add this further word on the significance of Part VI of his opinion. . . .

The right of expressive association does not, of course, turn on the popularity of the views advanced by a group that claims protection. Whether the group appears to this Court to be in the vanguard or rearguard of social thinking is irrelevant to the group's rights. I conclude that BSA has not made out an expressive association claim, therefore, not because of what BSA may espouse, but because of its failure to make sexual orientation the subject of any unequivocal advocacy, using the channels it customarily employs to state its message. . . .

How the Court Works

The Constitution makes the Supreme Court the final arbiter in "cases" and "controversies" arising under the Constitution or the laws of the United States. As the interpreter of the law, the Court often is viewed as the least mutable and most tradition-bound of the three branches of the federal government. But the Court has undergone innumerable changes in its history, some of which have been mandated by law. Some of these changes are embodied in Court rules; others are informal adaptations to needs and circumstances.

The Schedule of the Term

Annual Terms

By law the Supreme Court begins its regular annual term on the first Monday in October, and the term lasts approximately nine months. This session is known as the October term. The summer recess, which is not determined by statute or Court rules, generally begins in late June or early July of the following year. This system—staying in continuous session throughout the year, with periodic recesses—makes it unnecessary to convene a special term to deal with matters arising in the summer.

The justices actually begin work before the official opening of the term. They hold their initial conference during the last week in September. When the justices formally convene on the first Monday in October, oral arguments begin.

Arguments and Conferences

At least four justices must request that a case be argued before it can be accepted. Arguments are heard on Monday, Tuesday, and Wednesday for seven two-week sessions, beginning in the first week in October and ending in mid-April. Recesses of two weeks or longer occur between the sessions of oral arguments so that justices can consider the cases and deal with other Court business.

The schedule for oral arguments is 10:00 A.M. to noon and 1 P.M. to 3 P.M. Because most cases receive one hour apiece for argument, the Court can hear up to twelve cases a week.

The Court holds conferences on the Friday just before the two-week oral argument periods and on Wednesday and Friday during the weeks when oral arguments are scheduled. The conferences are designed for consideration of cases already heard in oral argument.

Before each of the Friday conferences, the chief justice circulates a "discuss" list—a list of cases deemed important enough for discussion and a vote. Appeals are placed on the discuss list almost automatically, but as many as three-quarters of the petitions for certiorari are denied. No case is denied review during conference, however, without an initial examination by the justices and their law clerks. Any justice can have a case placed on the Court's conference agenda for review. Most of the cases scheduled for the discuss list also are denied review in the end but only after discussion by the justices during the conference.

Although the last oral arguments have been heard by mid-April each year, the conferences of the justices continue until the end of the term to consider cases remaining on the Court's agenda. All conferences are held in secret, with no legal assistants or other staff present. The attendance of six justices constitutes a quorum. Conferences begin with handshakes all around. In discussing a case, the chief justice speaks first, followed by each justice in order of seniority.

Decision Days

Opinions are released on Tuesdays and Wednesdays during the weeks that the Court is hearing oral arguments; during other weeks, they are released on Mondays. In addition to opinions, the Court also releases an "orders" list—the summary of the Court's action granting or denying review. The orders list is posted at the beginning of the Monday session. It is not announced orally but can be obtained from the clerk's office or the public information office. When urgent or important matters arise, the Court's summary orders may be made available on a day other than Monday.

Unlike its orders, decisions of the Court are announced orally in open Court. The justice who wrote the opinion announces the Court's decision; and justices writing dissenting opinions may deliver a summary in order to

---

Visiting the Supreme Court

The Supreme Court building has six levels, two of which—the ground and main floors—are accessible to the public. The basement contains a parking garage, a printing press, and offices for security guards and maintenance personnel. On the ground floor are the John Marshall statue, the exhibition area, the public information office, and a cafeteria. The main corridor, known as the Great Hall, the courtroom, and justices' offices are on the main floor. The second floor contains dining rooms, the justices' reading room, and other offices; the third floor, the Court library; and the fourth floor, the gym and storage areas.

From October to mid-April, the Court hears oral arguments Monday through Wednesday for about two weeks a month. These sessions begin at 10 a.m. and continue until 3 P.M., with a one-hour recess starting at noon. They are open to the public on a first-come, first-served basis.

Visitors may inspect the Supreme Court chamber any time the Court is not in session. Historical exhibits and a free motion picture on how the Court works also are available throughout the year. The Supreme Court building is open from 9 A.M. to 4:30 P.M. Monday through Friday, except for legal holidays. When the Court is not in session, lectures are given in the courtroom every hour on the half hour between 9:30 A.M. and 3:30 P.M.

---

emphasize their views. When more than one decision is to be rendered, the justices who wrote the opinions make their announcements in reverse order of seniority. Occasionally, all or a large portion of the opinion is read aloud; more often, the author summarizes the opinion more or less briefly.

Reviewing Cases

In determining whether to accept a case for review, the Court has considerable discretion, subject only to the restraints imposed by the Constitution and Congress. Article III, section 2, of the Constitution provides that "In all Cases affecting Ambassadors, other public Ministers and Consuls, and those in which a State shall be Party, the supreme Court shall have original Jurisdiction. In all the other Cases . . . the supreme Court shall have appellate Jurisdiction, both as to Law and Fact, with such Exceptions, and under such Regulations as the Congress shall make."

Original jurisdiction refers to the right of the Supreme Court to hear a case before any other court does. Appellate jurisdiction is the right to review the decision of a lower court. The vast majority of cases reaching the Supreme Court are appeals from rulings of the lower courts; generally only a handful of original jurisdiction cases are filed each term.

After enactment of the Judiciary Act of 1925, the Supreme Court gained broad discretion to decide for itself what cases it would hear. In 1988 Congress virtually eliminated the Court's mandatory jurisdiction, which obliged it to hear most appeals. Since then that discretion has been nearly unlimited.

Methods of Appeal

Cases come to the Supreme Court in several ways: through petitions for writs of certiorari, appeals, and requests for certification.

In petitioning for a writ of certiorari, a litigant who has lost a case in a lower court sets out the reasons why the Supreme Court should review the case. If a writ is granted, the Court requests a certified record of the case from the lower court.

The main difference between the certiorari and appeal routes is that the Court has complete discretion to grant a request for a writ of certiorari but is under more obligation to accept and decide a case that comes to it on appeal.

Most cases reach the Supreme Court by means of the writ of certiorari. In the relatively few cases to reach the Court by means of appeal, the appellant must file a jurisdictional statement explaining why the case qualifies for review and why the Court should grant it a hearing. Often the justices dispose of these cases by deciding them summarily, without oral argument or formal opinion.

Those whose petitions for certiorari have been granted must pay the Court's standard $300 fee for docketing the case. The U.S. government does not have to pay these fees, nor do persons too poor to afford them. The latter may file in forma pauperis (in the character or manner of a pauper) petitions. Another, seldom used, method of appeal is certification, the request by a lower court—usually a court of appeals—for a final answer to questions of law in a particular case. The Court, after examining the certificate, may order the case argued before it.

Process of Review

In recent terms the Court has been asked to review around 8,000 cases. All petitions are examined by the staff of the clerk of the Court; those found to be in reasonably proper form are placed on the docket and given a number. All cases, except those falling within the Court's original jurisdiction, are placed on a single docket, known simply as "the docket." Only in the numbering of the cases is a distinction made between prepaid and in forma pauperis cases on the docket. The first case filed in the 2000–2001 term, for example, would be designated 00–1. In forma pauperis cases contain the year and begin with the number 5001. The second in forma pauperis case filed in the 2000–2001 term would thus be number 00–5002.

Each justice, aided by law clerks, is responsible for reviewing all cases on the docket. In recent years a number of justices have used a "cert pool" system in this review. Their clerks work together to examine cases, writing a pool memo on several petitions. The memo then is given to the justices who determine if more research is needed. Other justices may prefer to review each petition themselves or have their clerks do it.

Petitions on the docket vary from elegantly printed and bound documents, of which multiple copies are submitted to the Court, to single sheets of prison stationery scribbled in pencil. The decisions to grant or deny review of cases are made in conferences, which are held in the conference room adjacent to the chief justice's chambers. Justices are summoned to the conference room by a buzzer, usually between 9:30 and 10:00 A.M. They shake hands with each other and take their appointed seats, and the chief justice then begins the discussion.

Discuss and Orders Lists

A few days before the conference convenes, the chief justice compiles the discuss list of cases deemed important enough for discussion and a vote. As many as three-quarters of the petitions for certiorari are denied a place on the list and thus rejected without further consideration. Any justice can have a case placed on the discuss list simply by requesting that it be placed there.

Only the justices attend conferences; no legal assistants or staff are present. The junior associate justice acts as doorkeeper and messenger, sending for reference material and receiving messages and data. Unlike with other parts of the federal government, few leaks have occurred about what transpires during the conferences.

At the start of the conference, the chief justice makes a brief statement outlining the facts of each case. Then each justice, beginning with the senior associate justice, comments on the case, usually indicating in the course of the comments how he or she intends to vote. A traditional but unwritten rule is that four affirmative votes puts a case on the schedule for oral argument.

Petitions for certiorari, appeals, and in forma pauperis motions that are approved for review or denied review during conference are placed on a certified orders list to be released the next Monday in open court.

Arguments

Once the Court announces it will hear a case, the clerk of the Court arranges the schedule for oral argument. Cases are argued roughly in the order in which they were granted review, subject to modification if more time is needed to acquire all the necessary documents. Cases generally are heard not sooner than three months after the Court has agreed to review them. Under special circumstances the date scheduled for oral argument can be advanced or postponed.

Well before oral argument takes place, the justices receive the briefs and records from counsel in the case. The measure of attention the brief receives—from a thorough and exhaustive study to a cursory glance—depends both on the nature of the case and the work habits of the justice.

As one of the two public functions of the Court, oral arguments are viewed by some as very important. Others dispute the significance of oral arguments, contending that by the time a case is heard most of the justices already have made up their minds.

Time Limits

The time allowed each side for oral argument is thirty minutes. Because the time allotted must accommodate any questions the justices may wish to ask, the actual time for presentation may be considerably shorter than thirty minutes. Under the current rules of the Court, one counsel only will be heard for each side, except by special permission.

An exception is made for an amicus curiae, a "friend of the court," a person who volunteers or is invited to take part in matters before a court but is not a party in the case. Counsel for an amicus curiae may participate in oral argument if the party supported by the amicus allows use of part of its argument time or the Court grants a motion permitting argument by this counsel. The motion must show, the rules state, that the amicus's argument "is thought to provide assistance to the Court not otherwise available." The Court is generally unreceptive to such motions by private parties, but the government is often allowed to argue in cases where it has filed an amicus brief.

Court rules provide advice to counsel presenting oral arguments before the Court: "Oral argument should emphasize and clarify the written arguments appearing in the briefs on the merits." That same rule warns—with italicized emphasis—that the Court "looks with disfavor on oral argument read from a prepared text." Most attorneys appearing before the Court use an outline or notes to make sure they cover the important points.

Circulating the Argument

The Supreme Court has tape-recorded oral arguments since 1955. In 1968 the Court, in addition to its own recording, began contracting with private firms to tape and transcribe all oral arguments. The contract stipulates that the transcript "shall include everything spoken in argument, by Court, counsel, or others, and nothing shall be omitted from the transcript unless the Chief Justice or Presiding Justice so directs." But "the names of Justices asking questions shall not be recorded or transcribed; questions shall be indicated by the letter 'Q.'"

The marshal of the Court keeps the tapes during the term, and their use usually is limited to the justices and their law clerks. At the end of the term, the tapes are sent to the National Archives. Persons wishing to listen to the tapes or buy a copy of a transcript can apply to the Archives for permission to do so.

Transcripts made by a private firm can be acquired more quickly. These transcripts usually are available at the Court a week after arguments are heard. Transcripts can be read in the Court's library or public information office. Those who purchase the transcripts must agree that they will not be photographically reproduced. In addition, transcripts of oral arguments are available on the Westlaw and Lexis electronic data retrieval systems a month or more after argument.

Proposals have been made to tape arguments for television and radio use or to permit live broadcast coverage of arguments. The Court has rejected these proposals. But the Court began posting transcripts of arguments on its new Web site (www.supremecourtus.gov) on October 24, 2000. The transcripts are posted two weeks following the argument.

Use of Briefs

The brief of the petitioner or appellant must be filed within forty-five days of the Court's announced decision to hear the case. Except for in forma pauperis cases, forty copies of the brief must be filed with the Court. For in forma pauperis proceedings, the Court requires only that documents be legible. The opposing brief from the respondent or appellee is to be filed within thirty days of receipt of the brief of the petitioner or appellant. Either party may file with the clerk a request for an extension of time in filing the brief.

Court Rule 24 sets forth the elements that a brief should contain. These are: the questions presented for review; a list of all parties to the proceeding; a table of contents and table of authorities; citations of the opinions and judgments delivered in the lower courts; "a concise statement of the grounds on which the jurisdiction of this Court is invoked"; constitutional provisions, treaties, statutes, ordinances, and regulations involved; "a concise statement of the case containing all that is material to the consideration of the questions presented"; a summary of argument; the argument, which exhibits "clearly the points of fact and of law being presented and citing the authorities and statutes relied upon"; and a conclusion "specifying with particularity the relief which the party seeks."

The form and organization of the brief are covered by rules 33 and 34. The rules limit the number of pages in various types of briefs. The rules also set out a color code for the covers of different kinds of briefs. Petitions are white; motions opposing them are orange. Petitioner's briefs on the merits are light blue, while those of respondents are red. Reply briefs are yellow; amicus curiae, green (light green, supporting petitioner; dark green, supporting respondent); and documents filed by the United States, gray.

Questioning

During oral argument the justices may interrupt with questions or remarks as often as they wish. Unless counsel has been granted special permission extending the thirty-minute limit, he or she can continue talking after the time has expired only to complete a sentence or answer to a question.

The frequency of questioning, as well as the manner in which questions are asked, depends on the style of the justices and their interest in a particular case. Of the current justices, all but Clarence Thomas participate, more or less actively, in questioning during oral arguments; Thomas asks questions very, very rarely.

Questions from the justices may upset and unnerve counsel by interrupting a well-rehearsed argument and introducing an unexpected element. Nevertheless, questioning has several advantages. It serves to alert counsel about what aspects of the case need further elaboration or more information. For the Court, questions can bring out weak points in an argument—and sometimes strengthen it.

Conferences

Following oral argument, the justices deal with cases in conference. During the Wednesday afternoon conference, the cases that were argued the previous Monday are discussed and tentatively decided. At the all-day Friday conference, the cases argued on the preceding Tuesday and Wednesday are discussed and tentatively decided. Justices also consider new motions, appeals, and petitions while in conference.

Conferences are conducted in complete secrecy. No secretaries, clerks, stenographers, or messengers are allowed into the room. This practice began many years ago when the justices became convinced that decisions were being disclosed prematurely.

The justices meet in an oak-paneled, book-lined conference room adjacent to the chief justice's suite. Nine chairs surround a large rectangular table, each chair bearing the nameplate of the justice who sits there. The chief justice sits at the east end of the table, and the senior associate justice at the west end. The other justices take their places in order of seniority. The junior justice is charged with sending for and receiving documents or other information the Court needs.

On entering the conference room the justices shake hands with each other, a symbol of harmony that began in the 1880s. The chief justice begins the conference by calling the first case to be decided and discussing it. When the chief justice is finished, the senior associate justice speaks, followed by the other justices in order of seniority.

The justices can speak for as long as they wish, but they practice restraint because of the amount of business to be completed. By custom each justice speaks without interruption. Other than these procedural arrangements, little is known about what transpires in conference. Although discussions generally are said to be polite and orderly, occasionally they can be acrimonious. Likewise, consideration of the issues in a particular case may be full and probing, or perfunctory, leaving the real debate on the question until later when the written drafts of opinions are circulated between chambers.

Generally the discussion of the case clearly indicates how a justice plans to vote on it. A majority vote is needed to decide a case—five votes if all nine justices are participating.

Opinions

After the justices have voted on a case, the writing of the opinion or opinions begins. An opinion sets out the factual background of the case and the legal basis for the decision. Soon after a case is decided in conference, the task of writing the majority opinion is assigned. When in the majority, the chief justice designates the writer. When the chief justice is in the minority, the senior associate justice voting with the majority assigns the job of writing the majority opinion.

Any justice may write a separate opinion. If in agreement with the Court's decision but not with some of the reasoning in the majority opinion, the justice writes a concurring opinion giving his or her reasoning. If in disagreement with the majority, the justice writes a dissenting opinion or simply goes on record as a dissenter without an opinion. More than one justice can sign a concurring opinion or a dissenting opinion.

The amount of time between the vote on a case and the announcement of the decision varies from case to case. In simple cases where few points of law are at issue, the opinion sometimes can be written and cleared by the other justices in a week or less. In more complex cases, especially those with several dissenting or concurring opinions, the process can take six months or more. Some cases may have to be reargued or the initial decision changed after the drafts of opinions have been circulated.

The assigning justice may consider the points made by majority justices during the conference discussion, the workload of the other justices, the need to avoid the more extreme opinions within the majority, and expertise in the particular area of law involved in a case.

The style of writing a Court opinion—majority, concurring, or dissenting—depends primarily on the individual justice. In some cases, the justice may prefer to write a restricted and limited opinion; in others, he or she may take a broader approach to the subject. The decision likely is to be influenced by the need to satisfy the other justices in the majority.

When a justice is satisfied that the written opinion is conclusive or "unanswerable," it goes into print. Draft opinions are circulated, revised, and printed on a computerized typesetting system. The circulation of the drafts—whether computer-to-computer or on paper—provokes further discussion in many cases. Often the suggestions and criticisms require the writer to juggle opposing views. To retain a majority, the author of the draft opinion frequently feels obliged to make major emendations to satisfy justices who are unhappy with the initial draft. Some opinions have to be rewritten several times.

One reason for the secrecy surrounding the circulation of drafts is that some of the justices who voted with the majority may find the majority draft opinion so unpersuasive—or one or more of the dissenting drafts so convincing—that they change their vote. If enough justices alter their votes, the majority may shift, so that a former dissent becomes the majority opinion. When a new majority emerges from this process, the task of writing, printing, and circulating a new majority draft begins all over again.

When the drafts of an opinion—including dissents and concurring views—have been written, circulated, discussed, and revised, if necessary, the final versions then are printed. Before the opinion is produced, the reporter of decisions adds a "headnote" or syllabus summarizing the decision and a "lineup" showing how the justices voted.

As soon as a decision is announced from the bench, the Court's public information office distributes copies of the opinion to journalists and others. Members of the press and public can also obtain copies of a decision from the public information office until the supply runs out. Copies of opinions are also sent to federal and state courts and agencies. The Government Printing Office (GPO) also prints opinions for inclusion in United States Reports, the official record of Supreme Court opinions; these volumes are published well after the time of the decision. The private reporting service U.S. Law Week publishes new Supreme Court opinions the week after they are issued.

The Court also makes opinions available electronically. In 1991 it began making opinions available in electronic format to a number of large legal publishers, the GPO, and other information services. A number of law schools established sites on the World Wide Web that included current as well as past Supreme Court decisions. In 1996 the Court also established its own electronic bulletin board system (BBS). It provided anyone with a personal computer access to the Court's current opinions, docket, argument calendar, and other information and publications. The telephone number is (202) 554-2570. Most recently, the Court on April 17, 2000, launched its own Web site: www.supremecourtus.gov. The site provides access to opinions and orders on the day of their release, Court calendars, schedules, rules, visitors' guides, press releases, and other information. Initially, the Web site did not include docket information, such as the status of a case or the names of attorneys; that information was added in September 2000. The Court intended to close the BBS once that transition was complete.

Brief Biographies

William Hubbs Rehnquist

Born: October 1, 1924, Milwaukee, Wisconsin.

Education: Stanford University, B.A., Phi Beta Kappa, and M.A., 1948; Harvard University, M.A., 1949; Stanford University Law School, LL.B., 1952.

Family: Married Natalie Cornell, 1953; died, 1991; two daughters, one son.

Career: Law clerk to Justice Robert H. Jackson, U.S. Supreme Court, 1952–1953; practiced law, 1953–1969; assistant U.S. attorney general, Office of Legal Counsel, 1969–1971.

Supreme Court Service: Nominated as associate justice of the U.S. Supreme Court by President Richard Nixon, October 21, 1971; confirmed, 68–26, December 10, 1971; nominated as chief justice of the United States by President Ronald Reagan June 17, 1986; confirmed, 65–33, September 17, 1986.

President Reagan's appointment of William H. Rehnquist as chief justice in 1986 was a deliberate effort to shift the Court to the right. Since his early years as an associate justice in the 1970s, Rehnquist had been the Court's strongest conservative voice. And as chief justice, Rehnquist has helped move the Court to the right in a number of areas, including criminal law, states' rights, civil rights, and church-state issues.

Rehnquist, the fourth associate justice to become chief, argues that the original intent of the Framers of the Constitution and the Bill of Rights is the proper standard for interpreting those documents today. He also takes a literal approach to individual rights. These beliefs have led him to dissent from the Court's rulings protecting a woman's privacy-based right to abortion, to argue that no constitutional barrier exists to school prayer, and to side with police and prosecutors on questions of criminal law. In 1991 he wrote the Court's decision upholding an administration ban on abortion counseling at publicly financed clinics. The next year he vigorously dissented from the Court's affirmation of *Roe v. Wade*, the 1973 opinion that made abortion legal nationwide.

A native of Milwaukee, Rehnquist attended Stanford University, where he earned both a B.A. and an M.A. He received a second M.A. from Harvard before returning to Stanford for law school. His classmates there recalled him as an intelligent student with already well-entrenched conservative views.

After graduating from law school in 1952, Rehnquist came to Washington, D.C., to serve as a law clerk to Supreme Court justice Robert H. Jackson. There he wrote a memorandum that later came back to haunt him during his Senate confirmation hearings. In the memo Rehnquist favored separate but equal schools for blacks and whites. Asked about those views by the Senate Judiciary Committee in 1971, Rehnquist repudiated them, declaring that they were Justice Jackson's, not his own.

Following his clerkship, Rehnquist decided to practice law in the Southwest. He moved to Phoenix and immediately became immersed in Arizona Republican politics. From his earliest days in the state, he was associated with the party's conservative wing. A 1957 speech denouncing the liberalism of the Warren Court typified his views at the time.

During the 1964 presidential race, Rehnquist campaigned ardently for Barry Goldwater. It was then that Rehnquist met and worked with Richard G. Kleindienst, who later, as President Richard Nixon's deputy attorney general, appointed Rehnquist to head the Justice Department's Office of Legal Counsel as an assistant attorney general. In 1971 Nixon nominated him to the Supreme Court.

Rehnquist drew opposition from liberals and civil rights organizations before winning confirmation and again before being approved as chief justice in 1986. The Senate voted to approve his nomination in December 1971 by a vote of 68–26 at the same time that another Nixon nominee, Lewis F. Powell Jr., was winning nearly unanimous confirmation.

In 1986 Rehnquist faced new accusations of having harassed voters as a Republican poll watcher in Phoenix in the 1950s and 1960s. He was also found to have accepted anti-Semitic restrictions in a property deed to a Vermont home. Despite the charges, the Senate approved his appointment as chief justice 65–33. Liberal Democratic senators cast most of the no votes in both confirmations.

Despite his strong views, Rehnquist is popular among his colleagues and staff. When he was nominated for chief justice, Justice William J. Brennan Jr., the leader of the Court's liberal bloc, said Rehnquist would be "a splendid chief justice." After becoming chief justice, Rehnquist was credited with speeding up the Court's conferences, in which the justices decide what cases to hear, vote on cases, and assign opinions.

Rehnquist was married to Natalie Cornell, who died in 1991. They had two daughters and a son.

John Paul Stevens

Born: April 20, 1920, Chicago, Illinois.

Education: University of Chicago, B.A., Phi Beta Kappa, 1941; Northwestern University School of Law, J.D., 1947.

Family: Married Elizabeth Jane Sheeren, 1942; three daughters, one son; divorced 1979; married Maryan Mulholland Simon, 1980.

Career: Law clerk to Justice Wiley B. Rutledge, U.S. Supreme Court, 1947–1948; practiced law, Chicago, 1949–1970; judge, U.S. Court of Appeals for the Seventh Circuit, 1970–1975.

Supreme Court Service: Nominated as associate justice of the U.S. Supreme Court by President Gerald R. Ford November 28, 1975; confirmed, 98–0, December 17, 1975.

When President Gerald R. Ford nominated federal appeals court judge John Paul Stevens to the Supreme Court seat vacated by veteran liberal William O. Douglas in 1975, Court observers struggled to pin an ideological label on the new nominee. The consensus that finally emerged was that Stevens was neither a doctrinaire liberal nor conservative, but a judicial centrist. His subsequent opinions bear out this description, although in recent years he has moved steadily toward the liberal side.

Stevens is a soft-spoken, mild-mannered man who often sports a bow tie under his judicial robes. A member of a prominent Chicago family, he had a long record of excellence in scholarship, graduating Phi Beta Kappa from the University of Chicago in 1941. He earned the Bronze Star during a wartime stint in the navy and then returned to Chicago to enter Northwestern University Law School, from which he was graduated magna cum laude in 1947. From there Stevens left for Washington, where he served as a law clerk to Supreme Court justice Wiley B. Rutledge. He returned to

Chicago to join the prominent law firm of Poppenhusen, Johnston, Thompson & Raymond, which specialized in antitrust law. Stevens developed a reputation as a pre-eminent antitrust lawyer and three years later in 1952 formed his own firm, Rothschild, Stevens, Barry & Myers. He remained there, engaging in private practice and teaching part-time at Northwestern and the University of Chicago law schools, until his appointment by President Richard Nixon in 1970 to the U.S. Court of Appeals for the Seventh Circuit.

Stevens developed a reputation as a political moderate during his undergraduate days at the University of Chicago, then an overwhelmingly liberal campus. Although he is a registered Republican, he has never been active in partisan politics. Nevertheless, Stevens served as Republican counsel in 1951 to the House Judiciary Subcommittee on the Study of Monopoly Power. He also served from 1953 to 1955, during the Eisenhower administration, as a member of the attorney general's committee to study antitrust laws.

In his five years on the federal appeals court, Stevens earned a reputation as an independent-minded judicial craftsman. President Ford, who took office after Nixon's forced resignation, wanted to nominate a moderate of impeccable legal reputation to help restore confidence in government after the Watergate scandals. Stevens was confirmed without dissent, 98–0, on December 17, 1975, and took office two days later.

Stevens has frequently dissented from the most conservative rulings of the Burger and Rehnquist Courts. For example, he dissented from the Burger Court's 1986 decision upholding state antisodomy laws and the Rehnquist Court's 1989 decision permitting states to execute someone for committing a murder at the age of sixteen or seventeen. He has taken liberal positions on abortion rights, civil rights, and church-state issues.

In his second full term on the Court, Stevens wrote the main opinion in a case upholding the right of the Federal Communications Commission to penalize broadcasters for airing indecent material at times when children are in the audience. But in 1997, he led the Court in a major victory for First Amendment interests by striking down a newly enacted law aimed at blocking sexually explicit materials from children on the Internet. In the same year, he wrote the opinion holding that presidents have no immunity while in office from civil suits for private conduct unrelated to their office.

In 1942 Stevens married Elizabeth Jane Sheeren. They have four children. They were divorced in 1979. Stevens subsequently married Maryan Mulholland Simon, a longtime neighbor in Chicago.

Sandra Day O'Connor

Born: March 26, 1930, El Paso, Texas.
Education: Stanford University, B.A., 1950; Stanford University Law School, LL.B., 1952.
Family: Married John J. O'Connor III, 1952; three sons.
Career: Deputy county attorney, San Mateo, California, 1952–1953; assistant attorney general, Arizona, 1965–1969; Arizona state senator, 1969–1975; Arizona Senate majority leader, 1972–1975; judge, Maricopa County Superior Court, 1974–1979; judge, Arizona Court of Appeals, 1979–1981.
Supreme Court Service: Nominated as associate justice of the U.S. Supreme Court by President Ronald Reagan August 19, 1981; confirmed, 99–0, September 21, 1981.

Sandra Day O'Connor, the first woman to serve on the Court, has been a pivotal figure in forming a conservative majority on a range of issues but has also moderated the Rehnquist Court's stance on some questions, including abortion rights and affirmative action.

Pioneering came naturally to O'Connor. Her grandfather left Kansas in 1880 to take up ranching in the desert land that eventually became the state of Arizona. O'Connor, born in El Paso, Texas, where her mother's parents lived, was raised on the Lazy B Ranch, the 198,000-acre spread that her grandfather founded in southeastern Arizona near Duncan. She spent her school years in El Paso, living with her grandmother. She graduated from high school at age sixteen and then entered Stanford University.

Six years later, in 1952, Sandra Day had won degrees with great distinction, both from the university, in economics, and from Stanford Law School. At Stanford she met John J. O'Connor III, her future husband, and William H. Rehnquist, a future colleague on the Supreme Court. While in law school, Sandra Day was an editor of the *Stanford Law Review* and a member of Order of the Coif, the academic honor society.

Despite her record, O'Connor had difficulty finding a job as an attorney in 1952 when relatively few women were practicing law. She applied, among other places, to the firm in which William French Smith—first attorney general in the Reagan administration—was a partner, only to be offered a job as a secretary.

After she completed a short stint as deputy county attorney for San Mateo County (California) while her new husband completed law school at Stanford, the O'Connors moved with the U.S. Army to Frankfurt, Germany. There Sandra O'Connor worked as a civilian attorney for the army, while John O'Connor served his tour of duty. In 1957 they returned to Phoenix, where, during the next eight years, their three sons were born. O'Connor's life was a mix of parenthood, homemaking, volunteer work, and some "miscellaneous legal tasks" on the side.

In 1965 she resumed her legal career on a full-time basis, taking a job as an assistant attorney general for Arizona. After four years in that post she was appointed to fill a vacancy in the state Senate, where she served on the judiciary committee. In 1970 she was elected to the same body and two years later was chosen its majority leader, the first woman in the nation to hold such a post. O'Connor was active in Republican Party politics, serving as co-chair of the Arizona Committee for the Re-election of the President in 1972.

In 1974 she was elected to the Superior Court for Maricopa County, where she served for five years. Then in 1979 Democratic governor Bruce Babbitt appointed O'Connor to the Arizona Court of Appeals. It was from that post that President Reagan chose her as his first nominee to the Supreme Court, succeeding Potter Stewart, who retired. Reagan described her as "a person for all seasons." The Senate confirmed her on September 21, 1981, by a vote of 99–0.

O'Connor brings to the Court a conservative viewpoint and a cautious, case-by-case decisionmaking style. On criminal law issues, she has generally voted to give broader discretion to police, uphold death penalty cases, and restrict the use of federal habeas corpus to challenge state court convictions. She was a strong supporter of limiting punitive damage awards in state courts and relaxing restrictions on government support for religion.

In two important areas, however, O'Connor's cautious approach has disappointed conservatives. While she voted in many decisions in the 1980s to limit abortion rights, she joined in 1992 with two other Republican-appointed justices, Anthony M. Kennedy and David H. Souter, to form a majority for preserving a modified form of the Court's original abortion rights ruling, *Roe v. Wade*. In a jointly authored opinion the three justices said that *Roe*'s "essential holding"—guaranteeing a woman's right to an abortion during most of her pregnancy—should be reaffirmed. But the joint opinion also said that states could regulate abortion procedures as long as they did not impose "an undue burden" on a woman's choice—a test that O'Connor had advocated in previous opinions.

O'Connor has also voted to limit racial preferences in employment and government contracting and wrote the Court's first opinion restricting the use of race in drawing legislative and congressional districts. But she also joined the majority in a critical 1987 case upholding voluntary affirmative action by government employers to remedy past discrimination against women. And she has refused to limit all consideration of race in redistricting cases.

Antonin Scalia

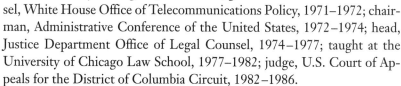

Born: March 11, 1936, Trenton, New Jersey.

Education: Georgetown University, A.B., 1957; Harvard University Law School, LL.B., 1960.

Family: Married Maureen McCarthy, 1960; five sons, four daughters.

Career: Practiced law, Cleveland, 1960–1967; taught at the University of Virginia, 1967–1971; general counsel, White House Office of Telecommunications Policy, 1971–1972; chairman, Administrative Conference of the United States, 1972–1974; head, Justice Department Office of Legal Counsel, 1974–1977; taught at the University of Chicago Law School, 1977–1982; judge, U.S. Court of Appeals for the District of Columbia Circuit, 1982–1986.

Supreme Court Service: Nominated as associate justice of the U.S. Supreme Court by President Ronald Reagan June 17, 1986; confirmed, 98–0, September 17, 1986.

After Warren E. Burger retired from the Court and Ronald Reagan named William H. Rehnquist to succeed him as chief justice, the president's next move—appointing Antonin Scalia as associate justice—was not surprising. On issues dear to Reagan, Scalia clearly met the president's tests for conservatism. Scalia, whom Reagan had named to the U.S. Court of Appeals for the District of Columbia Circuit in 1982, became the first Supreme Court justice of Italian ancestry. A Roman Catholic, he opposes abortion. He has also strongly opposed "affirmative action" preferences for minorities.

In contrast to the heated debate over Rehnquist's nomination as chief justice, only a few, brief speeches were given before the Senate confirmed the equally conservative Scalia, 98–0. He has since become the scourge of some members of Congress because of his suspicion of committee reports, floor speeches, and other elements of legislative history that courts traditionally use to interpret statutes.

Born in Trenton, New Jersey, March 11, 1936, Scalia grew up in Queens, New York. His father was a professor of Romance languages at Brooklyn College, and his mother was a schoolteacher. He was first in his graduating class at an all-male military academy in Manhattan, St. Francis Xavier, and class valedictorian at Georgetown University, where he graduated in 1957. He received his law degree in 1960 from Harvard Law School, where he served as note editor of the *Harvard Law Review*. He worked for six years for the firm of Jones, Day, Cockley & Reavis in Cleveland and then taught contract, commercial, and comparative law at the University of Virginia Law School.

Scalia was a specialist in administrative law and a strong advocate of deregulation. He served as general counsel of the White House Office of Telecommunications Policy from 1971 to 1972. He then headed the Administrative Conference of the United States, a group that advises the government on questions of administrative law and procedure. From 1974 through the Ford administration he headed the Justice Department's Office of Legal Counsel, a post Rehnquist had held three years earlier. Scalia then returned to academia to teach at the University of Chicago Law School. From 1977 to 1982 he was editor of the magazine *Regulation*, published by the American Enterprise Institute for Public Policy Research.

President Ronald Reagan appointed Scalia to the U.S. Court of Appeals for the District of Columbia Circuit in 1982. There, Scalia showed himself to be a hard worker, an aggressive interrogator, and an articulate advocate. He had a marked impatience with what he saw as regulatory or judicial overreaching. In 1983 he dissented from a ruling requiring the Food and Drug Administration (FDA) to consider whether drugs used for lethal injections met FDA standards as safe and effective. The Supreme Court agreed, reversing the appeals court in 1985.

Scalia was thought to be the principal author of an unsigned decision in 1986 that declared major portions of the Gramm-Rudman-Hollings budget-balancing act unconstitutional. The Supreme Court upheld the decision later in the year.

On the Supreme Court Scalia quickly became a forceful voice for conservative positions. He joined in conservative decisions limiting procedural rights in criminal cases and in a series of rulings in 1989 limiting remedies in employment discrimination cases. He also strongly dissented from rulings upholding affirmative action and reaffirming abortion rights. In 1997, he wrote an important decision that struck down on states' rights grounds a federal law requiring state and local law enforcement agencies to conduct background checks on prospective gun purchasers.

In many of his constitutional law opinions, Scalia argued for an "original intent" approach that limited rights to those intended when the Constitution was adopted. He also sharply challenged the use of legislative history in interpreting statutes. He argued that judges should look only to the words of the statute itself.

Scalia expressed his conservative views in aggressive questioning from the bench and in frequently acerbic opinions, especially in dissent.

Anthony McLeod Kennedy

Born: July 23, 1936, Sacramento, California.

Education: Stanford University, A.B., Phi Beta Kappa, 1958; Harvard University Law School, LL.B., 1961.

Family: Married Mary Davis, 1963; two sons, one daughter.

Career: Practiced law, San Francisco, 1961–1963, Sacramento, 1963–1975; professor of constitutional law, McGeorge School of Law, University of the Pacific, 1965–1988; judge, U.S. Court of Appeals for the Ninth Circuit, 1975–1988.

Supreme Court Service: Nominated as associate justice of the U.S. Supreme Court by President Ronald Reagan November 11, 1987; confirmed, 97–0, February 3, 1988.

Quiet, scholarly Anthony M. Kennedy, President Reagan's third choice for his third appointment to the Supreme Court, helped form a conservative majority on many issues in his initial years after joining the Court in 1988. While he adheres to generally conservative views, Kennedy has taken moderate stands on some issues that often make him a pivotal vote between the Court's conservative and liberal blocs.

Before Kennedy's nomination in November 1987, the Senate and the country had agonized through Reagan's two unsuccessful attempts to replace retiring Justice Lewis F. Powell Jr., first with Robert H. Bork and then with Douglas H. Ginsburg. The Senate rejected Bork's nomination after contentious hearings, where opponents depicted the federal appeals court judge as a conservative ideologue. Reagan then turned to Ginsburg, a colleague of Bork's on the federal appeals court in Washington, but he withdrew his name amid controversy about his admitted past use of marijuana.

A quiet sense of relief prevailed when Reagan finally selected a nominee who could be confirmed without another wrenching confrontation.

Kennedy spent twelve years as a judge on the U.S. Court of Appeals for the Ninth Circuit. But unlike Bork, who wrote and spoke extensively for twenty years, Kennedy's record was confined mostly to his approximately five hundred judicial opinions, where he generally decided issues narrowly instead of using his opinions as a testing ground for constitutional theories. The Senate voted to confirm him without dissent, 97–0, on February 3, 1988.

A native Californian, Kennedy attended Stanford University from 1954 to 1957 and the London School of Economics from 1957 to 1958. He received an A.B. from Stanford in 1958 and an LL.B. from Harvard Law School in 1961. Admitted to the California bar in 1962, he was in private law practice until 1975, when President Gerald R. Ford appointed him to the appeals court. From 1965 to 1988 he taught constitutional law at McGeorge School of Law, University of the Pacific.

In his first full term on the Court, Kennedy provided a crucial fifth vote for the Court's conservative wing in a number of civil rights cases. He generally favored law enforcement in criminal cases. And in a closely watched abortion-rights case, he voted along with Chief Justice William H. Rehnquist and Justices Byron R. White and Antonin Scalia to overturn the 1973 ruling, *Roe v. Wade*, that first established a constitutional right to abortion.

Many observers viewed Kennedy's arrival as ushering in a new conservative era. But in 1992 he sorely disappointed conservatives in two major cases. In one he provided the critical fifth vote and wrote the majority opinion in a decision barring officially sponsored prayers at public high school graduation ceremonies. In the other he reversed himself on the abortion issue, joining with Justices Sandra Day O'Connor and David H. Souter in an opinion that upheld a modified version of *Roe v. Wade*.

Kennedy has proved to be a strong free speech advocate in First Amendment cases. In 1989 he helped form the 5–4 majority that overturned state laws against burning or desecrating the U.S. flag. The former constitutional law professor has also displayed a special interest in equal protection and federalism issues. He has voted with other conservatives in rulings that limited racially motivated congressional districting and backed states in disputes over federal power. But he was the swing vote in a 1995 decision to bar the states from imposing term limits on members of Congress. And in 1996 he wrote the opinion striking down Colorado's anti-gay rights amendment prohibiting enactment of any laws to bar discrimination against homosexuals.

David Hackett Souter

Born: September 17, 1939, Melrose, Massachusetts.

Education: Harvard College, B.A., 1961; Rhodes scholar, Oxford University, 1961–1963; Harvard University Law School, LL.B., 1966.

Family: Unmarried.

Career: Private law practice, Concord, New Hampshire, 1966–1968; assistant attorney general, New Hampshire, 1968–1971; deputy attorney general, New Hampshire, 1971–1976; attorney general, New Hampshire, 1976–1978; associate justice, New Hampshire Superior Court, 1978–1983; associate justice, New Hampshire Supreme Court, 1983–1990; judge, U.S. Court of Appeals for the First Circuit, 1990.

Supreme Court Service: Nominated as associate justice of the U.S. Supreme Court by President George Bush July 23, 1990; confirmed, 90–9, October 2, 1990.

At first the Senate did not know what to make of David H. Souter, a cerebral, button-down nominee who was President Bush's first appointment to the Court. Souter was little known outside his home state of New Hampshire, where he had been attorney general, a trial judge, and a state supreme court justice. He had virtually no scholarly writings to dissect and little federal court experience to scrutinize. Only three months earlier Bush had appointed him to the U.S. Court of Appeals for the First Circuit. Souter had yet to write a legal opinion on the appeals court.

During his confirmation hearings, the Harvard graduate and former Rhodes scholar demonstrated intellectual rigor and a masterly approach to constitutional law. His earlier work as state attorney general and New Hampshire Supreme Court justice had a conservative bent, but he came across as more moderate during the hearings.

Under persistent questioning from Democratic senators, Souter refused to say how he would vote on the issue of abortion rights. Abortion rights supporters feared he would provide a fifth vote for overturning the 1973 *Roe v. Wade* decision. Senators in both parties, however, said they were impressed with his legal knowledge. He was confirmed by the Senate 90–9; dissenting senators cited his refusal to take a stand on abortion.

On the bench Souter proved to be a tenacious questioner but reserved in his opinions. He generally voted with the Court's conservative majority in his first term. But in the 1991–1992 term he staked out a middle ground with Justices Sandra Day O'Connor and Anthony M. Kennedy in two crucial cases. In a closely watched abortion case Souter joined with the other two Republican-appointed justices in writing the main opinion reaffirming the "essential holding" of *Roe v. Wade*. The three also joined in forming a 5–4 majority to prohibit school-sponsored prayers at public high school graduation ceremonies.

In the Court's next several terms Souter moved markedly to the left. He joined with liberals in dissenting from cases that restricted racial redistricting. He also voted with the Court's liberal bloc on church-state and some criminal law issues.

Despite his experience in state government, Souter has proved to be a strong supporter of federal power in cases affecting states' rights. He joined the dissenters in a 1995 decision striking down on states' rights grounds a federal law banning the possession of guns near schools. And in 1996 he wrote a massive and scholarly dissent from the Court's decision limiting Congress's power to authorize private citizens to sue states in federal courts to enforce federal law.

Souter is known for his intensely private, ascetic life. He was born September 17, 1939, in Melrose, Massachusetts. An only child, he moved with his parents to Weare, New Hampshire, at age eleven. Except for college, he lived in Weare until 1990.

Graduating from Harvard College in 1961, Souter attended Oxford University on a Rhodes Scholarship from 1961 to 1963, then returned to Cambridge for Harvard Law School. Graduating in 1966, he worked for two years in a Concord law firm. In 1968 he became an assistant attorney general, rose to deputy attorney general in 1971, and in 1976 was appointed attorney general. Souter served as attorney general until 1978, when he was named to the state's trial court. Five years later Gov. John H. Sununu appointed Souter to the state supreme court. Sununu was Bush's chief of staff when Souter was named to the U.S. Supreme Court.

Souter, a bachelor, is a nature enthusiast and avid hiker.

Clarence Thomas

Born: June 23, 1948, Savannah, Georgia.

Education: Immaculate Conception Seminary, 1967–1968; Holy Cross College, B.A., 1971; Yale University Law School, J.D., 1974.

Family: Married Kathy Grace Ambush, 1971; one son; divorced 1984; married Virginia Lamp, 1987.

Career: Assistant attorney general, Missouri, 1974–1977; attorney, Monsanto Co., 1977–1979; legislative assistant to Sen. John C. Danforth, R-Mo., 1979–1981; assistant secretary of education for civil rights, 1981–1982; chairman, Equal Employment Opportunity Commission, 1982–1990; judge, U.S. Court of Appeals for the District of Columbia Circuit, 1990–1991.

Supreme Court Service: Nominated as associate justice of the U.S. Supreme Court by President George Bush July 1, 1991; confirmed, 52–48, October 15, 1991.

Clarence Thomas won a narrow confirmation to the Supreme Court in 1991 after surviving dramatic accusations of sexual harassment. He generated continuing controversy with outspoken conservative views as a justice.

The Senate's 52–48 vote on Thomas was the closest Supreme Court confirmation vote in more than a century. It followed a tumultuous nomination process that included close scrutiny of Thomas's judicial philosophy and sensational charges of sexual harassment brought by a former aide. Thomas denied the charges and accused the Senate Judiciary Committee of conducting a "high-tech lynching."

President George Bush nominated Thomas to succeed Thurgood Marshall, the Court's first black justice and a pioneer of the civil rights movement. Thomas came to prominence as a black conservative while serving as chairman of the Equal Employment Opportunity Commission during the Reagan and Bush administrations. Bush appointed him to the U.S. Court of Appeals for the District of Columbia Circuit in 1990.

Thomas was only forty-three at the time of his nomination to the Court, and senators noted that he likely would be affecting the outcome of major constitutional rulings well into the twenty-first century. Democratic senators closely questioned him on a range of constitutional issues—in particular, abortion. Thomas declined to give his views on abortion, saying he had never discussed the issue.

The committee decided to end its hearings even though it had received an allegation from a University of Oklahoma law professor, Anita Hill, that Thomas had sexually harassed her while she worked for him at the U.S. Department of Education and the EEOC. When the accusation leaked out, the Judiciary Committee reopened the hearing to take testimony from Hill, Thomas, and other witnesses.

In the end most senators said they could not resolve the conflict between Hill's detailed allegations and Thomas's categorical denials. Instead, senators fell back on their previous positions. Supporters praised his determined character and rise from poverty in rural Georgia. Opponents questioned whether Thomas had been candid with the committee in discussing his judicial philosophy.

After joining the Court, Thomas became one of the Court's most conservative members. He closely aligned himself with fellow conservative Antonin Scalia, voting with Scalia about 90 percent of the time. In 1992 he voted as his opponents had warned to overturn the 1973 abortion rights ruling, *Roe v. Wade*, but the Court reaffirmed the decision by a 5–4 vote.

In later cases Thomas wrote lengthy opinions sharply challenging existing legal doctrines. In 1994 he called for scrapping precedents that allowed courts to order the creation of majority-black districts for legislative or congressional seats. In 1995 he authored opinions that called for restricting the basis for Congress to regulate interstate commerce and for reexamining federal courts' role in desegregating public schools. In a campaign finance case in 1996, he urged the Court to overturn all laws limiting political contributions as an infringement on the First Amendment.

Thomas graduated from Yale Law School in 1974 and became an assistant attorney general of Missouri and, three years later, a staff attorney for Monsanto Company. He worked for Sen. John C. Danforth, R-Mo., as a legislative assistant and served in the Department of Education as assistant secretary for civil rights for one year before being named chairman of the EEOC.

Thomas's wife, the former Virginia Lamp, is a lawyer who served as a legislative official with the U.S. Department of Labor during the Bush administration and since 1993 as a senior policy analyst with the House Republican Conference. They were married in 1987. He has a son from his first marriage, which ended in divorce in 1984.

Ruth Bader Ginsburg

Born: March 15, 1933, Brooklyn, New York.

Education: Cornell University, B.A., 1954; attended Harvard University Law School, 1956–1958; graduated Columbia Law School, J.D., 1959.

Family: Married Martin D. Ginsburg, 1954; one daughter, one son.

Career: Law clerk to U.S. District Court Judge Edmund L. Palmieri, 1959–1961; Columbia Law School Project on International Procedure, 1961–1963; professor, Rutgers University School of Law, 1963–1972; director, Women's Rights Project, American Civil Liberties Union, 1972–1980; professor, Columbia Law School, 1972–1980;

judge, U.S. Court of Appeals for the District of Columbia Circuit, 1980–1993.

Supreme Court Service: Nominated as associate justice of the U.S. Supreme Court by President Bill Clinton June 22, 1993; confirmed, 96–3, August 3, 1993.

Ruth Bader Ginsburg's path to the U.S. Supreme Court is a classic American story of overcoming obstacles and setbacks through intelligence, persistence, and quiet hard work. Her achievements as a student, law teacher, advocate, and judge came against a background of personal adversity and institutional discrimination against women. Ginsburg not only surmounted those hurdles for herself but also charted the legal strategy in the 1970s that helped broaden opportunities for women by establishing constitutional principles limiting sex discrimination in the law.

Born into a Jewish family of modest means in Brooklyn, Ruth Bader was greatly influenced by her mother, Celia, who imparted a love of learning and a determination to be independent. Celia Bader died of cancer on the eve of her daughter's high school graduation in 1948.

Ruth Bader attended Cornell University, where she graduated first in her class and met her future husband, Martin Ginsburg, who became a tax lawyer and later a professor at Georgetown University Law Center in Washington.

At Harvard Law School Ruth Bader Ginsburg made law review, cared for an infant daughter, and then helped her husband complete his studies after he was diagnosed with cancer. He recovered, graduated, and got a job in New York, and she transferred to Columbia for her final year of law school.

Although she was tied for first place in her class when she graduated, Ginsburg was unable to land a Supreme Court clerkship or job with a top New York law firm. Instead, she won a two-year clerkship with a federal district court judge. She then accepted a research position at Columbia that took her to Sweden, where she studied civil procedure and began to be stirred by feminist thought.

Ginsburg taught at Rutgers law school in New Jersey from 1963 to 1972. She also worked with the New Jersey affiliate of the American Civil Liberties Union (ACLU), where her caseload included several early sex discrimination complaints. In 1972 Ginsburg became the first woman to be named to a tenured position on the Columbia Law School faculty. As director of the national ACLU's newly established Women's Rights Project, she also handled the cases that over the course of several years led the Supreme Court to require heightened scrutiny of legal classifications based on sex. Ginsburg won five of the six cases she argued before the Court.

President Jimmy Carter named Ginsburg to the U.S. Court of Appeals for the District of Columbia Circuit in 1980. There she earned a reputation as a judicial moderate on a sharply divided court. When Justice Byron R. White announced plans for his retirement in March 1993, Ginsburg was among the large field of candidates President Bill Clinton considered for the vacancy. Clinton considered and passed over two other leading candidates for the position before deciding to interview Ginsburg. White House aides told reporters later that Clinton had been especially impressed with Ginsburg's life story. Reaction to the nomination was overwhelmingly positive.

In three days of confirmation hearings before the Senate Judiciary Committee, Ginsburg depicted herself as an advocate of judicial restraint, but she also said courts sometimes had a role to play in bringing about social change. On specific issues she strongly endorsed abortion rights, equal rights for women, and the constitutional right to privacy. But she declined to give her views on many other issues, including capital punishment. Some senators said that she had been less than forthcoming, but the committee voted unanimously to recommend her for confirmation. The full Senate confirmed her four days later by a vote of 96–3.

Ginsburg was sworn in August 10, 1993, as the Court's second female justice—joining Justice Sandra Day O'Connor—and the first Jewish justice since 1969.

In her first weeks on the bench, Ginsburg startled observers and drew some criticism with her unusually active questioning, but she eased up later. In her voting, she took liberal positions on women's rights, civil rights, church-state, states' rights, and First Amendment issues, but she had a more mixed record in other areas, including criminal law. In 1996 she wrote the Court's opinion in an important sex discrimination case, requiring the all-male Virginia Military Institute to admit women or give up its public funding.

Stephen Gerald Breyer

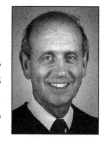

Born: August 15, 1938, San Francisco, California.
Education: Stanford University, A.B., Phi Beta Kappa, 1959; Oxford University, B.A. (Marshall scholar), 1961; Harvard Law School, LL.B., 1964.
Family: Married Joanna Hare, 1967; two daughters, one son.

Career: Law clerk to Justice Arthur J. Goldberg, U.S. Supreme Court, 1964–1965; assistant to assistant attorney general, antitrust, U.S. Justice Department, 1965–1967; professor, Harvard Law School, 1967–1981; assistant special prosecutor, Watergate Special Prosecution Force, 1973; special counsel, Senate Judiciary Committee, 1974–1975; chief counsel, Senate Judiciary Committee, 1979–1980; judge, U.S. Court of Appeals for the First Circuit, 1980–1994.

Supreme Court Service: Nominated as associate justice of the U.S. Supreme Court by President Bill Clinton May 17, 1994; confirmed, 87–9, July 29, 1994.

When President Bill Clinton introduced Stephen G. Breyer, his second Supreme Court nominee, at a White House ceremony on May 16, 1994, he described the federal appeals court judge as a "consensus-builder." The reaction to the nomination proved his point. Senators from both parties quickly endorsed Breyer. The only vocal dissents came from a few liberals and consumer advocates, who said Breyer was too probusiness.

Breyer, chosen to replace the retiring liberal justice Harry A. Blackmun, won a reputation as a centrist in fourteen years on the federal appeals court in Boston and two earlier stints as a staff member for the Senate Judiciary Committee. Breyer's work crossed ideological lines. He played a critical role in enacting airline deregulation in the 1970s and writing federal sentencing guidelines in the 1980s.

Born in 1938 to a politically active family in San Francisco, Breyer earned degrees from Stanford University and Harvard Law School. He clerked for Supreme Court Justice Arthur J. Goldberg and helped draft Goldberg's influential opinion in the 1965 case establishing the right of married couples to use contraceptives. Afterward he served two years in the Justice Department's antitrust division and then took a teaching position at Harvard Law School in 1967.

Breyer took leave from Harvard to serve as an assistant prosecutor in the Watergate investigation in 1973, special counsel to the Judiciary Committee's Administrative Practices Subcommittee from 1974 to 1975, and the full committee's chief counsel from 1979 to 1980. He worked for Sen. Edward Kennedy, D-Mass., but also had good relationships with Republican committee members. His ties to senators paid off when President Jimmy Carter nominated him for the federal appeals court in November 1980. Even though Ronald Reagan had been elected president, GOP senators allowed a vote on Breyer's nomination.

As a judge, Breyer was regarded as scholarly, judicious, and openminded, with generally conservative views on economic issues and more liberal views on social questions. He wrote two books on regulatory reform that criticized economic regulations as anticompetitive and questioned priorities in some environmental and health rulemaking. He also served as a member of the newly created United States Sentencing Commission from 1985 to 1989. Later he defended the commission's guidelines against criticism from judges and others who viewed them as overly restrictive.

President Clinton interviewed Breyer before his first Supreme Court appointment in 1993 but chose Ruth Bader Ginsburg instead. He picked Breyer in 1994 after Senate Majority Leader George Mitchell took himself out of consideration and problems developed with two other leading candidates.

In his confirmation hearings before the Senate Judiciary Committee, Breyer defused two potential controversies by saying that he accepted Supreme Court precedents upholding abortion rights and capital punishment. The only contentious issue in the confirmation process concerned Breyer's investment in the British insurance syndicate Lloyd's of London. Some senators said Breyer should have recused himself from several environmental pollution cases because of the investment. Breyer told the committee that the cases could not have affected his holdings but also promised to get out of Lloyd's as soon as possible. The panel went on to recommend the nomination unanimously.

One Republican senator, Indiana's Richard Lugar, raised the Lloyd's issue during debate, but Breyer was strongly supported by senators from both parties. The Senate voted to confirm Breyer 87–9. Breyer disposed of his investment in Lloyd's shortly after taking office.

Breyer has compiled a moderately liberal record on the Court. He dissented from several conservative rulings on race and religion and wrote the dissenting opinion for the four liberal justices in a decision that struck down a federal law prohibiting the possession of firearms near schools. But he had a more conservative record on criminal law issues and joined the Court's 1995 opinion permitting random drug testing of high school athletes.

Breyer joined Ginsburg as the Court's second Jewish justice. The Court had two Jewish members only once before, in the 1930s when Louis Brandeis and Benjamin Cardozo served together for six years.

Glossary of Legal Terms

Accessory. In criminal law, a person not present at the commission of an offense who commands, advises, instigates, or conceals the offense.

Acquittal. A person is acquitted when a jury returns a verdict of not guilty. A person also may be acquitted when a judge determines that insufficient evidence exists to convict him or that a violation of due process precludes a fair trial.

Adjudicate. To determine finally by the exercise of judicial authority, to decide a case.

Affidavit. A voluntary written statement of facts or charges affirmed under oath.

A fortiori. With stronger force, with more reason.

Amicus curiae. Friend of the court; a person, not a party to litigation, who volunteers or is invited by the court to give his or her views on a case.

Appeal. A legal proceeding to ask a higher court to review or modify a lower court decision. In a civil case, either the plaintiff or the defendant can appeal an adverse ruling. In criminal cases a defendant can appeal a conviction, but the Double Jeopardy Clause prevents the government from appealing an acquittal. In Supreme Court practice an appeal is a case that falls within the Court's mandatory jurisdiction as opposed to a case that the Court agrees to review under the discretionary writ of certiorari. With the virtual elimination of the Court's mandatory jurisdiction in 1988, the Court now hears very few true appeals, but petitions for certiorari are often referred to imprecisely as appeals.

Appellant. The party who appeals a lower court decision to a higher court.

Appellee. One who has an interest in upholding the decision of a lower court and is compelled to respond when the case is appealed to a higher court by an appellant.

Arraignment. The formal process of charging a person with a crime, reading that person the charge, asking whether he or she pleads guilty or not guilty, and entering the plea.

Attainder, Bill of. A legislative act pronouncing a particular individual guilty of a crime without trial or conviction and imposing a sentence.

Bail. The security, usually money, given as assurance of a prisoner's due appearance at a designated time and place (as in court) to procure in the interim the prisoner's release from jail.

Bailiff. A minor officer of a court, usually serving as an usher or a messenger.

Brief. A document prepared by counsel to serve as the basis for an argument in court, setting out the facts of and the legal arguments in support of the case.

Burden of proof. The need or duty of affirmatively providing a fact or facts that are disputed.

Case law. The law as defined by previously decided cases, distinct from statutes and other sources of law.

Cause. A case, suit, litigation, or action, civil or criminal.

Certiorari, Writ of. A writ issued from the Supreme Court, at its discretion, to order a lower court to prepare the record of a case and send it to the Supreme Court for review.

Civil law. Body of law dealing with the private rights of individuals, as distinguished from criminal law.

Class action. A lawsuit brought by one person or group on behalf of all persons similarly situated.

Code. A collection of laws, arranged systematically.

Comity. Courtesy, respect; usually used in the legal sense to refer to the proper relationship between state and federal courts.

Common law. Collection of principles and rules of action, particularly from unwritten English law, that derive their authority from longstanding usage and custom or from courts recognizing and enforcing these customs. Sometimes used synonymously with case law.

Consent decree. A court-sanctioned agreement settling a legal dispute and entered into by the consent of the parties.

Contempt (civil and criminal). Civil contempt arises from a failure to follow a court order for the benefit of another party. Criminal contempt occurs when a person willfully exhibits disrespect for the court or obstructs the administration of justice.

Conviction. Final judgment or sentence that the defendant is guilty as charged.

Criminal law. The branch of law that deals with the enforcement of laws and the punishment of persons who, by breaking laws, commit crimes.

Declaratory judgment. A court pronouncement declaring a legal right or interpretation but not ordering a specific action.

De facto. In fact, in reality.

Defendant. In a civil action, the party denying or defending itself against charges brought by a plaintiff. In a criminal action, the person indicted for commission of an offense.

De jure. As a result of law or official action.

De novo. Anew; afresh; a second time.

Deposition. Oral testimony from a witness taken out of court in response to written or oral questions, committed to writing, and intended to be used in the preparation of a case.

Dicta. *See* Obiter dictum.

Dismissal. Order disposing of a case without a trial.

Docket. A calendar prepared by the clerks of the court listing the cases set to be tried.

Due process. Fair and regular procedure. The Fifth and Fourteenth amendments guarantee persons that they will not be deprived of life, liberty, or property by the government until fair and usual procedures have been followed.

Error, Writ of. A writ issued from an appeals court to a lower court requiring it to send to the appeals court the record of a case in which it has entered a final judgment and which the appeals court will review for error.

Ex parte. Only from, or on, one side. Application to a court for some ruling or action on behalf of only one party.

Ex post facto. After the fact; an ex post facto law makes an action a crime after it already has been committed, or otherwise changes the legal consequences of some past action.

Ex rel. Upon information from; the term is usually used to describe legal proceedings begun by an official in the name of the state but at the instigation of, and with information from, a private individual interested in the matter.

Grand jury. Group of twelve to twenty-three persons impanelled to hear, in private, evidence presented by the state against an individual or persons accused of a criminal act and to issue indictments when a majority of the jurors find probable cause to believe that the accused has committed a crime. Called a "grand" jury because it comprises a greater number of persons than a "petit" jury.

Grand jury report. A public report, often called "presentments," released by a grand jury after an investigation into activities of public officials that fall short of criminal actions.

Guilty. A word used by a defendant in entering a plea or by a jury in returning a verdict, indicating that the defendant is legally responsible as charged for a crime or other wrongdoing.

Habeas corpus. Literally, "you have the body"; a writ issued to inquire whether a person is lawfully imprisoned or detained. The writ demands that the persons holding the prisoner justify the detention or release the prisoner.

Immunity. A grant of exemption from prosecution in return for evidence or testimony.

In camera. In chambers. Refers to court hearings in private without spectators.

In forma pauperis. In the manner of a pauper, without liability for court costs.

In personam. Done or directed against a particular person.

In re. In the affair of, concerning. Frequent title of judicial proceedings in which there are no adversaries but instead where the matter itself—such as a bankrupt's estate—requires judicial action.

In rem. Done or directed against the thing, not the person.

Indictment. A formal written statement, based on evidence presented by the prosecutor, from a grand jury. Decided by a majority vote, an indictment charges one or more persons with specified offenses.

Information. A written set of accusations, similar to an indictment, but filed directly by a prosecutor.

Injunction. A court order prohibiting the person to whom it is directed from performing a particular act.

Interlocutory decree. A provisional decision of the court before completion of a legal action that temporarily settles an intervening matter.

Judgment. Official decision of a court based on the rights and claims of the parties to a case that was submitted for determination.

Juries. *See* Grand jury; Petit jury.

Jurisdiction. The power of a court to hear a case in question, which exists when the proper parties are present and when the point to be decided is within the issues authorized to be handled by the particular court.

Magistrate. A judicial officer having jurisdiction to try minor criminal cases and conduct preliminary examinations of persons charged with serious crimes.

Majority opinion. An opinion joined by a majority of the justices explaining the legal basis for the Court's decision and regarded as binding precedent for future cases.

Mandamus. "We command." An order issued from a superior court directing a lower court or other authority to perform a particular act.

Moot. Unsettled, undecided. A moot question also is one that no longer is material; a moot case is one that has become hypothetical.

Motion. Written or oral application to a court or a judge to obtain a rule or an order.

Nolo contendere. "I will not contest it." A plea entered by a defendant at the discretion of the judge with the same legal effect as a plea of guilty, but it may not be cited in other proceedings as an admission of guilt.

Obiter dictum. Statements by a judge or justice expressing an opinion and included with, but not essential to, an opinion resolving a case before the court. Dicta are not necessarily binding in future cases.

Parole. A conditional release from imprisonment under conditions that, if the prisoner abides by the law and other restrictions that may be imposed, the prisoner will not have to serve the remainder of the sentence.

Per curiam. "By the court." An unsigned opinion of the court, or an opinion written by the whole court.

Petit jury. A trial jury, originally a panel of twelve persons who tried to reach a unanimous verdict on questions of fact in criminal and civil proceedings. Since 1970 the Supreme Court has upheld the legality of state juries with fewer than twelve persons. Fewer persons serve on a "petit" jury than on a "grand" jury.

Petitioner. One who files a petition with a court seeking action or relief, including a plaintiff or an appellant. But a petitioner also is a person who files for other court action where charges are not necessarily made; for example, a party may petition the court for an order requiring another person or party to produce documents. The opposite party is called the respondent.

When a writ of certiorari is granted by the Supreme Court, the parties to the case are called petitioner and respondent in contrast to the appellant and appellee terms used in an appeal.

Plaintiff. A party who brings a civil action or sues to obtain a remedy for injury to his or her rights. The party against whom action is brought is termed the defendant.

Plea bargaining. Negotiations between a prosecutor and the defendant aimed at exchanging a plea of guilty from the defendant for concessions by the prosecutor, such as reduction of the charges or a request for leniency.

Pleas. *See* Guilty; Nolo contendere.

Plurality opinion. An opinion supported by the largest number of justices but less than a majority. A plurality opinion typically is not regarded as establishing a binding precedent for future cases.

Precedent. A judicial decision that may be used as a basis for ruling on subsequent similar cases.

Presentment. *See* Grand jury report.

Prima facie. At first sight; referring to a fact or other evidence presumably sufficient to establish a defense or a claim unless otherwise contradicted.

Probation. Process under which a person convicted of an offense, usually a first offense, receives a suspended sentence and is given freedom, usually under the guardianship of a probation officer.

Quash. To overthrow, annul, or vacate; as to quash a subpoena.

Recognizance. An obligation entered into before a court or magistrate requiring the performance of a specified act—usually to appear in court at a later date. It is an alternative to bail for pretrial release.

Remand. To send back. When a decision is remanded, it is sent back by a higher court to the court from which it came for further action.

Respondent. One who is compelled to answer the claims or questions posed in court by a petitioner. A defendant and an appellee may be called respondents, but the term also includes those parties who answer in court during actions where charges are not necessarily brought or where the Supreme Court has granted a writ of certiorari.

Seriatim. Separately, individually, one by one.

Stare decisis. "Let the decision stand." The principle of adherence to settled cases, the doctrine that principles of law established in earlier judicial decisions should be accepted as authoritative in similar subsequent cases.

Statute. A written law enacted by a legislature. A collection of statutes for a particular governmental division is called a code.

Stay. To halt or suspend further judicial proceedings.

Subpoena. An order to present oneself before a grand jury, court, or legislative hearing.

Subpoena duces tecum. An order to produce specified documents or papers.

Tort. An injury or wrong to the person or property of another.

Transactional immunity. Protects a witness from prosecution for any offense mentioned in or related to his or her testimony, regardless of independent evidence against the witness.

Use immunity. Protects a witness from the use of his or her testimony against the witness in prosecution.

Vacate. To make void, annul, or rescind.

Writ. A written court order commanding the designated recipient to perform or not perform specified acts.

United States Constitution

We the People of the United States, in Order to form a more perfect Union, establish Justice, insure domestic Tranquility, provide for the common defence, promote the general Welfare, and secure the Blessings of Liberty to ourselves and our Posterity, do ordain and establish this Constitution for the United States of America.

Article I

Section 1. All legislative Powers herein granted shall be vested in a Congress of the United States, which shall consist of a Senate and House of Representatives.

Section 2. The House of Representatives shall be composed of Members chosen every second Year by the People of the several States, and the Electors in each State shall have the Qualifications requisite for Electors of the most numerous Branch of the State Legislature.

No Person shall be a Representative who shall not have attained to the age of twenty five Years, and been seven Years a Citizen of the United States, and who shall not, when elected, be an Inhabitant of that State in which he shall be chosen.

[Representatives and direct Taxes shall be apportioned among the several States which may be included within this Union, according to their respective Numbers, which shall be determined by adding to the whole Number of free Persons, including those bound to Service for a Term of Years, and excluding Indians not taxed, three fifths of all other Persons.][1] The actual Enumeration shall be made within three Years after the first Meeting of the Congress of the United States, and within every subsequent Term of ten Years, in such Manner as they shall by Law direct. The Number of Representatives shall not exceed one for every thirty Thousand, but each State shall have at Least one Representative; and until such enumeration shall be made, the State of New Hampshire shall be entitled to chuse three, Massachusetts eight, Rhode-Island and Providence Plantations one, Connecticut five, New-York six, New Jersey four, Pennsylvania eight, Delaware one, Maryland six, Virginia ten, North Carolina five, South Carolina five, and Georgia three.

When vacancies happen in the Representation from any State, the Executive Authority thereof shall issue Writs of Election to fill such Vacancies.

The House of Representatives shall chuse their Speaker and other Officers; and shall have the sole Power of Impeachment.

Section 3. The Senate of the United States shall be composed of two Senators from each State, [chosen by the Legislature thereof,]² for six Years; and each Senator shall have one Vote.

Immediately after they shall be assembled in Consequence of the first Election, they shall be divided as equally as may be into three Classes. The Seats of the Senators of the first Class shall be vacated at the Expiration of the second Year, of the second Class at the Expiration of the fourth Year, and of the third Class at the Expiration of the sixth Year, so that one third may be chosen every second Year; [and if Vacancies happen by Resignation, or otherwise, during the Recess of the Legislature of any State, the Executive thereof may make temporary Appointments until the next Meeting of the Legislature, which shall then fill such Vacancies.]³

No Person shall be a Senator who shall not have attained to the Age of thirty Years, and been nine Years a Citizen of the United States, and who shall not, when elected, be an Inhabitant of that State for which he shall be chosen.

The Vice President of the United States shall be President of the Senate, but shall have no Vote, unless they be equally divided.

The Senate shall chuse their other Officers, and also a President pro tempore, in the Absence of the Vice President, or when he shall exercise the Office of President of the United States.

The Senate shall have the sole Power to try all Impeachments. When sitting for that Purpose, they shall be on Oath or Affirmation. When the President of the United States is tried, the Chief Justice shall preside: And no Person shall be convicted without the Concurrence of two thirds of the Members present.

Judgment in Cases of Impeachment shall not extend further than to removal from Office, and disqualification to hold and enjoy any Office of honor, Trust or Profit under the United States: but the Party convicted shall nevertheless be liable and subject to Indictment, Trial, Judgment and Punishment, according to Law.

Section 4. The Times, Places and Manner of holding Elections for Senators and Representatives, shall be prescribed in each State by the Legislature thereof; but the Congress may at any time by Law make or alter such Regulations, except as to the Places of chusing Senators.

The Congress shall assemble at least once in every Year, and such Meeting shall [be on the first Monday in December],⁴ unless they shall by Law appoint a different Day.

Section 5. Each House shall be the Judge of the Elections, Returns and Qualifications of its own Members, and a Majority of each shall constitute a Quorum to do Business; but a smaller Number may adjourn from day to day, and may be authorized to compel the Attendance of absent Members, in such Manner, and under such Penalties as each House may provide.

Each House may determine the Rules of its Proceedings, punish its Members for disorderly Behaviour, and, with the Concurrence of two thirds, expel a Member.

Each House shall keep a Journal of its Proceedings, and from time to time publish the same, excepting such Parts as may in their Judgment require Secrecy; and the Yeas and Nays of the Members of either House on any question shall, at the Desire of one fifth of those Present, be entered on the Journal.

Neither House, during the Session of Congress, shall, without the Consent of the other, adjourn for more than three days, nor to any other Place than that in which the two Houses shall be sitting.

Section 6. The Senators and Representatives shall receive a Compensation for their Services, to be ascertained by Law, and paid out of the Treasury of the United States. They shall in all Cases, except Treason, Felony and Breach of the Peace, be privileged from Arrest during their Attendance at the Session of their respective Houses, and in going to and returning from the same; and for any Speech or Debate in either House, they shall not be questioned in any other Place.

No Senator or Representative shall, during the Time for which he was elected, be appointed to any civil Office under the Authority of the United States, which shall have been created, or the Emoluments whereof shall have been encreased during such time; and no Person holding any Office under the United States, shall be a Member of either House during his Continuance in Office.

Section 7. All Bills for raising Revenue shall originate in the House of Representatives; but the Senate may propose or concur with Amendments as on other Bills.

Every Bill which shall have passed the House of Representatives and the Senate, shall, before it become a Law, be presented to the President of the United States; If he approve he shall sign it, but if not he shall return it, with his Objections to that House in which it shall have originated, who shall enter the Objections at large on their Journal, and proceed to reconsider it. If after such Reconsideration two thirds of that House shall agree to pass the Bill, it shall be sent, together with the Objections, to the other House, by which it shall likewise be reconsidered, and if approved by two thirds of that House, it shall become a Law. But in all such Cases the Votes of both Houses shall be determined by yeas and Nays, and the Names of the Persons voting for and against the Bill shall be entered on the Journal of each House respectively. If any Bill shall not be returned by the President within ten Days (Sundays excepted) after it shall have been presented to him, the Same shall be a Law, in like Manner as if he had signed it, unless the Congress by their Adjournment prevent its Return, in which Case it shall not be a Law.

Every Order, Resolution, or Vote to which the Concurrence of the Senate and House of Representatives may be necessary (except on a question of Adjournment) shall be presented to the President of the United States; and before the Same shall take Effect, shall be approved by him, or being disapproved by him, shall be repassed by two thirds of the Senate and House of Representatives, according to the Rules and Limitations prescribed in the Case of a Bill.

Section 8. The Congress shall have Power To lay and collect Taxes, Duties, Imposts and Excises, to pay the Debts and provide for the common Defence and general

Welfare of the United States; but all Duties, Imposts and Excises shall be uniform throughout the United States;

To borrow Money on the credit of the United States;

To regulate Commerce with foreign Nations, and among the several States, and with the Indian Tribes;

To establish an uniform Rule of Naturalization, and uniform Laws on the subject of Bankruptcies throughout the United States;

To coin Money, regulate the Value thereof, and of foreign Coin, and fix the Standard of Weights and Measures;

To provide for the Punishment of counterfeiting the Securities and current Coin of the United States;

To establish Post Offices and post Roads;

To promote the Progress of Science and useful Arts, by securing for limited Times to Authors and Inventors the exclusive Right to their respective Writings and Discoveries;

To constitute Tribunals inferior to the supreme Court;

To define and punish Piracies and Felonies committed on the high Seas, and Offences against the Law of Nations;

To declare War, grant Letters of Marque and Reprisal, and make Rules concerning Captures on Land and Water;

To raise and support Armies, but no Appropriation of Money to that Use shall be for a longer Term than two Years;

To provide and maintain a Navy;

To make Rules for the Government and Regulation of the land and naval Forces;

To provide for calling forth the Militia to execute the Laws of the Union, suppress Insurrections and repel Invasions;

To provide for organizing, arming, and disciplining, the Militia, and for governing such Part of them as may be employed in the Service of the United States, reserving to the States respectively, the Appointment of the Officers, and the Authority of training the Militia according to the discipline prescribed by Congress;

To exercise exclusive Legislation in all Cases whatsoever, over such District (not exceeding ten Miles square) as may, by Cession of particular States, and the Acceptance of Congress, become the Seat of the Government of the United States, and to exercise like Authority over all Places purchased by the Consent of the Legislature of the State in which the Same shall be, for the Erection of Forts, Magazines, Arsenals, dock-Yards, and other needful Buildings;—And

To make all Laws which shall be necessary and proper for carrying into Execution the foregoing Powers, and all other Powers vested by this Constitution in the Government of the United States, or in any Department or Officer thereof.

Section 9. The Migration or Importation of such Persons as any of the States now existing shall think proper to admit, shall not be prohibited by the Congress prior to the Year one thousand eight hundred and eight, but a Tax or duty may be imposed on such Importation, not exceeding ten dollars for each Person.

The Privilege of the Writ of Habeas Corpus shall not be suspended, unless when in Cases of Rebellion or Invasion the public Safety may require it.

No Bill of Attainder or ex post facto Law shall be passed.

No Capitation, or other direct, Tax shall be laid, unless in Proportion to the Census or Enumeration herein before directed to be taken.[5]

No Tax or Duty shall be laid on Articles exported from any State.

No Preference shall be given by any Regulation of Commerce or Revenue to the Ports of one State over those of another; nor shall Vessels bound to, or from, one State, be obliged to enter, clear, or pay Duties in another.

No Money shall be drawn from the Treasury, but in Consequence of Appropriations made by Law; and a regular Statement and Account of the Receipts and Expenditures of all public Money shall be published from time to time.

No Title of Nobility shall be granted by the United States: And no Person holding any Office of Profit or Trust under them, shall, without the Consent of the Congress, accept of any present, Emolument, Office, or Title, of any kind whatever, from any King, Prince, or foreign State.

Section 10. No State shall enter into any Treaty, Alliance, or Confederation; grant Letters of Marque and Reprisal; coin Money; emit Bills of Credit; make any Thing but gold and silver Coin a Tender in Payment of Debts; pass any Bill of Attainder, ex post facto Law, or Law impairing the Obligation of Contracts, or grant any Title of Nobility.

No State shall, without the Consent of the Congress, lay any Imposts or Duties on Imports or Exports, except what may be absolutely necessary for executing it's inspection Laws: and the net Produce of all Duties and Imposts, laid by any State on Imports or Exports, shall be for the Use of the Treasury of the United States; and all such Laws shall be subject to the Revision and Controul of the Congress.

No State shall, without the Consent of Congress, lay any Duty of Tonnage, keep Troops, or Ships of War in time of Peace, enter into any Agreement or Compact with another State, or with a foreign Power, or engage in War, unless actually invaded, or in such imminent Danger as will not admit of delay.

Article II

Section 1. The executive Power shall be vested in a President of the United States of America. He shall hold his Office during the Term of four Years, and, together with the Vice President, chosen for the same Term, be elected, as follows

Each State shall appoint, in such Manner as the Legislature thereof may direct, a Number of Electors, equal to the whole Number of Senators and Representatives to which the State may be entitled in the Congress: but no Senator or Representative, or Person holding an Office of Trust or Profit under the United States, shall be appointed an Elector.

[The Electors shall meet in their respective States, and vote by Ballot for two Persons, of whom one at least shall not be an Inhabitant of the same State with themselves. And they shall make a List of all the Persons voted for, and of the Number of Votes for each; which List they shall sign and certify, and transmit sealed to the Seat of the Government of the United States, directed to the President of the Senate. The President of the Senate shall, in the Presence of the Senate and House of Representatives, open all the Certificates, and the Votes shall then be counted. The Person having the greatest Number of Votes shall be the President, if such

Number be a Majority of the whole Number of Electors appointed; and if there be more than one who have such Majority, and have an equal Number of Votes, then the House of Representatives shall immediately chuse by Ballot one of them for President; and if no Person have a Majority, then from the five highest on the list the said House shall in like Manner chuse the President. But in chusing the President, the Votes shall be taken by States, the Representation from each State having one Vote; A quorum for this Purpose shall consist of a Member or Members from two thirds of the States, and a Majority of all the States shall be necessary to a Choice. In every Case, after the Choice of the President, the Person having the greatest Number of Votes of the Electors shall be the Vice President. But if there should remain two or more who have equal Votes, the Senate shall chuse from them by Ballot the Vice President.][6]

The Congress may determine the Time of chusing the Electors, and the Day on which they shall give their Votes; which Day shall be the same throughout the United States.

No Person except a natural born Citizen, or a Citizen of the United States, at the time of the Adoption of this Constitution, shall be eligible to the Office of President; neither shall any Person be eligible to that Office who shall not have attained to the Age of thirty five Years, and been fourteen Years a Resident within the United States.

In Case of the Removal of the President from Office, or of his Death, Resignation, or Inability to discharge the Powers and Duties of the said Office,[7] the Same shall devolve on the Vice President, and the Congress may by Law provide for the Case of Removal, Death, Resignation or Inability, both of the President and Vice President, declaring what Officer shall then act as President, and such Officer shall act accordingly, until the Disability be removed, or a President shall be elected.

The President shall, at stated Times, receive for his Services, a Compensation, which shall neither be encreased nor diminished during the Period for which he shall have been elected, and he shall not receive within that Period any other Emolument from the United States, or any of them.

Before he enter on the Execution of his Office, he shall take the following Oath or Affirmation:—"I do solemnly swear (or affirm) that I will faithfully execute the Office of President of the United States, and will to the best of my Ability, preserve, protect and defend the Constitution of the United States."

Section 2. The President shall be Commander in Chief of the Army and Navy of the United States, and of the Militia of the several States, when called into the actual Service of the United States; he may require the Opinion, in writing, of the principal Officer in each of the executive Departments, upon any Subject relating to the Duties of their respective Offices, and he shall have Power to grant Reprieves and Pardons for Offences against the United States, except in Cases of Impeachment.

He shall have Power, by and with the Advice and Consent of the Senate, to make Treaties, provided two thirds of the Senators present concur; and he shall nominate, and by and with the Advice and Consent of the Senate, shall appoint Ambassadors, other public Ministers and Consuls, Judges of the supreme Court, and all other Officers of the United States, whose Appointments are not herein otherwise provided for, and which shall be established by Law: but the Congress may by Law vest the Appointment of such inferior Officers, as they think proper, in the President alone, in the Courts of Law, or in the Heads of Departments.

The President shall have Power to fill up all Vacancies that may happen during the Recess of the Senate, by granting Commissions which shall expire at the End of their next Session.

Section 3. He shall from time to time give to the Congress Information of the State of the Union, and recommend to their Consideration such Measures as he shall judge necessary and expedient; he may, on extraordinary Occasions, convene both Houses, or either of them, and in Case of Disagreement between them, with Respect to the Time of Adjournment, he may adjourn them to such Time as he shall think proper; he shall receive Ambassadors and other public Ministers; he shall take Care that the Laws be faithfully executed, and shall Commission all the Officers of the United States.

Section 4. The President, Vice President and all civil Officers of the United States, shall be removed from Office on Impeachment for, and Conviction of, Treason, Bribery, or other high Crimes and Misdemeanors.

Article III

Section 1. The judicial Power of the United States, shall be vested in one supreme Court, and in such inferior Courts as the Congress may from time to time ordain and establish. The Judges, both of the supreme and inferior Courts, shall hold their Offices during good Behaviour, and shall, at stated Times, receive for their Services, a Compensation, which shall not be diminished during their Continuance in Office.

Section 2. The judicial Power shall extend to all Cases, in Law and Equity, arising under this Constitution, the Laws of the United States, and Treaties made, or which shall be made, under their Authority;—to all Cases affecting Ambassadors, other public Ministers and Consuls;—to all Cases of admiralty and maritime Jurisdiction;—to Controversies to which the United States shall be a Party;—to Controversies between two or more States;—between a State and Citizens of another State;8—between Citizens of different States;—between Citizens of the same State claiming Lands under Grants of different States, and between a State, or the Citizens thereof, and foreign States, Citizens or Subjects.[8]

In all Cases affecting Ambassadors, other public Ministers and Consuls, and those in which a State shall be Party, the supreme Court shall have original Jurisdiction. In all the other Cases before mentioned, the supreme Court shall have appellate Jurisdiction, both as to Law and Fact, with such Exceptions, and under such Regulations as the Congress shall make.

The Trial of all Crimes, except in Cases of Impeachment, shall be by Jury; and such Trial shall be held in the State where the said Crimes shall have been committed; but when not committed within any State, the Trial shall be at such Place or Places as the Congress may by Law have directed.

Section 3. Treason against the United States, shall consist only in levying War against them, or in adhering to their Enemies, giving them Aid and Comfort. No Person shall be convicted of Treason unless on the Testimony of two Witnesses to the same overt Act, or on Confession in open Court.

The Congress shall have Power to declare the Punishment of Treason, but no Attainder of Treason shall work Corruption of Blood, or Forfeiture except during the Life of the Person attainted.

Article IV

Section 1. Full Faith and Credit shall be given in each State to the public Acts, Records, and judicial Proceedings of every other State. And the Congress may by general Laws prescribe the Manner in which such Acts, Records and Proceedings shall be proved, and the Effect thereof.

Section 2. The Citizens of each State shall be entitled to all Privileges and Immunities of Citizens in the several States.

A Person charged in any State with Treason, Felony, or other Crime, who shall flee from Justice, and be found in another State, shall on Demand of the executive Authority of the State from which he fled, be delivered up, to be removed to the State having Jurisdiction of the Crime.

[No Person held to Service or Labour in one State, under the Laws thereof, escaping into another, shall, in Consequence of any Law or Regulation therein, be discharged from such Service or Labour, but shall be delivered up on Claim of the Party to whom such Service or Labour may be due.][9]

Section 3. New States may be admitted by the Congress into this Union; but no new State shall be formed or erected within the Jurisdiction of any other State; nor any State be formed by the Junction of two or more States, or Parts of States, without the Consent of the Legislatures of the States concerned as well as of the Congress.

The Congress shall have Power to dispose of and make all needful Rules and Regulations respecting the Territory or other Property belonging to the United States; and nothing in this Constitution shall be so construed as to Prejudice any Claims of the United States, or of any particular State.

Section 4. The United States shall guarantee to every State in this Union a Republican Form of Government, and shall protect each of them against Invasion; and on Application of the Legislature, or of the Executive (when the Legislature cannot be convened) against domestic Violence.

Article V

The Congress, whenever two thirds of both Houses shall deem it necessary, shall propose Amendments to this Constitution, or, on the Application of the Legislatures of two thirds of the several States, shall call a Convention for proposing Amendments, which, in either Case, shall be valid to all Intents and Purposes, as Part of this Constitution, when ratified by the Legislatures of three fourths of the several States, or by Conventions in three fourths thereof, as the one or the other Mode of Ratification may be proposed by the Congress; Provided [that no Amendment which may be made prior to the Year One thousand eight hundred and eight shall in any Manner affect the first and fourth Clauses in the Ninth Section of the first Article; and][10] that no State, without its Consent, shall be deprived of its equal Suffrage in the Senate.

Article VI

All Debts contracted and Engagements entered into, before the Adoption of this Constitution, shall be as valid against the United States under this Constitution, as under the Confederation.

This Constitution, and the Laws of the United States which shall be made in Pursuance thereof; and all Treaties made, or which shall be made, under the Authority of the United States, shall be the supreme Law of the Land; and the Judges in every State shall be bound thereby, any Thing in the Constitution or Laws of any State to the Contrary notwithstanding.

The Senators and Representatives before mentioned, and the Members of the several State Legislatures, and all executive and judicial Officers, both of the United States and of the several States, shall be bound by Oath or Affirmation, to support this Constitution; but no religious Test shall ever be required as a Qualification to any Office or public Trust under the United States.

Article VII

The Ratification of the Conventions of nine States, shall be sufficient for the Establishment of this Constitution between the States so ratifying the Same.

Done in Convention by the Unanimous Consent of the States present the Seventeenth Day of September in the Year of our Lord one thousand seven hundred and Eighty seven and of the Independence of the United States of America the Twelfth. IN WITNESS whereof We have hereunto subscribed our Names,

George Washington,
President and
deputy from Virginia.

New Hampshire: John Langdon,
Nicholas Gilman.

Massachusetts: Nathaniel Gorham,
Rufus King.

Connecticut: William Samuel Johnson,
Roger Sherman.

New York: Alexander Hamilton.

New Jersey:	William Livingston,
	David Brearley,
	William Paterson,
	Jonathan Dayton.
Pennsylvania:	Benjamin Franklin,
	Thomas Mifflin,
	Robert Morris,
	George Clymer,
	Thomas FitzSimons,
	Jared Ingersoll,
	James Wilson,
	Gouverneur Morris.
Delaware:	George Read,
	Gunning Bedford Jr.,
	John Dickinson,
	Richard Bassett,
	Jacob Broom.
Maryland:	James McHenry,
	Daniel of St. Thomas Jenifer,
	Daniel Carroll.
Virginia:	John Blair,
	James Madison Jr.
North Carolina:	William Blount,
	Richard Dobbs Spaight,
	Hugh Williamson.
South Carolina:	John Rutledge,
	Charles Cotesworth Pinckney,
	Charles Pinckney,
	Pierce Butler.
Georgia:	William Few,
	Abraham Baldwin.

[The language of the original Constitution, not including the Amendments, was adopted by a convention of the states on September 17, 1787, and was subsequently ratified by the states on the following dates: Delaware, December 7, 1787; Pennsylvania, December 12, 1787; New Jersey, December 18, 1787; Georgia, January 2, 1788; Connecticut, January 9, 1788; Massachusetts, February 6, 1788; Maryland, April 28, 1788; South Carolina, May 23, 1788; New Hampshire, June 21, 1788.

Ratification was completed on June 21, 1788.

The Constitution subsequently was ratified by Virginia, June 25, 1788; New York, July 26, 1788; North Carolina, November 21, 1789; Rhode Island, May 29, 1790; and Vermont, January 10, 1791.]

Amendments

Amendment I

(First ten amendments ratified December 15, 1791.)

Congress shall make no law respecting an establishment of religion, or prohibiting the free exercise thereof; or abridging the freedom of speech, or of the press; or the right of the people peaceably to assemble, and to petition the Government for a redress of grievances.

Amendment II

A well regulated Militia, being necessary to the security of a free State, the right of the people to keep and bear Arms, shall not be infringed.

Amendment III

No Soldier shall, in time of peace be quartered in any house, without the consent of the Owner, nor in time of war, but in a manner to be prescribed by law.

Amendment IV

The right of the people to be secure in their persons, houses, papers, and effects, against unreasonable searches and seizures, shall not be violated, and no Warrants shall issue, but upon probable cause, supported by Oath or affirmation, and particularly describing the place to be searched, and the persons or things to be seized.

Amendment V

No person shall be held to answer for a capital, or otherwise infamous crime, unless on a presentment or indictment of a Grand Jury, except in cases arising in the land or naval forces, or in the Militia, when in actual service in time of War or public danger; nor shall any person be subject for the same offence to be twice put in jeopardy of life or limb; nor shall be compelled in any criminal case to be a witness against himself, nor be deprived of life, liberty, or property, without due process of law; nor shall private property be taken for public use, without just compensation.

Amendment VI

In all criminal prosecutions, the accused shall enjoy the right to a speedy and public trial, by an impartial jury of the State and district wherein the crime shall have been committed, which district shall have been previously ascertained by law, and to be informed of the nature and cause of the accusation; to be confronted with the witnesses against him; to have compulsory process for obtaining witnesses in his favor, and to have the Assistance of Counsel for his defence.

Amendment VII

In Suits at common law, where the value in controversy shall exceed twenty dollars, the right of trial by jury shall be preserved, and no fact tried by a jury, shall be otherwise re-examined in any Court of the United States, than according to the rules of the common law.

Amendment VIII

Excessive bail shall not be required, nor excessive fines imposed, nor cruel and unusual punishments inflicted.

Amendment IX

The enumeration in the Constitution, of certain rights, shall not be construed to deny or disparage others retained by the people.

Amendment X

The powers not delegated to the United States by the Constitution, nor prohibited by it to the States, are reserved to the States respectively, or to the people.

Amendment XI

(Ratified February 7, 1795)

The Judicial power of the United States shall not be construed to extend to any suit in law or equity, commenced or prosecuted against one of the United States by Citizens of another State, or by Citizens or Subjects of any Foreign State.

Amendment XII

(Ratified June 15, 1804)

The Electors shall meet in their respective states and vote by ballot for President and Vice-President, one of whom, at least, shall not be an inhabitant of the same state with themselves; they shall name in their ballots the person voted for as President, and in distinct ballots the person voted for as Vice-President, and they shall make distinct lists of all persons voted for as President, and of all persons voted for as Vice-President, and of the number of votes for each, which lists they shall sign and certify, and transmit sealed to the seat of the government of the United States, directed to the President of the Senate;—The President of the Senate shall, in the presence of the Senate and House of Representatives, open all the certificates and the votes shall then be counted;—The person having the greatest number of votes for President, shall be the President, if such number be a majority of the whole number of Electors appointed; and if no person have such majority, then from the persons having the highest numbers not exceeding three on the list of those voted for as President, the House of Representatives shall choose immediately, by ballot, the President. But in choosing the President, the votes shall be taken by states, the representation from each state having one vote; a quorum for this purpose shall consist of a member or members from two-thirds of the states, and a majority of all the states shall be necessary to a choice. [And if the House of Representatives shall not choose a President whenever the right of choice shall devolve upon them, before the fourth day of March next following, then the Vice-President shall act as President, as in the case of the death or other constitutional disability of the President.—][11] The person having the greatest number of votes as Vice-President, shall be the Vice-President, if such number be a majority of the whole number of Electors appointed, and if no person have a majority, then from the two highest numbers on the list, the Senate shall choose the Vice-President; a quorum for the purpose shall consist of two-thirds of the whole number of Senators, and a majority of the whole number shall be necessary to a choice. But no person constitutionally ineligible to the office of President shall be eligible to that of Vice-President of the United States.

Amendment XIII

(Ratified December 6, 1865)

Section 1. Neither slavery nor involuntary servitude, except as a punishment for crime whereof the party shall have been duly convicted, shall exist within the United States, or any place subject to their jurisdiction.

Section 2. Congress shall have power to enforce this article by appropriate legislation.

Amendment XIV

(Ratified July 9, 1868)

Section 1. All persons born or naturalized in the United States, and subject to the jurisdiction thereof, are citizens of the United States and of the State wherein they reside. No State shall make or enforce any law which shall abridge the privileges or immunities of citizens of the United States; nor shall any State deprive any person of life, liberty, or property, without due process of law; nor deny to any person within its jurisdiction the equal protection of the laws.

Section 2. Representatives shall be apportioned among the several States according to their respective numbers, counting the whole number of persons in each State, excluding Indians not taxed. But when the right to vote at any election for the choice of electors for President and Vice President of the United States, Representatives in Congress, the Executive and Judicial officers of a State, or the members of the Legislature thereof, is denied to any of the male inhabitants of such State, being twenty-one years of age,[12] and citizens of the United States, or in any way abridged, except for participation in rebellion, or other crime, the basis of representation therein shall be reduced in the proportion which the number of such male citizens shall bear to the whole number of male citizens twenty-one years of age in such State.

Section 3. No person shall be a Senator or Representative in Congress, or elector of President and Vice President, or hold any office, civil or military, under the United States, or under any State, who, having previously taken an oath, as a member of Congress, or as an officer of the United States, or as a member of any State legislature, or as an executive or judicial officer of any State, to support the Constitution of the United States, shall have engaged in insurrection or rebellion against the same, or given aid or comfort to the enemies thereof. But Congress may by a vote of two-thirds of each House, remove such disability.

Section 4. The validity of the public debt of the United States, authorized by law, including debts incurred for payment of pensions and bounties for services in suppressing insurrection or rebellion, shall not be questioned. But neither the United States nor any State shall assume or pay any debt or obligation incurred in aid of insurrection or rebellion against the United States, or any claim for the loss or emancipation of any slave; but all such debts, obligations and claims shall be held illegal and void.

Section 5. The Congress shall have power to enforce, by appropriate legislation, the provisions of this article.

Amendment XV

(Ratified February 3, 1870)

Section 1. The right of citizens of the United States to vote shall not be denied or abridged by the United States or by any State on account of race, color, or previous condition of servitude.

Section 2. The Congress shall have power to enforce this article by appropriate legislation.

Amendment XVI

(Ratified February 3, 1913)

The Congress shall have power to lay and collect taxes on incomes, from whatever source derived, without apportionment among the several States, and without regard to any census or enumeration.

Amendment XVII

(Ratified April 8, 1913)

The Senate of the United States shall be composed of two Senators from each State, elected by the people thereof, for six years; and each Senator shall have one vote.

The electors in each State shall have the qualifications requisite for electors of the most numerous branch of the State legislatures.

When vacancies happen in the representation of any State in the Senate, the executive authority of such State shall issue writs of election to fill such vacancies: *Provided,* That the legislature of any State may empower the executive thereof to make temporary appointments until the people fill the vacancies by election as the legislature may direct.

This amendment shall not be so construed as to affect the election or term of any Senator chosen before it becomes valid as part of the Constitution.

Amendment XVIII

(Ratified January 16, 1919)[13]

Section 1. After one year from the ratification of this article the manufacture, sale, or transportation of intoxicating liquors within, the importation thereof into, or the exportation thereof from the United States and all territory subject to the jurisdiction thereof for beverage purposes is hereby prohibited.

Section 2. The Congress and the several States shall have concurrent power to enforce this article by appropriate legislation.

Section 3. This article shall be inoperative unless it shall have been ratified as an amendment to the Constitution by the legislatures of the several States, as provided in the Constitution, within seven years from the date of the submission hereof to the States by the Congress.

Amendment XIX

(Ratified August 18, 1920)

The right of citizens of the United States to vote shall not be denied or abridged by the United States or by any State on account of sex.

Congress shall have power to enforce this article by appropriate legislation.

Amendment XX

(Ratified January 23, 1933)

Section 1. The terms of the President and Vice President shall end at noon on the 20th day of January, and the terms of Senators and Representatives at noon on the 3d day of January, of the years in which such terms would have ended if this article had not been ratified; and the terms of their successors shall then begin.

Section 2. The Congress shall assemble at least once in every year, and such meeting shall begin at noon on the 3d day of January, unless they shall by law appoint a different day.

Section 3.[14] If, at the time fixed for the beginning of the term of the President, the President elect shall have died, the Vice President elect shall become President. If a President shall not have been chosen before the time fixed for the beginning of his term, or if the President elect shall have failed to qualify, then the Vice President elect shall act as President until a President shall have qualified; and the Congress may by law provide for the case wherein neither a President elect nor a Vice President elect shall have qualified, declaring who shall then act as President, or the manner in which one who is to act shall be selected, and such person shall act accordingly until a President or Vice President shall have qualified.

Section 4. The Congress may by law provide for the case of the death of any of the persons from whom the House of Representatives may choose a President whenever the right of choice shall have devolved upon them, and for the case of the death of any of the persons from whom the Senate may choose a Vice President whenever the right of choice shall have devolved upon them.

Section 5. Sections 1 and 2 shall take effect on the 15th day of October following the ratification of this article.

Section 6. This article shall be inoperative unless it shall have been ratified as an amendment to the Constitution by the legislatures of three-fourths of the several States within seven years from the date of its submission.

Amendment XXI

(Ratified December 5, 1933)

Section 1. The eighteenth article of amendment to the Constitution of the United States is hereby repealed.

Section 2. The transportation or importation into any State, Territory, or possession of the United States for delivery or use therein of intoxicating liquors, in violation of the laws thereof, is hereby prohibited.

Section 3. This article shall be inoperative unless it shall have been ratified as an amendment to the Constitution by conventions in the several States, as provided in the Constitution, within seven years from the date of the submission hereof to the States by the Congress.

Amendment XXII

(Ratified February 27, 1951)

Section 1. No person shall be elected to the office of the President more than twice, and no person who has held the office of President, or acted as President, for more than two years of a term to which some other person was elected President shall be elected to the office of the President more than once. But this Article shall not apply to any person holding the office of President when this Article was proposed by the Congress, and shall not prevent any person who may be holding the office of President, or acting as President, during the term within which this Article become operative from holding the office of President or acting as President during the remainder of such term.

Section 2. This article shall be inoperative unless it shall have been ratified as an amendment to the Constitution by the legislatures of three-fourths of the several States within seven years from the date of its submission to the States by the Congress.

Amendment XXIII

(Ratified March 29, 1961)

Section 1. The District constituting the seat of Government of the United States shall appoint in such manner as the Congress may direct:

A number of electors of President and Vice President equal to the whole number of Senators and Representatives in Congress to which the District would be entitled if it were a State, but in no event more than the least populous State; they shall be in addition to those appointed by the States, but they shall be considered, for the purposes of the election of President and Vice President, to be electors appointed by a State; and they shall meet in the District and perform such duties as provided by the twelfth article of amendment.

Section 2. The Congress shall have power to enforce this article by appropriate legislation.

Amendment XXIV

(Ratified January 23, 1964)

Section 1. The right of citizens of the United States to vote in any primary or other election for President or Vice President, for electors for President or Vice President, or for Senator or Representative in Congress, shall not be denied or abridged by the United States or any State by reason of failure to pay any poll tax or other tax.

Section 2. The Congress shall have power to enforce this article by appropriate legislation.

Amendment XXV

(Ratified February 10, 1967)

Section 1. In case of the removal of the President from office or of his death or resignation, the Vice President shall become President.

Section 2. Whenever there is a vacancy in the office of the Vice President, the President shall nominate a Vice President who shall take office upon confirmation by a majority vote of both Houses of Congress.

Section 3. Whenever the President transmits to the President pro tempore of the Senate and the Speaker of the House of Representatives his written declaration that he is unable to discharge the powers and duties of his office, and until he transmits to them a written declaration to the contrary, such powers and duties shall be discharged by the Vice President as Acting President.

Section 4. Whenever the Vice President and a majority of either the principal officers of the executive departments or of such other body as Congress may by law provide, transmit to the President pro tempore of the Senate and the Speaker of the House of Representatives their written declaration that the President is unable to discharge the powers and duties of his office, the Vice President shall immediately assume the powers and duties of the office as Acting President.

Thereafter, when the President transmits to the President pro tempore of the Senate and the Speaker of the House of Representatives his written declaration that no inability exists, he shall resume the powers and duties of his office unless the Vice President and a majority of either the principal officers of the executive department or of such other body as Congress may by law provide, transmit within four days to the President pro tempore of the Senate and the Speaker of the House of Representatives their written declaration that the President is unable to discharge the powers and duties of his office. Thereupon Congress shall decide the issue, assembling within forty-eight hours for that purpose if not in session. If the Congress, within twenty-one days after receipt of the latter written declaration, or, if Congress is not in session, within twenty-one days after Congress is required to assemble, determines by two-thirds vote of both Houses that the President is unable to discharge the powers and duties of his office, the Vice President shall continue to discharge the same as Acting President; otherwise, the President shall resume the powers and duties of his office.

Amendment XXVI

(Ratified July 1, 1971)

Section 1. The right of citizens of the United States, who are eighteen years of age or older, to vote shall not be denied or abridged by the United States or by any State on account of age.

Section 2. The Congress shall have power to enforce this article by appropriate legislation.

Amendment XXVII

(Ratified May 7, 1992)

No law varying the compensation for the services of the Senators and Representatives shall take effect, until an election of Representatives shall have intervened.

Notes

1. The part in brackets was changed by section 2 of the Fourteenth Amendment.
2. The part in brackets was changed by the first paragraph of the Seventeenth Amendment.
3. The part in brackets was changed by the second paragraph of the Seventeenth Amendment.
4. The part in brackets was changed by section 2 of the Twentieth Amendment.
5. The Sixteenth Amendment gave Congress the power to tax incomes.
6. The material in brackets has been superseded by the Twelfth Amendment.
7. This provision has been affected by the Twenty-fifth Amendment.
8. These clauses were affected by the Eleventh Amendment.
9. This paragraph has been superseded by the Thirteenth Amendment.
10. Obsolete.
11. The part in brackets has been superseded by section 3 of the Twentieth Amendment.
12. See the Nineteenth and Twenty-sixth Amendments.
13. This Amendment was repealed by section 1 of the Twenty-first Amendment.
14. See the Twenty-fifth Amendment.

Source: U.S. Congress, House, Committee on the Judiciary, *The Constitution of the United States of America, as Amended,* 100th Cong., 1st sess., 1987, H Doc 100-94.

Index